IPSec VPN Design

Vijay Bollapragada

Mohamed Khalid

Scott Wainner

Cisco Press

800 East 96th Street
Indianapolis, IN 46240 USA

IPSec VPN Design

Vijay Bollapragada, Mohamed Khalid, Scott Wainner

Copyright© 2005 Cisco Systems, Inc.

Cisco Press logo is a trademark of Cisco Systems, Inc.

Published by:
Cisco Press
800 East 96th Street
Indianapolis, IN 46240 USA

Printed in the United States of America 1 2 3 4 5 6 7 8 9 0

First Printing   April 2005

Library of Congress Cataloging-in-Publication Number: 2002106378

ISBN: 1-58705-111-7

Warning and Disclaimer

This book is designed to provide information about IPSec VPN design. Every effort has been made to make this book as complete and as accurate as possible, but no warranty or fitness is implied.

The information is provided on an "as is" basis. The authors, Cisco Press, and Cisco Systems, Inc. shall have neither liability nor responsibility to any person or entity with respect to any loss or damages arising from the information contained in this book or from the use of the discs or programs that may accompany it.

The opinions expressed in this book belong to the author and are not necessarily those of Cisco Systems, Inc.

Corporate and Government Sales

Cisco Press offers excellent discounts on this book when ordered in quantity for bulk purchases or special sales.

For more information, please contact U.S. Corporate and Government Sales, 1-800-382-3419, corpsales@pearsontechgroup.com.

For sales outside the U.S., please contact International Sales at international@pearsoned.com.

Trademark Acknowledgments

All terms mentioned in this book that are known to be trademarks or service marks have been appropriately capitalized. Cisco Press or Cisco Systems, Inc. cannot attest to the accuracy of this information. Use of a term in this book should not be regarded as affecting the validity of any trademark or service mark.

Feedback Information

At Cisco Press, our goal is to create in-depth technical books of the highest quality and value. Each book is crafted with care and precision, undergoing rigorous development that involves the unique expertise of members from the professional technical community.

Readers' feedback is a natural continuation of this process. If you have any comments regarding how we could improve the quality of this book, or otherwise alter it to better suit your needs, you can contact us through email at feedback@ciscopress.com. Please make sure to include the book title and ISBN in your message.

We greatly appreciate your assistance.

Publisher	John Wait
Editor-in-Chief	John Kane
Cisco Representative	Anthony Wolfenden
Cisco Press Program Manager	Jeff Brady
Executive Editor	Brett Bartow
Production Manager	Patrick Kanouse
Development Editor	Grant Munroe
Project Editor	Sheila Schroeder
Copy Editor	Michelle Grandin
Technical Editors	Anthony Kwan, Suresh Subbarao, Michael Sullenberger
Team Coordinator	Tammi Barnett
Cover Designer	Louisa Adair
Composition	Mark Shirar
Indexer	Tim Wright

CISCO SYSTEMS

Corporate Headquarters
Cisco Systems, Inc.
170 West Tasman Drive
San Jose, CA 95134-1706
USA
www.cisco.com
Tel: 408 526-4000
      800 553-NETS (6387)
Fax: 408 526-4100

European Headquarters
Cisco Systems International BV
Haarlerbergpark
Haarlerbergweg 13-19
1101 CH Amsterdam
The Netherlands
www-europe.cisco.com
Tel: 31 0 20 357 1000
Fax: 31 0 20 357 1100

Americas Headquarters
Cisco Systems, Inc.
170 West Tasman Drive
San Jose, CA 95134-1706
USA
www.cisco.com
Tel: 408 526-7660
Fax: 408 527-0883

Asia Pacific Headquarters
Cisco Systems, Inc.
Capital Tower
168 Robinson Road
#22-01 to #29-01
Singapore 068912
www.cisco.com
Tel: +65 6317 7777
Fax: +65 6317 7799

Cisco Systems has more than 200 offices in the following countries and regions. Addresses, phone numbers, and fax numbers are listed on the
Cisco.com Web site at www.cisco.com/go/offices.

Argentina • Australia • Austria • Belgium • Brazil • Bulgaria • Canada • Chile • China PRC • Colombia • Costa Rica • Croatia • Czech Republic
Denmark • Dubai, UAE • Finland • France • Germany • Greece • Hong Kong SAR • Hungary • India • Indonesia • Ireland • Israel • Italy
Japan • Korea • Luxembourg • Malaysia • Mexico • The Netherlands • New Zealand • Norway • Peru • Philippines • Poland • Portugal
Puerto Rico • Romania • Russia • Saudi Arabia • Scotland • Singapore • Slovakia • Slovenia • South Africa • Spain • Sweden
Switzerland • Taiwan • Thailand • Turkey • Ukraine • United Kingdom • United States • Venezuela • Vietnam • Zimbabwe

About the Authors

Vijay Bollapragada, CCIE No. 1606, is a director in the Network Systems Integration and Test Engineering group at Cisco Systems, where he works on the architecture, design, and validation of complex network solutions. An expert in router architecture and IP Routing, Vijay is a co-author of another Cisco Press publication titled *Inside Cisco IOS Software Architecture*. Vijay is also an adjunct professor in the Electrical Engineering department at Duke University.

Mohamed Khalid, CCIE No. 2435, is a technical leader working with IP VPN solutions at Cisco Systems. He works extensively with service providers across the globe and their associated Cisco account teams to determine technical and engineering requirements for various IP VPN architectures.

Scott Wainner is a Distinguished Systems Engineer in the U.S. Service Provider Sales Organization at Cisco Systems, where he focuses on VPN architecture and solution development. In this capacity, he works directly with customers in a consulting role by providing guidance on IP VPN architectures while interpreting customer requirements and driving internal development initiatives within Cisco Systems. Scott has more than 18 years of experience in the networking industry in various roles including network operations, network installation/provisioning, engineering, and product engineering. Most recently, he has focused his efforts on L2VPN and L3VPN service models using MPLS VPN, Pseudowire Emulation, and IPSec/SSL to provide VPN services to both enterprises and service providers. He holds a B.S. in Electrical Engineering from the United States Air Force Academy and a M.S. in Electronics and Computer Engineering from George Mason University in Fairfax, Virginia. Scott is currently an active member of the IEEE and the IETF.

About the Technical Editors

Anthony Kwan is the director and executive project manager of infrastructure for HTA; CCNP, CCDP, MCSE, Master ASE, MCNE, CCIE(written). He has ten years of experience in the internetworking industry. He designed and built a number of secured enterprise datacenters with an upward budget of $120 million. He also directed a number of consulting firms in building a Network Infrastructure and Technology consulting practice. He is a frequent contributor to Cisco Press and other publications specializing in networking technology. He can be reached at atonio888@yahoo.com.

Suresh Subbarao has worked in the networking area for the last 10 years. He is currently a network engineer at Cisco Systems focusing on security services for Service Providers with a special emphasis on IPSec VPNs.

Michael Sullenberger received a bachelor of science degree in mathematics from Harvey Mudd College in 1981. He started working with computer networks at the Stanford Linear Accelerator Center (SLAC) in 1981 as a Fortran programmer and as a user of the BITnet network, an early world wide 9600 baud network. At SLAC Michael also managed DEC VMS computers and gained knowledge of the DECnet and LAT protocol. He was also part of the introduction of Ethernet and FDDI networks to SLAC. In 1988 Michael moved to the networking group, where he assisted in transforming a large bridged, primarily DECnet, network to a routed multi-protocol, primarily TCP/IP, network. In 1994, he left SLAC to work for a small company, TGV, that wrote TCP/IP stacks and applications for OpenVMS and Windows systems. At TGV he worked in technical support where he learned the details of TCP/IP from the IP layer through the Application layer. TGV was bought by Cisco in 1996, and Michael moved into the Routing Protocols group, where he enhanced his knowledge of TCP/IP by adding information on the link-layer and IP routing protocols. In 1998, Michael moved to the Escalation Team at Cisco, where he continues to expand his TCP/IP knowledge in areas such as NAT, HSRP, GRE and IPsec Encryption. In 2000, he started a project, as the principle architect, that became the Cisco Dynamic Multipoint VPN (DMVPN) solution for scaling IPsec VPN networks. In 2004, the DMVPN solution won the Cisco Pioneer Award. Michael continues to this day working on enhancing DMVPN as well as designing and troubleshooting DMVPN and IPsec networks. Also starting in 2000 Michael has been a speaker each year at the Cisco Networkers Conferences in the area of site-to-site IPsec and DMVPN networks.

Dedications

Vijay Bollapragada: To my best friend and wife, Leena, for her love and encouragement and for allowing me to take precious family time away to write this book. To my two lovely children, Amita and Abhishek, to my parents for instilling the right values in me, and all my wonderful friends.

Thanks to my coauthors, Mo and Scott, for bearing with me during the trials and tribulations of book writing and teaching me things along the way. And thanks to the awesome folks I work with at Cisco that constantly keep me challenged and remind me that there is something new to learn everyday.

Mohamed Khalid: First and foremost, I would like to acknowledge my parents—their dedication, sacrifice, and encouragement have been instrumental in all my achievements and success. Thanks to my wife Farhath, who gave me the time and constant encouragement to finish the book.

Thanks to Scott Wainner, Haseeb, and Sunil who provided valuable technical insights. Last but not least, I am deeply grateful to my friend and co-author, Vijay Bollapragada, who cajoled, encouraged, and assisted me in completing this book.

Scott Wainner: I would like to acknowledge my wife, Jill, for her love, patience, and encouragement. There are never enough hours in the day, so I thank her for caring for our family. I'd also like to thank my children—Craig, Brett, Natalie, and Caroline—for their patience and inspiration in exploring life's possibilities.

Special thanks go to my father and late mother—Tom and Zenith—for being an inspiration and guiding force in my life. To my colleagues, Vijay and Mo, you guys rock and it's been an honor working with you all these years. And finally, I'd like acknowledge my God for granting me the gifts to fulfill this dream.

Acknowledgments

This book would have not been possible without the help of many people whose many comments and suggestions improved the end result. First, we would like to thank the technical reviewers for the book, which include Anthony Kwan, Mike Sullenberger, and Suresh Subbarao. Their knowledge of the subject, attention to detail, and suggestions were invaluable. We would like to thank Brett Bartow of Cisco Press for constantly keeping the pressure and pulling all of this together. Without his help, this project would have never seen the light of day. We would also like to thank Grant Munroe and Chris Cleveland from Cisco Press for their attention to detail and editorial comments that improved the quality of the book tremendously. We would also like to thank the IPSec development team at Cisco—they are the ones that write and perfect the code that makes all the features discussed in this book possible.

This Book Is Safari Enabled

The Safari® Enabled icon on the cover of your favorite technology book means the book is available through Safari Bookshelf. When you buy this book, you get free access to the online edition for 45 days.

Safari Bookshelf is an electronic reference library that lets you easily search thousands of technical books, find code samples, download chapters, and access technical information whenever and wherever you need it.

To gain 45-day Safari Enabled access to this book:

- Go to http://www.ciscopress.com/safarienabled
- Complete the brief registration form
- Enter the coupon code Z8HY-WQDH-PUGS-B2HS-GRCF

If you have difficulty registering on Safari Bookshelf or accessing the online edition, please e-mail customer-service@safaribooksonline.com.

Contents at a Glance

Contents

Icons Used in This Book

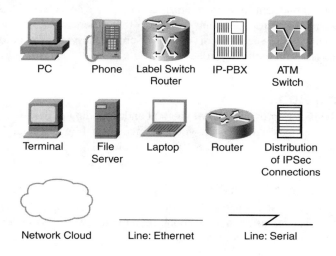

PC	Phone	Label Switch Router	IP-PBX	ATM Switch
Terminal	File Server	Laptop	Router	Distribution of IPSec Connections

Network Cloud   Line: Ethernet   Line: Serial

Command Syntax Conventions

The conventions used to present command syntax in this book are the same conventions used in the IOS Command Reference. The Command Reference describes these conventions as follows:

- **Boldface** indicates commands and keywords that are entered literally as shown. In actual configuration examples and output (not general command syntax), boldface indicates commands that are manually input by the user (such as a **show** command).

- *Italics* indicate arguments for which you supply actual values.

- Vertical bars (I) separate alternative, mutually exclusive elements.

- Square brackets [ ] indicate optional elements.

- Braces { } indicate a required choice.

- Braces within brackets [{ }] indicate a required choice within an optional element.

Introduction

VPNs are becoming more important for both enterprises and service providers. IPSec specifically is one of the more popular technologies for deploying IP-based VPNs. There are many books in the market that go into technical details of IPSec protocols and cover product level configuration, but they do not address overall design issues for deploying IPSec VPNs.

The Goals of This Book

The objective of this book is to provide you with a good understanding of design and architectural issues of IPSec VPNs. This book will also give you guidance on enabling value-added services and integrating IPSec VPNs with other Layer 3 (MPLS VPN) technologies.

Who Should Read This Book

The primary audience for this book is network engineers involved in design, deployment, and trouble-shooting of IPSec VPNs. The assumption in this book is that you have a good understanding of basic IP routing, although IPSec knowledge is not a prerequisite.

How This Book Is Organized

The book is divided into three general parts. Part I covers the general architecture of IPSec, including its protocols and Cisco IOS IPSec implementation details. Part II, beginning with Chapter 5, examines the IPSec VPN design principles covering hub-and-spoke, full-mesh, and fault-tolerant designs. Part II also covers dynamic configuration models used to simplify IPSec VPNs designs, and presents a case study. Part III, beginning with Chapter 8, covers design issues in adding services to an IPSec VPN such as voice, multicast, and integrating IPSec VPNs with MPLs VPNs. The book is organized as follows:

- **Part I, "Introduction and Concepts"**

  - **Chapter 1, "Introduction to VPNs"**—Provides an introduction to VPN concepts and covers a brief introduction to various VPN technologies.

  - **Chapter 2, "IPSec Overview"**—Gives an overview of IPSec protocols and describes differences between transport mode and tunnel mode. Cisco IOS IPSec packet processing is also explained in this chapter.

  - **Chapter 3, "Enhanced IPSec Features"**—Introduces advanced IPSec features that improve IPSec VPN scalability and fault tolerance, such as dead peer detection and control plane keepalives. This chapter also explains the challenges of IPSec interoperating with Network Address Translation (NAT) and Path Maximum Transmission Unit detection (PMTUD) and how to overcome these challenges.

- **Chapter 4, "IPSec Authentication and Authorization Models"**—Explores IPSec features that are primarily called upon for the remote access users such as Extended Authentication (XAUTH) and Mode-configuration (MODE-CFG). It also explains the Cisco EzVPN connection model and digital certificate concepts.

- **Part II, "Design and Deployment"**

  - **Chapter 5, "IPSec VPN Architectures"**—Covers various IPSec connections models such as native IPSec, GRE, and remote access. Deployment architectures for each of the connection models are explored with pros and cons for each architecture.

  - **Chapter 6, "Designing Fault-Tolerant IPSec VPNs"**—Discusses how to introduce fault tolerance into VPN architectures and describes the caveats with the various fault-tolerance methods.

  - **Chapter 7, "Auto-Configuration Architectures for Site-to-Site IPSec VPNs"**—Covers mechanisms to alleviate the configuration complexity of a large-scale IPSec VPN; Tunnel Endpoint Discovery (TED) and Dynamic Multipoint VPNs (DMVPN) are the two mechanisms discussed in depth.

- **Part III, "Service Enhancements"**

  - **Chapter 8, "IPSec and Application Interoperability"**— Examines the issues with IPSec VPNs in the context of the running applications such as voice and multicast over the VPN.

  - **Chapter 9, "Network-Based IPSec VPNs"**—Concludes by introducing the concept of network-based VPNs.

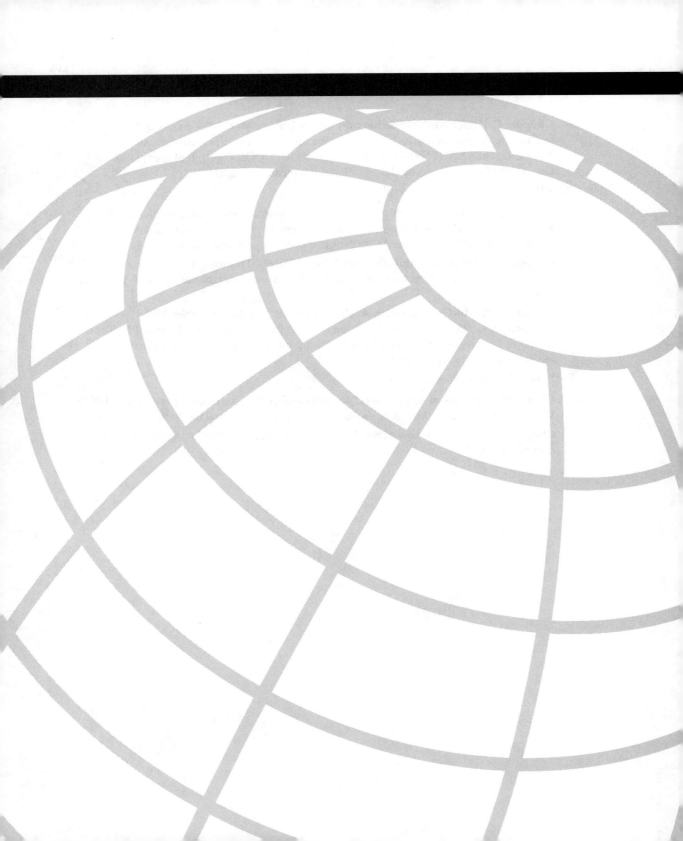

CHAPTER 1

Introduction to VPNs

Virtual private networks, commonly referred to as VPNs, are not an entirely new concept in networking. As the name suggests, a VPN can be defined as a private network service delivered over a public network infrastructure. A telephone call between two parties is the simplest example of a virtual private connection over a public telephone network. Two important characteristics of a VPN are that it is virtual and private.

There are many types of VPNs, such as Frame Relay and ATM, and entire books can and have been written about each of these VPN technologies. The focus of this book is on a VPN technology known as *IPSec*.

Motivations for Deploying a VPN

This chapter introduces some of the VPN technologies and helps to explain the motivations for deploying a VPN. The primary reason for deploying a VPN is cost savings. Corporations with offices all over the world often need to interconnect them in order to conduct everyday business. For these connections, they can either use dedicated leased lines that run between the offices or have each site connect locally to a public network, such as the Internet, and form a VPN over the public network.

Figure 1-1 shows an international corporation that connects to each site using leased lines. Each connection is point-to-point and requires a dedicated leased line to connect it to another site. If each site needs to be connected to every other site (a situation also known as any-to-any or full-mesh connectivity), *n-1* leased lines would be required at each site where *n* is the number of sites. Leased lines are typically priced based on the distance between the sites and bandwidth offered. Cross-country and intercontinental links are typically very expensive, making full-mesh connectivity with leased lines very expensive.

Figure 1-2 shows an alternate method of connecting the same sites of the corporation, this time over a public network such as the Internet. In this model, each site is connected to the public network at its closest point, possibly via a leased line, but all connections between sites are virtual connections. The cloud in the figure represents a virtual connection between the sites, as opposed to a physical dedicated connection between sites in the leased-line model.

Figure 1-1 *Connecting Sites of a Corporation over Leased Lines*

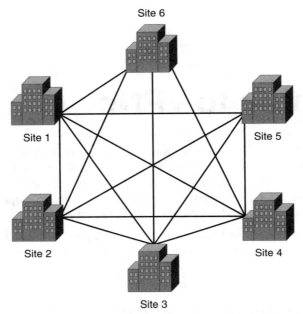

Sites of a Corporation in Full Mesh over Leased Lines

NOTE A public network can be defined as a network with an infrastructure shared by many users of that network. Bear in mind that the word "public" does not mean that the network is available free to anyone. Many service providers have large ATM and Frame Relay public networks, and the Internet is probably the most ubiquitous public network of them all.

Although connecting the sites over a public network has obvious cost advantages over the dedicated leased line model and provides significant cost savings to the corporation, this model also introduces risks, such as the following:

- Data security
- Lack of dedicated bandwidth between sites

In the VPN model, the corporation's data is being transported across a public network, which means other users of the public network can potentially access the corporation's data and thereby pose a security risk.

Figure 1-2   *Connecting Sites of a Corporation over a Public Network*

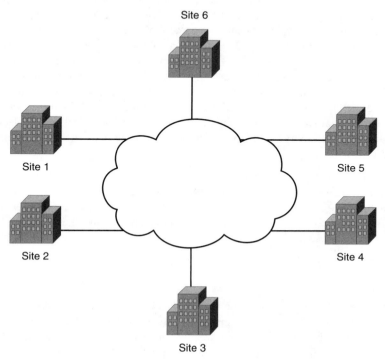

The second risk in the VPN model is the lack of dedicated bandwidth availability between sites that the leased line model provides. Because the VPN model connects sites using a virtual connection and the physical links in the public network are shared by many sites of many different VPNs. Bandwidth between the sites is not guaranteed unless the VPN allows some form of connection admission control and bandwidth reservation schemes. Both risks can be mitigated—the next section introduces some VPN technologies that overcome these risks.

VPN Technologies

In the simplest sense, a VPN connects two endpoints over a public network to form a logical connection. The logical connections can be made at either Layer 2 or Layer 3 of the OSI model, and VPN technologies can be classified broadly on these logical connection models as Layer 2 VPNs or Layer 3 VPNs. Conceptually, establishing connectivity between sites over a Layer 2 or Layer 3 VPN is the same. The concept involves adding a "delivery header" in front of the payload to get it to the destination site. In the case of Layer 2 VPNs, the delivery header is at Layer 2, and in the case of Layer 3 VPNs, it is (obviously) at Layer 3. ATM and Frame Relay are examples of Layer 2 VPNs; GRE, L2TP, MPLS, and IPSec are examples of Layer 3 VPN technologies.

Layer 2 VPNs

Layer 2 VPNs operate at Layer 2 of the OSI reference model; they are point-to-point and establish connectivity between sites over a virtual circuit. A virtual circuit is a logical end-to-end connection between two endpoints in a network, and can span multiple elements and multiple physical segments of a network. The virtual circuit is configured end-to-end and is usually called a permanent virtual circuit (PVC). A dynamic point-to-point virtual circuit is also possible and is known as a switched virtual circuit (SVC); SVCs are used less frequently because of the complexity involved in troubleshooting them. ATM and Frame Relay are two of the most popular Layer 2 VPN technologies. ATM and Frame Relay providers can offer private site-to-site connectivity to a corporation by configuring permanent virtual circuits across a shared backbone.

One of the advantages of a Layer 2 VPN is the independence of the Layer 3 traffic payload that can be carried over it. A Frame Relay or ATM PVC between sites can carry many different types of Layer 3 traffic such as IP, IPX, AppleTalk, IP multicast, and so on. ATM and Frame Relay also provide good quality of service (QoS) characteristics, which is especially critical for delay-sensitive traffic such as voice.

Layer 3 VPNs

A connection between sites can be defined as a Layer 3 VPN if the delivery header is at Layer 3 of the OSI model. Common examples of Layer 3 VPNs are GRE, MPLS, and IPSec VPNs. Layer 3 VPNs can be point-to-point to connect two sites such as GRE and IPSec, or may establish any-to-any connectivity to many sites using MPLS VPNs.

GRE Tunnels

Generic routing encapsulation (GRE) was originally developed by Cisco and later standardized as RFC 1701. An IP delivery header for GRE is defined in RFC 1702. A GRE tunnel between two sites that have IP reachability can be described as a VPN, because the private data between the sites is encapsulated in a GRE delivery header.

Because the public Internet is probably the most ubiquitous public network in the world, it is possible to connect many sites of a corporation using GRE tunnels. In this model, each site of the corporation requires only physical connectivity to its Internet service provider, as all of the connections between sites are over GRE tunnels. Although VPNs built over the Internet using GRE are possible, they are rarely used for corporate data due to the inherent risks and lack of strong security mechanisms associated with GRE.

MPLS VPNs

Pioneered by Cisco, Multiprotocol Label Switching was originally known as Tag Switching and later standardized via the IETF as MPLS. Service providers are increasingly deploying MPLS to offer MPLS VPN services to customers. A common principle among all VPN technologies is encapsulation of private data with a delivery header; MPLS VPNs use labels to encapsulate the original data, or payload, to form a VPN between sites.

NOTE   Creating an MPLS VPN is the most popular application and the primary motivation for deploying MPLS; other applications of MPLS include traffic engineering offering Layer 2 VPN services over MPLS.

RFC 2547 defines a scheme for offering VPN service using MPLS. One of the key advantages of MPLS VPNs over other VPN technologies is that it offers the flexibility to configure arbitrary topologies between VPN sites. For example, if three sites of a corporation all must be connected to one another in a full-mesh (any-to-any) configuration using ATM, Frame Relay, GRE, or IPSec technologies, each site requires two virtual circuits, or tunnels, to every other site. The addition of a fourth site to this full-mesh configuration requires that three tunnels, or virtual circuits, exist at each site, and calls for modification in the configurations at all the sites. If n is the number of sites in a VPN, the configuration complexity for this model is $O(n)$ and the scalability is $O(n^2)$. If the same three sites are connected over an MPLS VPN, the addition of the fourth site requires configuration change at only the fourth site. The configuration complexity of this model with n sites is always a constant and is $O(1)$.

The fact that there are virtually no point-to-point tunnels for connecting sites of an MPLS VPN renders them very scalable. Any-to-any connectivity between sites of a VPN and extranet connectivity across VPNs are easy to achieve using MPLS VPNs compared to other tunneling techniques such as GRE. One of the drawbacks of an MPLS VPN is that connectivity between the sites of a VPN is restricted to sites where the provider has points of presence. Although a GRE tunnel could be used across the Internet to extend its reach, GRE by itself has minimal security. We address this issue in Chapter 9, "Network-Based IPSec VPNs."

IPSec VPNs

One of the main concerns for anyone using any VPN is security of data when it traverses a public network. In other words, how does one prevent malicious eavesdropping of data in a VPN?

Encrypting the data is one way to protect it. Data encryption may be achieved by deploying encryption/decryption devices at each site. IPSec is a suite of protocols developed under the auspices of the IETF to achieve secure services over IP packet-switched networks. The Internet is the most ubiquitous packet-switched public network; therefore, an IPSec VPN deployed over the public Internet can mean significant cost savings to a corporation as compared to a leased-line VPN.

IPSec services allow for authentication, integrity, access control, and confidentiality. With IPSec, the information exchanged between remote sites can be encrypted and verified. Both remote access clients and site-to-site VPNs can be deployed using IPSec. Subsequent chapters focus on the IPSec protocols and deployment models that use IPSec.

Remote Access VPNs

As stated previously, VPNs can be classified into site-to-site VPNs and remote access VPNs. Frame Relay, ATM, GRE, and MPLS VPN can be considered site-to-site VPNs because information relevant to the configuration between sites is known in advance at both sides and, more importantly, are static and therefore do not change dynamically. On the other hand, consider a telecommuter who needs VPN access to corporate data over the Internet. The information required to establish a VPN connection such as an IP address of the telecommuter changes dynamically depending on the location of the telecommuter and is not known in advance to the other side of the VPN. This type of VPN can be classified as a remote access VPN.

Remote access to corporate data resources has been a critical enabler for improved productivity, especially for mobile workers. Telecommuters, "road warriors," and remote offices rely on timely access to mission-critical information in order to maintain a competitive advantage in the marketplace. The reliance on remote access has driven demand for higher capacity connections with extended durations from end users. As a result, increased costs are incurred, primarily in the form of telephony charges, for access to the corporate data.

Although dial-up networking provides a universal local access solution, it can be very expensive for long distance and metered local access calls. Remote access VPN connections provide the best solution, mitigating metered telephone charges while allowing the corporation to leverage new last-mile access technologies such as cable and DSL.

Two of the most common remote access methods for VPN access are Layer 2 tunneling protocol (L2TP) and IPSec. L2TP is an IETF standard (RFC 2661) for transporting PPP frames over IP. L2TP provides dial-up users with a virtual connection to a corporate gateway over an IP network, which could be the Internet. Figure 1-3 shows the L2TP model.

The remote user initiates a PPP session to the closest access server, known as a local access concentrator (LAC) via a local telephone call. The LAC authenticates the remote user and determines which local network server (LNS) will terminate the remote user. An L2TP tunnel is established between the LAC and the LNS, and once the LNS authenticates the user, a virtual interface for PPP termination is created on the LNS analogous to a direct-dialed connection to the LNS.

IPSec is another VPN technology that can be used to connect remote access users. This entire book is devoted to the topic of IPSec VPNs, and remote access is specifically covered in detail in Chapter 4, "IPSec Authentication and Authorization Models."

Figure 1-3   *Remote Access VPN Using L2TP*

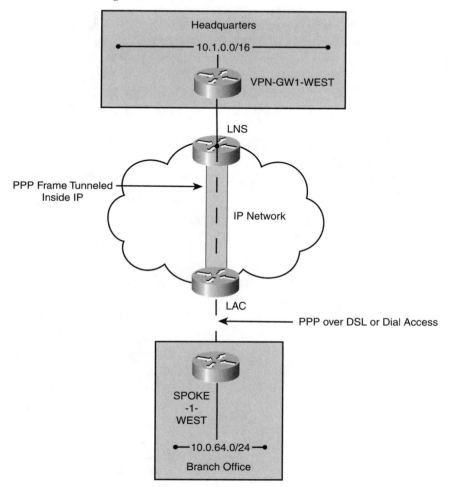

Summary

In this brief introduction to VPNs, you learned that network designers can choose from a wide range of technologies to create VPNs which can be classified into Layer 2 or Layer 3 VPNs, and further into site-to-site and remote access VPNs. Technologies such as Frame Relay, ATM, GRE, and MPLS are used with site-to-site VPNs. The most common remote access VPN technology is L2TP, and IPSec can be used for both remote access and site-to-site VPNs.

CHAPTER 2

IPSec Overview

Chapter 1, "Introduction to VPNs," introduced VPN concepts at a high level and presented an overview of several technologies that use VPNs. In this chapter, you will explore the building blocks of an IPSec VPN and obtain an understanding of IPSec architecture and how the various components of IPSec interact with each other to create a VPN. You will also look at some Cisco-specific IPSec implementation details and how IPSec packet processing is performed on Cisco IOS platforms.

A common misconception about IPSec is that it is a single protocol for providing these security services for IP traffic. In fact, IPSec is really a *suite*, or collection, of protocols for security defined by the IPSec working group in the IETF. The baseline IPSec architecture and fundamental components of IPSec are defined in RFC2401 as the following:

- **Security protocols**—Authentication header (AH) and encapsulation security payload (ESP)
- **Key management**—ISAKMP, IKE, SKEME
- **Algorithms**—for encryption and authentication

The interaction between these components of IPSec is intertwined in such a way that it is a bit hard to understand one of the components without understanding another. A quote from a draft submitted to the IPSec IETF working group sums it up pretty well: "Perhaps IPSec is well understood by some, but frequent questions on the developers' mailing list confirm that one cannot become an IPSec expert merely by reading the RFCs. Much valuable information is buried deep in the list archives or in the minds of its designers."

You will start your IPSec journey with an introduction to encryption terminology, followed by an examination of the IPSec security protocols (AH and ESP), and lastly, an explanation of security associations and key management.

Encryption Terminology

Security and data confidentiality are prime requirements for any VPN. One of the primary reasons for choosing IPSec as your VPN technology is the confidentiality of data provided by the encryption that is built in.

NOTE   *Encryption* is the transformation of plain text into a form that makes the original text incomprehensible to an unauthorized recipient that does not hold a matching key to decode or decrypt the encrypted message.

Decryption is the reverse of encryption; it is the transformation of encrypted data back into plain text. Encryption techniques are as old as history—in fact, Julius Cæsar apparently did not trust his messengers and therefore encrypted his military messages to his generals with a simple encryption scheme; he replaced every A by D, every B by E, and so on. Only someone who knew the *key* (to shift each alphabetical letter by three, in this case) would be able to decrypt the message.

A *cryptographic algorithm*, also called a *cipher*, is the mathematical function used for encryption and decryption. Generally, there are two related functions—one for encryption and the other for decryption. Security of data in modern cryptographic algorithms is based on the *key* (or keys). It doesn't matter if an eavesdropper knows your algorithm; if he or she doesn't know your particular key, an eavesdropper will be unable read your messages.

Cryptographic algorithms can be classified into two categories:

- Symmetric
- Asymmetric

Symmetric Algorithms

Symmetric cryptographic algorithms are based on the sender and receiver of the message knowing and using the same secret key. The sender uses a secret key to encrypt the message, and the receiver uses the same key to decrypt it. The main problem with using the symmetric key approach is finding a way to distribute the key without anyone else finding it out. Anyone who overhears or intercepts the key in transit can later read and modify messages encrypted or authenticated using that key, and can forge new messages. DES, 3DES, and AES are popular symmetric encryption algorithms. A detailed explanation of these algorithms is beyond the scope of this book.

NOTE   DES uses a 56-bit key and is not considered secure anymore; in 1999, the DES key was cracked in less than 24 hours by using an exhaustive key search. Triple DES (3DES) and AES are the recommended encryption algorithms as of this writing.

Asymmetric Algorithms

Asymmetrical encryption algorithms, also known as public key algorithms, use separate keys—
one for encryption and another for decryption. The encryption key is called the *public key* and
can be made public. Only the *private key*, used for decryption, needs to be kept secret. Although
the public and private keys are mathematically related, it is not feasible to derive one from the
other. Anyone with a recipient's public key can encrypt a message, but the message can only be
decrypted with a private key that only the recipient knows. Therefore, a secure communication
channel to transmit the secret key is no longer required as in the case of symmetric algorithms.

Figure 2-1   *Public Key Encryption*

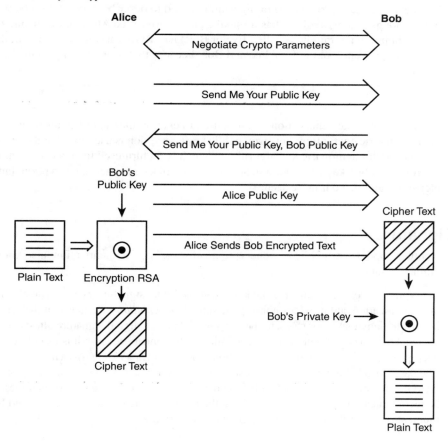

Figure 2-1 illustrates how public key encryption algorithms work. Bob and Alice communicate securely using public key encryption as follows:

1 Alice and Bob agree on a public key algorithm.

2 Bob sends Alice his public key and Alice sends Bob her public key.

3 Alice sends Bob a message, encrypting the message using Bob's public key.

4 Bob receives the message and decrypts Alice's message using his private key.

NOTE	Whenever an encryption theory or algorithm is used to describe a transaction between two parties, longstanding tradition has it that the parties are called Alice and Bob, and the eavesdropper in the middle is called Eve or Blackhat. Rumor has it that early on, the FBI and CIA actually went looking for Alice and Bob, because they were passing so many encrypted messages.

In reality, public key encryption is rarely used to encrypt messages because it is much slower than symmetric encryption; however, public key encryption is used to solve the problem of key distribution for symmetric key algorithms, which is, in turn used to encrypt actual messages. Therefore, public key encryption is not meant to replace symmetric encryption, but can supplement it and make it more secure.

Digital Signatures

Another good use of public key encryption is for message authentication, also known as a digital signature.

Encrypting a message with a private key creates a digital signature, which is an electronic means of authentication and provides non-repudiation. *Non-repudiation* means that the sender will not be able to deny that he or she sent the message. That is, a digital signature attests not only to the contents of a message, but also to the identity of the sender. Because it is usually inefficient to encrypt an actual message for authentication, a document *hash* known as a message digest is used. The basic idea behind a message digest is to take a variable length message and convert it into a fixed length compressed output called the message digest. Because the original message cannot be reconstructed from the message digest, the hash is labeled "one-way." Alice and Bob's communication using digital signature is shown in Figure 2-2.

Figure 2-2   *Signed Message Digest*

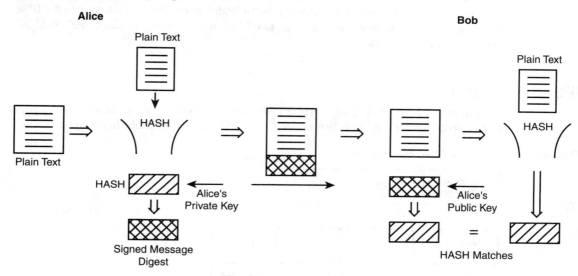

1 Alice computes a one-way hash of a document that she wishes to send Bob.

2 Alice encrypts the hash with her private key. The encrypted message digest becomes the digital signature.

3 Alice sends the document along with the digital signature to Bob.

4 Bob decrypts the digital signature using Alice's public key and also computes a one-way hash of the document received from Alice. If the two values match, Bob can be sure that the document came from Alice and the document was not tampered with in transit. The slightest change in the document will cause the values to not match and will cause the authentication to fail.

NOTE   When the message digest generated is encrypted using a key, it's called a keyed message digest. Another definition for a keyed message digest is *message authentication code* (HMAC).

IPSec Security Protocols

The objective of IPSec is to provide security services for IP packets at the network layer. These services include access control, data integrity, authentication, protection against replay, and data confidentiality.

Encapsulating security payload (ESP) and authentication header (AH) are the two IPSec security protocols used to provide this security for an IP datagram. Before looking into the IPSec security protocols, you must understand the two IPSec modes, transport and tunnel mode, and what services each provides.

IPSec Transport Mode

In transport mode, an IPSec header (AH or ESP) is inserted between the IP header and the upper layer protocol header. Figure 2-3 shows an IP packet protected by IPSec in transport mode.

Figure 2-3   *IP Packet in IPSec Transport Mode*

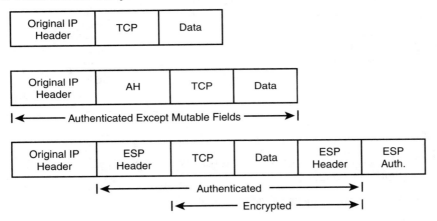

In this mode, the IP header is the same as that of the original IP packet except for the IP protocol field, which is changed to ESP (50) or AH (51), and the IP header checksum, which is recalculated. IPSec assumes the IP endpoints are reachable. In this mode, the destination IP address in the IP header is not changed by the source IPSec endpoint; therefore, this mode can only be used to protect packets in scenarios in which the IP endpoints and the IPSec endpoints are the same.

From an IPSec VPN point of view, this mode is most useful when traffic between two hosts must be protected, rather than when traffic moves from site-to-site, and each site has many hosts. The biggest challenge when using IPSec transport mode in the site-to-site model is the complexity involved in managing IPSec protection from any given host to all the possible peer hosts. Additionally, the two hosts' IP addresses must be routable across the entire IP routing path. Due to the complexities of building an IPSec transport mode VPN from host to host, the typical VPN will use a VPN gateway to protect all the hosts from one site to all the hosts at a peer site. A typical IPSec VPN deployment occurs between sites where each site has multiple hosts behind a VPN gateway and the IPSec tunnel endpoints serve as the VPN gateway routers. With the VPN gateway protecting a set of host IP addresses, the IPSec transport mode has limited utility. IPSec transport mode can still be used for VPN connectivity if Generic Route Encapsulation (GRE) IP tunnels are used between the VPN gateways. The GRE tunnel endpoints serve as "host" endpoints. IPSec protects the GRE tunnel traffic in transport mode. Chapter 3, "Enhanced IPSec Features," explores more about GRE and IPSec.

NOTE   Another limitation of transport mode is that it cannot be used with NAT translation of packets between IPSec peers. Also, for most hardware encryption engines, it is less efficient to encrypt transport mode than tunnel mode, because transport mode requires displacement of the IP header to make room for the ESP or AH header.

IPSec Tunnel Mode

IPSec VPN service using transport mode and GRE encapsulation between the VPN gateways at each site is a very popular option for site-to-site VPNs. But what about an IP node that has no GRE support, yet requires the establishment IPSec VPN connectivity with another site? The most common example of this is a telecommuter. IPSec tunnel mode helps address this situation.

In tunnel mode, the original IP packet is encapsulated in another IP datagram, and an IPSec header (AH or ESP) is inserted between the outer and inner headers. Because of this encapsulation with an "outer" IP packet, tunnel mode can be used to provide security services between sites on behalf of IP nodes behind the gateway router at each site. Also, this mode can be used for the telecommuter scenario of connecting from an end host to an IPSec gateway at a site. Figure 2-4 shows an IP packet protected by IPSec in tunnel mode.

Figure 2-4   *IP Packet in IPSec Tunnel Mode*

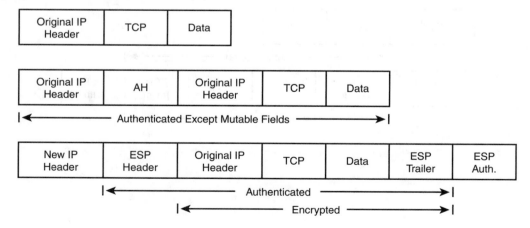

Encapsulating Security Header (ESP)

ESP provides confidentiality, data integrity, and optional data origin authentication and anti-replay services. It provides these services by encrypting the original payload and encapsulating the packet between a header and a trailer, as shown in Figure 2-5.

Figure 2-5   *IP Packet Protected by ESP*

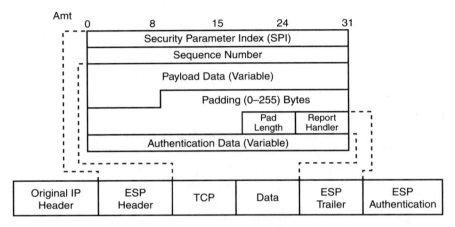

ESP is identified by a value of 50 in the IP header. The ESP header is inserted after the IP header and before the upper layer protocol header. The IP header itself could be a new IP header in tunnel mode or the original IP packet's header in transport mode. Figures 2-6 and 2-7 show the position of the ESP header in transport and tunnel mode, respectively.

Figure 2-6   *IP Packet Protected by ESP in Transport Mode*

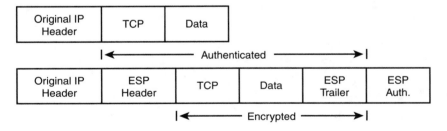

Figure 2-7 *IP Packet Protected by ESP in Tunnel Mode*

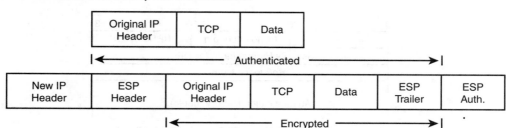

The *security parameter index (SPI)* in the ESP header is a 32-bit value that, combined with the destination address and protocol in the preceding IP header, identifies the security association (SA) to be used to process the packet. The SPI is an arbitrary number chosen by the destination peer during Internet Key Exchange (IKE) negotiation between the peers. It functions like an index number that can be used to look up the SA in the security association database (SADB).

The sequence number is a unique monotonically increasing number inserted into the header by the sender. Sequence numbers, along with the sliding receive window, provide anti-replay services. The anti-replay protection scheme is common to both ESP and AH.

The data being protected (or, more specifically, being encrypted by ESP) is in the payload data field. The algorithm used to encrypt the payload may require an initialization vector (IV), which is also carried in the data payload. Note that the IV is authenticated but not encrypted. If the encryption algorithm used is DES, then the first eight bytes of the protected data field is the IV; 3DES and AES also have an 8-byte IV.

Padding in the ESP header is the addition of bits to the ESP header; the number of bits to be padded depends on the encryption algorithm that is used. The Pad Length field indicates the number of pad bytes added so that the original data can be restored on decryption.

The next header payload identifies the type of data in the payload. For example, if ESP is used in tunnel mode, this value will be 4.

Authentication digest in the ESP header is used to verify data integrity. Because authentication is always applied after encryption, a check for validity of the data is done upon receipt of the packet and before decryption.

Authentication Header (AH)

AH provides connectionless integrity, data authentication, and optional replay protection but, unlike ESP, it does not provide confidentiality. Consequently, it has a much simpler header than ESP. Figure 2-8 shows an AH-protected IP packet.

Figure 2-8 *IP Packet Protected by AH*

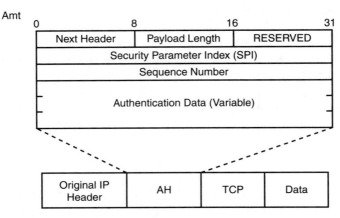

AH is an IP protocol, identified by a value of 51 in the IP header. The Next header field indicates what follows the AH header. In transport mode, it will be the value of the upper layer protocol being protected (for example, UDP or TCP). In tunnel mode, this value is 4. The positions of AH in transport and tunnel mode are shown in Figure 2-9 and Figure 2-10, respectively.

Figure 2-9 *IP Packet Protected by AH in Transport Mode*

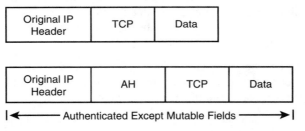

Figure 2-10 *IP Packet Protected by AH in Tunnel Mode*

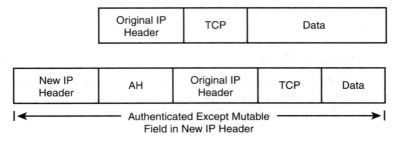

AH in transport mode is useful if the communication endpoints are also the IPSec endpoints. In tunnel mode, AH encapsulates the IP packet and an additional IP header is added before the AH header. Although the tunnel mode of AH could be used to provide IPSec VPN end-to-end security, there is no data confidentiality in AH and hence this mode is not too useful.

The payload length field in the AH header in Figure 2-9 indicates the length of the header. The Reserved field is not used, and is, therefore, set to zeroes. The SPI and sequence numbers have the same significance as in ESP. The authentication digest has one key difference from ESP: With AH, authentication is provided to the IP header in addition to the payload. As AH creates the authentication data on the entire packet, including the IP header, some of the IP fields will change in transit; therefore, all those fields in the IP header that may change in transit are zeroed out before the authentication digest is hashed. The fields that zero out include type of service (ToS) bits, flags, fragment offset, time-to-live (TTL), and header checksum. These fields are zeroed out because authenticating a changed value in transit (for example, TTL) will cause the authentication hash to have a mismatch from the sender and the packet will be dropped.

Key Management and Security Associations

You learned that there are two types of encryption algorithms—symmetric and asymmetric. You also know that IPSec VPNs are typically deployed across a public infrastructure because IPSec offers encryption services to keep the data confidential from non-intended recipients of the data. DES and 3DES are two of the most popular encryption algorithms used for IPSec VPNs; both are symmetric algorithms and, therefore, have to deal with the challenge of secure key distribution. Problems arise when the key distribution must be done over a public infrastructure such as the Internet.

Collectively, the generation, distribution, and storage of keys is called key management. All crypto systems must deal with key management issues. The default IPSec method for secure key negotiation is the Internet Key Exchange (IKE) protocol. IKE is designed to provide mutual authentication of systems, as well as to establish a shared secret key to create IPSec security associations. Before delving into how IKE works, it may be helpful to review the Diffie-Hellman key management protocol that is used by IKE to exchange a secret key over an insecure medium (such as the Internet).

The Diffie-Hellman Key Exchange

Whitfield Diffie and Martin Hellman first published their algorithm in 1976. This algorithm is based on the difficulty of solving the discrete logarithm problem. In short, the situation is as follows (using the classic cryptographic characters of Alice, Bob, and Eve):

- Alice wishes to communicate with Bob securely.

- In order to achieve this secure communication, Alice needs to establish a session key with Bob, but they have to somehow agree on a shared key over a public medium that is insecure.

- To make matters worse, Eve wishes to monitor this communication.

In this section, you'll see how the Diffie-Hellman key exchange can help this situation. The algorithm has two system parameters, p and g. The parameters are both public and, therefore, may be used by all the users in a system. Parameter p is a large prime number and parameter g (usually called a generator) is an integer less than p, which is capable of generating every element from 1 to $p-1$ when multiplied by itself a certain number of times modulo the prime p.

First, Alice generates the random private value a and Bob generates the random private value b. Then they derive their public values using parameters p and g and their private values. Alice's public value is $X=g^a \bmod p$ and Bob's public value is $Y=g^b \bmod p$. They then exchange their public values. Finally, Alice computes $k_{ab}=(g^b)^a \bmod p$, and Bob computes $k_{ba}=(g^a)^b \bmod p$. Because $k_{ab}=k_{ba}=k$, Alice and Bob now have a shared secret key k. The protocol depends on the discrete logarithm problem for its security. It assumes that it is computationally infeasible to calculate the shared secret key $k=g^{ab} \bmod p$ given the two public values $g^a \bmod p$ and $g^b \bmod p$ when the prime p is sufficiently large. Although all of this has been accomplished with Eve monitoring, she cannot determine the value of the shared key. Figure 2-11 illustrates a graphical representation of the Diffie-Hellman key exchange.

Figure 2-11 *Diffie-Hellman Key Exchange*

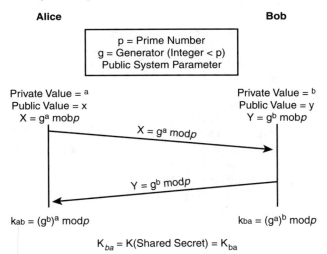

NOTE   The possibility of a "man-in-the-middle" attack remains a serious security problem for public key–based algorithms. Suppose Alice wishes to communicate with Bob and Eve wishes to eavesdrop on the conversation or possibly deliver a false message to Bob. To get communications started, Alice must ask Bob for his public key. If Bob sends his public key to Alice and Eve is able to intercept it, a man-in-the-middle attack can begin. In order to perpetrate the attack, Eve sends Alice a public key for which she has the private, matching, key. Believing this public key to be Bob's, Alice encrypts her message with Eve's key and sends the encyphered message back to Bob. Eve again intercepts and decyphers the message, keeps a copy, and reencyphers it (after alteration, if desired) using the public key Bob originally sent to Alice. When Bob receives the newly encyphered message, he will believe it came from Alice. Strong authentication is required between the peers to mitigate these types of attacks.

Security Associations and IKE Operation

A security association, more commonly referred to as an SA, is a basic building block of IPSec. An SA is an entry in the SA database (SADB), which contains information about the security that has been negotiated between two parties for IKE or IPSec. There are two types of SAs:

- IKE or ISAKMP SA
- IPSec SA

Although it is common practice to use the term SA to encompass both types, it is important to make the distinction for troubleshooting purposes, because each type of SA achieves a different purpose. Both SA types are established between IPSec peers using the IKE protocol.

IKE SAs between peers are used for control traffic, such as negotiating algorithms to use to encrypt IKE traffic and authenticate peers. There is only one IKE SA between peers, and it usually has less traffic and a longer lifetime than IPSec SAs.

IPSec SAs are used for negotiating encryption algorithms to apply for IP traffic between the peers, based on policy definitions that define the type of traffic to be protected. Because they are unidirectional, at least two IPSec SAs are needed (one for inbound traffic and the other for outbound traffic). It is possible to have multiple pairs of IPSec SAs between peers to describe unique disjoint sets of IP hosts or IP data traffic. IPSec SAs also usually have more traffic and a shorter lifetime than IKE SAs.

The establishment and maintenance of both ISAKMP/IKE SAs and IPSec SAs is a major function of the IKE protocol. The number of RFCs in the IETF IPSec working group related to key exchange and negotiation can be intimidating and confusing, as it is spread over four RFC documents: IKE (RFC 2409), ISAKMP (RFC 2408), OAKLEY (RFC 2412), and the ISAKMP Domain of Interpretation (RFC 2407). The relationships between these standards are not clearly defined in the documents themselves. This chapter attempts to clarify this quagmire of terminology and its related concepts.

IKE operates in two phases to establish these IKE and IPSec SAs:

- Phase 1 provides mutual authentication of the IKE peers and establishment of the session key. This phase creates an ISAKMP SA (a security association for IKE, sometimes referred to as an *IKE SA*) using a DH exchange, cookies, and an ID exchange. Once an ISAKMP SA is established, all IKE communication between the initiator and responder is protected with encryption and an integrity check that is authenticated. The purpose of IKE phase 1 is to facilitate a secure channel between the peers so that phase 2 negotiations can occur securely.

- Phase 2 provides for the negotiation and establishment of the IPSec SAs using ESP or AH to protect IP data traffic.

NOTE   Even though we use ISAKMP and IKE interchangeably, they are different. ISAKMP defines how IPSec peers communicate, the constructs of the message exchange between the peers, and the state transitions they go through to establish their connection. ISAKMP provides the means to authenticate a peer and to exchange information for key exchange. However, ISAKMP does not define *how* an authenticated key exchange is done; IKE defines *how* the key exchange is done.

Before we delve into IKE phase 1 and phase 2 operations, we will quickly review the ISAKMP header, which is shown in Figure 2-12.

Figure 2-12   *ISAKMP Header*

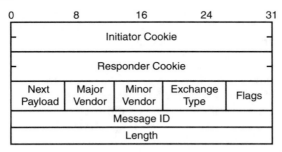

IKE messages are constructed by chaining ISAKMP payloads to an ISAKMP header. The initiator and responder cookies in the header are created by each peer and are used in conjunction with the message ID to determine the state of an in-progress ISAKMP exchange. The cookies are eight bytes of random values that are used to identify the IKE SA. The cookies are formed by a hash of the peer identity (IP address, port, and protocol), a locally generated secret number, the date, and the time. The cookies serve as a sort of ISAKMP SPI.

The Next payload field indicates that the ISAKMP payload immediately follows the header. ISAKMP versions are identified by Major and Minor fields. So far, the Major version is only 1, and the Minor version is zero. The exchange type shows the type of message being used. The flags are one octet in length. There are only three bits that are used, starting with the least significant bit. Bit 0 is the encryption bit. When set to 1, it means the payload is encrypted. Bit 1 is the commit bit and, if set, it ensures that encrypted material is not received prior to SA establishment. Bit 2 is the authentication bit and implies, if set, that the payload will be only authenticated and not encrypted. The length field, which is four octets in length, indicates the length of the total message, which is the header plus the payloads. Refer to RFC 2408 for more information on the header.

IKE Phase 1 Operation

IKE phase 1 offers two modes—Main and Aggressive. The result of each mode is the establishment of an ISAKMP/IKE SA. The IKE SA has various parameters that are negotiated between two peers. The mandatory parameters are the encryption algorithm, hash algorithm, authentication method, Diffie-Hellman group, and optional parameters such as lifetime. Example 2-1 shows how to configure these IKE phase 1 parameters on a Cisco IOS router.

Example 2-1   *Configuring IKE Phase 1 Parameters on a Cisco IOS Router*

```
crypto isakmp policy 1
encryption 3des
hash md5
group2
lifetime
authentication pre-shared
Show cry isakmp policy
```

Bear in mind that the configuration in Example 2-1 shows only one set of possible parameters. Each parameter has a range of values, and there can be many possibilities for the encryption algorithm parameter. The base encryption algorithms that are supported by IKE are DES, 3DES, and AES. Other encryption algorithms, defined in the IKE RFC, can also be used. The hash algorithm used is always an HMAC version of the negotiated hash algorithm. The Diffie-Hellman group determines the parameters to use when the peers engage in DH exchange. The group number implicitly defines these parameters. The optional parameter lifetime, which determines the life of the IKE SA, can be configured in either seconds or kilobytes.

NOTE   It should be noted that you can configure multiple sets of IKE policy parameters (by changing the index number 1 in Example 2-1). The initiator can offer more than one IKE policy and the responder can match the offered policies against all of its policy sets.

The parameter with the most impact on the IKE exchange itself is the *authentication method.* There are four types of authentication methods available with IKE: pre-shared key, digital signature, public key encryption with four encryptions, and public key encryption with two encryptions. You will explore these methods further in this chapter.

Main Mode

Main Mode consists of six messages—three in each direction—exchanged between the initiator and responder. It offers identity protection and considerable flexibility in terms of the parameters and configurations that can be negotiated. Figure 2-13 illustrates the Main Mode operation.

Figure 2-13   *IKE Phase 1 Main Mode Using Pre-shared Keys*

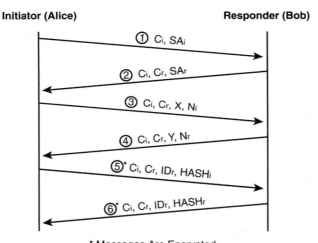

In the first exchange, initiator sends an ISAKMP header with a cookie Ci (initiator cookie) and an SA payload (SAi). The SAi is used for communicating the various phase 1 parameters (encryption algorithm, hash algorithm, authentication method, lifetime, and so on). In the second exchange, the responder replies with selected parameters for each of the proposals along with the SA header response (SAr) and the ISAKMP header with a cookie Cr (responder cookie). The responder picks one of the offered proposals in its entirety and returns that—it is not allowed to pick and choose attributes from different proposals. If none of the proposals match, then the responder will return a notify payload rejecting the proposals. The third and fourth exchanges occur when the keying materials are exchanged.

Once the keying materials are exchanged, four different keys are derived. The value SKEYID (Shared Key ID) and the key resulting from the DH exchange, K, are used to derive three additional keys:

$$SKEYID_d = \text{hashfunc}(SKEYID, K|C_I|C_R|0)$$
$$SKEYID_a \ \text{hashfunc}(SKEYID, SKEYID_d|K|C_I|C_R|1)$$
$$SKEYID_e = \text{hashfunc}(SKEYID, SKEYID_a|K|C_I|C_R|2)$$

SKEYID is derived differently for each authentication where *hashfunc(key, data)* is the negotiated hash function using the key over the data mechanism. $SKEYID_d$ is used to derive more keying material if such material is required and perfect forward secrecy (PFS) is not required. $SKEYID_a$ is used as the key to provide data integrity for ISAKMP messages. $SKEYID_e$ is used as the key for encryption of IKE messages.

The fifth and sixth messages are encrypted with $SKEYID_e$ and authenticated using the hashes derived, *HASH_i* and *HASH_r*, along with the different phase 1 encryption and hash algorithm that was negotiated as part of the first two exchanges and use of $SKEYID_e$ and $SKEYID_a$. The main part of the exchange is the identification of the initiator and responder *IDi* and *IDr*.

$$HASH_i = \text{hash}(SKEYID, X|Y|C_i|C_r|SAr|\textbf{\textit{IDi}})$$
$$HASH_r = \text{hash}(SKEYID, X|Y|C_r|C_i|SAi|\textbf{\textit{IDr}})$$

One point to note in Main Mode is that that because the ID payload is encrypted, the responder has no idea who he is talking to. Therefore, in the case of Main Mode using a pre-shared key, the identity can be based only on the source IP address of the initiating peer.

Aggressive Mode

IKE Aggressive Mode needs only three exchanges, unlike Main Mode's six exchanges, that perform key negotiation and authentication, speeding up the IKE transaction processing. The increase in speed comes at the cost of some security, however. Figure 2-14 shows Aggressive Mode negotiation.

Figure 2-14   *IKE Phase 1 Aggressive Mode*

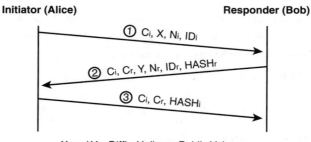

X and Y—Diffie-Hellman Public Values
N_i and N_r—Nonce (Random Data Used to Guarantee Liveness)

In the first message, the initiator sends the ISAKMP header, security association, DH public value, nonce, and the identification ID (IDi). In the second message, the responder replies with all the chosen transforms for each of the proposals and DH half key. This message is authenticated but not encrypted.

The third message is sent by the initiator back to the responder with the message authenticated such that the responder can make sure that the hash matches the hash calculated, which would confirm that all is well. One of the primary uses of Aggressive Mode is for remote access IKE clients when the responder has no prior knowledge of the address of the initiator and pre-shared keys are used as the authentication method. Aggressive Mode is less secure than Main Mode because identities are passed in the clear and DH parameters cannot be negotiated.

Authentication Methods

As mentioned earlier, one of the parameters with the most impact on the IKE phase 1 exchange itself is the *authentication method*. Next, you'll look at the two widely deployed authentication methods: pre-shared key and digital signatures.

Pre-shared Key Authentication

In this method, both the initiator and responder must have the same pre-shared keys; otherwise, the IKE tunnel will not be built due to the pre-shared key mismatch. The keys are agreed upon typically using an out-of-band technique. In a previous section in this chapter, you reviewed the DH exchange and saw how SKEYIDs are generated. The other keys are generated from SKEYID. The value of *SKEYID* generated for pre-shared key is

$$SKEYID = \text{hash (Pre-Shared Key, Ni|Nr)}$$

One disadvantage of using pre-shared keys in IKE Main Mode is that, because the ID payloads are encrypted, the responder is not aware of the identity of the initiator. In remote access scenarios (such as telecommuting), the source IP address of the initiator is not known in advance to the responder. In such cases, Aggressive Mode is the only choice with pre-shared key authentication.

Due to its simplicity, this authentication method is widely deployed for mass IPSec VPN deployment. The Cisco IOS configuration for this method is shown in Example 2-2.

Example 2-2   *Cisco IOS Configuration for Setting Pre-shared Keys*

```
crypto isakmp policy 1
encryption 3des
hash md5
group2
lifetimez
authentication pre-shared
crypto isakmp key ciscovpn 9.1.1.35
crypto isakmp key wildvpn address 0.0.0.0 0.0.0.0
```

Digital Signature Authentication

In the case of digital signatures, peers can be authenticated with public key signatures—either DSS or RSA. Currently, Cisco IOS only supports RSA. Public keys are usually obtained using certificates. IKE allows for the exchange of certificates between the initiator and responder. Figure 2-15 shows an IKE exchange with a digital signature.

Figure 2-15   *IKE Phase 1 Authentication Using Digital Signatures*

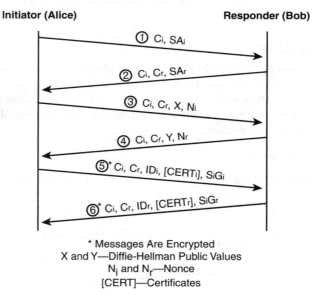

```
                    * Messages Are Encrypted
         X and Y—Diffie-Hellman Public Values
                  Nᵢ and Nᵣ—Nonce
                  [CERT]—Certificates
```

The important thing to point out in Figure 2-15 is that in the third and fourth message exchanges, a request for the certificate is sent by the initiator to the responder, and vice versa, along with a nonce (Ni,Nr) and the DH public values. In the fifth and sixth message exchanges, the certificates are actually exchanged. Although the use of certificate is optional, it has become a standard implementation, as shown below.

$$SIG_i = \text{PRIVATEKEY\_i}(HASH_i)$$
$$SIGr = \text{PRIVATEKEY\_r}(HASH_r)$$

The key thing is the HASH_i and HASH_r are signed by the corresponding private keys to form the message digest SIG_i and SIG_r. Recipients of the signature will use the signer's public key to decrypt and verify the message. The public keys, along with proof of identity (ID), are in the certificates. The fifth and sixth message exchanges are encrypted using $SKEYID_e$; therefore, the certificate payload is also encrypted. The recipient must decrypt the packet and get the public key from the certificate before the signed hash is authenticated. The method for generating *SKEYID* is as follows:

SKEYID = hash(Ni|Nr|K)

We have already shown how the other keys are generated from SKEYID.

The creation and management of certificates using a Certificate Authority (CA) server is beyond the scope of the IPSec standard. One thing worth mentioning, however, is that certificates contain public keys signed by a trusted CA, which provides a third-party relationship trusted by both the authenticating peers. The Public Key Infrastructure (PKI) is a good example of a certificate management system. For more information on PKI, refer to the RFC material managed within the IETF PKIX group, or obtain a reference book on PKI.

IKE Phase 2 Operation

IKE phase 1 creates the IKE/ISAKMP SAs and phase 2 establishes the IPSec SA in each direction. Phase 2 is also referred to as Quick Mode. At the completion of Quick Mode, the two peers should be ready to pass traffic using ESP or AH modes. Because an IPSec SA is unidirectional, there will be a minimum of two IPSec SA between two IPSec peers. Figure 2-16 shows the Quick Mode exchange.

Figure 2-16   *IKE Phase 2 – Quick Mode*

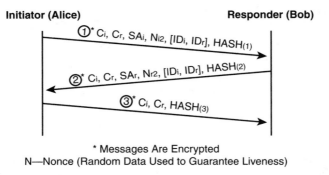

* Messages Are Encrypted
N—Nonce (Random Data Used to Guarantee Liveness)

Quick Mode

Quick Mode has three exchanges. All of these messages are protected by IKE, which means that all of the packets are encrypted and authenticated by *SKEYID_e* and *SKEYID_a*—the same keys derived in IKE phase 1.

The first message from the initiator has the ISAKMP header and the IPSec SA payload with all the proposals and transforms that will be used for bulk data. A new nonce (Ni2) will be exchanged between the initiator and responder. The new nonce is used to generate fresh key material and may also prevent replay attacks. All the IPSec keys are derived from SKEYID_d; therefore, an attacker with knowledge of SKEYID_d will be able to derive all the current and future keys in use for IPSec until IKE renegotiates. To improve the protection of IPSec keys, Perfect Forward Secrecy (PFS) is used to decouple the relation of future keys from existing keys. When PFS is enabled, new DH public values (X,Y) will be exchanged and the resulting shared secret K will be used to generate new key material as follows:

$HASH(1)$ = hash (SKEYIDa, Mid|SAi|Ni2) without PFS
$HASH(1)$ = hash (SKEYIDa, Mid|SAi|Ni2|X||IDi|IDr) with PFS

The *Message ID (Mid)* is important because there may be multiple Quick Mode transactions between two peers, and a unique identifier is needed to distinguish them. The Mid, which is part of the ISAKMP header, serves as this unique identifier.

The second message is sent from the responder to the initiator with the chosen proposal along with the ISAKMP header, nonce (Nr2), and *HASH(2)*:

$HASH(2)$ = hash (SKEYID_a, Mid|Sar|Ni2|Nr2) without PFS
$HASH(2)$ = hash (SKEYIDa, Mid|SAr|Ni2|Nr2|Y||IDi||IDr)with PFS

In the third and final message, the initiator authenticates with *HASH3*. This is to validate the communication channel prior to passing IPSec traffic. If the third message is not validated, an attacker could use previous packets of a Quick Mode transaction and replay them, thereby consuming resources. The third message is as follows:

$HASH(3)$ = hash(SKEYIDa, 0|Mid|Ni2|Nr2)

An important point to highlight is that following the second exchange, the initiator has enough information to derive key material and to actually start sending traffic. Once the initiator sends the third message, it may start sending IPSec traffic. If the responder has not received the third message, or if it is still authenticating the third message when the data packets start arriving, the packets will be dropped. To avoid this scenario, the responder sets the commit bit during the second message exchange, which states that the initiator must wait for the recipient's response. In the third exchange, the initiator acknowledges the commit requirement by setting the commit bit. Once the responder has authenticated the third message, it sends a fourth message back to the initiator stating that it is now ready for the IPSec traffic.

NOTE   Cisco IOS routers will respect commit bit if it is passed on from another vendor box, but will never initiate with commit bit.

At the completion of the third message exchange, the keying material can be generated for the data transfer:

$KEYMAT$ = HASH(SKEYIDd, protocol, SPI|Ni2|Nr2) without PFS

The protocol assigned is ESP or AH and the SPI is the random number that forms part of the security protocol header. Alternatively, KEYMAT may be defined as:

$KEYMAT$ = HASH(SKEYIDd, K|protocol, SPI|Ni2|Nr2) with PFS

Note that here, K is the new shared secret created between the two peers using a new DH key exchange.

At the start of this section, it was noted that there will be a minimum of two IPSec SAs created on each peer—an inbound SA and an outbound SA. Both SAs will have their own KEYMAT, as the SPI will be different for the inbound and outbound direction; each peer chooses its outbound SPI, which is the other peer's inbound SPI. If we consider two peers, the inbound SPI assigned to each peer is created by itself in order to avoid collision of SPI values. That is, if the destination peer created the inbound SPI, the two peers could potentially create the same SPI values, and therefore inbound SAs/SPIs are created by the IPSec gateway, which creates them for all the peers that it talks to. The outbound SA/SPI of one peer is the inbound SA/SPI for the other peer.

IPSec Packet Processing

Processing of packets on a router or a host is typically an implementation issue. Interestingly, RFC 2401 describes a general model for implementation in support of interoperability and achieving the functional goals of IPSec. The model describes two databases that all IPSec implementations will implement:

- Security Policy Database (SPD)
- Security Association Database (SADB)

The SPD holds the policy definitions that determine the disposition of all IP traffic—inbound or outbound—between two IPSec peers. The SADB contains parameters that are associated with each (active) security association.

Security Policy Database

Security policies applied to inbound and outbound IP packets are stored in the database called Security Policy Database (SPD). The security policy database defines various selectors to identify packets that require IPSec services. The selectors are as follows:

- Destination IP address
- Source IP address
- Name
- Data sensitivity level
- Transport Layer protocols
- Source and destination ports

One or more of these selectors define the set of IP traffic encompassed by this policy entry where each policy is represented in the SPD. Each entry includes an indication of whether traffic matching this policy will be bypassed, discarded, or subject to IPSec processing. If IPSec processing is to be applied, the entry includes an SA (or SA bundle) specification that lists the IPSec protocols, modes, and algorithms to be employed.

Security Association Database (SADB)

Each entry in the SADB defines the parameters associated with one SA. When an IPSec SA is created, the SADB is updated with all the parameters associated with the Security Association (SA). The SA entry for an inbound IPSec packet is obtained by indexing into the SADB with the destination IP address in the outer IP header, SPI, and IPSec security protocol (ESP or AH). The SA entry for outbound IPSec packets is obtained by a pointer to the SADB in the SPD. The SADB contains the following nine parameters for IPSec processing:

- **Sequence number**—The 32-bit value provided in the ESP or AH header.

- **Sequence number overflow**—A flag that indicates that the sequence number value has gone beyond the 2^{32} value and, hence, the SA must be deleted and a new SA negotiated between the IPSec peers.

- **Anti-replay window**—A 32- or 64-bit counter, used to determine if an inbound IPSec packet is a replayed packet.

- **SA lifetime**—Determined by a time-frame or byte count. The first lifetime to expire causes the SA to be deleted and a new one to be created. The SADB is responsible for management of an SA's lifetime. There are two lifetime triggers— one is a soft lifetime and the other is hard lifetime. A *soft lifetime* determines the point in time prior to a *hard lifetime* expiration when a new IPSec SA should be initiated. This allows the creation of a new SA before the old SA's expiration of the hard lifetime, thereby preventing loss of data.

- **Modes**—Determines whether tunnel mode or transport mode is used.

- **AH authentication algorithm**—Determines the choice of MD5 or SHA authentication and defines the keys to create the authentication digest.

- **ESP authentication algorithm**—Determines the choice of MD5 or SHA authentication and defines the keys to create the authentication digest.

- **ESP encryption algorithm**—The algorithm used for encryption DES, 3DES, or AES and defines the keys and IV for encryption.

- **Path MTU**—Any observed PMTU and aging variables.

Example 2-3 shows the SADB in a Cisco router running IOS.

Example 2-3 *Security Association Database (SADB)*

```
vpn-gw1-east#show cry ipsec sa
interface: FastEthernet0/0
   Crypto map tag: vpn, local addr. 9.1.1.35
   local  ident (addr/mask/prot/port): (10.1.1.0/255.255.255.0/0/0)
   remote ident (addr/mask/prot/port): (10.0.68.0/255.255.255.0/0/0)
   current_peer: 9.1.1.146:500
     PERMIT, flags={origin_is_acl,}
    #pkts encaps: 10, #pkts encrypt: 10, #pkts digest 10
    #pkts decaps: 19, #pkts decrypt: 19, #pkts verify 19
    #pkts compressed: 0, #pkts decompressed: 0
    #pkts not compressed: 0, #pkts compr. failed: 0
    #pkts not decompressed: 0, #pkts decompress failed: 0
```

continues

Example 2-3 *Security Association Database (SADB) (Continued)*

```
#send errors 0, #recv errors 0
local crypto endpt.: 9.1.1.35, remote crypto endpt.: 9.1.1.146
path mtu 1500, media mtu 1500
current outbound spi: A8992968
inbound esp sas:
 spi: 0xDFCB9E37(3754663479)
   transform: esp-3des esp-sha-hmac ,
   in use settings ={Tunnel, }
   slot: 0, conn id: 2000, flow_id: 1, crypto map: vpn
   sa timing: remaining key lifetime (k/sec): (4607997/3368)
   IV size: 8 bytes
   replay detection support: Y
inbound ah sas:
inbound pcp sas:
outbound esp sas:
 spi: 0xA8992968(2828609896)
   transform: esp-3des esp-sha-hmac ,
   in use settings ={Tunnel, }
   slot: 0, conn id: 2001, flow_id: 2, crypto map: vpn
   sa timing: remaining key lifetime (k/sec): (4607998/3368)
   IV size: 8 bytes
   replay detection support: Y
outbound ah sas:
outbound pcp sas:
```

Cisco IOS IPSec Packet Processing

Next, you step through the IPSec packet processing on a Cisco router. See Figure 2-17 for this example.

Figure 2-17 *IPSec Packet Processing Between Two IPSec Peers*

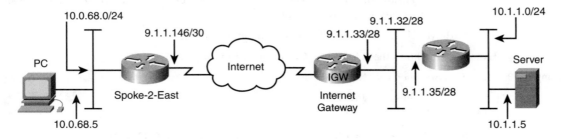

The configuration of the routers shown in Figure 2-17 is shown in Example 2-4 and Example 2-5.

Example 2-4 *Spoke Configuration*

```
SPOKE-1-EAST
hostname spoke-1-east
!
!
```

Example 2-4 *Spoke Configuration (Continued)*

```
ip domain-name cisco.com
!
!
crypto isakmp policy 1
 authentication pre-share
crypto isakmp key cisco address 9.1.1.35
!
!
crypto IPSec transform-set test esp-3des esp-sha-hmac
!
crypto map vpn 1 IPSec-isakmp
 set peer 9.1.1.35
 set transform-set test
 match address 100
!
!
!
interface Serial0/0
 ip address 9.1.1.146 255.255.255.252
 crypto map vpn
!
interface Ethernet0/1
 ip address 10.0.68.1 255.255.255.0
 half-duplex
!
ip classless
ip route 0.0.0.0 0.0.0.0 9.1.1.145
!
!
access-list 100 permit ip 10.0.68.0 0.0.0.255 10.1.1.0 0.0.0.255
!
!
line con 0
line aux 0
line vty 0 4
 login
!
!
end
```

Example 2-5 *Hub Configuration*

```
VPN-GW1-EAST
hostname vpn-gw1-east
!
!
ip cef
ip audit notify log
ip audit po max-events 100
!
crypto isakmp policy 1
```

continues

Example 2-5 *Hub Configuration (Continued)*

```
 authentication pre-share
crypto isakmp key cisco address 9.1.1.146
!
!
crypto IPSec transform-set test esp-3des esp-sha-hmac
!
crypto map vpn 1 IPSec-isakmp
 description spoke-1-east
 set peer 9.1.1.146
 set transform-set test
 match address 100
!
!
controller ISA 1/1
!
!
interface FastEthernet4/0
 ip address 10.1.1.1 255.255.255.0
 duplex full
 no cdp enable
!
interface FastEthernet5/0
 ip address 9.1.1.35 255.255.255.240
 duplex full
 no cdp enable
 crypto map vpn
!
ip classless
ip route 0.0.0.0 0.0.0.0 9.1.1.33
!
!
access-list 100 permit ip 10.1.1.0 0.0.0.255 10.0.68.0 0.0.0.255
!
!
line con 0
line aux 0
line vty 0 4
 login
!
!
end
```

In this example, we assume that a device (10.0.68.5) on the router SPOKE-1-EAST's LAN 10.0.68.0/24 wants to communicate with another device (10.1.1.5) on the LAN 10.1.1.0/24 on the VPN-GW1-EAST router. We'll also assume that the communication is in the direction of spoke to hub.

1   When an IP packet is destined from the spoke device to the hub site, the IP configuration on the device on the spoke LAN site delivers the IP packet to the SPOKE-1-EAST. The IP routing configuration on the spoke router determines that the IP packet is to be routed out of the interface serial0/0.

2 Before the packet is transmitted out of this interface, notice that there is a crypto-map configured on the serial0/0 interface. This means that this packet may need to be processed by IPSec on the router.

3 The next step is to consult the SPD to see if there is a policy match for this packet (Source:10.0.68.5, Destination: 10.1.1.5). The Access List 100, which was configured as a policy match under the crypto-map, matches all packets with a source in the range of 10.0.68.0/24 and a destination in the range of 10.1.1.0/24. Our packet matches this policy; therefore, the packet needs to be IPSec protected. If the access list does not match a packet, the packet will be sent in the clear without any further IPSec processing.

4 The following configuration shows the data sensitivity level needed if the packet needs to be secured per SPD:

```
crypto IPSec transform-set test esp-3des esp-sha-hmac
```
The configuration specifies the use of 3DES encryption with ESP and SHA-HMAC for data integrity and that tunnel mode will be used for encapsulating this packet. The command **show crypto ipsec transform-set** can be used to verify the configuration:

```
spoke-1-east#show cry ipsec transform-set
Transform set test: { esp-3des esp-sha-hmac  }
   will negotiate = { Tunnel,  },
```

5 The next step is to see if an IKE or IPSec SA is already established to the IPSec peer. Assume this is the first packet to this destination; hence, there will be no SA existing in the SADB. All packets that match this policy can be queued or dropped until the IKE and IPSec SA are established. IOS IPSec drops all packets while waiting for IKE and IPSec SAs to be established.

6 IKE phase 1 negotiation is performed between the peers to establish the IKE/ISAKMP SA. The parameters used for phase 1 are defined in the following configuration:

```
crypto isakmp policy 1
 authentication pre-share
crypto isakmp key s0n0f1ke1sc0m1ng address 9.1.1.35
!
spoke-1-east# show cry isakmp policy
Protection suite of priority 1
        encryption algorithm:   DES - Data Encryption Standard
        hash algorithm:         Secure Hash Standard
        authentication method:  Pre-Shared Key
        Diffie-Hellman group:   #1 (768 bit)
        lifetime:               86400 seconds, no volume limit
Default protection suite
        encryption algorithm:   DES - Data Encryption Standard
        hash algorithm:         Secure Hash Standard
        authentication method:  Rivest-Shamir-Adleman Signature
        Diffie-Hellman group:   #1 (768 bit)
        lifetime:               86400 seconds, no volume limit
```

7 After the IKE and IPSec SA are established as shown in the following configuration, the original IP packet is encapsulated in IPSec tunnel mode using an ESP header. Recall that in tunnel mode, a new IP header is added. In this case, the source IP address of 9.1.1.150 and destination IP address of 9.1.1.35 are used in the IPSec encapsulating header. This packet is handed back to usual IP forwarding routines to process the packet.

```
spoke-1-east# show cry isakmp sa
dst                src              state          conn-id    slot
9.1.1.146          9.1.1.35         QM_IDLE              1       0
vpn-gw1-east# show cry eng conn act
  ID Interface    IP-Address     State    Algorithm        Encrypt  Decrypt
1 FastEthernet0/0    9.1.1.146    set    HMAC_SHA+DES_56_CB  0          0
2000 FastEthernet0/0 9.1.1.146    set    HMAC_SHA+3DES_56_C  0         19
2001 FastEthernet0/0 9.1.1.146    set    HMAC_SHA+3DES_56_C  19         0
```

8 Next, the encrypted IPSec packet arrives into the hub router, and the presence of an IPSec header in the IP packet indicates that it must receive IPSec processing on the hub.

9 The outer header destination address (9.1.1.35), the security protocol ESP, and the SPI in the ESP header are used as indexes into the SADB to find the SA for this packet.

10 Once there is a hit in the SADB, the packet is authenticated and then decrypted using the proper transforms.

11 Once the packet is decrypted, the 5-tuple check of the policy corresponding to the packet is checked. The 5-tuple is the source address of the inner IP header, destination address of inner IP header, source port of inner header, destination port of inner header, and the IP protocol ID. Querying the SPD validates the 5-tuple. The lifetime counter in bytes is decremented and the anti-replay window is updated.

The packet would have been dropped in the following cases:

- The SA was not in the SADB
- The sequence number was on the left of the sliding window; therefore, the packet fails the replay check
- Authentication fails
- The length is incorrect
- The SA lifetime has expired

12 If all goes well in the previous step, the packet is passed to usual IP packet processing on the hub router.

NOTE	Not only does IPSec require outgoing packets to be encrypted (if they match the proxy or access list), but also any incoming packets that match the reverse of the proxy or access list must be encrypted. If packets that match the reverse are received in clear text, they will be dropped.

Summary

In this chapter, you read an introduction to the IPSec architecture and explored concepts and terminology in enough detail to understand IPSec VPNs from a deployment and design perspective. You learned about the IPSec protocols ESP and AH and the difference between transport and tunnel mode, as well as how IKE and IPSec SAs are established between peers. You also saw how Cisco IOS processes IPSec packets.

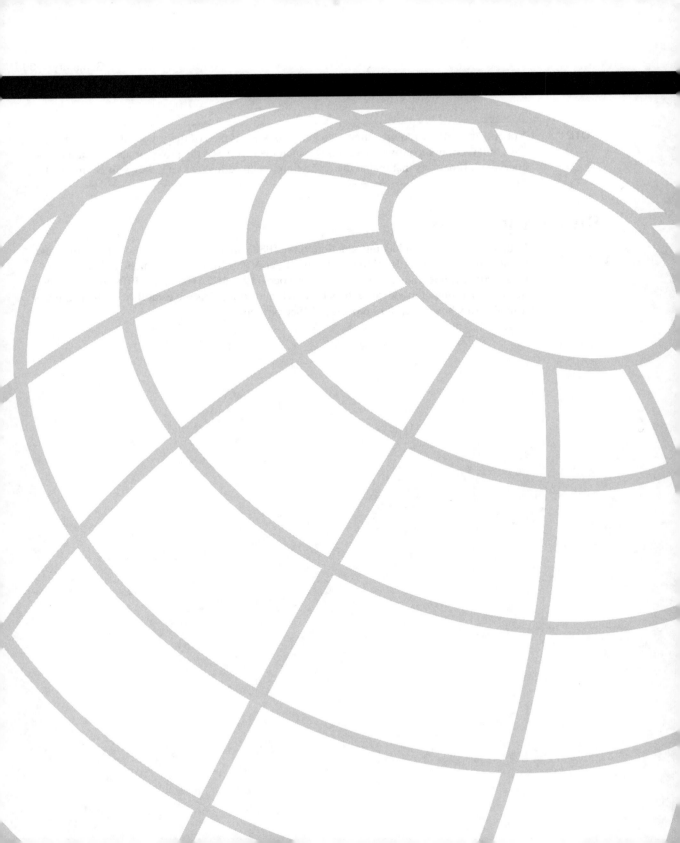

CHAPTER 3

Enhanced IPSec Features

Chapter 2, "IPSec Overview," described the IPSec architecture and the basic building blocks necessary to create a VPN. In this chapter, you will read about advanced IPSec features that will both improve the scalability and fault tolerance of IPSec VPNs and mitigate some of its inherent limitations. The base topology shown in Figure 3-1 will be used to explain the advanced IPSec features in this chapter.

Figure 3-1   *Topology*

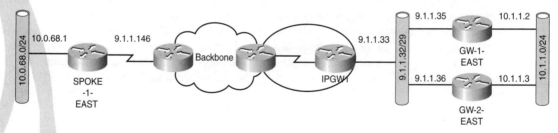

IKE Keepalives

IPSec is a peer-to-peer type of technology; IP reachability between IPSec peers is required for an IPSec session to be established between them. It is possible that IP connectivity may be lost between the peers due to routing problems, peer reloading, or some other situation. In such cases, there is often no way for IKE and IPSec to identify the loss of peer connectivity. The IPSec control plane protocol (IKE) is based on UDP and is, therefore, inherently connectionless; the IKE and IPSec security associations (SAs) established between the peers can remain until their lifetimes naturally expire. This lack of IPSec session liveliness creates "black holes" where traffic is lost. It is highly desirable to recognize these "black holes" as soon as possible, primarily because the IPSec SAs consume expensive CPU cycles when one side of the session continues to encrypt traffic to its unreachable peer. Also, the lack of failure detection of a peer may prevent the activation of an alternate backup peer. Finally, when reachability to the peer is restored, the peer may have no IKE or IPSec SAs, and the encrypted packets destined to the peer will be dropped by the peer, as it has no valid SA. Hence, the old IKE and IPSec SAs that are still present are really invalid and may preclude the creation of new IPSec SAs.

A *keepalive* mechanism, wherein the peers exchange some type of message to inform each other that they are alive, will help resolve these issues. Interestingly enough, the IKE protocol specification has no notion of such a keepalive mechanism. Cisco IOS allows the configuration of an IKE periodic keepalive mechanism that can be configured between IOS IPSec peers. Example 3-1 shows the configuration of an IKE keepalive in IOS from SPOKE-1-EAST's standpoint.

Example 3-1 *IKE Keepalive Configuration on SPOKE-1-EAST*

```
spoke-1-east

crypto isakmp policy 1
 authentication pre-share
!
crypto isakmp key cisco address 9.1.1.35
crypto isakmp key Cisco address 9.1.1.36

crypto isakmp keepalive 60 3
```

IKE keepalive messages are exchanged periodically by each peer to declare their availability. If three consecutive keepalive messages are unacknowledged, the associated peer is unreachable and the associated SAs should be removed and an IPSec tunnel built to a backup peer if one is present. In the above example, keepalives are sent every 60 seconds and the retry is a default value of 3, which means that it will take 180 seconds (60 times 3) to declare the IPSec endpoint dead. IKE keepalives are encrypted and authenticated, just like other IKE IPSec packets.

NOTE   The IKE keepalive mechanism has its limitations. The mechanism is able to detect the status of only the IKE SAs and endpoints. However, there may be cases in which the IKE peer is reachable, but its protected networks behind the peer are not. In that case, IKE keepalives do not help.

The IKE keepalive mechanism works fine to detect dead IKE peers and prevent "black holes" and conserve expensive CPU resources; however, one of the limitations of the IKE keepalive mechanism is its scalability. An IPSec router that is terminating a few thousand site-to-site IPSec sessions with IKE keepalives turned on will consume expensive CPU cycles for the housekeeping of the IKE keepalive messages, thereby limiting the scalability of the number of IPSec sessions that can be terminated by this router. An alternative mechanism to the IKE keepalive is known as Dead Peer Detection (DPD), discussed in the next section.

Dead Peer Detection

Dead peer detection (DPD), defined in RFC 3706, is an alternative mechanism that is more scalable than the IKE keepalives in detecting dead IPSec peers. Unlike the keepalive mechanism, DPD does not send periodic messages to check liveliness of a peer. The fundamental premise behind DPD is that DPD is a traffic-based detection method. In other words, DPD specifies that when traffic is occurring between the peers; there is no need to send a keepalive to check for liveliness of the peer, as the IPSec traffic serves as implicit proof of the availability of the peer.

If, on the other hand, a period of time elapses during which no traffic is exchanged between the peers, the liveliness of each peer is questionable. Note also that liveliness of a peer is needed only if traffic is to be sent to the peer. For example, if SPOKE-1-EAST in Figure 3-1 has sent outbound IPSec packets towards the VPN-GW1-EAST and has not received any IPSec packets inbound from VPN-GW1-EAST for a period of idle time, you might expect that SPOKE-1-EAST will initiate a DPD exchange. However, if SPOKE-1-EAST does not have data traffic to send to VPN-GW1-EAST, it really does not need to know if it is alive.

By delaying the DPD exchange (which, when sent, is sent in parallel with the start of the data traffic), DPD avoids sending extra messages and allows more time for an intermediate network outage to recover. After all, if the intermediate network is not needed at a given time, why detect that it is currently down? Doing so might force IPSec re-keying before it is necessary.

DPD capability is negotiated between IPSec peers during IKE negotiation by using a DPD vendor ID, as shown in Figure 3-2.

Figure 3-2   *DPD Vendor ID*

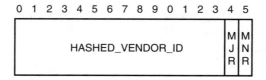

The DPD vendor ID is 16 bytes long. The first 14 bytes are the HASHED_VENDOR_ID field, and take the value HASHED_VENDOR_ID = {0xAF, 0xCA, 0xD7, 0x13, 0x68, 0xA1, 0xF1, 0xC9, 0x6B, 0x86, 0x96, 0xFC, 0x77, 0x57}. Even though this field is called HASHED_VENDOR_ID, the value of that this field is fixed, so it is not really vendor-specific. The last two bytes represent the current major (MJR) and minor (MNR) version of the protocol. An IKE peer must send the vendor ID if it wishes to take part in DPD exchanges.

Figure 3-3 shows the bidirectional DPD message exchange between the initiator and the responder, which means that for an R_U_THERE message, there should be a corresponding ACK.

Figure 3-3 *DPD Message Exchange*

Initiator   Responder

HDR*, NOTIFY(R-U-THERE), HASH ------>

<------ HDR*, NOTIFY(R-U-THERE-ACK), HASH

The DPD message format is shown in Figure 3-4.

Figure 3-4 *DPD Message Format*

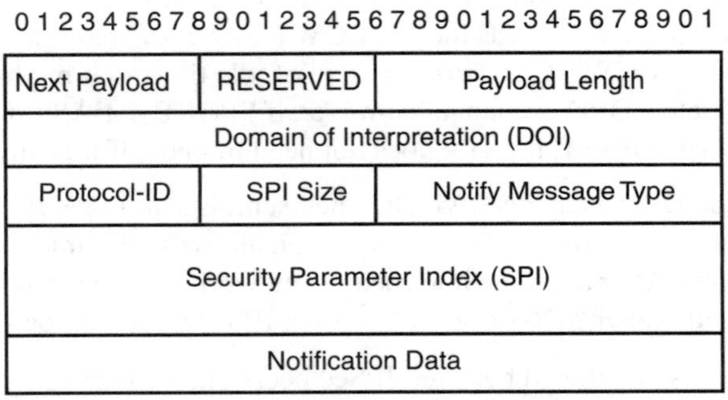

```
0 1 2 3 4 5 6 7 8 9 0 1 2 3 4 5 6 7 8 9 0 1 2 3 4 5 6 7 8 9 0 1
```

Next Payload	RESERVED	Payload Length
Domain of Interpretation (DOI)		
Protocol-ID	SPI Size	Notify Message Type
Security Parameter Index (SPI)		
Notification Data		

The protocol ID is set to 500 for ISAKMP, and the SPI length should be set to 16, which is equal to the length of the ISAKMP cookies—which, as we know from Chapter 2, "IPSec Overview," serves as the SPI for IKE/ISAKMP. Table 3-1 lists the ISAKMP Notify message types.

Table 3-1 *DPD ISAKMP Notify Message Types*

Notify	Message Value
R-U-THERE	36136
R-U-THERE-ACK	36137

Example 3-2 shows the DPD configuration on SPOKE-1-EAST. The configuration is essentially the same as the IKE keepalive configuration, except that two more timer parameters are provided to configure idle interval and retransmit interval.

Example 3-2 *DPD Configuration*

```
spoke-1-east

version 12.2
service log backtrace
```

Example 3-2   *DPD Configuration (Continued)*

```
service timestamps debug uptime
service timestamps log uptime
no service password-encryption
!
hostname spoke-1-east
!
enable password lab
!
clock timezone EST 0
ip subnet-zero
!
!
ip domain name cisco.com
!
!
crypto isakmp policy 1
 authentication pre-share
crypto isakmp key cisco address 9.1.1.35
crypto isakmp key Cisco address 9.1.1.36
crypto isakmp keepalive 60 2
!
!
crypto ipsec transform-set test esp-3des esp-sha-hmac
!
crypto map vpn 1 ipsec-isakmp
 set peer 9.1.1.35
 set peer 9.1.1.36
 set transform-set test
 match address 100
!
interface Serial0/0
 ip address 9.1.1.146 255.255.255.252
 crypto map vpn
!
interface Ethernet0/1
 ip address 10.0.68.1 255.255.255.0
 half-duplex
!
ip classless
ip route 0.0.0.0 0.0.0.0 9.1.1.145

!
access-list 100 permit ip 10.0.68.0 0.0.0.255 10.1.1.0 0.0.0.255
!
!
line con 0
line aux 0
line vty 0 4
 password lab
 login
!
```

continues

Example 3-2 *DPD Configuration (Continued)*

```
!
end

spoke-1-east#


spoke-1-east#show cry isa sa det
Codes: C - IKE configuration mode, D - Dead Peer Detection
       K - Keepalives, N - NAT-traversal
       X - IKE Extended Authentication

Conn id Local            Remote            Encr Hash Auth DH Lifetime Capabilities
1        9.1.1.146        9.1.1.35          des  sha  psk  1  23:59:39 D

spoke-1-east# debug crypto isakmp

ISAKMP (0:1): purging node 942371640
ISAKMP: received ke message (4/1)
ISAKMP: DPD received kei with flags 0x8
ISAKMP (0:1): more than 60 seconds since last inbound data. Sending DPD.
ISAKMP (0:1): DPD Sequence number 0x17815542
ISAKMP: set new node -1912932512 to QM_IDLE
ISAKMP (0:1): sending packet to 9.1.1.35 my_port 500 peer_port 500 (I) QM_IDLE
ISAKMP (0:1): purging node -1912932512
ISAKMP (0:1): received packet from 9.1.1.35 dport 500 sport 500 (I) QM_IDLE
ISAKMP: set new node -1385918665 to QM_IDLE
ISAKMP (0:1): processing HASH payload. message ID = -1385918665
ISAKMP (0:1): processing NOTIFY R_U_THERE_ACK protocol 1
       spi 0, message ID = -1385918665, sa = 82CFB8F8
ISAKMP (0:1): DPD/R_U_THERE_ACK received from peer 9.1.1.35, sequence 0x17815542
ISAKMP (0:1): deleting node -1385918665 error FALSE reason "informational (in) state 1"
ISAKMP (0:1): Input = IKE_MESG_FROM_PEER, IKE_INFO_NOTIFY
ISAKMP (0:1): Old State = IKE_P1_COMPLETE  New State = IKE_P1_COMPLETE
```

The *idle interval* timer facilitates the fault detection and recovery of idle resources in the absence of a valid connection. Idle interval is the configured time wherein the peer (SPOKE-1-EAST) has not received any inbound data on its SA from the remote peer (VPN-GW1-EAST). As you can see from the debugs in Example 3-2, once the interval is hit, an R_U_THERE_MESSAGE is sent and the initiator expects an ACK back. If the ACK is not received, the R_U_THERE message will be retransmitted three times, depending on the retransmit interval, before the initiator declares the remote peer dead. In the case of Example 3-2, you can see that R_U_THERE_ACK was received from VPN-GW1-EAST.

NOTE   Note that two conditions have to be met before a DPD R_U_THERE_MESSAGE is sent. First, the idle timer must expire, and second, the router has to have data going out to the peer. If the second condition is not met, the message is not sent. This policy conserves resources.

The lack of data or a response from the remote peer (VPN-GW1-EAST) will cause the local peer (SPOKE-1-EAST) to clear the local IPSec connection and recover the security association resources assigned. After clearing the resources, it may attempt to reestablish a connection with the same peer or with an alternate peer (VPN-GW2-EAST).

The characteristics of dead peer detection make the protocol a much more scalable fault-detection mechanism than IKE keepalives, especially in the context of addressing the state of IPSec connections to thousands of remote peers. The detection of an invalid IPSec security association may occur quickly by setting the idle interval and retry interval to a fairly low value with relatively few retries. The key advantage to DPD is that the periodic polling that is seen in IKE keepalives is suppressed in DPD, saving system resources.

NOTE   If one of peers supports only the original IKE keepalive mechanism while the other peer supports the DPD mechanism, the peer running DPD will fall back to the traditional periodic ISAKMP keepalive method. It is important to note that there are cases in which periodic IKE keepalives are necessary. These cases occur when there is Network Address Translation (NAT) or a firewall between the two peers. In such cases, periodic keepalives are required to refresh the state entries on the NAT or the firewall box. In the section "NAT Traversal (NAT-T)," which appears later in this chapter, you will examine a feature known as NAT Traversal. NAT Traversal has a NAT keepalive mechanism that negates the need for periodic IKE keepalive messages for maintaining state information on the NAT or firewall box.

Both IKE keepalives and DPD are useful mechanisms, but each has its limitations. For instance, they only detect if the IKE SAs and the endpoints are alive. They are useful if the path between the IKE peer fails for some reason, and the peer endpoints are not reachable from one another. On the other hand, if the IKE endpoints are reachable but the protected networks behind the endpoints are not, then these mechanisms cannot prevent the black-holing of traffic after it reaches the IKE endpoint.

Idle Timeout

When an IOS router creates an IPSec SA for a peer, it allocates a certain amount of resources to maintain the SA; the SA requires both memory and several managed timers. For idle peers, these resources are wasteful and consume expensive resources. Furthermore, these wasted resources could eventually prevent the router from creating new SAs with other active peers. The solution to this problem is to monitor the SAs for activity, removing idle SAs after a specified period of inactivity. The configuration of the SA idle timeout is shown in Example 3-3 along with the debug output.

Example 3-3 *Idle Timeout Configuration*

```
vpn-gw1-east


version 12.2
service timestamps debug datetime msec
service timestamps log datetime msec
no service password-encryption
!
hostname vpn-gw1-east
!
logging queue-limit 100
!
ip subnet-zero
!
ip domain name cisco.com
!


crypto isakmp policy 1
 authentication pre-share
crypto isakmp key cisco address 9.1.1.146
!
crypto ipsec security-association idle-time 120
!
crypto ipsec transform-set test esp-3des esp-sha-hmac
crypto map vpn 1 ipsec-isakmp
 set peer 9.1.1.33
 set transform-set test
 match address 100
!
!
!
interface FastEthernet0/0
 ip address 9.1.1.35 255.255.255.248
 speed 100
 full-duplex
 no cdp enable
 crypto map vpn
!
interface FastEthernet0/1
 ip address 10.1.1.2 255.255.255.0
 speed 100
 full-duplex
 no cdp enable
!
router ospf 1
 log-adjacency-changes
 network 10.1.1.0 0.0.0.255 area 0
 redistribute static
!
ip http server
no ip http secure-server
```

Example 3-3   *Idle Timeout Configuration (Continued)*

```
ip classless
ip route 0.0.0.0 0.0.0.0 9.1.1.33
!
!
!
access-list 100 permit ip 10.1.1.0 0.0.0.255 10.0.68.0 0.0.0.255
!

line con 0
line aux 0
line vty 0 4
 login
!
!
end



vpn-gw1-east#show cry isa sa
Codes: C - IKE configuration mode, D - Dead Peer Detection
       K - Keepalives, N - NAT-traversal
       X - IKE Extended Authentication
       psk - Preshared key, rsig - RSA signature
       renc - RSA encryption
Conn id Local            Remote         Encr Hash Auth DH Lifetime Capabilities
1       9.1.1.35         9.1.1.146      des  sha  psk  1  23:59:20
vpn-gw1-east# debug crypto ipsec

 ipsec(create_sa): starting idle timer, 120 seconds
  ISAKMP: Created a peer struct for 9.1.1.146, peer port 500
  ISAKMP: Locking peer struct 0x82A461D8, ipsec refcount 1 for from create_transfor


ipsecipsecipsec(delete_sa): deleting SA,
  (sa) sa_dest= 9.1.1.35, sa_prot= 50,
    sa_spi= 0x2CA9A57F(749315455),
    sa_trans= esp-3des esp-sha-hmac , sa_conn_id= 2000
ipsec(delete_sa): deleting SA,
  (sa) sa_dest= 9.1.1.146, sa_prot= 50,
    sa_spi= 0x7F4A6D6C(2135584108),
    sa_trans= esp-3des esp-sha-hmac , sa_conn_id= 2001
ipsec(lifetime_expiry): SA idletime reached; deleting ipsec SA
ipsec(lifetime_expiry): notifying END_TUNNEL
        local: 9.1.1.35 / ivrf: 0
        remote: 9.1.1.146 / fvrf: 0 / peer port: 500

spoke-1-east# debug crypto ipsec
ISAKMP (0:1): received packet from 9.1.1.35 dport 500 sport 500 (I) QM_IDLE
ISAKMP: set new node -329991077 to QM_IDLE
ISAKMP (0:1): processing HASH payload. message ID = -329991077
ISAKMP (0:1): processing DELETE payload. message ID = -329991077
```

continues

Example 3-3 *Idle Timeout Configuration (Continued)*

```
ipsec(key_engine): got a queue event...
ipsec(key_engine_delete_sas): rec'd delete notify from ISAKMP
ipsec(key_engine_delete_sas): delete SA with spi 749315455/50 for 9.1.1.35
ipsec(delete_sa): deleting SA,
  (sa) sa_dest= 9.1.1.146, sa_prot= 50,
    sa_spi= 0x7F4A6D6C(2135584108),
    sa_trans= esp-3des esp-sha-hmac , sa_conn_id= 2000
ipsec(delete_sa): deleting SA,
  (sa) sa_dest= 9.1.1.35, sa_prot= 50,
    sa_spi= 0x2CA9A57F(749315455),
    sa_trans= esp-3des esp-sha-hmac , sa_conn_id= 2001
ISAKMP: received ke message (4/1)
ISAKMP: Unlocking ipsec struct 0x82E0D92C notified by ipsec, count 0
```

Idle timeout is an important IPSec feature for IPSec scalability, especially on hub sites where there may be thousands of tunnel terminations, but only a few that are active.

NOTE The default SA idle-timeout in older versions of IOS code that did not have support for the idle timeout feature used to be equivalent to the IPSec security association lifetime.

Reverse Route Injection

Reverse Route Injection (*RRI*) is a mechanism used to integrate route availability to IPSec state. Without RRI, routing decisions are made independent of the IPSec peer state. A route to the secure subnet of the remote peer must exist. The route might be statically configured or derived through some form of end-to-end dynamic routing exchange. Coupling the IPSec security association state with the viability of a route path simplifies the end-to-end fault recovery process. The Cisco RRI process inserts a static route associated with an IPSec peer into the forwarding information base. The availability of the route in the forwarding information base may be propagated to adjacent routers by redistributing the static routes. In this section, you'll review two scenarios for RRI:

- Static IPSec peers
- Dynamic IPSec peers

A static IPSec peer is one in which the crypto maps and the corresponding IPSec security policies and proxies are pre-defined (site-to-site). In the static IPSec peer case, an IPSec session can be initiated either from the hub or the spoke. A dynamic IPSec peer is one in which the spoke side or client initiates IPSec (telecommuter) session and the receiver's IPSec proxies are not pre-defined.

Figure 3-5 shows an application for RRI for static IPSec peers.

Figure 3-5   *Application of RRI in the Context of IPSec*

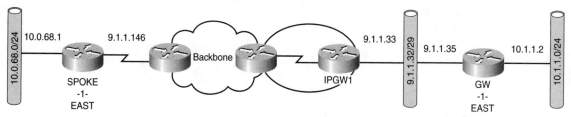

In Figure 3-5, VPN-GW1-EAST is the head-end router, which terminates IPSec from SPOKE-1-EAST. With RRI configured on VPN-GW1-EAST, the remote subnet protected by SPOKE-1-EAST (that is, 10.0.68.0/24) is inserted into VPN-GW1-EAST's forwarding table as a static route. These subnets can be advertised further by redistributing the static route to the routing protocol of choice; in example 3-4, it is redistributed into OSPF. Example 3-4 shows VPN-GW1-EAST's configuration along with a snapshot of the routing table.

Example 3-4   *RRI Configuration*

```
vpn-gw1-east

!
version 12.2
service timestamps debug datetime msec
service timestamps log datetime msec
no service password-encryption
!
hostname vpn-gw1-east
!
logging queue-limit 100
!
ip subnet-zero
!
!
ip domain name cisco.com
!
!
crypto isakmp policy 1
 authentication pre-share
crypto isakmp key cisco address 9.1.1.146
crypto ipsec security-association idle-time 120
!
crypto ipsec transform-set test esp-3des esp-sha-hmac
!
crypto map vpn 1 ipsec-isakmp
 set peer 9.1.1.146
 set transform-set test
 match address 100
 reverse-route remote-peer 9.1.1.33
!
!
```

continues

Example 3-4 *RRI Configuration (Continued)*

```
interface FastEthernet0/0
 ip address 9.1.1.35 255.255.255.248
 speed 100
 full-duplex
 no cdp enable
 crypto map vpn
!
interface FastEthernet0/1
 ip address 10.1.1.2 255.255.255.0
 speed 100
 full-duplex
 no cdp enable
!
router ospf 1
 log-adjacency-changes
 network 10.1.1.0 0.0.0.255 area 0
 redistribute static subnets
!
ip classless
ip route 0.0.0.0 0.0.0.0 9.1.1.33
!
!
access-list 100 permit ip 10.1.1.0 0.0.0.255 10.0.68.0 0.0.0.255
!
!
line con 0
line aux 0
line vty 0 4
 login
!
end

vpn-gw1-east#show ip route
Codes: C - connected, S - static, R - RIP, M - mobile, B - BGP
       D - EIGRP, EX - EIGRP external, O - OSPF, IA - OSPF inter area
       N1 - OSPF NSSA external type 1, N2 - OSPF NSSA external type 2
       E1 - OSPF external type 1, E2 - OSPF external type 2
       i - IS-IS, L1 - IS-IS level-1, L2 - IS-IS level-2, ia - IS-IS inter area

       * - candidate default, U - per-user static route, o - ODR
       P - periodic downloaded static route

Gateway of last resort is 9.1.1.33 to network 0.0.0.0

     9.0.0.0/8 is variably subnetted, 2 subnets, 2 masks
C       9.1.1.32/29 is directly connected, FastEthernet0/0
S       9.1.1.146/32 [1/0] via 9.1.1.33
     10.0.0.0/24 is subnetted, 2 subnets
C       10.1.1.0 is directly connected, FastEthernet0/1
S       10.0.68.0 [1/0] via 9.1.1.146
S*   0.0.0.0/0 [1/0] via 9.1.1.33
```

NOTE	The behavior of RRI injecting a route into the routing table has changed as of Cisco IOS Software Release 12.3(14)T onwards. A new option has been added in the RRI command **reverse-route remote-peer <ip address> static**. Without the static keyword, a route is injected into the routing table only after successful establishment of IPSec SA. The "static" keyword is required if the static route has to be injected into the routing table without an SA being established in advance (which was the legacy behavior discussed in example 3-4).

RRI functionality for dynamic peers behaves exactly the same way as the static IPSec peers, except that the route to the spoke subnet is injected only after the IPSec SAs are successfully established.

RRI also gives the option of adding a route to the destination tunnel endpoint address, which is important in case the interface where the crypto map is applied is a broadcast interface, such as Ethernet. If an IP address is not specified, the route will point to the interface where the crypto map is bound. For remote access clients (for example, telecommuter clients) that use dynamic crypto maps, the route injection is tightly coupled with creation of IPSec security associations. In this case, a route will be dynamically created based on the source proxy ID and mask passed by the client during Quick Mode.

Today, when the physical link of an IPSec gateway (hub) goes down, SAs are not cleared until the IPSec SA timer expires (idle timeout or IPSec SA lifetime). For dynamic IPSec peers, RRI routes are purged from the routing table when the SAs are cleared; if a redundant hub site is present, the spokes automatically initiate IKE/IPSec toward the new hub, and all is fine. However, on static IPSec peers, the failure of a link on the IPSec gateway causes some issues with RRI.

You saw earlier that for static peers (with the static keyword), the RRI routes are injected into the routing table irrespective of whether SAs are established. This means that even if the SAs time out, the RRI route is never purged from the original hub's routing table. Since the RRI route is never purged, traffic destined to the RRI-injected subnet is always drawn to the original hub where the SAs no longer exist. If the IPSec SAs cannot be reestablished by the original hub for the destination spoke, the traffic will be "black-holed" at this hub. This issue is resolved by combining RRI with the Cisco Hot Standby Routing Protocol (HSRP), which is discussed in the next section.

RRI and HSRP

HSRP is commonly used to provide failover between routers. HSRP tracks the state of router interfaces and provides a failover mechanism between primary and secondary devices. This functionality can be exploited to provide IPSec redundancy. A simple mechanism to provide IPSec redundancy using HSRP is illustrated in Figure 3-6.

Figure 3-6 *IPSec Redundancy Using HSRP*

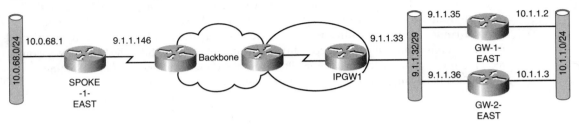

Figure 3-6 shows two routers, VPN-GW1-EAST and VPN-GW2-EAST, at the hub site with a common Ethernet on both the Internet-facing and corporate-facing sides. The remote router, in this case, SPOKE-1-EAST has an IPsec peering with the HSRP address at the hub. The active HSRP router will terminate the IPSec connection from the remote router. If the active router fails, the standby router becomes the active router and the remote router renegotiates a new IPSec session with the new active router. So far, this redundancy scheme will work fine. One problem with this scheme is the assumption that routing is symmetric. In other words, all traffic from the remote router to the active HSRP peer and the reverse traffic flow from the hub site back to the remote router is assumed to be traversing the same IPSec hub router; however, this may not be the case. RRI configuration integrated with HSRP on the hub routers ensures that routing is indeed symmetric. This solution will be explored further in Chapter 6, "Designing Fault-Tolerant IPSec VPNs." Example 3-5 illustrates how you would map the standby IP address to the crypto map on VPN-GW1-EAST followed by the configuration on SPOKE-1-EAST. The configuration would be the same on VPN-GW2-EAST, aside from the IP address on the physical interface and the HSRP standby priority.

NOTE   HSRP runs only over Ethernet interfaces. Although it cannot run over serial interfaces, it can track the state of any interface.

Example 3-5 *IPSec and HSRP Configuration*

```
vpn-gw1-east


crypto isakmp policy 1
 authentication pre-share
crypto isakmp key cisco address 9.1.1.146
crypto isakmp keepalive 60 3

!
!
crypto ipsec transform-set test esp-3des esp-sha-hmac
!
crypto map vpn 1 ipsec-isakmp
```

Example 3-5   *IPSec and HSRP Configuration (Continued)*

```
 set peer 9.1.1.146
 set transform-set test
 match address 100
 reverse-route remote-peer 9.1.1.33
!
!
interface FastEthernet0/0
 ip address 9.1.1.35 255.255.255.248
 duplex full
 random-detect
 standby delay minimum 30 reload 60
 standby ip 9.1.1.34
 standby priority 105
 standby preempt
 standby name ipsec
 standby track FastEthernet2/0
 crypto map vpn redundancy ipsec
!
interface FastEthernet2/0
 ip address 10.1.1.2 255.255.255.0
 duplex full
 standby 1 ip 10.1.1.1
 standby 1 priority 105
 standby 1 preempt
 standby 1 name ip
 standby 1 track FastEthernet0/0
!
router ospf 1
 log-adjacency-changes
 redistribute static subnets
 network 10.1.1.0 0.0.0.255 area 0
!
ip classless
ip route 0.0.0.0 0.0.0.0 9.1.1.33
no ip http server
!
access-list 100 permit ip 10.1.1.0 0.0.0.255 10.0.68.0 0.0.0.255
!
!
line con 0
 stopbits 1
line aux 0
 stopbits 1
line vty 0 4
 login
!
end

spoke-1-east:

crypto map vpn 1 ipsec-isakmp
```

continues

Example 3-5   *IPSec and HSRP Configuration (Continued)*

```
set peer 9.1.1.34
set transform-set test
match address 100
!
interface Serial0/0
 ip address 9.1.1.146 255.255.255.252
 crypto map vpn
!
interface Ethernet0/1
 ip address 10.0.68.1 255.255.255.0
 half-duplex
!
ip classless
ip route 0.0.0.0 0.0.0.0 9.1.1.145

!
access-list 100 permit ip 10.0.68.0 0.0.0.255 10.1.1.0 0.0.0.255
```

HSRP's interaction with RRI IPSec provides a good IPSec high-availability solution. The state of several important interfaces associated with routing and crypto on VPN-GW1-EAST may be mutually tracked such that a failure on any of the interfaces is synchronized; the routes and crypto termination are all revoked on VPN-GW1-EAST such that the responsibility may be transferred to the secondary router, VPN-GW2-EAST. One thing this solution does not provide is IPSec statefulness. This means that, from the perspective of SPOKE-1-EAST, it has to initiate a completely new IKE and IPSec security association to VPN-GW2-EAST's HSRP address because VPN-GW2-EAST has no IKE or IPSec SA to SPOKE-1-EAST. Also, the spoke won't re-initiate the IKE/IPSec SAs with the standby router until IKE or DPD times out.

A better high-availability solution is one in which the connection state can be shared between the IPSec gateways VPN-GW1-EAST and VPN-GW2-EAST. The principle benefit to the stateful failover model is that the remote spoke (VPN-SPOKE1-EAST) doesn't need to renegotiate an IPSec security association with a standby peer because a valid security association already exists. Stateful failover is further discussed in the next section.

Stateful Failover

You have seen in Chapter 2, "IPSec Overview," that the establishment of an IPSec security association between two endpoints requires the creation of security state information that is used to encrypt or authenticate traffic. The security association state is stored in data structures referred to as the security association database (SADB). In the event of a communications failure between two IPSec peers, the SADB must be cleared for the peer and re-created as the IPSec security association is restored. Obviously, it would be very useful for redundancy if the SADB can be duplicated and kept in synch on another peer. This is exactly the intent of the stateful failover model. Stateful failover is accomplished via a SADB transfer and synchronization process.

SADB Transfer

The IPSec state stored for a remote peer on an active router may be transferred to a standby router such that the standby router may assume the responsibilities for communicating with the active router's remote peers. The active router and the standby router must synchronize the SADB between themselves. By synchronizing the state of the SADB between the two active and standby peers, the remote peer may maintain its IPSec state with either of the active or standby routers without requiring the renegotiation of IKE and IPSec security associations. Of course, the security transform associated with the remote peers is specified in the SADB; therefore, the IPSec policies will be identical.

SADB Synchronization

Two IPSec gateways engaged in the stateful failover model must be configured such that the IKE identity address is consistent because the IPSec policy between the routers must not change. The standby router must assume the IKE identity of the active router during failover. By synchronizing the state of the SABD between the two potential remote peers, the loss of an active peer allows the standby peer to assume the role of the active peer without the remote peer's knowledge of the transfer of responsibility. The information that the active router transmits to the standby router includes:

- IKE cookie's stamp
- Session keys
- Sequence number counter and window state
- Kilobyte (KB) lifetime expirations
- Dead peer detection (DPD) sequence number updates

Shown in Example 3-6 is the configuration of VPN-GW1-EAST and VPN-GW2-EAST with stateful IPSec using the State Synchronization Protocol (SSP) configured between them. The example also includes snapshots of various relevant show commands on both the gateways showing the SADB synchronization.

Example 3-6 *Configuration for Stateful Switchover using SSP*

```
vpn-gw1-east

version 12.2
service timestamps debug datetime msec
service timestamps log datetime msec
no service password-encryptionf
!
hostname vpn-gw1-east
```

continues

Example 3-6 *Configuration for Stateful Switchover using SSP (Continued)*

```
!
ip subnet-zero
!
ip cef
!
ssp group 1
 remote 9.1.1.36
 redundancy ipsec
!
!
crypto isakmp policy 1
 authentication pre-share
crypto isakmp key cisco address 9.1.1.146
crypto isakmp keepalive 10 10
crypto isakmp ssp 1
 !
 !
 !
crypto ipsec transform-set test esp-3des esp-sha-hmac
!
crypto map vpn ha replay-interval inbound 100 outbound 1
crypto map vpn 1 ipsec-isakmp
 set peer 9.1.1.146
 set transform-set test
 match address 100
 reverse-route remote-peer 9.1.1.33
 !
 !
interface FastEthernet0/0
 ip address 9.1.1.35 255.255.255.248
 duplex full
 random-detect
 standby delay minimum 30 reload 60
 standby ip 9.1.1.34
 standby priority 105
 standby preempt
 standby name ipsec
 standby track FastEthernet2/0
 crypto map vpn ssp 1
 !
interface FastEthernet2/0
 ip address 10.1.1.2 255.255.255.0
 duplex full
 standby 1 ip 10.1.1.1
 standby 1 priority 105
 standby 1 preempt
 standby 1 name ip
 standby 1 track FastEthernet0/0
 !
router ospf 1
 log-adjacency-changes
```

Example 3-6   *Configuration for Stateful Switchover using SSP (Continued)*

```
 redistribute static subnets
 network 10.1.1.0 0.0.0.255 area 0
 !
ip classless
ip route 0.0.0.0 0.0.0.0 9.1.1.33
no ip http server
!
access-list 100 permit ip 10.1.1.0 0.0.0.255 10.0.68.0 0.0.0.255
!
!
end

vpn-gw1-east#show cry isa sa
dst              src              state          conn-id    slot
9.1.1.34         9.1.1.146        QM_IDLE              1       0



vpn-gw1-east#show cry eng conn act

  ID Interface        IP-Address     State  Algorithm            Encrypt  Decrypt
   1 FastEthernet0/0 9.1.1.35        set    HMAC_SHA+DES_56_CB         0        0
2000 FastEthernet0/0 9.1.1.35        set    HMAC_SHA+3DES_56_C         0     4631
2001 FastEthernet0/0 9.1.1.35        set    HMAC_SHA+3DES_56_C      4610        0


vpn-gw1-east#show cry ipsec sa

interface: FastEthernet0/0
   Crypto map tag: vpn, local addr. 9.1.1.34

   local  ident (addr/mask/prot/port): (10.1.1.0/255.255.255.0/0/0)
   remote ident (addr/mask/prot/port): (10.0.68.0/255.255.255.0/0/0)
   current_peer: 9.1.1.146
     PERMIT, flags={origin_is_acl,}
   #pkts encaps: 6893, #pkts encrypt: 6893, #pkts digest 6893
   #pkts decaps: 6893, #pkts decrypt: 6893, #pkts verify 6893
   #pkts compressed: 0, #pkts decompressed: 0
   #pkts not compressed: 0, #pkts compr. failed: 0, #pkts decompress failed: 0
   #send errors 0, #recv errors 0

   local crypto endpt.: 9.1.1.34, remote crypto endpt.: 9.1.1.146
   path mtu 1500, media mtu 1500
   current outbound spi: DE0F857C

   inbound esp sas:
    spi: 0x5E9B7765(1587246949)
       transform: esp-3des esp-sha-hmac ,
       in use settings ={Tunnel, }
       slot: 100, conn id: 2000, flow_id: 1, crypto map: vpn
       sa timing: remaining key lifetime (k/sec): (4607260/3534)
```

continues

Example 3-6 *Configuration for Stateful Switchover using SSP (Continued)*

```
                IV size: 8 bytes
                replay detection support: Y

        inbound ah sas:

        inbound pcp sas:

        outbound esp sas:
          spi: 0xDE0F857C(3725559164)
                transform: esp-3des esp-sha-hmac ,
                in use settings ={Tunnel, }
                slot: 100, conn id: 2001, flow_id: 2, crypto map: vpn
                sa timing: remaining key lifetime (k/sec): (4607622/3534)
                IV size: 8 bytes
                replay detection support: Y

        outbound ah sas:

        outbound pcp sas:


vpn-gw1-east#show ssp packet
SSP packet Information
      Socket creation time: 00:01:42
      Local port: 3249       Server port: 3249
      Packets Sent = 43, Bytes Sent = 2232
      Packets Received = 5, Bytes Received = 92

vpn-gw1-east#show ssp peer
SSP Peer Information
      IP Address        Connection State    Local Interface
      9.1.1.36          Connected           FastEthernet0/0


vpn-gw1-east#show cry ipsec ha
Interface            VIP              SAs    ipsec HA State
FastEthernet0/0      9.1.1.34          2     Active since 16:09:50

vpn-gw2-east#  show running-config
Building configuration...

Current configuration : 1587 bytes
!
version 12.2
service timestamps debug datetime msec
service timestamps log datetime msec
no service password-encryption
!
hostname vpn-gw2-east
!
ip subnet-zero
```

Example 3-6   *Configuration for Stateful Switchover using SSP (Continued)*

```
!
!
ip cef
!
ssp group 1
 remote 9.1.1.35
 redundancy ipsec
!
!
crypto isakmp policy 1
 authentication pre-share
crypto isakmp key cisco address 9.1.1.146
crypto isakmp keepalive 10 10
crypto isakmp ssp 1
!
!
!
crypto ipsec transform-set test esp-3des esp-sha-hmac
!
crypto map vpn ha replay-interval inbound 100 outbound 1
crypto map vpn 1 ipsec-isakmp
 set peer 9.1.1.146
 set transform-set test
 match address 100
 reverse-route remote-peer 9.1.1.33

!
interface FastEthernet0/0
 ip address 9.1.1.36 255.255.255.248
 duplex full
 standby delay minimum 30 reload 60
 standby ip 9.1.1.34
 standby preempt
 standby name ipsec
 standby track FastEthernet2/0
 crypto map vpn ssp 1
!
interface FastEthernet2/0
 ip address 10.1.1.3 255.255.255.0
 duplex full
 standby 1 ip 10.1.1.1
 standby 1 preempt
 standby 1 name ip
 standby 1 track FastEthernet0/0
!
router ospf 1
 log-adjacency-changes
 redistribute static subnets
 network 10.1.1.0 0.0.0.255 area 0
!
ip classless
```

continues

Example 3-6 *Configuration for Stateful Switchover using SSP (Continued)*

```
ip route 0.0.0.0 0.0.0.0 9.1.1.33
no ip http server
ip pim bidir-enable
!
access-list 100 permit ip 10.1.1.0 0.0.0.255 10.0.68.0 0.0.0.255
!
!
line con 0
 stopbits 1
line aux 0
 stopbits 1
line vty 0 4
 login
!
end

vpn-gw2-east#show cry isa sa
dst             src             state           conn-id    slot
9.1.1.34        9.1.1.146       QM_IDLE               1      0




vpn-gw2-east#show ssp packet
SSP packet Information
    Socket creation time: 00:05:19
    Local port: 11001       Server port: 3249
    Packets Sent = 5, Bytes Sent = 92
    Packets Received = 121, Bytes Received = 5664


vpn-gw2-east#show cry isa ha

VIP             SAs     Stamp       HA State

9.1.1.34         1      6F2BFDBB    Standby since 16:10:44 UTC



vpn-gw2-east#show cry ipsec sa

interface: FastEthernet0/0
    Crypto map tag: vpn, local addr. 9.1.1.34

   local  ident (addr/mask/prot/port): (10.1.1.0/255.255.255.0/0/0)
   remote ident (addr/mask/prot/port): (10.0.68.0/255.255.255.0/0/0)
   current_peer: 9.1.1.146
     PERMIT, flags={origin_is_acl,}
    #pkts encaps: 162402, #pkts encrypt: 162402, #pkts digest 162402
    #pkts decaps: 162404, #pkts decrypt: 162404, #pkts verify 162404
    #pkts compressed: 0, #pkts decompressed: 0
    #pkts not compressed: 0, #pkts compr. failed: 0, #pkts decompress failed: 0
```

Example 3-6   *Configuration for Stateful Switchover using SSP (Continued)*

```
#send errors 57, #recv errors 0

local crypto endpt.: 9.1.1.34, remote crypto endpt.: 9.1.1.146
path mtu 1500, media mtu 1500
current outbound spi: DE0F857C

inbound esp sas:
  spi: 0x5E9B7765(1587246949)
    transform: esp-3des esp-sha-hmac ,
    in use settings ={Tunnel, }
    slot: 100, conn id: 2000, flow_id: 1, crypto map: vpn
    sa timing: remaining key lifetime (k/sec): (4142627/3552)
    IV size: 8 bytes
    replay detection support: Y
    HA Status: STANDBY

inbound ah sas:

inbound pcp sas:

outbound esp sas:
  spi: 0xDE0F857C(3725559164)
    transform: esp-3des esp-sha-hmac ,
    in use settings ={Tunnel, }
    slot: 100, conn id: 2001, flow_id: 2, crypto map: vpn
    sa timing: remaining key lifetime (k/sec): (4147199/3552)
    IV size: 8 bytes
    replay detection support: Y
    HA Status: STANDBY

outbound ah sas:

outbound pcp sas:
```

Example 3-6 shows the configuration of stateful IPSec using SSP. An alternate way to configure IPSec failover using an alternate mechanism known as Stateful Switch Over (SSO) is shown in Example 3-7.

Example 3-7   *Configuration for Stateful Switchover using SSO*

```
vpn-gw1-east

version 12.2
service timestamps debug datetime msec
service timestamps log datetime msec
no service password-encryptionyf
!
hostname vpn-gw1-east
!
ip subnet-zero
!
```

continues

Example 3-7 *Configuration for Stateful Switchover using SSO (Continued)*

```
redundancy inter-device
 scheme standby ipsec
!
ipc zone default
 association 1
   no shutdown
protocol sctp
local-port 5000
local-ip 9.1.1.35
retransmit-timeout 300 1000
path-retransmit 10
assoc-retransmit 20
remote-port 5000
   remote-ip 9.1.1.36
 !
ip cef
!
crypto isakmp policy 1
 authentication pre-share
crypto isakmp key cisco address 9.1.1.146
crypto isakmp keepalive 10 10
!
crypto ipsec transform-set test esp-3des esp-sha-hmac
!
crypto map vpn ha redundancy replay-interval inbound 1000 outbound 1000
crypto map vpn 1 ipsec-isakmp
 set peer 9.1.1.146
 set transform-set test
 match address 100
 reverse-route remote-peer 9.1.1.33
 !
 !
interface FastEthernet0/0
 ip address 9.1.1.35 255.255.255.248
 duplex full
 random-detect
 standby delay minimum 30 reload 60
 standby ip 9.1.1.34
 standby priority 105
 standby preempt
 standby name ipsec
 standby track FastEthernet2/0
 crypto map vpn redundancy ipsec stateful
 !
interface FastEthernet2/0
 ip address 10.1.1.2 255.255.255.0
 duplex full
 standby 1 ip 10.1.1.1
 standby 1 priority 105
 standby 1 preempt
 standby 1 name ip
```

Example 3-7   *Configuration for Stateful Switchover using SSO (Continued)*

```
 standby 1 track FastEthernet0/0
 !
router ospf 1
 log-adjacency-changes
 redistribute static subnets
 network 10.1.1.0 0.0.0.255 area 0
 !
ip classless
ip route 0.0.0.0 0.0.0.0 9.1.1.33
no ip http server
 !
access-list 100 permit ip 10.1.1.0 0.0.0.255 10.0.68.0 0.0.0.255
 !
 !
end
```

The objective of both configurations shown in Example 3-6 and 3-7 is the same, which is to provide IPSec stateful failover. From an end-user perspective, other than the configuration syntax, there is not much difference between the two mechanisms. The SSP mechanism was developed specifically for IPSec stateful failover, whereas the SSO mechanism uses a more generic High Availability infrastructure which is used for providing stateful failover mechanisms for many other protocols in Cisco IOS such as OSPF, BGP, IP and others, in addition to IPSec.

IPSec and Fragmentation

A router fragments IP packets when the packet size exceeds the MTU of the outgoing interface. With IPSec, the addition of an IPSec header may cause IP fragmentation. IPSec RFCs state that this fragmentation, if needed, is performed after encryption for outbound processing. For inbound processing when an IPSec endpoint receives fragmented packets, the IPSec layer gets a reassembled packet from the IP layer before decryption.

NOTE   Fragmentation works in the Cisco Express Forwarding (CEF) switching path in all high-end routers such as the Cisco 7200, whereas reassembly of fragmented IP packets occurs in the IOS process switch path on all Cisco routers. Also, remember that reassembly of fragmented packets is performed only for packets that are destined to the router; fragmented packets that transit the routers are switched in the CEF path.

It is always desirable to avoid IP fragmentation between endpoints. Path MTU Discovery (PMTUD), stated in RFC 1191, was developed for this purpose. PMTUD dynamically determines the lowest MTU between two endpoints by using the Don't Fragment (DF) bit in the IP header to dynamically discover the PMTU of a path. The basic idea of PMTU is that a source initially assumes that the PMTU of a path is the (known) MTU of its first hop, and sends all packets on that path with the DF bit set. If any of the IP packets need to be fragmented by some router along the path, that router will discard the packet and send an ICMP Destination Unreachable message to the host with a code meaning "fragmentation needed and DF set." Upon receipt of such a message, the source host reduces its assumed PMTU for the path. PMTU is only supported for TCP, in which case the source host, upon reception of the ICMP unreachable message, sets the TCP maximum segment size (MSS). PMTU has some issues with IPSec, which will be explored in the next section.

IPSec and PMTUD

As described in RFC 1191, PMTU works on the premise that an ICMP unreachable packet informs the host with a code meaning "fragmentation needed and DF set." The amount of information that is returned in the ICMP message is limited, and with an IPSec packet this affects what selectors are available to identify security associations, originating hosts, and other aspects for use in further propagating the PMTU information. An ICMP PMTU may identify only the first (outermost) security association because the ICMP PMTU may contain only 64 bits of the "offending" packet beyond the IP header, which would capture only the first SPI from AH or ESP.

You can see this issue illustrated using Figure 3-6. Assume a host connected to subnet 10.0.68.0 is sending traffic to destination 10.1.1.0 with the DF bit set. IPSec policy on SPOKE-1-EAST encapsulates all traffic from this subnet to the destination subnet. The DF bit from the original IP packet is copied to the IPSec header. Also assume that the MTU of an intermediate router in the backbone requires fragmentation of the IPSec-encapsulated packet. The DF bit is set on this packet and therefore cannot be fragmented. It must be dropped by the backbone router and an ICMP unreachable (PMTU message) is sent back to the source. The source address in the PMTU message is that of the IPSec endpoint (SPOKE-1-EAST), because this router is the source of the IPSec-encapsulated packet. The ICMP PMTU message carries the SPI information, which points to the IPSec SA. In this case, a single SA is used for all hosts on the subnet. Therefore, the IPSec router has no way to figure out which host to send the Path MTU message to. To figure this out, you have two options:

- The IPSec router sends the PMTU message to all hosts on this subnet.

- The IPSec router stores the PMTU with the SPI and waits until the next packet(s) arrives from the originating host(s) for the relevant security association. If the packets are bigger than the PMTU, drop the packet(s), and compose ICMP PMTU message(s) with the new packet(s) and the updated PMTU, and send the originating host(s) the ICMP message(s) about the problem. This involves a delay in notifying the originating host(s), but avoids the problems of the first bullet.

The second option is more feasible than the first and is, in fact, required by the IPSec RFCs. Cisco IOS behavior mimics this option. Example 3-8 shows how SPOKE-1-EAST reacts to change in PMTU by updating the SADB.

Example 3-8   *Change in PMTU in the IPSec SA*

```
spoke-1-east# show cry ipsec sa
interface: Serial0/0
    Crypto map tag: vpn, local addr. 9.1.1.146
   local  ident (addr/mask/prot/port): (10.0.68.0/255.255.255.0/0/0)
   remote ident (addr/mask/prot/port): (10.1.1.0/255.255.255.0/0/0)
   current_peer: 9.1.1.35:500
     PERMIT, flags={origin_is_acl,}
    #pkts encaps: 4, #pkts encrypt: 4, #pkts digest 4
    #pkts decaps: 4, #pkts decrypt: 4, #pkts verify 4
    #pkts compressed: 0, #pkts decompressed: 0
    #pkts not compressed: 0, #pkts compr. failed: 0
    #pkts not decompressed: 0, #pkts decompress failed: 0
    #send errors 1, #recv errors 0
     local crypto endpt.: 9.1.1.146, remote crypto endpt.: 9.1.1.35
     path mtu 1500, media mtu 1500
     current outbound spi: BBB91DFA
     inbound esp sas:
      spi: 0x99E52DE4(2581933540)
        transform: esp-3des esp-sha-hmac ,
        in use settings ={Tunnel, }
        slot: 0, conn id: 2000, flow_id: 1, crypto map: vpn
        sa timing: remaining key lifetime (k/sec): (4607999/3589)
        IV size: 8 bytes
        replay detection support: Y
     inbound ah sas:
     inbound pcp sas:
     outbound esp sas:
      spi: 0xBBB91DFA(3149471226)
        transform: esp-3des esp-sha-hmac ,
        in use settings ={Tunnel, }
        slot: 0, conn id: 2001, flow_id: 2, crypto map: vpn
        sa timing: remaining key lifetime (k/sec): (4607999/3589)
        IV size: 8 bytes
        replay detection support: Y
     outbound ah sas:
     outbound pcp sas:

spoke-1-east#
ICMP: dst (9.1.1.146) frag. needed and DF set unreachable rcv from 9.1.1.145
ipsec(adjust_mtu): adjusting path mtu from 1500 to 1400,
  (identity) local= 9.1.1.146, remote= 9.1.1.35,
    local_proxy= 10.0.68.0/255.255.255.0/0/0 (type=4),
    remote_proxy= 10.1.1.0/255.255.255.0/0/0 (type=4)
ICMP: dst (10.1.1.10) frag. needed and DF set unreachable sent to 10.0.68.5
ICMP: dst (10.1.1.10) frag. needed and DF set unreachable sent to 10.0.68.5

spoke-1-east# show cry ipsec sa
```

continues

Example 3-8 *Change in PMTU in the IPSec SA (Continued)*

```
interface: Serial0/0
  Crypto map tag: vpn, local addr. 9.1.1.146
 local  ident (addr/mask/prot/port): (10.0.68.0/255.255.255.0/0/0)
 remote ident (addr/mask/prot/port): (10.1.1.0/255.255.255.0/0/0)
 current_peer: 9.1.1.35:500
   PERMIT, flags={origin_is_acl,}
 #pkts encaps: 35, #pkts encrypt: 35, #pkts digest 35
 #pkts decaps: 39, #pkts decrypt: 39, #pkts verify 39
 #pkts compressed: 0, #pkts decompressed: 0
 #pkts not compressed: 0, #pkts compr. failed: 0
 #pkts not decompressed: 0, #pkts decompress failed: 0
 #send errors 1, #recv errors 0
   local crypto endpt.: 9.1.1.146, remote crypto endpt.: 9.1.1.35
   path mtu 1400, media mtu 1500
   current outbound spi: BBB91DFA
   inbound esp sas:
    spi: 0x99E52DE4(2581933540)
      transform: esp-3des esp-sha-hmac ,
      in use settings ={Tunnel, }
      slot: 0, conn id: 2000, flow_id: 1, crypto map: vpn
      sa timing: remaining key lifetime (k/sec): (4607987/3020)
      IV size: 8 bytes
      replay detection support: Y
   inbound ah sas:
   inbound pcp sas:
   outbound esp sas:
    spi: 0xBBB91DFA(3149471226)
      transform: esp-3des esp-sha-hmac ,
      in use settings ={Tunnel, }
      slot: 0, conn id: 2001, flow_id: 2, crypto map: vpn
      sa timing: remaining key lifetime (k/sec): (4607986/3020)
      IV size: 8 bytes
      replay detection support: Y
   outbound ah sas:
   outbound pcp sas:
```

NOTE   Another option to deal with PMTU for TCP packets is to configure the TCP MSS size on the interface facing the host using the command **ip tcp mss adjust <value>**. This option still will not solve the PMTU if an intermediate router along the path needs to fragment the IPSec packet.

One of the assumptions for PMTU to work is that the ICMP unreachables can reach the source. It is possible that firewalls may block ICMP messages from reaching the sources, which will break PMTUD. A workaround for this situation is to override the DF bit using the following IOS command:

```
Spoke-1-east(config)# crypto ipsec df-bit [clear ¦ set ¦ copy]
```

In the first case, with the DF bit clear option, no path MTU is performed and the DF bit in the IPSec header is set to 0 and fragmented if required. The default behavior is to copy the DF bit from the IP packet to the IPSec header.

Look Ahead Fragmentation

The IPSec RFCs state that IP fragmentation for IPSec-encapsulated packet should happen after encryption. It would be immensely helpful if the encrypting router looks ahead and knows that after encryption and addition of the IPSec header, the resulting packet will exceed the MTU of the outbound interface and would need fragmentation. By looking ahead, the packet can be fragmented before encryption, which saves the decrypting IPSec router from the CPU-intensive job of reassembling the IPSec fragments. Reassembly of the IP packet is off-loaded to the end host. The Cisco IOS feature that performs this function is known as Look Ahead Fragmentation. The feature is quite intuitively simple; a packet arriving into an IPSec gateway will have its length plus IPSec encapsulation overhead compared to the encrypting interface's MTU. If the expected packet size is larger than the MTU of the outbound interface, the IPSec gateway will fragment the IP packet prior to encryption. Otherwise, the packet is forwarded with encryption without fragmentation.

Example 3-9 shows the configuration of this feature. It can be configured on an interface or globally.

Example 3-9   *Look Ahead Fragmentation Configuration*

```
vpn-spoke1-east

crypto isakmp policy 1
 authentication pre-share
crypto isakmp key cisco address 9.1.1.34
crypto isakmp keepalive 60 3

crypto ipsec fragmentation before-encryption
```

Look Ahead Fragmentation configuration works for IP traffic using IPSec tunnel mode only, and will not work in case of transport mode. The reason is that in transport mode, the IP header of the original packet is used in each of the fragments, which results in the More Fragment bit set in the first fragment's IP header and the fragment offset in the subsequent fragments. The receiving IPSec peer has no way of knowing whether an individual packet was fragmented before encryption or after encryption. Therefore, in case of transport mode, the fragments are reassembled before decryption.

GRE and IPSec

Designing a VPN using IPSec for connectivity between peers has inherent limitations. These are:

- IPSec can encrypt/decrypt only IP traffic.

- IP traffic destined to a multicast or broadcast IP address cannot be handled by IPSec, which means that IP multicast traffic cannot traverse the IPSec tunnel. Also, many routing protocols (such as EIGRP, OSPF, and RIPv2) use a multicast or a broadcast address; therefore, dynamic routing using these routing protocols cannot be configured between IPSec peers.

These limitations can be overcome by configuring an IP-encapsulated GRE tunnel between the peers and applying IPSec protection on the GRE/IP tunnel. RFC 2784 covers GRE in detail. It essentially GRE-encapsulates any payload in an IP unicast packet destined to the GRE endpoint. A GRE-encapsulated packet is shown in Figure 3-7.

Figure 3-7 *GRE-Encapsulated Packet*

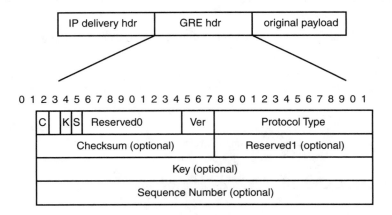

When GRE is used in conjunction with IPSec, either tunnel mode or transport mode can be used. Tunnel mode adds an IPSec IP header to the GRE packet whereas IPSec transport mode uses the original GRE packet's IP header. Figures 3-8 and 3-9 show GRE with IPSec in tunnel mode and transport mode, respectively.

Figure 3-8   *GRE-Encapsulated Packet in IPSec Tunnel Mode*

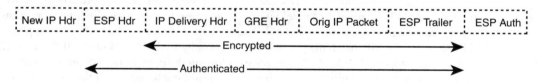

Figure 3-9   *GRE-Encapsulated Packet in IPSec Transport Mode*

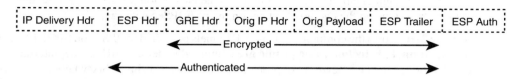

IPSec transport mode is the most efficient way to combine GRE and IPSec together because GRE encapsulation already places a new IP header on the payload. The use of IPSec transport mode, however, requires that the GRE encapsulation use an IP source and destination address that is reachable via the IP path to its peer. GRE adds 24 bytes of overhead to the original IP packet. In conjunction with IPSec transport mode, GRE encapsulation adds 4 bytes of extra overhead in comparison to the 20 bytes of overhead added by IPSec tunnel mode. Although the additional overhead and extra processing for GRE encapsulation reduce the overall throughput and may impact the latency of the connection, the benefits of using GRE with IPSec far outweigh the impact.

Use of GRE with IPSec also has the useful side effect of making IPSec VPN configuration simpler. Traditional IPSec configuration between peers requires IPSec policy configuration to specify the protected subnets so that traffic destined to the protected subnets is encrypted or decrypted. Every time a new protected subnet is added or deleted, the IPSec policy configuration needs to be updated on both peers. Also, the security policy database (SPD) and security association database (SADB) size can get quite large depending on the IPSec SA bundles negotiated and installed. This usually has an impact on the overall performance and scalability of the security gateway. Using GRE with IPSec significantly reduces the configuration complexity, as the policy in the SPD needs to match the traffic only to the GRE endpoint addresses. The addition or deletion of the protected subnets requires no change in the configuration of the IPSec SPD peers. The protected subnet traffic is directed to be encrypted by being routed out the GRE tunnel interface (everything that goes through the GRE tunnel will be encrypted). This does mean that the granularity for what gets encrypted is now at the IP address level rather than the port level in the transport header. In general, this is not an issue because usually all traffic for hosts on protected subnets is to be encrypted.

The GRE encapsulation does increase the size of the packet and potentially causes fragmentation issues. Packet fragmentation can be avoided by ensuring that PMTUD is enabled. To ensure that PMTUD works as expected, ICMP code 3 type 4 messages must be allowed through the network. If ICMP code 3 type 4 messages are not supported in the network, setting a lower MTU size on the tunnel interface will cause fragmentation before encryption to happen, achieving the same effect as Look Ahead Fragmentation. If the end hosts support PMTUD, then they will match the packet size to the configured MTU. Both the IPSec and GRE specifications support Path MTU Discovery by allowing the copy of the DF bit of the original IP header into the newly built IP header. This is usually a configuration option of the devices.

If the end host does not support PMTUD and the DF bit is not set, the packet will be fragmented and sent over the GRE-encrypted tunnel. One benefit to reducing the MTU on the GRE tunnel is that packet fragmentation occurs before it hits the encryption process; therefore, the reassembly is done on the end host and not on the peer IPSec gateway.

Example 3-10 shows the configuration of GRE tunnels protected by IPSec on SPOKE-1-EAST. Note the **tunnel protection ipsec profile gre** command under the GRE tunnel interface configuration, which is a new way of protecting GRE tunnels using IPSec wherein the physical interface that the GRE tunnel traverses does not need the crypto map configuration. Compare this configuration with Example 3-11, which shows the old way of IPSec-protected GRE in IOS.

Example 3-10 *GRE and IPSec Using Tunnel Protection CLI*

```
spoke-1-east

!
crypto isakmp policy 1
 authentication pre-share
crypto isakmp key cisco address 9.1.1.35
crypto isakmp keepalive 60 2
!
crypto ipsec transform-set test esp-3des esp-sha-hmac
!
crypto ipsec profile gre
 set transform-set test
!
int tu0
 ip address 192.168.1.1 255.255.255.0
 ip mtu 1400
 ip tcp adjust-mss 1360
 tunnel source s0/0
 tunnel destination 9.1.1.35
 tunnel path-mtu-discovery
 tunnel protection ipsec profile gre
!
interface Serial0/0
 ip address 9.1.1.146 255.255.255.252
 crypto map vpn
!
interface Ethernet0/1
 ip address 10.0.68.1 255.255.255.0
```

Example 3-10 *GRE and IPSec Using Tunnel Protection CLI (Continued)*

```
 half-duplex
!
ip classless
ip route 0.0.0.0 0.0.0.0 9.1.1.145
ip route 10.0.1.0 0.0.0.255 tu0
```

The primary motivation for using GRE with IPSec is its ability to run dynamic routing protocols such as OSPF or EIGRP between sites for advertising the protected subnets. Dynamic routing also implicitly helps in failover situations. On the other hand, if static routes are used for the reachability of the protected subnets with GRE, then there is no way for the IPSec peers to know that the protected subnets are not reachable when the GRE tunnel endpoints are not reachable anymore. To facilitate knowledge of the tunnel status, GRE keepalive messages can be configured on the GRE peers. Example 3-11 shows configuration of GRE keepalive under the tunnel interface. GRE tunnel comes up as soon as it sees the default route in the routing table on SPOKE-1-EAST. Now, if VPN-GW1-EAST goes down, you want the tunnel interface on SPOKE-1-EAST to go down—this is facilitated by GRE keepalives.

Example 3-11 *GRE Tunnel Keepalive*

```
spoke-1-east

!
crypto isakmp policy 1
 authentication pre-share
crypto isakmp key cisco address 9.1.1.35
crypto isakmp keepalive 60 2
!
crypto ipsec transform-set test esp-3des esp-sha-hmac
mode transport
!
crypto map vpn 1 ipsec-isakmp
 set peer 9.1.1.35
 set transform-set test
 match address 100

!
int tunnel0
ip address 192.168.1.1 255.255.255.0
ip mtu 1400
ip tcp adjust-mss 1360
tunnel path-mtu-discovery
tunnel source s0/0
tunnel destination 9.1.1.35
keepalive 20 3
!
interface Serial0/0
 ip address 9.1.1.146 255.255.255.252
 crypto map vpn
```

continues

Example 3-11 *GRE Tunnel Keepalive (Continued)*

```
!
interface Ethernet0/1
 ip address 10.0.68.1 255.255.255.0
 half-duplex
!
ip classless
ip route 0.0.0.0 0.0.0.0 9.1.1.145
ip route 10.0.1.0 0.0.0.255 tu0
!
access-list 100 permit gre host 9.1.1.146 host 9.1.1.35


spoke-1-east#show cry isa sa
dst              src             state          conn-id    slot
9.1.1.35         9.1.1.146       QM_IDLE             82       0


spoke-1-east#show int tu0
Tunnel0 is up, line protocol is up
  Hardware is Tunnel
  Interface is unnumbered. Using address of Ethernet0/1 (10.0.68.1)
  MTU 1514 bytes, BW 9 Kbit, DLY 500000 usec,
     reliability 255/255, txload 1/255, rxload 1/255
  Encapsulation TUNNEL, loopback not set
  Keepalive set (20 sec), retries 3
  Tunnel source 9.1.1.146 (Serial0/0), destination 9.1.1.35
  Tunnel protocol/transport GRE/IP, key disabled, sequencing disabled
  Tunnel TTL 255
  Checksumming of packets disabled,  fast tunneling enabled
  Last input 00:00:07, output 00:00:07, output hang never
  Last clearing of "show interface" counters never
  Input queue: 0/75/0/0 (size/max/drops/flushes); Total output drops:14
  Queueing strategy: fifo
  Output queue: 0/0 (size/max)
  5 minute input rate 0 bits/sec, 0 packets/sec
  5 minute output rate 0 bits/sec, 0 packets/sec
     483 packets input, 36396 bytes, 0 no buffer
     Received 0 broadcasts, 0 runts, 0 giants, 0 throttles
     0 input errors, 0 CRC, 0 frame, 0 overrun, 0 ignored, 0 abort
     168 packets output, 8596 bytes, 0 underruns
     0 output errors, 0 collisions, 0 interface resets
     0 output buffer failures, 0 output buffers swapped out

Tunnel0: sending keepalive, 9.1.1.35->9.1.1.146 (len=24 ttl=255), counter=1
Tunnel0: GRE/IP encapsulated 9.1.1.146->9.1.1.35 (linktype=7, len=48)
IP: s=9.1.1.146 (Tunnel0), d=9.1.1.35 (Serial0/0), len 48, sending, proto =47
IP: s=9.1.1.35 (Serial0/0), d=9.1.1.146 (Serial0/0), len 24, rcvd 3, proto=47
Tunnel0: GRE/IP to decaps 9.1.1.35->9.1.1.146 (len=24 ttl=253)
Tunnel0: keepalive received, 9.1.1.35->9.1.1.146 (len=24 ttl=253), reset
```

NOTE GRE keepalives are not supported with the **tunnel protection IPsec** configuration syntax. Therefore, for GRE keepalive functionality, you need to use the old-style crypto map configuration.

Figure 3-10 shows the format of a GRE keepalive packet from SPOKE-1-EAST's perspective.

Figure 3-10 *GRE Keepalive Packet*

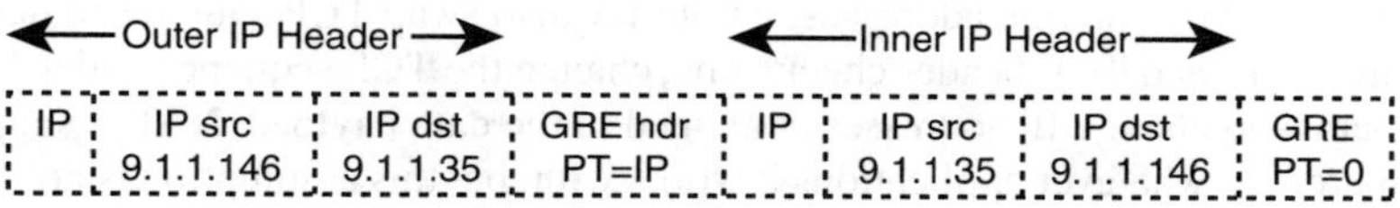

Notice that the destination IP address in the inner IP header is SPOKE-1-EAST's tunnel source address (9.1.1.146) and the source IP address in the inner IP header is that of the tunnel destination address of VPN-GW1-EAST (9.1.1.35). The protocol type (PT) in the inner header is set to 0. This payload is sent in a GRE tunnel with a protocol type of IP in the outer header with source and destination addresses as configured on the tunnel interface shown in Example 3-11. The tunnel keepalive counter is incremented by one as shown in the debug snapshots in Example 3-11. As the GRE tunnel is protected via the crypto map, this keepalive packet will be encrypted when it leaves SPOKE-1-EAST. The packet will reach the far end tunnel endpoint peer (VPN-GW1-EAST) via normal routing Upon arrival on VPN-GW1-EAST, the packet will get decrypted and then decapsulated; the resulting packet will have a source IP address of VPN-GW1-EAST and a destination IP address of SPOKE-1-EAST. This packet will now make its way back to SPOKE-1-EAST through the GRE tunnel, which is again encrypted. The packet, on reaching SPOKE-1-EAST after decryption and GRE decapsulation, will result in a PT of 0, which will signify that this is a keepalive packet that it originally constructed. The receipt of this packet signifies the GRE tunnel is up. The tunnel keepalive counter will be reset to 0 and the packet will be discarded. This process is repeated periodically by each GRE peer.

When VPN-GW1-EAST becomes unreachable from SPOKE-1-EAST for whatever reason, SPOKE-1-EAST will continue to construct and send the keepalive packets as well as normal traffic. Because the keepalives do not come back, the tunnel line protocol will stay up as long as the tunnel keepalive counter is less than the configured retry value. When the number of retries exceeds the configured value, the line protocol will be brought down on the tunnel interface on VPN-SPOKE1-EAST.

In the up/down state, the tunnel will not forward or process any traffic apart from the keepalive packets. The reception of a keepalive packet from VPN-GW1-EAST would imply that the tunnel endpoint is again reachable; when this happens, the tunnel keepalive counter will be reset to 0 and the line protocol will change state back to up, resuming data traffic.

One thing worth mentioning is that GRE keepalive packets are sent out with the TOS bit set to 5 so that the routers process those packets with higher priority, even during congestion.

IPSec and NAT

Network Address Translation (NAT) is typically used to connect a private network such as a corporate network with private IP addresses to a public network such as the Internet. Because private addresses are not routable on the Internet, NAT replaces the private IP addresses with routable addresses in the public network. Keep in mind that to function, NAT doesn't just swap IP source and destination addresses, but it may also swap TCP source and destination ports, change the IP and TCP header checksums, change the TCP sequence and acknowledgment numbers, and change IP addresses contained in the data payload. NAT is supposed to be transparent to whatever applications it works with, but this assumption is not true when NAT is used in conjunction with IPSec. Next, you'll see how NAT affects IPSec protocols.

Effect of NAT on AH

You may recall from Chapter 2, "IPSec Overview," that AH protects the entire IP packet, including invariant header fields such as the source and destination IP address, through a message digest algorithm to produce a keyed hash. The recipient uses the hash to authenticate the packet. If any field in the original IP packet is modified, authentication will fail and the recipient will discard the packet. AH is intended to prevent unauthorized modification, source spoofing, and man-in-the-middle attacks. But NAT, by definition, modifies IP packets. Therefore, NAT on AH does not work.

Effect of NAT on ESP

Like AH, ESP also employs a message digest algorithm for packet authentication. But unlike AH, the hash created by ESP does not include the outer packet IP header fields. This solves one problem, but leaves other problems with ESP. When TCP or UDP are involved, as they are in transport mode ESP, there are two caveats for ESP and NAT to work together. First, because NAT modifies the TCP packet, NAT must also recalculate the checksum used to verify integrity. On the other hand, ESP authentication will fail if NAT updates the TCP checksum. If NAT does not update the checksum (for example, if the payload is encrypted), TCP verification will fail.

In tunnel mode, however, ESP has no issues with NAT. In this mode, the original IP address and transport information is included as payload. So, NAT and ESP can work together in tunnel mode when the NAT translation is 1:1 on addresses with no multiplexing of inside addresses to a single outside address using the transport layer port for differentiation.

Effect of NAT on IKE

IKE has problems when NAT devices transparently modify outgoing packets. The first issue is that some devices might depend on IKE negotiation being made by incoming packets sent from UDP port 500. If a NAT device is introduced, the final packet port will, most surely, not be the expected port; therefore, IKE negotiation will not even begin. Another issue comes about when IKE includes IP addresses as part of the authentication process, which depends on which IKE mode is used. If the authentication is based on the IP address, the changes made by a NAT device will cause IKE negotiation to fail.

IPSec and NAT Solutions

The easiest way to get around IPSec issues with NAT is to avoid the problem by performing NAT before IPSec, but this is not always possible. In this section, you will examine other options for tackling IPSec issues with NAT.

NAT Traversal (NAT-T)

The IPSec NAT Traversal (NAT-T) feature introduces support for IPSec traffic to travel through NAT points in the network. There are three parts to NAT Traversal. The first is to determine if the remote peer supports NAT Traversal. The second is to detect the presence of a NAT function along the path between the peers. The third is to determine how to deal with NAT using UDP encapsulation.

The ability of a peer to support NAT-T and detection of NAT along the path is performed as part of the IKE phase 1 negotiation process. NAT-T capability exchange is done in the first two messages of the IKE phase 1 exchange with the addition of a new vendor identification (ID) payload. Both peers need to exchange the ID for the NAT-T support between the peers. Once the NAT-T capability is successfully exchanged, the detection of NAT along the path is accomplished.

To detect whether a NAT device exists along the network path, the peers send a payload with hashes of the IP address and port of both the source and destination address from each end. If both ends calculate the hashes and the hashes match, each peer knows that a NAT device does not exist on the network path between them. If the hashes do not match (that is, if the address or port have been translated), then each peer needs to perform NAT Traversal to get the IPSec packet through the network. The hashes are sent as a series of NAT-D payloads. Each payload contains one hash. If multiple hashes exist, multiple NAT-D payloads are sent. In most environments, there are only two NAT-D payloads—one for the source address and port and one for the destination address and port. The destination NAT-D payload is sent first, followed by the source NAT-D payload, which implies that the receiver should expect to process the local NAT-D payload first and the remote NAT-D payload second. The NAT-D payloads are included in the third and fourth messages in Main Mode and in the second and third messages in Aggressive Mode. Once the responder sends the NAT-D payload, the initiator *must* change ports when sending the ID payload if there is NAT between the hosts. The initiator must set both UDP source and destination ports to 4500. All subsequent packets sent to this peer *must* be sent on port 4500. The changing of the port by IKE is called floating IKE. Figure 3-11 shows the IKE phase 1 exchange using pre-shared keys and NAT-T.

Figure 3-11   *IKE Phase 1 Key Exchange Using Pre-shared Keys and NAT*

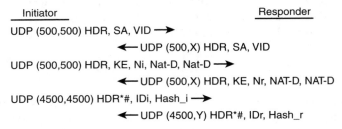

Similarly, if the responder needs to rekey the phase 1 SA, then it *must* start the negotiation using UDP (4500,Y). Any implementation that supports NAT traversal *must* support negotiations that begin on port 4500. If a negotiation starts on 4500, then it doesn't need to change anywhere else in the exchange.

After IKE phase 1 is complete, both peers know if there is NAT between them. The final decision of using the NAT-T is left to IKE phase 2 (that is, Quick Mode). The use of NAT-T is negotiated inside the SA payloads of Quick Mode. In Quick Mode, both ends can also send the original addresses of the IPSec packets (in case of the transport mode) to the other end such that the other end has the possibility to fix the TCP/IP checksum field after NAT. Let's now look at the packet format of an actual data packet once IKE and IPSec SAs have been negotiated between the peers using UDP encapsulation. Shown in Figure 3-12 is an UDP-encapsulated ESP packet in tunnel mode.

The UDP header is a standard header where the source port and destination port *must* be the same as used by floated IKE traffic. The checksum *should* be transmitted as a zero value. The ESP encapsulation is unchanged from what you learned in Chapter 2, "IPSec Overview." After ESP, the UDP header is inserted and the total length, protocol, and header checksum is recalculated in the new IP outer header.

At the decryption end, the UDP header is first removed from the packet and the total length, protocol, and header checksum field is edited to match the new resulting IP packet and processed for decryption.

One more thing worth mentioning is that most NAT devices expire the translation after an idle period of time. To ensure that the translations do not expire, NAT keepalive messages are sent between the peers with a payload that resembles the one shown in Figure 3-13.

Figure 3-12   *UDP-encapsulated ESP Packet in Tunnel Mode*

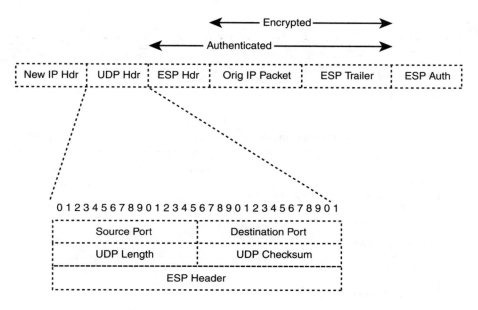

Figure 3-13   *NAT Keepalive Packet*

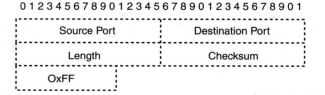

The only field that is different here compared to the other UDP-encapsulated packets is the checksum field. The sender *should* use a one-octet long payload with the value 0xFF. The receiver *should* ignore a received NAT keepalive packet.

A topology with a NAT device in front of SPOKE-1-EAST is shown in Figure 3-14. Example 3-12 shows the configuration and debugs for SPOKE-1-EAST doing NAT-T negotiation. Peers that run IOS code that support NAT-T automatically exchange this capability. The CLI to control the NAT keepalive timer to disable NAT-T is also indicated in Example 3-12.

Figure 3-14 *NAT Device Introduced in the Topology*

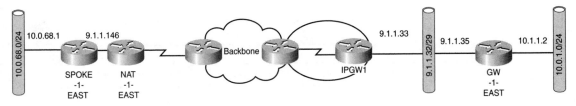

Example 3-12 *NAT Keepalive Configuration in IOS*

```
spoke-1-east

version 12.2
service timestamps debug uptime
service timestamps log uptime
no service password-encryption
!
hostname spoke-1-east
!
enable password lab
!
ip domain name cisco.com
!
!
crypto isakmp policy 1
 authentication pre-share
crypto isakmp key cisco address 9.1.1.35
crypto isakmp keepalive 60
crypto isakmp nat keepalive 60
!
!
crypto ipsec transform-set test esp-3des esp-sha-hmac
!
crypto map vpn 1 ipsec-isakmp
 set peer 9.1.1.35
 set transform-set test
 match address 100
!
!
interface Serial0/0
 ip address 9.1.1.146 255.255.255.252
 crypto map vpn
!
interface Ethernet0/1
 ip address 10.0.68.1 255.255.255.0
 half-duplex
 no keepalive
!
ip classless
ip route 0.0.0.0 0.0.0.0 9.1.1.145
```

Example 3-12   *NAT Keepalive Configuration in IOS (Continued)*

```
no ip http server
ip pim bidir-enable
!
!
access-list 100 permit ip 10.0.68.0 0.0.0.255 10.1.1.0 0.0.0.255
!
!
line con 0
line aux 0
line vty 0 4
 password lab
 login
!
!
end
spoke-1-east#
ISAKMP (0:1): constructed NAT-T vendor-03 ID
ISAKMP (0:1): vendor ID is NAT-T
ISAKMP (0:1): found peer pre-shared key matching 9.1.1.35
ISAKMP (0:1) local preshared key found
ISAKMP (0:1): Checking ISAKMP transform 1 against priority 1 policy
ISAKMP:        encryption DES-CBC
ISAKMP:        hash SHA
ISAKMP:        default group 1
ISAKMP:        auth pre-share
ISAKMP:        life type in seconds
ISAKMP:        life duration (VPI) of  0x0 0x1 0x51 0x80
ISAKMP (0:1): atts are acceptable. Next payload is 0
ISAKMP (0:1): constructed HIS NAT-D
ISAKMP (0:1): constructed MINE NAT-D
ISAKMP
ISAKMP:received payload type 17
ISAKMP (0:1): Detected NAT-D payload
ISAKMP (0:1): NAT does not match MINE hash
hash received: 1 76 36 D8 8B 88 BA D6 8E C9 AC B1 B1 7 AB C6 C0 66 DF BE
my nat hash  : 77 7D 44 40 FA D0 7D A1 29 54 91 A9 D7 EC 40 A4 38 18 F1 EA
ISAKMP:received payload type 17
ISAKMP (0:1): Detected NAT-D payload
ISAKMP (0:1): NAT match HIS hash
ISAKMP (0:1): Input = IKE_MESG_INTERNAL, IKE_PROCESS_MAIN_MODE
ISAKMP (0:1): Old State = IKE_I_MM4 New State = IKE_I_MM4

ISAKMP (0:1): sending packet to 9.1.1.35 my_port 4500 peer_port 4500 (I) MM_KEY_EXCH
ISAKMP (0:1): Input = IKE_MESG_INTERNAL, IKE_PROCESS_COMPLETE
ISAKMP (0:1): Old State = IKE_I_MM4  New State = IKE_I_MM5

ISAKMP (0:1): received packet from 9.1.1.35 dport 4500 sport 4500 (I) MM_KEY_EXCH

spoke-1-east#show cry isa sa det
Codes: C - IKE configuration mode, D - Dead Peer Detection
       K - Keepalives, N - NAT-traversal
```

continues

Example 3-12 *NAT Keepalive Configuration in IOS (Continued)*

```
              X - IKE Extended Authentication

Conn id Local           Remote          Encr Hash Auth DH Lifetime Capabilities
1       9.1.1.146       9.1.1.35        des  sha  psk  1  23:59:09 DN


spoke-1-east#show cry ipsec sa

interface: Serial0/0
    Crypto map tag: vpn, local addr. 9.1.1.146

    local  ident (addr/mask/prot/port): (10.0.68.0/255.255.255.0/0/0)
    remote ident (addr/mask/prot/port): (10.1.1.0/255.255.255.0/0/0)
    current_peer: 9.1.1.35:4500
      PERMIT, flags={origin_is_acl,}
     #pkts encaps: 4, #pkts encrypt: 4, #pkts digest 4
     #pkts decaps: 0, #pkts decrypt: 0, #pkts verify 0
     #pkts compressed: 0, #pkts decompressed: 0
     #pkts not compressed: 0, #pkts compr. failed: 0
     #pkts not decompressed: 0, #pkts decompress failed: 0
     #send errors 1, #recv errors 0

      local crypto endpt.: 9.1.1.146, remote crypto endpt.: 9.1.1.35
      path mtu 1500, media mtu 1500
      current outbound spi: 8531E6D1

      inbound esp sas:
       spi: 0x8BC80991(2345142673)
         transform: esp-3des esp-sha-hmac ,
         in use settings ={Tunnel UDP-Encaps, }
         slot: 0, conn id: 2000, flow_id: 1, crypto map: vpn
         sa timing: remaining key lifetime (k/sec): (4608000/3483)
         IV size: 8 bytes
         replay detection support: Y

      inbound ah sas:

      inbound pcp sas:

      outbound esp sas:
       spi: 0x8531E6D1(2234640081)
         transform: esp-3des esp-sha-hmac ,
         in use settings ={Tunnel UDP-Encaps, }
         slot: 0, conn id: 2001, flow_id: 2, crypto map: vpn
         sa timing: remaining key lifetime (k/sec): (4607999/3483)
         IV size: 8 bytes
         replay detection support: Y

      outbound ah sas:
```

NOTE   IPSec over TCP encapsulation is also supported on the VPN 3000 Concentrator to pass through NAT devices. The reason is most firewalls allow TCP ports.

IPSec Pass-through

This section deals with another method for resolving IPSec and NAT incompatibilities. This method, however, applies only to ESP-based IPSec traffic.

The feature, IPSec pass-through, supports IKE and ESP (IP protocol 50) only in tunnel mode through an IOS PAT box. AH or ESP in transport mode are not supported.

With ESP, we know that the IP header is not authenticated, so NAT can change the IP addresses. In case of AH, authentication includes the IP header of the packet as seen in Chapter 2, "IPSec Overview. There is no way to perform address translation on a packet using NAT and recover it. NAT will change the source address, destination address, or port; therefore, authentication will fail at the remote peer. The same reason holds true for ESP in transport mode. There are two issues to be considered here—one is IKE and the other is ESP in tunnel mode. We will again refer to Figure 3-13 to explain these issues.

IKE Passing Through PAT

IKE uses UDP port 500. If there is just one device behind the NAT/PAT box, then there is nothing that needs to be done by the PAT gateway, as the IKE flow will pass unmodified as standard UDP traffic. When there is more than one IPSec device behind the PAT gateway, a unique delimiter is required to identify the IKE session for each of the IPSec endpoints. The delimiter used is the initiator cookie that is part of IKE header.

ESP Passing Through PAT

In the case of ESP, PAT needs to use some other field in the packet to multiplex. The only field that is accessible to PAT and is unique is the security parameter index (SPI) that is part of the ESP header.

The same principles apply if there is just one IPSec endpoint passing through the PAT gateway. The SPI of the endpoint can be used to map to the translation. The problem arises when more than one IPSec endpoint exists behind the PAT gateway and they all establish connections to the same remote peer. The IPSec SA is unidirectional. When the packets return from the remote peer, it will have a different SPI. The PAT gateway sitting in the middle has no way to associate inbound and outbound SPIs and decide that they belong to same ESP connection of one IPSec endpoint. Next, you examine one of the most commonly used methods to overcome this problem.

Restricted ESP Through PAT Mode

The first method, referred to as the restricted method, allows PAT to serially establish translation tables on ESP traffic initiated from inside IPSec endpoints to an outside IPSec endpoint. Once the outside endpoint starts replying, PAT assumes the packets are associated with the only outstanding IPSec session allowed to go, and "binds" the two SPIs in the translation. From this moment on, the next inside IPSec endpoint is allowed to send ESP traffic and establish its unique translation map, and so on.

Refer to the topology shown in Figure 3-14, which explains the workings of restricted ESP. The NAT translation on INTERNET-PAT-ROUTER is shown in Example 3-13. You can see that the there is both in and out mapping of the translation along with SPIs.

Example 3-13 *NAT/PAT Translation with ESP*

```
NAT-ROUTER#show ip nat translations

Pro Inside global  Inside local      Outside local     Outside global
esp 100.1.1.2:0      9.1.1.146:0      9.1.1.35:0        9.1.1.35:5D826FB2
esp 100.1.1.2:0      9.1.1.146:62BC13C  9.1.1.35:0        9.1.1.35:0
```

From this point on, all ESP traffic between 9.1.1.146 and 9.1.1.35 using SPI1 and SPI2 uses these translations. If the endpoints decide to change SPI values, essentially a new ESP translation must be established. The one critical restriction with this approach is that PAT must first see the in-to-out connection requesting a new SPI in order to create the in-to-out translation capable of mapping the returning out-to-in reply packets.

Example 3-14 shows the configuration that is needed on the PAT box to allow ESP in a restricted way. You can see that the SPIs from the NAT translation on the NAT-ROUTER match the inbound and outbound SPIs of IPSec SAs created between VPN-GW1-EAST and SPOKE-1-EAST.

Example 3-14 *PAT Configuration to Allow ESP*

```
NAT-ROUTER#

version 12.2
service timestamps debug uptime
service timestamps log uptime
no service password-encryption
!
hostname NAT-ROUTER
!
ip subnet-zero
!


!
interface FastEthernet0/0
 ip address 100.1.1.1 255.255.255.252
 ip nat outside
 duplex full
```

Example 3-14 *PAT Configuration to Allow ESP (Continued)*

```
!
interface Serial1/1:0
 ip address 9.1.1.145 255.255.255.252
 ip nat inside
!
router ospf 1
 log-adjacency-changes
 network 100.1.1.0 0.0.0.255 area 0

ip nat service list 1 IKE preserve-port
ip nat service list 1 ESP spi-match
ip nat inside source list 1 interface FastEthernet0/0 overload
ip classless
ip route 0.0.0.0 0.0.0.0 100.1.1.1
no ip http server
no ip http secure-server
!
!
!
access-list 1 permit 9.1.1.146
!
!
line con 0
 exec-timeout 0 0
 stopbits 1
line aux 0
 stopbits 1
line vty 0 4
 login
line vty 5 15
 login
!
!
end


NAT-ROUTER# debug ip nat ipsec

NAT: ipsec: using mapping to create outbound ESP IL=9.1.1.146, SPI=62BC13C,
IG=100.1.1.2
NAT: ipsec: created In->Out ESP translation IL=9.1.1.146 SPI=0x62BC13C, IG=100.1.1.2,
OL=9.1.1.34, OG=9.1.1.34
NAT: ipsec: Inside host (IL=9.1.1.146) trying to open an ESP connection to Outside host
(OG=9.1.1.34), wait for Out->In reply
NAT: ipsec: new Out->In ESP transl OG=9.1.1.34 SPI=0x5D826FB2, IG=100.1.1.2,
IL=9.1.1.146


NAT-ROUTER#show ip nat translations
```

continues

Example 3-14 *PAT Configuration to Allow ESP (Continued)*

```
Pro Inside global  Inside local      Outside local     Outside global
esp 100.1.1.2:0     9.1.1.146:0       9.1.1.34:0        9.1.1.34:5D826FB2
esp 100.1.1.2:0     9.1.1.146:62BC13C 9.1.1.34:0          9.1.1.34:0
udp 100.1.1.2:500   9.1.1.146:500     9.1.1.34:500        9.1.1.34:500


NAT-ROUTER#show ip nat translations esp verbose
Pro Inside global  Inside local      Outside local     Outside global
esp 9.1.1.33:0      9.1.1.146:0        9.1.1.34:0      9.1.1.34:5D826FB2
    create 00:04:01, use 00:04:01, timing-out,
    flags:
extended, 0x100000, use_count: 1
esp 9.1.1.33:0          9.1.1.146:62BC13C 9.1.1.34:0        9.1.1.34:0
    create 00:04:01, use 00:04:01, left 00:00:58, Map-Id(In): 2,
    flags:
extended, use_count: 0

vpn-gw1-east:

vpn-gw1-east#show cry isa sa
dst             src             state          conn-id   slot
9.1.1.34        100.1.1.2       QM_IDLE           10       0

vpn-gw1-east#show cry ipsec sa

interface: FastEthernet0/0
    Crypto map tag: vpn, local addr. 9.1.1.34

   local  ident (addr/mask/prot/port): (10.1.1.0/255.255.255.0/0/0)
   remote ident (addr/mask/prot/port): (10.0.68.0/255.255.255.0/0/0)
   current_peer: 9.1.1.33
     PERMIT, flags={origin_is_acl,}
    #pkts encaps: 4, #pkts encrypt: 4, #pkts digest 4
    #pkts decaps: 4, #pkts decrypt: 4, #pkts verify 4
    #pkts compressed: 0, #pkts decompressed: 0
    #pkts not compressed: 0, #pkts compr. failed: 0, #pkts decompress failed: 0
    #send errors 0, #recv errors 0

    local crypto endpt.: 9.1.1.34, remote crypto endpt.: 100.1.1.2
    path mtu 1500, media mtu 1500
    current outbound spi: 5D826FB2

    inbound esp sas:
     spi: 0x62BC13C(103530812)
       transform: esp-3des esp-sha-hmac ,
       in use settings ={Tunnel, }
       slot: 100, conn id: 2000, flow_id: 1, crypto map: vpn
       sa timing: remaining key lifetime (k/sec): (4607998/3507)
       IV size: 8 bytes
       replay detection support: Y
```

Example 3-14 *PAT Configuration to Allow ESP (Continued)*

```
     inbound ah sas:

     inbound pcp sas:

     outbound esp sas:
      spi: 0x5D826FB2(1568829362)
        transform: esp-3des esp-sha-hmac ,
        in use settings ={Tunnel, }
        slot: 100, conn id: 2001, flow_id: 2, crypto map: vpn
        sa timing: remaining key lifetime (k/sec): (4607999/3507)
        IV size: 8 bytes
        replay detection support: Y

     outbound ah sas:

     outbound pcp sas:
```

Summary

This chapter covered many advanced IPSec features, some of which are specific to Cisco IOS, which help IPSec VPNs scale better and be more fault tolerant. You also explored how to use GRE in combination with IPSec to work around implicit limitations of native IPSec. Finally, you looked at how to solve IPSec issues with NAT. The concepts covered in this chapter lay the foundation for future chapters on IPSec scalability and fault tolerance. Subsequent chapters include case studies to help you understand the features within the context of design and deployment scenarios.

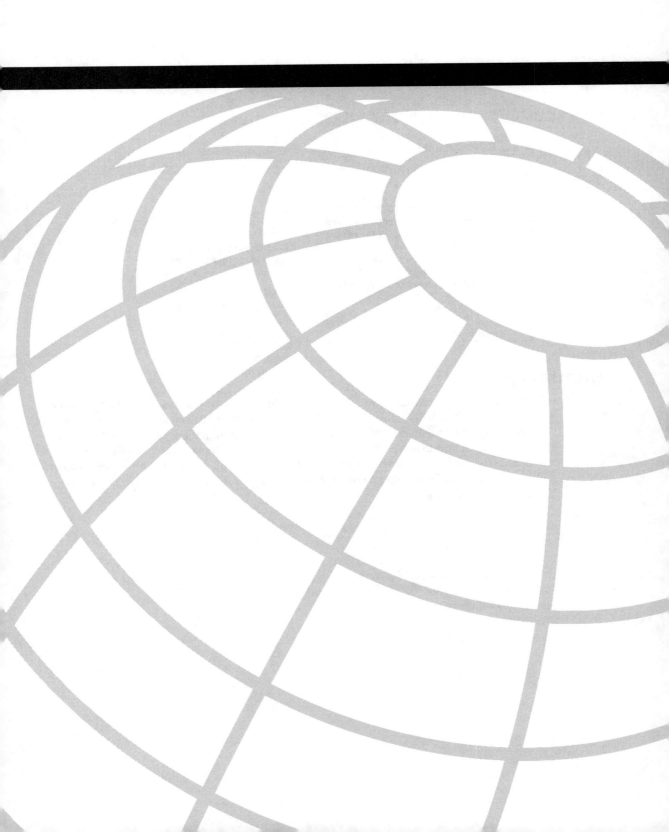

CHAPTER 4

IPSec Authentication and Authorization Models

Telecommuting is increasingly becoming a part of everyday life, and IPSec connectivity is arguably the most popular connection method that telecommuters use to connect to a VPN across the public Internet. Given that telecommuters can be anywhere in the Internet, the successful completion of authorization and authentication is critical for granting access to the VPN. This chapter explores authentication and authorization models for the IPSec telecommuter.

Extended Authentication (XAUTH) and Mode Configuration (MODE-CFG)

Authentication schemes such as Remote Authentication Dial-In User Service (RADIUS) and SecureID are commonly used for providing secure remote access. It is highly desirable to leverage these authentication mechanisms for IPSec remote access. But Internet Key Exchange (IKE) protocol, which you learned about in Chapter 2, "IPSec Overview," does not provide a method to leverage these unidirectional authentication schemes. Extended Authentication, commonly referred to as XAUTH, was developed to leverage these legacy authentication schemes with IKE.

XAUTH provides an additional level of authentication by allowing the IPSec gateway to request extended authentication from remote users, thus forcing remote users to respond with their credentials before being allowed access to the VPN. It should be noted that XAUTH functions by first forming an IKE phase 1 SA using conventional IKE, and then by extending the IKE exchange to include additional user authentication exchanges. Figure 4-1 shows an XAUTH exchange using a generic username and password authentication scheme.

Figure 4-1 *Extended Authentication (XAUTH) Exchange*

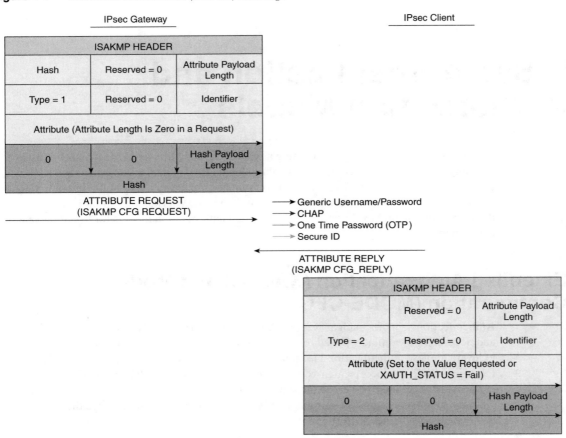

As shown in Figure 4-1, XAUTH uses a Request/Reply mechanism to provide the extended authentication. The XAUTH process is terminated, either when the gateway starts a SET/ACK exchange, which includes an XAUTH_STATUS attribute, or when the remote device sends a XAUTH_STATUS attribute in a REPLY message.

The XAUTH protocol defines four message types that are exchanged between the remote user and the IPSec gateway. These messages carry various attributes for the extended authentication process to work. The four XAUTH message types are:

- ISAKMP_CFG_REQUEST
- ISAKMP_CFG_REPLY
- ISAKMP_CFG_SET
- ISAKMP_CFG_ACK

A description of the XAUTH message types follows:

- **ISAKMP_CFG_REQUEST**—This message is sent from the IPSec gateway to the IPSec client requesting extended authentication of the client.

- **ISAKMP_CFG_REPLY**—This message must contain the filled-in authentication attributes that were requested by the gateway or, if the proper authentication attributes cannot be retrieved, this message must contain the XAUTH_STATUS attribute with a value of FAIL.

- **ISAKMP_CFG_SET**—This message is sent from the gateway and is used only to state the success or failure of the authentication.

- **ISAKMP_CFG_ACK**—This message is sent from the IPSec client, acknowledging receipt of the authentication result.

The XAUTH message types defined above carry various attributes. A brief description of the attributes is shown in Table 4-1.

Table 4-1   *XAUTH Attributes*

Attribute	Description
XAUTH_TYPE	This attribute describes the type of extended authentication method requested. Four authentication methods are defined in the protocol: Generic, RADIUS_CHAP, One Time password (OTP), and Secure ID. This is an optional attribute for the ISAKMP_CFG_REQUEST and ISAKMP_CFG_REPLY messages. The XAUTH_TYPE in a REPLY must be identical to the XAUTH_TYPE in the REQUEST. However, an XAUTH transaction may have multiple REQUEST/REPLY pairs with different XAUTH_TYPE values in each pair.
XAUTH_USER_NAME	The username may be any unique identifier of the user, such as a login name, an email address, or a X.500 Distinguished Name.
XAUTH_USER_PASSWORD	The user's password.
XAUTH_PASSCODE	A token card's passcode.

continues

Table 4-1 *XAUTH Attributes (Continued)*

Attribute	Description
XAUTH_MESSAGE	A textual message from the gateway to the IPSec client. The message may contain a textual challenge or instruction.
XAUTH_CHALLENGE	A challenge string sent from the gateway to the IPSec client to be included in its calculation of a password. This attribute should be sent only in an ISAKMP_CFG_REQUEST message. Typically, ' the XAUTH_TYPE attribute dictates how the receiving device should handle the challenge. For example, RADIUS-CHAP uses the challenge to hide the password.
XAUTH_STATUS	A variable that is used to denote authentication success (OK=1) or failure (FAIL=0). This attribute *must* be sent in the ISAKMP_CFG_SET message, in which case it may be set to either OK or FAIL, and *may* be sent in a REPLY message by a remote peer, in which case it *must* be set to FAIL.

When a remote access user connects to an IPSec gateway and XAUTH is required by the gateway, configuration on the gateway initiates the XAUTH messages before IKE phase 2 negotiation begins. If the remote access client does not have support for the authentication method requested by the gateway, the client would send back a REPLY with the XAUTH_STATUS attribute set to FAIL, thus failing the authentication.

Example 4-1 shows the configuration of XAUTH using the RADIUS/AAA authentication method.

Example 4-1 *Cisco IOS XAUTH Configuration on the IPSec Gateway*

```
vpn-gw1-east#
!
hostname vpn-gw1-east
!
username ezvpn password 0 east
username ezvpn1@vpngroup password 0 ezvpn1east
username ezvpn2@vpngroup password 0 ezvpn2east
aaa new-model
!
aaa authentication login vpn local
aaa authorization network vpn local
aaa session-id common
ip subnet-zero
!
crypto isakmp policy 1
 encr 3des
 authentication pre-share
 group 2
crypto isakmp keepalive 10 10
```

Example 4-1   *Cisco IOS XAUTH Configuration on the IPSec Gateway (Continued)*

```
!
crypto ipsec transform-set vpn esp-3des esp-sha-hmac
!
crypto dynamic-map dynamic 1
 set transform-set vpn
 reverse-route remote-peer 9.1.1.33
!
!
crypto map vpn client authentication list vpn
crypto map vpn isakmp authorization list vpn
crypto map vpn client configuration address respond
crypto map vpn 3 ipsec-isakmp dynamic dynamic
```

The addition of the following command on the crypto map enables XAUTH and triggers the XAUTH transaction after IKE phase 1 and before IKE phase 2:

```
crypto map map-name client authentication list list-name
```

As you learned in Chapter 2, "IPSec Overview," a very common deployment scenario for IPSec telecommuters is the use of IKE pre-shared key authentication with Aggressive Mode. The primary motivation for this scenario is that the IP address of an IPSec remote access user connecting to an IPSec gateway over the public Internet is typically not known in advance to the gateway. In most deployments using pre-shared keys, a single shared group key is used for all users of the VPN. What this means is that without employing some form of additional user authentication, there is no way to verify that the person connecting with that VPN client is indeed a valid user.

Imagine, for example, a situation where a laptop with a VPN client is stolen—because the VPN client is already configured with a valid group key, anyone with the laptop can connect to the VPN without any problems, as no further authentication is required! Extended Authentication (XAUTH) is widely employed to address this serious security gap. XAUTH forces users to identify themselves with a user id and a password *after* the group pre-shared key has been verified.

XAUTH is also referred to as "two factor authentication." The password could be a "one-time password" (for example, from a SecureID card) adding further security to such a deployment. Although the usage of XAUTH is very common and desired for the telecommuter scenario using pre-shared keys and Aggressive Mode, it can also be used with Main Mode and other authentication methods such as digital certificates. It is important to note that although XAUTH is deployed very commonly, it has not been established as a standard by the IPSec working group in the IETF, which means that it may present interoperability issues among different vendor implementations.

Mode-Configuration (MODECFG)

In remote access scenarios, it is highly desirable to be able to push configuration information such as the private IP address, a DNS server's IP address, and so forth, to the client. The IPSec Mode-configuration (MODECFG) allows this functionality. Configuration for MODECFG using Cisco IOS is shown in Example 4-2.

Example 4-2 *Cisco IOS MODECFG Configuration on the IPSec Gateway*

```
vpn-gw1-east#
!
hostname vpn-gw1-east
!
username ezvpn password 0 east
username ezvpn1@vpngroup password 0 ezvpn1east
username ezvpn2@vpngroup password 0 ezvpn2east
aaa new-model
!
aaa authentication login vpn local
aaa authorization network vpn local
aaa session-id common
ip subnet-zero
!
crypto isakmp policy 1
 encr 3des
 authentication pre-share
 group 2
crypto isakmp keepalive 10 10
!
crypto isakmp client configuration group vpngroup
 key ciscoezvpn
 dns 10.1.1.10
 wins 10.1.1.11
 pool vpnpool
 include-local-lan
 backup-gateway 9.1.1.36
!
crypto ipsec transform-set vpn esp-3des esp-sha-hmac
!
crypto dynamic-map dynamic 1
 set transform-set vpn
 reverse-route remote-peer 9.1.1.33
!
!
crypto map vpn client authentication list vpn
crypto map vpn isakmp authorization list vpn
crypto map vpn client configuration address respond
crypto map vpn 3 ipsec-isakmp dynamic dynamic
```

Some of the key attributes that can be pushed to a remote user using MODECFG follow:

- **INTERNAL_IP4_ADDRESS**, **INTERNAL_IP6_ADDRESS**—Specifies an address within the internal network. The requested address is valid until the expiration of the ISAKMP SA that was used to secure the request. The address may also expire when the IPSec phase 2 SA expires, if the request is associated with a phase 2 negotiation.

- **INTERNAL_IP4_NETMASK**, **INTERNAL_IP6_NETMASK**—The internal network's netmask.

- **INTERNAL_IP4_DNS**, **INTERNAL_IP6_DNS**—Specifies an address of a DNS server or multiple DNS servers within the network. The responder may respond with zero, one, or more DNS server attributes.

- **INTERNAL_IP4_NBNS**, **INTERNAL_IP6_NBNS**—Specifies an address of a NetBios Name Server (NBNS) within the network. Multiple NBNSs may be requested. The responder may respond with zero, one, or more NBNS attributes.

Like XAUTH, MODECFG is not a standard of the IPSec working group in the IETF. Although Cisco defined this protocol and most client implementations work with the Cisco implementation, given that this not a standard, there are no guarantees for interoperability.

Easy VPN (EzVPN)

As you saw in Chapter 2, "IPSec Overview," for an IPSec tunnel to be established between two peers, there is a significant amount of configuration required on both peers. This includes IPSec policies, Diffie-Hellman parameters, encryption algorithms, and so on. In a large corporate environment with hundreds of sites, managing the IPSec configuration can get quite tedious. The Cisco Easy VPN feature, also known as EzVPN, eases IPSec configuration by allowing an almost no-touch configuration of the IPSec client.

EzVPN uses the Unity client protocol, which allows most IPSec VPN parameters to be defined at an IPSec gateway, which is also the EzVPN server. When an EzVPN client initiates an IPSec tunnel connection, the EzVPN server pushes the IPSec policies and other attributes required to form the IPSec tunnel to the EzVPN client and creates the corresponding IPSec tunnel connection. The tunnel on the EzVPN client can be initiated automatically or manually, or it could be traffic triggered, depending on the configuration or type of EzVPN client used. Minimal configuration is required at the EzVPN client. EzVPN provides the following general functions in order to simplify the configuration process:

- **Negotiating tunnel parameters**—This is done with encryption algorithms, SA lifetimes, and so on.

- **User authentication**—This entails validating user credentials by way of XAUTH.

- **Automatic configuration**—Performed by pushing attributes such as IP address, DNS, WINs, and so on, using MODECFG.

| NOTE | The term EzVPN client is used for both Cisco Unity VPN clients, called EzVPN software clients, and the Unity client protocol running on smaller Cisco routers like the 800, 1700, and 2600 series, commonly referred to as EzVPN hardware clients. |

The Cisco Easy VPN feature supports two modes of operation:

- Client Mode
- Network Extension Mode

You will examine each of these modes in detail in the following sections.

EzVPN Client Mode

Figure 4-2 shows an IPSec Unity client configured for Client Mode in order to establish an IPSec VPN tunnel to the gateway.

Figure 4-2   *EzVPN IPSec Client Mode Connection*

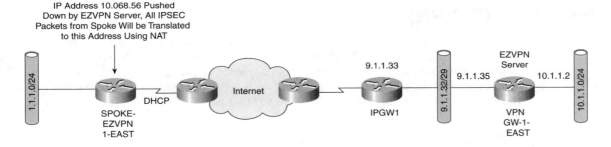

EzVPN Client Mode is also known as Network/Port Address Translation (NAT/PAT) Mode. In this mode, all traffic from the client side uses a single IP address for all hosts on the private network. In Figure 4-2, all traffic from the hosts on the FastEthernet interface on the EzVPN client is translated by NAT to a source IP address of 10.0.68.5, which is assigned by the EzVPN server as an attribute using MODECFG. The client keeps track of the mappings so that it can be forwarded to the correct host on the private network.

The configuration of the EzVPN hardware client is shown in Example 4-3.

Example 4-3   *EzVPN Client Mode Configuration*

```
spoke-ezvpn1-east#
!
hostname spoke-ezvpn1-east
!
```

Example 4-3   *EzVPN Client Mode Configuration (Continued)*

```
crypto ipsec client ezvpn vpn
 connect auto
 group vpngroup key ciscoezvpn
 local-address Ethernet0
 mode client
 peer 9.1.1.35
 username ezvpn1@vpngroup password  ezvpn1east
!
!
interface Ethernet0
 ip address dhcp
 load-interval 30
 half-duplex
 crypto ipsec client ezvpn vpn outside
!
interface FastEthernet0
 ip address 1.1.1.1 255.255.255.0
 load-interval 30
 speed 100
 full-duplex
 no keepalive
 crypto ipsec client ezvpn vpn inside
!
ip route 0.0.0.0 0.0.0.0 Ethernet0
!
end
```

Notice that in the EzVPN client configuration, none of the IPSec policies, encryption algorithms, and so forth are configured. Example 4-4 shows how to monitor an EzVPN client configuration.

Example 4-4   *Verification of EzVPN Client Mode Configuration*

```
spoke-ezvpn1-east#show crypto isakmp sa
dst             src             state           conn-id slot
9.1.1.35        9.1.1.146       QM_IDLE             4    0
spoke-ezvpn1-east#show crypto ipsec client ezvpn
Easy VPN Remote Phase: 2
Tunnel name : vpn
Inside interface list: FastEthernet0,
Outside interface: Ethernet0
Current State: IPSEC_ACTIVE
Last Event: SOCKET_UP
Address: 10.0.68.56
Mask: 255.255.255.255
DNS Primary: 10.1.1.10
NBMS/WINS Primary: 10.1.1.11
```

The configuration of the EzVPN server is shown in Example 4-5.

Example 4-5 *EzVPN Server-side Configuration*

```
vpn-gw1-east#
!
hostname vpn-gw1-east
!
username ezvpn password 0 east
username ezvpn1@vpngroup password 0 ezvpn1east
username ezvpn2@vpngroup password 0 ezvpn2east
aaa new-model
!
aaa authentication login vpn local
aaa authorization network vpn local
aaa session-id common
ip subnet-zero
!
crypto isakmp policy 1
 encr 3des
 authentication pre-share
 group 2
crypto isakmp keepalive 10 10
!
crypto isakmp client configuration group vpngroup
 key ciscoezvpn
 dns 10.1.1.10
 wins 10.1.1.11
 pool vpnpool
 include-local-lan
 backup-gateway 9.1.1.36
!
!
crypto ipsec transform-set vpn esp-3des esp-sha-hmac
!
crypto dynamic-map dynamic 1
 set transform-set vpn
 reverse-route remote-peer 9.1.1.33
!
!
crypto map vpn client authentication list vpn
crypto map vpn isakmp authorization list vpn
crypto map vpn client configuration address respond
crypto map vpn 3 ipsec-isakmp dynamic dynamic
!
!
interface Loopback0
 ip address 9.2.1.100 255.255.255.255
!
interface FastEthernet0/0
 ip address 9.1.1.35 255.255.255.248
 duplex full
 crypto map vpn
!
```

Example 4-5   *EzVPN Server-side Configuration (Continued)*

```
interface FastEthernet2/0
 ip address 100.1.1.147 255.255.255.0
 duplex full
!
interface FastEthernet4/0
 ip address 10.1.1.1 255.255.255.0
 duplex full
!
router ospf 1
 log-adjacency-changes
 redistribute static subnets
 network 10.1.1.0 0.0.0.255 area 0
!
ip local pool vpnpool 10.0.68.1 10.0.68.100
ip classless
ip route 0.0.0.0 0.0.0.0 9.1.1.33
!
radius-server host 100.1.1.4 auth-port 1645 acct-port 1646
radius-server key cisco
end
```

The IOS command **crypto isakmp client configuration group vpngroup** defines the attributes for the VPN group that was assigned to the EzVPN client.

Network Extension Mode

Figure 4-3 shows an EzVPN client in Network Extension Mode. This mode allows the EzVPN client to present a full, routable network to the tunneled network.

Figure 4-3   *EzVPN IPSec Network Extension Mode Connection*

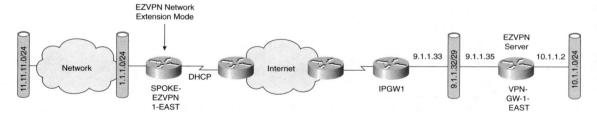

IPSec encapsulates all traffic from the EzVPN client's private network, which is marked as 'inside' to networks behind the IPSec gateway. Therefore, devices behind the gateway have direct access to devices on the EzVPN client's private network via the tunnel and vice versa without the need for NAT or PAT. As there is no reason for NAT or PAT, the EzVPN server does not push down an IP address for tunneled traffic, but all other attributes like ACLs, DNS, and

WINS, can be pushed down. Example 4-6 shows the configuration of Network Extension Mode on the EzVPN client shown in Figure 4-3.

Example 4-6   *EzVPN Client Configuration for Network Extension Mode*

```
spoke-ezvpn1-east#
!
hostname spoke-ezvpn1-east
!
crypto ipsec client ezvpn vpn
 connect auto
 group vpngroup key ciscoezvpn
 local-address Ethernet0
 mode network-extension
 acl 100
 peer 9.1.1.35
 username ezvpn1@vpngroup password  ezvpn1east
!
interface Ethernet0
 ip address dhcp
 load-interval 30
 half-duplex
 crypto ipsec client ezvpn vpn outside
!
interface FastEthernet0
 ip address 1.1.1.1 255.255.255.0
 load-interval 30
 speed 100
 full-duplex
 no keepalive
 crypto ipsec client ezvpn vpn inside
!
access-list 100 permit 11.1.1.0 0.0.0.255 any
ip route 0.0.0.0 0.0.0.0 dhcp
```

Note the ACL 100 under the mode network-extension in the configuration. The ACL 100 permits networks behind the "inside" network (11.1.1.0/24) and allows traffic to and from these subnets to be encrypted. Without the access list, only traffic to and from the "inside" subnet (1.1.1.0/24) is encrypted.

NOTE   The EzVPN server configuration is the same for both Client Extension Mode and Network Extension Mode. The client configuration determines which mode is being used.

Redundancy is always an integral part of any IPSec design and, in the case of EzVPN dead peer detection along with backup peer list, makes such a design possible. Example 4-7 shows the client configuration with multiple EzVPN server peer addresses manually configured on the client. An alternate mechanism to provide EzVPN server redundancy is to push the backup server's address list down to the client as an attribute. Dead peer detection is on by default on the EzVPN clients.

Example 4-7   *EzVPN Server Redundancy*

```
spoke-ezvpn1-east#
!
hostname spoke-ezvpn1-east
!
crypto ipsec client ezvpn vpn
 connect auto
 group vpngroup key ciscoezvpn
 local-address Ethernet0
 mode network-extension
 peer 9.1.1.35
 peer 9.1.1.45
 username ezvpn1@vpngroup password  ezvpn1east
```

EzVPN can be combined with XAUTH and MODECFG to provide extended authentication and thereby push all MODECFG attributes to the client. The attributes to be pushed can be defined locally on the EzVPN server or defined on a AAA server and defined either on a per-group or per-user basis. Example 4-8 shows the policies configured on a AAA server on a group basis.

Example 4-8   *Per-Group–based Policy Configuration on a AAA Server*

```
vpngroup Password = "cisco", Service-Type = Outbound
 cisco-avpair = "ipsec:tunnel-type=ESP"
 cisco-avpair = "ipsec:key-exchange=ike"
 cisco-avpair = "ipsec:tunnel-password=ciscoezvpn"
 cisco-avpair = "ipsec:addr-pool=vpnpool"
 cisco-avpair = "ipsec:default-domain=cisco"
 cisco-avpair = "ipsec:inacl=101"
 cisco-avpair = "ipsec:access-restrict=fastethernet 0/0"
 cisco-avpair = "ipsec:group-lock=1"
cisco-avpair = "ipsec:backup-server=9.1.1.35"

 cisco-avpair = "ipsec:dns-servers=10.1.1.10"
 cisco-avpair = "ipsec:firewall=1"
 cisco-avpair = "ipsec:include-local-lan=1"
 cisco-avpair = "ipsec:save-password=1"
 cisco-avpair = "ipsec:wins-servers=10.1.1.11"
 cisco-avpair = "ipsec:max-users = 100"
 cisco-avpair = "ipsec:max-logins = 2"
```

NOTE   When AAA is used for pushing the attributes, AAA between EzVPN server and the AAA server requires a hard-coded password of **cisco**. Therefore, notice the use of the string **cisco** as the vpngroup password. This is a requirement of the Cisco AAA implementation.

Example 4-9 shows the configuration of the policy attributes locally on the EzVPN server on a per-group basis.

Example 4-9 *Per-Group EzVPN Policy Attributes Configured Locally on an EzVPN Server*

```
crypto isakmp client configuration group vpngroup
 key ciscoezvpn
 dns 10.1.1.10
 wins 10.1.1.11
 domain cisco.com
 pool vpnpool
 group-lock
 save-password
 include-local-lan
 pfs
 backup-gateway 9.1.1.36
 max-users 100
 max-logins 2
 access-restrict fastEthernet 0/0
```

You've already seen described some attributes such as IP address, WINS, DNS, and backup server in the previous section. For a complete list of attributes and their description, refer to Cisco IOS EzVPN documentation. A couple of very useful attributes for telecommuter scenarios are max-logins and include-local-lan. The max-logins attribute allows the administrator to restrict the number of simultaneous IPSec connections from the same user to the gateway. The include-local-lan attribute is very useful in scenarios in which the telecommuter's LAN has resources, such as printers, attached to the LAN and access to these resources is required when the VPN tunnel is up.

The attributes may also be applied on a per-user basis. A user attribute overrides a group attribute value. These attributes are retrieved at the time user authentication occurs using XAUTH, and are then combined with group attributes and applied during Mode-Configuration. User-based attributes are available only if RADIUS is used as the database. Example 4-10 shows the RADIUS attributes that must be configured on a per-user basis.

Example 4-10 *User-Based Policy Control Using AAA*

```
ezvpn1@vpngroup Password = "ezvpn1east"
framed-Ip-Address=10.0.68.1
ipsec:user-save-password=1
ipsec:user-include-local-lan=1
ipsec:user-vpn-group=cisco
```

Note that EzVPN using the Cisco Unity protocol is not an IETF standard. The Cisco proprietary Unity protocol is supported by Cisco IOS devices, VPN 3000, and PIX devices for interoperability across Cisco devices.

Digital Certificates for IPSec VPNs

You have learned from Chapter 2, "IPSec Overview," that pre-shared keys and digital certificates are two primary authentication methods in IKE that can be used in the context of IPSec VPN deployments. You also saw that pre-shared keys with IKE Main Mode cannot be used for remote access scenarios in which the responder does not know the source IP address of the initiator in advance. Although Aggressive Mode can alleviate this issue, given that Aggressive Mode does not offer any form of ID protection, such a solution may not be acceptable. You also saw XAUTH provide an additional level of authentication for Aggressive Mode with pre-shared keys. Another solution for such a scenario is the use of digital certificates instead of pre-shared keys.

In addition to solving the authentication issue for remote access users, digital certificate–based authentication is also becoming increasingly popular for large IPSec VPN site-to-site deployments because it is more scalable than pre-shared keys. Without digital signatures, users must either manually exchange public keys or secrets between each pair of devices that use IPSec to protect communications. This is cumbersome because when a new device is added to the network, users are required to make configuration changes on every other device it securely communicates with. By using digital certificates, users simply enroll each new device with a Certificate Authority, and none of the other devices need modification. When the new device attempts an IPSec connection, IKE automatically exchanges certificates with the peer and the devices authenticate each other, thus making a large-scale IPSec VPN deployment very scalable using digital certificates. An entire book can be written on digital certificates and PKI. You will be introduced to some of the components of PKI in the remainder of this chapter.

Digital Certificates

Digital certificates provide a means to digitally authenticate devices and individual users. These certificates act kind of like an online passport—they are tamper proof and cannot be forged. An individual that wishes to send encrypted data obtains a digital certificate from a *Certificate Authority (CA)*. The CA issues an encrypted digital certificate containing the applicant's public key and a variety of other identification information. The CA makes its own public key readily available. The recipient of the encrypted message uses the CA's public key to decode the digital certificate attached to the message, verifies it as issued by the CA, and then obtains the sender's public key and identification information held within the certificate. With this information, the recipient can send an encrypted reply. Public key infrastructure (PKI) is the enabler for managing digital certificates for IPSec VPN deployment. The most widely used format for digital certificates is X.509, which is supported by Cisco IOS.

Certificate Authority—Enrollment

The Certificate Authority is the entity that issues the digital certificate. Enrollment is the process of obtaining a new certificate from a certificate authority. The IOS command **crypto ca trustpoint** is used to declare the specific CA that the router should use for enrollment.

As PKI is deployed on larger networks, enrollment becomes a big problem if it requires manual enrollment. The Cisco auto-enroll feature will be useful for this situation. With this feature, an IOS router can be configured to periodically contact the CA and request a new certificate. Auto enrollment may be configured to generate new encryption keys or to continue to use existing keys. Routers can initially auto-enroll with CA and when the certificate lifetime expires, the router re-enrolls automatically. Example 4-11 shows the configuration snippet for enrolling a Cisco router to a CA as well as the auto-enrollment command.

Example 4-11 *Cisco IOS Configuration for Enrolling with CA*

```
crypto ca trustpoint Public_CA
 enrollment url http://100.1.1.5:80
subject-name OU=Engineering., O=ABC

 auto-enroll 95 regenerate
 password cisco
 rsakeypair public-ca
```

Auto enrollment makes sure that the router re-enrolls with the CA after the certificate lifetime expires. However, while re-enrollment is occurring, new incoming IKE connections cannot be established because the existing certificate and key pairs are deleted immediately after the new key is generated, and the new key does not have a certificate to match it until the enrollment is complete. A simple workaround is to have the router re-enroll to the CA *before* the certificate lifetime expires, using the IOS command **auto enroll <*percent*> regenerate**."

It's possible that a router may be required to enroll with multiple certificate servers. Each CA server has an independent policy and may have different requirements as to general versus special purpose certificates or key length. Also, although it does not substantially affect the security of the system, VPN providers would like to use different key pairs for each VPN. Using the same key pair gives the impression of lower security, which is detrimental to end-user satisfaction. Example 4-12 shows an example of enrollment to multiple CAs using multiple key pairs.

Example 4-12 *Enrollment with Multiple CAs Using Multiple Key Pairs*

```
vpn-gw1-east#show running-config
!
crypto ca trustpoint Public_CA
 enrollment url http://100.1.1.5:80
 revocation-check crl
 rsakeypair public-ca
 match certificate engg
!
crypto ca trustpoint IOS_CA
```

Example 4-12   *Enrollment with Multiple CAs Using Multiple Key Pairs (Continued)*

```
enrollment url http://100.1.1.179:80
revocation-check none
rsakeypair ios-ca
!

vpn-gw1-east#show cry ca trustpoints
Trustpoint Public_CA:
    Subject Name:
    cn=Certificate Manager
    ou=nsite-rtp
    o=cisco-rtp
    l=rtp
    st=nc
    c=US
        Serial Number: 01
    Certificate configured.
    CEP URL: http://100.1.1.5

Trustpoint IOS_CA:
    Subject Name:
    cn=Certmanager O\=cisco OU\=nsite
        Serial Number: 01
    Certificate configured.
    CEP URL: http://100.1.1.179
```

Certificate Revocation

Situations may arise in which the certificate issued by a CA may need to be revoked before the lifetime of the certificate expires. One such situation would be if the certificate itself is known to have been compromised. Yet another more common situation in the context of IPSec VPNs is when temporary access to a VPN is desired. For example, assume that a user that belongs to Company A may want temporary access to Company B's VPN, and is granted a certificate for access. The access would need to be revoked after a short time in order to maintain integrity of the network.

Another precaution maintained prevents users whose certificate has been revoked from being granted access to a VPN. To achieve this, a list of certificates that have been revoked, known as a Certificate Revocation List (CRL), is sent periodically from the CA to the IPSec gateway. When an incoming IKE session is initiated for a user whose certificate is revoked, the CRL will be checked to see if the certificate is valid; if the certificate is revoked, IKE will fail and access to the VPN will be denied. Example 4-13 shows Cisco IOS configuration to check for a revoked certificate in the CRL.

Example 4-13 *Cisco IOS Configuration for Checking Certificate Status Using CRL*

```
crypto ca trustpoint Public_CA
 enrollment url http://100.1.1.5:80
 revocation-check crl
 rsakeypair public-ca
 match certificate eng
```

Once the CRL is obtained by the VPN endpoint from the CA, it will maintain it until the Certificate Revocation timer expires or if the endpoint reloads.

An alternate mechanism for checking the validity of a certificate is the use of the Online Certificate Status Protocol (OCSP). Unlike CRLs, which provide only periodic certificate status checks, OCSP can provide timely information regarding the status of a certificate. Example 4-14 shows the configuration to enable OCSP to check certificate status.

Example 4-14 *Cisco IOS Configuration for Checking Certificate Status Using OCSP*

```
crypto ca trustpoint Public_CA
 enrollment url http://100.1.1.5:80
 revocation-check ocsp
 rsakeypair public-ca
 match certificate eng
```

If the deployment needs more granular control over the permission to connect users (even those with valid certificates), certificate-based ACLs may be used. For example, there may be situations in which you wish to allow only a subset of users with a valid certificate to connect to the VPN. The configuration in Example 4-15 allows only users whose certificates contain "Engineering" in the subject name.

Example 4-15 *Cisco IOS Configuration for Certificate-Based ACLs*

```
crypto ca certificate map eng 10
 subject-name co Engineering

crypto ca trustpoint Public_CA
match certificate eng
 enrollment url http://100.1.1.5:80
 auto-enroll 95 regenerate
 password cisco
 rsakeypair public-ca
```

Digital certificates as an authentication method for large-scale IPSec VPNs is becoming increasingly popular for both remote access and site-to-site deployments. You learned in this section that the use of digital certificates requires some form of PKI infrastructure such as a CA server. Network administrators should be aware that managing the PKI infrastructure and digital certificates can be much more complicated than username-based password management. The benefits to be gained by the additional work by network administration should be carefully considered before using digital certificates.

Summary

This chapter covered IPSec features and mechanisms that are primarily targeted at the authentication of remote access users. You learned about XAUTH, which provides extended authentication for IPSec telecommuters by using authentication schemes such as RADIUS. MODECFG uses a push model to push attributes to the IPSec client. You also saw how EzVPN greatly simplifies configuration for IPSec clients and allows central configuration of the IPSec policies. You explored the use of digital certificates and PKI, which are becoming increasingly popular for scalable IPSec deployments for both remote access and site-to-site VPNs.

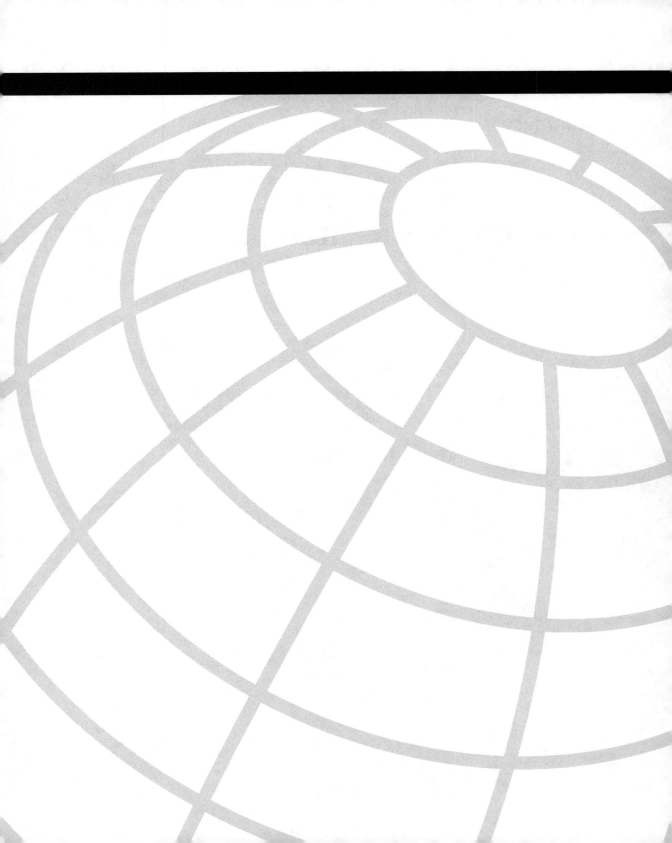

CHAPTER 5

IPSec VPN Architectures

In Chapter 2, "IPSec Overview," and Chapter 3, "Enhanced IPSec Features," you reviewed the fundamental concepts of IPSec VPNs. In this chapter, you will use those concepts to learn about IPSec VPN architectures. As you read in Chapter 1, "Introduction to VPNs," VPNs have been around for many years. Conceptually, the process of designing an IPSec VPN network is no different from the one used to determine any other VPN architecture, such as Frame Relay; however, IPSec adds a few more constraints and capabilities. In this chapter, you will be presented with the aspects that differentiate IPSec VPN networks from traditional VPN architectures, and understand key considerations when designing such a network.

IPSec VPN Connection Models

Before getting into IPSec VPN architectures, you'll review several IPSec connection models. These connection models are the mechanisms that are used to provide protected communication between VPN endpoints. You might think of them as the basic building blocks of an IPSec VPN architecture. We will explore three connectivity models:

- IPSec model
- GRE model
- Remote access client model

Each of these connection models has unique capabilities and constraints, which you will need to consider carefully when deciding which model will be most effective in the VPN architecture. Each of the models requires the presence of IP connectivity between the IPSec endpoints. The knowledgeable network designer will recognize that a scalable and reliable IPSec VPN architecture may leverage more than one connection model. The intent of this chapter is to guide the network designer in the choice of the connection model in order to achieve the optimal VPN architecture.

IPSec Model

As you learned in Chapter 2, "IPSec Overview," the simplest connectivity model is achieved by creating an IPSec VPN between two sites, which is commonly referred to as site-to-site connectivity using the IPSec model. The sites can be connected over private IP networks such as Frame Relay or ATM networks running IP using transport mode or over the public Internet using tunnel mode.

NOTE   IPSec encryption is applied after a clear text packet is received, a routing decision is made, and an interface is selected for egress transmission. The IPSec policy is applied to the egress interface where the encryption process is one of the last functions called upon prior to transmission of the packet. Similarly, encrypted packets received over an interface where an IPSec policy is applied are decrypted prior to the completion of the routing decision and forwarding action. Here, the focus is on the IPSec policy associated with the egress interface for encrypting packets and the ingress interface for decrypting packets. Usually, the egress and ingress interface is one and the same; therefore, the IPSec policy is consistent for both forward and reverse packet flows.

If the IPSec gateways have multiple egress interfaces, routing policy on the endpoints should ensure that the interface used for egress and ingress traffic is the same as the interface where the IPSec policy is applied. The issue of link redundancy and fault tolerance is discussed in detail in Chapter 6, "Designing Fault-Tolerant IPSec VPNs."

The IPSec model is conceptually simple to understand—it protects unicast traffic from one subnet to another. The IPSec model is generally the lowest common denominator from the perspective of capability of the IPSec nodes and their ability to establish connectivity between sites. Although the protection model is conceptually simple, the configuration of the model can get quite complex for large VPNs. Operators must explicitly configure a protect profile for traffic between every potential subnet. The addition of a single subnet in the VPN may require configuration updates to all the other VPN gateways in the network. Network designers must carefully allocate IP address blocks at each site in order to minimize the amount of explicit configuration of discrete IPSec proxy profiles. In some cases, network planners may have little control over the address allocation methods, which could result in a network with inefficient subnet addressing. A poorly architected network using the basic IPSec model will quickly become unmanageable. Clearly, there is a motivation to decouple the subnet address allocation from the IPSec policy definitions in order to simplify provisioning.

Another disadvantage of the IPSec model is the lack of support for IP multicast, as the original IPSec RFCs did not accommodate multicast in the IPSec proxy statements. Many IGP dynamic routing protocols (such as OSPF, EIGRP, and RIP) use IP multicast to establish routing adjacencies. Most enterprises rely on Interior Gateway Protocols (IGP) to dynamically discover the optimal paths through the VPN. The IPSec model mitigates the value of the IGP, essentially making the IPSec proxy statements behave as static routes.

NOTE   BGP may be used in lieu of an IGP because it uses TCP unicast packets to build adjacencies between peers. However, the use of BGP does not mitigate the requirement to explicitly define the IPSec proxy profiles for traffic flowing between all the distinct subnets.

It is evident that the requirement to explicitly define every potential IP flow on every VPN gateway is not a viable method for a large, complex network with hundreds, or even thousands, of subnets. In the next section, you'll explore how routing protocols can be exchanged over IPSec-enabled virtual interfaces in order to simplify the IPSec policies.

The GRE Model

In Chapter 2, "IPSec Overview," you saw that there are certain limitations for support of dynamic routing and IP multicast when using the IPSec model for site-to-site connectivity. One way to overcome these limitations is to use generic route encapsulation (GRE) tunneling of site-to-site traffic protected by IPSec. The notable advantage of this GRE model is that it simplifies configuration for site-to-site VPN connectivity. In the GRE model, all traffic between sites traverses a GRE tunnel that is protected by IPSec; therefore, IPSec profiles in this model are applied to packets that originate and terminate at the GRE tunnel interface. A VPN built with GRE and IPSec protection can be broken into four basic functions:

- Creating the GRE tunnel
- Protecting the GRE tunnel with IPSec
- Providing IP connectivity between the GRE tunnel and IPSec endpoints (routing outside the VPN)
- Providing a viable routing path for endsystems through the GRE tunnels (routing within the VPN)

The combination of GRE tunnel and IPSec protection decouples the dynamic routing requirements and subnet-to-subnet traffic flow from the IPSec protection policy. IPSec protection is dramatically simplified by virtue of the fact that a single IPSec proxy profile may be defined for the GRE tunnel that carries all traffic flowing between two VPN gateways regardless of the type, source, or destination. The compromise with using the GRE model, however, is that two routing planes are required:

- A routing plane between the VPN gateways routes encrypted tunnel packets
- A routing plane between the VPN gateways through the tunnel provides routing paths between the end-user subnets

Therefore, the GRE model minimizes the IPSec provisioning requirements while creating a tunnel overlay network that complicates management and introduces an entirely different set of scalability constraints.

The Remote Access Client Model

The requirement of encrypting traffic between software clients (for example, PCs, PDAs, kiosks, and the like) and VPN gateways presents a whole different set of challenges. The remote access client model requires a very different set of capabilities to accommodate dynamic host address assignment, lack of configuration control, and temporal connections. Both the IPSec model and the GRE model work well for site-to-site connectivity wherein all the IP addresses of all the IPSec endpoints are known in advance and pre-configured in the sites of the VPN gateway. However, these two models will not work for a telecommuter trying to connect to a corporate VPN, as the corporate site accepting the telecommuter's IPSec connection does not know the IP address in advance. You'll need an efficient and scalable manner to allow remote access clients to access the corporate VPN. In Chapter 3, "Enhanced IPSec Features," you saw how a remote access client initiates a connection to its IPSec endpoint, which is typically a hub. Using the advanced IPSec features, the remote access client model allows the client to use a dynamically assigned IP address. It also allows the network provisioning staff to define a policy that is pushed to the client to simplify network operations management. Neither the IPSec nor the GRE model provides this capability. You need a new method to exchange these capabilities and attributes during the establishment of the IPSec connection. You can accomplish the capability and attribute exchange using extensions to IKE. The IKE Mode Config process assigns connection attributes to the client, assuming that it is a single host. The typical attributes assigned include the following:

- Private IP address
- Private DNS server
- Private WINS server
- Private domain name

The private IP address is usually assigned from an address pool configured on the hub. Then, an IPSec proxy is created to protect traffic from the assigned private address to a range of addresses protected by the hub. The hub advertises the address pool to other network devices such that a return path is provided to the client. The client typically directs all user traffic to the hub when split tunneling is not allowed.

The remote access client model obviously simplifies the provisioning process by automating the policy distribution to the clients using IKE Mode Config. The protection policies may be centrally defined and managed such that the network operator is not required to configure each remote endpoint. There are a couple of disadvantages with this model. First, the IPSec connections can only be initiated from the client to the server. Second, the connection uses a simple IPSec proxy statement that doesn't support multicast.

IPSec Connection Model Summary

Three IPSec connection models have been presented, each with their own pros and cons. As a network designer, you must assess the scalability requirements, stability requirements, and application requirements in order to select the appropriate connection model. Often, a combination of the connection models is required in order to scale IPSec connectivity over a large enterprise network. Now that you've seen the basic capabilities of the various connection models, you'll see how these tools apply to the various network architectures.

In the remaining sections of this chapter, you will be presented with the variety of IPSec VPN architectures that are possible using the connection models previously discussed, and will delve into the pros and cons of each model. Figure 5-1 is provided as a reference network on which the various architecture models are applied. In many cases, a subset of routers from the reference network is used to provide clarity. Most of the possible architectures are a subset of the following two most common architectural models:

- Hub-and-spoke topology
- Full-mesh topology

The network designer's selection of topology is driven primarily by the application needs of the VPN. Other important factors are simplicity, scalability, efficiency, and—of course—cost.

Figure 5-1   *VPN Network Reference Model*

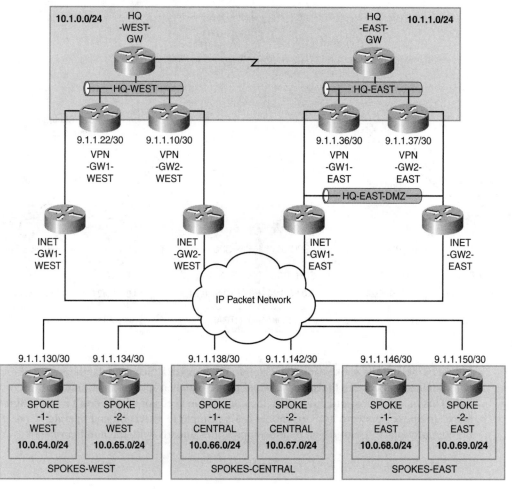

Hub-and-Spoke Architecture

One of the most common IPSec architectural models is the hub-and-spoke model shown in Figure 5-2.

Figure 5-2 *Hub-and-Spoke IPSec VPN Architecture*

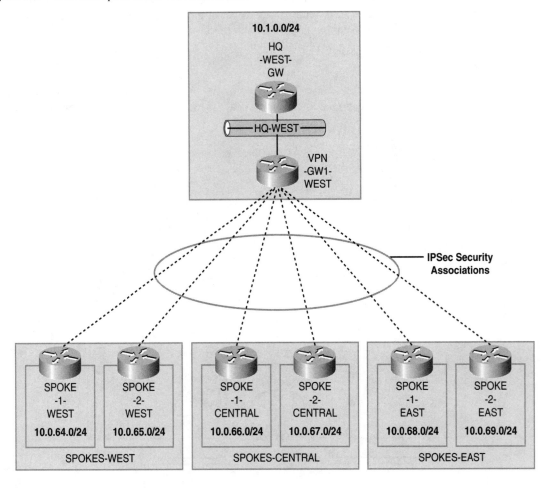

In this model, all the spokes are connected to the hub via IPSec tunnels; there is no direct communication between the spokes and all traffic between spokes must first pass through the hub. This model is cost-effective when the application needs of a VPN don't require significant spoke-to-spoke connectivity. This model is also simple to provision and operate because the number of point-to-point IPSec relationships scales linearly with the number of spokes. In this model, the *heart and soul* is obviously the *hub*, and thus any downtime on the hub will have a severe impact on the VPN connectivity. Fault-tolerant designs for hub failures are addressed in Chapter 6, "Designing Fault-Tolerant IPSec VPNs."

Using the IPSec Model

One of the most critical aspects of the IP network design process is the proper allocation of IP address subnets; this is also true for IPSec VPNs. Traditional Frame Relay or Asynchronous Transfer Mode (FR/ATM) hub-and-spoke networks place all the Layer 3 routing complexity at the hub, where hundreds—if not thousands—of remote sites connect. The network architect will typically assign the IP address ranges at each site such that the address space is assigned efficiently while simplifying the routing processes. The typical hub-and-spoke architecture requires an explicit route at the hub site for each remote spoke's address range. Likewise, each spoke will require a route to the IP address range assigned to the hub site. A reciprocal pair of static routes is all that is required on the connection between the hub and spoke. Dynamic routing may be used between the hub and its spokes to simplify the routing configuration, particularly at the hub site.

NOTE	Dynamically exchanging protected routes between IPSec sites generally requires GRE (or IP) encapsulation of the routing protocols. IPSec may then protect the IP-encapsulated routing exchanges.

It is easy to see how the scalability of the IPSec VPN comes into question at the hub side. Each site requires a minimum of two IPSec security associations (one for traffic in each direction) and an IKE security association. If the IP address ranges at either end of the site-to-site connection cannot be represented as a single IP address block because non-contiguous IP address ranges are used at the hub or spokes, then additional IPSec SAs may be required between each hub and spoke connection. Therefore, the proper allocation of IP address ranges is of paramount importance for scalability and reducing configuration complexity. Figure 5-3 shows the addressing used in the previous example of an IPSec VPN in a hub-and-spoke topology.

Example 5-1 shows the IPSec configuration for the hub site shown in Figure 5-3. Note that a single crypto map is used on the interface with multiple sequence numbers in the crypto map. Each sequence number represents a unique spoke. Associated with each sequence number is the access list that matches transit packets on the interface to the appropriate spoke. The access list associated with each spoke essentially "routes" the packets to that peer. Note also that the only routing statement is the default route to the backbone network.

Figure 5-3 *IPSec Proxy Profile for Hub-and-Spoke VPN Topology*

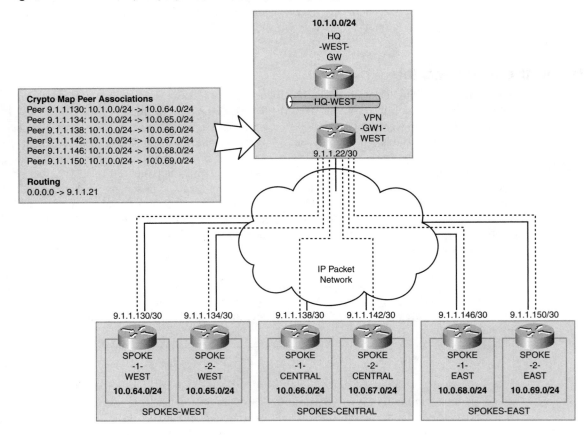

Example 5-1 *Native IPSec Hub Configuration*

```
hostname vpn-gw1-west
!
crypto isakmp policy 10
 hash md5
 authentication pre-share
 lifetime 3600
crypto isakmp key cisco address 9.1.1.130
crypto isakmp key cisco address 9.1.1.134
crypto isakmp key cisco address 9.1.1.138
crypto isakmp key cisco address 9.1.1.142
crypto isakmp key cisco address 9.1.1.146
crypto isakmp key cisco address 9.1.1.150
```

Example 5-1   *Native IPSec Hub Configuration (Continued)*

```
crypto isakmp keepalive 10 10
!
crypto ipsec transform-set esp-tunnel-internet esp-3des esp-md5-hmac
!
! Unique crypto map sequence associated with each spoke
crypto map vpn 10 ipsec-isakmp
 set peer 9.1.1.130
 set transform-set esp-tunnel-internet
 match address esp-spoke-1-west
!
crypto map vpn 20 ipsec-isakmp
 set peer 9.1.1.134
 set transform-set esp-tunnel-internet
 match address esp-spoke-2-west
!
crypto map vpn 30 ipsec-isakmp
 set peer 9.1.1.138
 set transform-set esp-tunnel-internet
 match address esp-spoke-1-central
!
crypto map vpn 40 ipsec-isakmp
 set peer 9.1.1.142
 set transform-set esp-tunnel-internet
 match address esp-spoke-2-central
!
crypto map vpn 50 ipsec-isakmp
 set peer 9.1.1.146
 set transform-set esp-tunnel-internet
 match address esp-spoke-1-east
!
crypto map vpn 60 ipsec-isakmp
 set peer 9.1.1.150
 set transform-set esp-tunnel-internet
 match address esp-spoke-2-east
!
interface Serial1/0:0
 ip address 9.1.1.22 255.255.255.252
 crypto map vpn
!
interface Ethernet4/0
 ip address 10.1.0.1 255.255.255.0
 duplex half
!
! Default route to the backbone
ip route 0.0.0.0 0.0.0.0 9.1.1.21
!
! Access list associated with each spoke
ip access-list extended esp-spoke-1-west
 permit ip 10.1.0.0 0.0.0.255 10.0.64.0 0.0.0.255
ip access-list extended esp-spoke-2-west
 permit ip 10.1.0.0 0.0.0.255 10.0.65.0 0.0.0.255
```

continues

Example 5-1 *Native IPSec Hub Configuration (Continued)*

```
ip access-list extended esp-spoke-1-central
 permit ip 10.1.0.0 0.0.0.255 10.0.66.0 0.0.0.255
ip access-list extended esp-spoke-2- central
 permit ip 10.1.0.0 0.0.0.255 10.0.67.0 0.0.0.255
ip access-list extended esp-spoke-1-east
 permit ip 10.1.0.0 0.0.0.255 10.0.68.0 0.0.0.255
ip access-list extended esp-spoke-2- east
 permit ip 10.1.0.0 0.0.0.255 10.0.69.0 0.0.0.255
!
```

Example 5-2 shows the output listing resulting from the configuration on the hub. A single crypto map is presented for clarity; however, there will be a unique crypto map instance for each spoke. Note also that the route listing does not specify a route to the spoke's protected address; only the default route is needed to force the traffic through the interface where the IPSec access list takes affect. Emphasis should be placed on the source address range that the hub is protecting. Note that the range includes only the LAN connected to the hub site.

Example 5-2 *Native IPSec Hub Configuration State*

```
vpn-gw1-west#show crypto map
Crypto Map "vpn" 10 ipsec-isakmp
        Peer = 9.1.1.130
        Extended IP access list esp-spoke-1-west
          access-list esp-spoke-1-west permit ip 10.1.0.0 0.0.0.255 10.0.64.0 0.0.0.255
        Current peer: 9.1.1.130
        Security association lifetime: 4608000 kilobytes/3600 seconds
        PFS (Y/N): N
        Transform sets={ esp-tunnel-internet, }
                Serial1/0:0
...

vpn-gw1-west#show ip route
Gateway of last resort is 9.1.1.21 to network 0.0.0.0

     9.0.0.0/8 is variably subnetted, 1 subnets
C       9.1.1.20/30 is directly connected, Serial1/0:0
     10.0.0.0/8 is variably subnetted, 1 subnets
C       10.1.0.0/24 is directly connected, Ethernet4/0
S*   0.0.0.0/0 [20/0] via 9.1.1.21, 3d15h
```

Example 5-3 provides the configuration listing for the spoke site with a reciprocal IPSec proxy statement. The spoke may also use a default route to the backbone network with a single crypto map to direct traffic to the hub site. The other spokes would use a similar configuration with the IPSec proxy modified for the address space protected by the spoke.

Example 5-3 *Native IPSec Spoke Configuration*

```
spoke-1-west #show running-config
!
hostname spoke-1-west
!
```

Example 5-3   *Native IPSec Spoke Configuration (Continued)*

```
crypto isakmp policy 10
 hash md5
 authentication pre-share
 lifetime 3600
crypto isakmp key cisco address 9.1.1.22
crypto isakmp keepalive 10
!
!
crypto ipsec transform-set esp-tunnel-internet esp-des esp-md5-hmac
!
! Crypto map for hub site peer
crypto map vpn 10 ipsec-isakmp
 set peer 9.1.1.22
 set transform-set esp-tunnel-internet
 match address esp-tunnel-list
!
!
interface Ethernet0
 ip address 10.0.64.1 255.255.255.0
!
interface Serial0
 ip address 9.1.1.130 255.255.255.252
 crypto map vpn
!
! default route to the backbone
ip route 0.0.0.0 0.0.0.0 9.1.1.129
!
! Protected address ranges from spoke to hub
ip access-list extended esp-tunnel-list
 permit ip 10.0.64.0 0.0.0.255 10.1.0.0 0.0.0.255
end
```

Example 5-4 provides the configuration state on SPOKE-1-WEST. Particular attention should be given to the address ranges that the spoke protects traffic from and to. This attribute will be exploited as additional functionality is provided. The current configuration protects traffic only destined to the IP address range assigned to the hub site, as opposed to traffic to any other spoke. Refer to Figure 5-3.

Example 5-4   *Native IPSec Spoke Configuration State*

```
spoke-1-west#show crypto map
Crypto Map "vpn" 10 ipsec-isakmp
        Peer = 9.1.1.22
        Extended IP access list esp-tunnel-list
          access-list esp-tunnel-list permit ip 10.0.64.0 0.0.0.255 10.1.0.0 0.0.0.255
        Current peer: 9.1.1.22
        Security association lifetime: 4608000 kilobytes/3600 seconds
        PFS (Y/N): N
        Transform sets={ esp-tunnel-internet, }
                Serial0
spoke-1-west#show ip route
```

continues

Example 5-4 *Native IPSec Spoke Configuration State (Continued)*

```
Gateway of last resort is 9.1.1.129 to network 0.0.0.0

     9.0.0.0/30 is subnetted, 1 subnets
C       9.1.1.128 is directly connected, Serial0
     10.0.0.0/8 is variably subnetted, 1 subnets
C       10.0.64.0/24 is directly connected, Ethernet0
S*   0.0.0.0/0 [1/0] via 9.1.1.129
```

One possible way to reduce the configuration complexity at the hub is to define a crypto profile at the hub that matches *any* remote site's address range. This approach works only when the spokes initiate the traffic to the hub. The hub cannot initiate a connection to the spokes because the crypto profile does not uniquely identify an appropriate spoke. When the spokes initiate connections to the hub, the inverse of the spoke's IPSec proxy statement will be installed on the hub; it must be a subset of the hub's crypto profile allowing return traffic to be directed to the appropriate spoke. For example, if SPOKE-1-WEST is initiating a connection to VPN-GW1-WEST with protection (FROM: 10.0.64.0/24, TO: 10.1.0.0/24), the inverse of this protection profile is (FROM: 10.1.0.0/24, TO: 10.0.64.0/24). The hub's profile must at least protect (FROM: 10.1.0.0/24, TO: 10.0.64.0/24). In order to support other spokes, the hub's protection profile might be increased to "cover" the addresses (FROM: 10.1.0.0/24, TO: 10.0.0.0/8). The hub's generic profile doesn't provide enough information for it to initiate IPSec connections for outbound traffic to the appropriate spokes; however, the hub can accept IPSec connections from any of the spokes that are protecting more specific subnets than 10.0.0.0/8. Assuming each spoke protects a unique address range and initiates the connection to the hub, the hub will have sufficient information to direct packets to the appropriate spoke if the packets are routed out this protected subnet.

NOTE   Mismatched crypto profiles commonly cause IKE phase 2 processing errors, so this model is not recommended. A more appropriate solution to reduce complexity at the hub might be to implement a dynamic crypto map on the hub.

In summary, the hub-and-spoke architecture using the native IPSec model provides encrypted simple IP connectivity between the hub-and-spoke sites. Contiguous address assignment of IP address ranges is critical for reducing the complexity of the VPN connectivity. The next section addresses transit routing at the hub site, which highlights the importance of address assignment.

Transit Spoke-to-Spoke Connectivity Using IPSec

The simple hub-and-spoke connectivity model described in the previous section provides remote site connectivity services only to the hub site. There is no connectivity enabled between the spokes in this model. Generally, this connectivity is sufficient for many applications such as customer–supplier extranets in which the suppliers have no need to communicate among themselves. But, this model doesn't meet the needs of enterprise VPNs where spoke-to-spoke connectivity is occasionally required.

This requirement adds an additional provisioning complexity on the IPSec VPN. One option is to build direct IPSec peer relationships between the spokes, effectively turning every spoke into a hub. The subsequent section explores this complex scenario using full-mesh VPNs. For this example, assume that the VPN topology will remain as hub-and-spoke.

To achieve spoke-to-spoke connectivity through the hub without building IPSec peer relationships directly between the spokes, the hub site VPN device must provide routing and IPSec protection for transit traffic. You have seen previously that the routing process in a private network provides sufficient information to the hub and spokes such that traffic is directed out the appropriate IPSec-protected interfaces. The same is true for Internet-connected devices for which default routes are common. However, the IPSec protection profiles must be modified to accommodate the new transit spoke-to-spoke traffic flows at the hub. The following sequence of events occurs for transit traffic flows as depicted in Figure 5-4:

1 Packets leaving SPOKE-1-WEST for a host protected by SPOKE-2-WEST will be encrypted by SPOKE-1-WEST with the security association for the VPN-GW1-WEST.

2 The hub VPN-GW1-WEST decrypts the packets arriving from SPOKE-1-WEST.

3 The hub VPN-GW1-WEST routing table decides that the packet is destined to another spoke that is accessible through the same IPSec-protected interface upon which the packet was received.

4 The hub VPN-GW1-WEST encrypts the packet again, which is destined for the remote spoke using the security association with the destination SPOKE-2-WEST.

5 SPOKE-2-WEST decrypts the packet from the hub VPN-GW1-WEST.

6 The remote SPOKE-2-WEST forwards the packet to the destination host.

In our previous hub-and-spoke example where no spoke-to-spoke connectivity was required, the hub site crypto profile was applied to traffic that originated or terminated at the hub site. For spoke-to-spoke connectivity via the hub, the profiles must be modified to protect every potential spoke-to-spoke source and destination pair. Although the simplest way to achieve this would appear to be by creating a crypto profile that matches *any-to-any* source-destination pair, unfortunately, this will not work. Recall that the IPSec profiles direct packets to remote crypto gateways following the routing function at the hub site. The key difference is that routing is only directing packets based on the destination address, whereas IPSec directs packets based on the 5-tuple — source address, destination address, IP protocol field, source port, and destination port. The IPSec profiles must associate the subnets assigned to a remote site with that site's IPSec peer endpoint. Likewise, the hub must match the security association with an inverse profile, which the spoke uses to protect its subnet. Figure 5-4 shows the transit routing requirements at the hub site. Note that this method is demonstrated using simple route aggregates in which there is an order of N provisioned crypto proxy statements, $O(N)$, where N represents the number of spokes. With inefficient address assignments, the provisioning may become as complex as configuring $O(N^2)$ proxy profiles. Clearly, you should, at all costs, avoid addressing schemes that don't leverage route aggregation.

Figure 5-4   *Transit IPSec Protection for Hub-and-Spoke Topology*

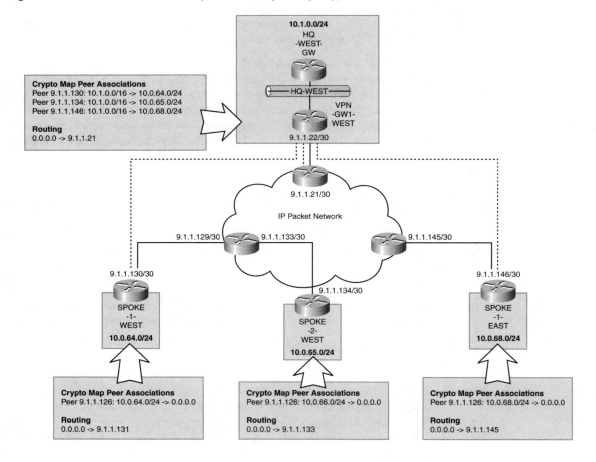

The topology provides some insight into how the crypto map profiles must be designed. The use of contiguous IP address ranges allows the aggregation of spoke routes using a single CIDR block of 10.0.0.0/16. Table 5-1 shows the discrete crypto proxy matrix required for any-to-any connectivity over the hub-and-spoke topology. Table 5-2 shows the aggregate crypto map profiles required.

Table 5-1   *IPSec Proxy Matrix for Transit Hub-and-Spoke Topology*

Hub Matrix				
To **From**	VPN-GW1-WEST 10.1.0.0/24	SPOKE-1-WEST 10.0.64.0/24	SPOKE-2-WEST 10.0.65.0/24	SPOKE-1-EAST 10.0.68.0/24
VPN-GW1-WEST 10.1.0.0/24	X	10.1.0.0/24 to 10.0.64.0/24	10.1.0.0/24 to 10.0.65.0/24	10.1.0.0/24 to 10.0.68.0/24
SPOKE-1-WEST 10.0.64.0/24	10.0.64.0/24 to 10.1.0.0/24	X	10.0.64.0/24 to 10.0.65.0/24	10.0.64.0/24 to 10.0.68.0/24
SPOKE-2-WEST 10.0.65.0/24	10.0.65.0/24 to 10.1.0.0/24	10.0.65.0/24 to 10.0.64.0/24	X	10.0.65.0/24 to 10.0.68.0/24
SPOKE-1-EAST 10.0.68.0/24	10.0.68.0/24 to 10.1.0.0/24	10.0.68.0/24 to 10.0.64.0/24	10.0.68.0/24 to 10.0.65.0/24	X

Table 5-2   *Crypto Map Profiles for Transit Hub Traffic*

Crypto Map Applied	Remote Site	Source
VPN-GW1-WEST	SPOKE-1-WEST	10.0.0.0/8 -> 10.0.64.0/24
VPN-GW1-WEST	SPOKE-2-WEST	10.0.0.0/8 -> 10.0.65.0/24
VPN-GW1-WEST	SPOKE-1-EAST	10.0.0.0/8 -> 10.0.68.0/24
SPOKE-1-WEST	VPN-GW1-WEST	10.0.64.0/24 -> 10.0.0.0/8
SPOKE-2-WEST	VPN-GW1-WEST	10.0.65.0/24 -> 10.0.0.0/8
SPOKE-1-EAST	VPN-GW1-WEST	10.0.68.0/24 -> 10.0.0.0/8

As seen in the tables, the aggregate crypto map (that is, 10.0.0.0/8) dramatically simplifies configuration complexity, especially in a large network. The introduction of addresses outside the aggregate address range of 10.0.0.0/0 will increase the configuration complexity. For example, the introduction of an address range of 192.168.0.0/24 on one of the spokes will double the configuration complexity. Also notice that the hub's outbound crypto map profile includes the reciprocal profile for traffic arriving from that spoke. Therefore, the hub knows which peer to use for encrypting traffic for each subnet and also knows which profile to associate for decrypting traffic arriving from each spoke. It is apparent that a properly assigned address space can dramatically simplify the configuration at the hub. The configuration samples that follow demonstrate how the crypto map profiles satisfy the any-to-any communication requirements through the hub-and-spoke topology.

The hub configuration for transit VPN traffic is modified such that traffic received from any spoke may be redirected out the same interface (by hair-pinning traffic—that is, by decrypting and re-encrypting a flow) to the appropriate spoke peer. The configuration listing in Example 5-5 is truncated to focus attention on the relevant changes from the previous configuration listing where spoke-to-spoke communication was not allowed. The only change made in the configuration in Example 5-5 is the masked address range for traffic from the hub site. This masked range highlights the importance of a VPN with proper IP address assignment. If any of the spokes protect an IP address range that is non-contiguous with 10.0.0.0/8, then a unique set of IPSec proxies must be defined for each non-contiguous IP address range.

Example 5-5 *IPSec Hub Configuration for Transit VPN Traffic*

```
hostname vpn-gw1-west
!
crypto map vpn 10 ipsec-isakmp
 set peer 9.1.1.130
 set transform-set esp-tunnel-internet
 match address esp-spoke-1-west
!
crypto map vpn 20 ipsec-isakmp
 set peer 9.1.1.134
 set transform-set esp-tunnel-internet
 match address esp-spoke-2-west
!
...
!
ip access-list extended esp-spoke-1-west
 permit ip 10.0.0.0 0.255.255.255 10.0.64.0 0.0.0.255
ip access-list extended esp-spoke-2-west
 permit ip 10.0.0.0 0.255.255.255 10.0.65.0 0.0.0.255
ip access-list extended esp-spoke-1-central
 permit ip 10.0.0.0 0.255.255.255 10.0.66.0 0.0.0.255
ip access-list extended esp-spoke-2- central
 permit ip 10.0.0.0 0.255.255.255 10.0.67.0 0.0.0.255
ip access-list extended esp-spoke-1-east
 permit ip 10.0.0.0 0.255.255.255 10.0.68.0 0.0.0.255
ip access-list extended esp-spoke-2- east
 permit ip 10.0.0.0 0.255.255.255 10.0.69.0 0.0.0.255
!
```

Example 5-6 shows the configuration state of the hub site with a source address range in the IPSec proxy that includes traffic from any other spoke. In addition, the IPSec proxy specifies the traffic to be directed to the appropriate spoke even though the hub router only uses a default route to the backbone network.

Example 5-6   *Native IPSec Hub Configuration State for Transit VPN Traffic*

```
vpn-gw1-west#show crypto map
Crypto Map "vpn" 10 ipsec-isakmp
        Peer = 9.1.1.130
        Extended IP access list esp-spoke-1-west
            access-list esp-spoke-1-west permit ip 10.0.0.0 0.255.255.255 10.0.64.0
0.0.0.255
        Current peer: 9.1.1.130
        Security association lifetime: 4608000 kilobytes/3600 seconds
        PFS (Y/N): N
        Transform sets={ esp-tunnel-internet, }
                Serial1/0:0
...
vpn-gw1-west#show ip route
Gateway of last resort is 9.1.1.21 to network 0.0.0.0

    9.0.0.0/8 is variably subnetted, 1 subnets
C       9.1.1.20/30 is directly connected, Serial1/0:0
    10.0.0.0/8 is variably subnetted, 1 subnets
C       10.1.0.0/24 is directly connected, Ethernet4/0
S*   0.0.0.0/0 [20/0] via 9.1.1.21, 3d15h
```

Examples 5-7 and 5-8 show the modified IPSec proxy profile for a selected spoke and the resulting configuration state. The configuration allows the spoke to encrypt and direct traffic to the hub site for traffic destined to any other spoke.

Example 5-7   *Native IPSec Spoke Configuration for Transit VPN Traffic*

```
spoke-1-west #show runring-config
!
hostname spoke-1-west
!
crypto map vpn 10 ipsec-isakmp
 set peer 9.1.1.22
 set transform-set esp-tunnel-internet
 match address esp-tunnel-list
!
...
!
ip access-list extended esp-tunnel-list
 permit ip 10.0.64.0 0.0.0.255 10.0.0.0 0.255.255.255
end
```

Example 5-8   *IPSec Spoke Configuration State for Transit VPN Traffic*

```
vpn-gw1-west#show crypto map
Crypto Map "vpn" 10 ipsec-isakmp
        Peer = 9.1.1.22
        Extended IP access list esp-tunnel-list
            access-list esp-tunnel-list permit ip 10.0.64.0 0.0.0.255 10.0.0.0
0.255.255.255
```

continues

Example 5-8   *IPSec Spoke Configuration State for Transit VPN Traffic (Continued)*

```
            Current peer: 9.1.1.22
            Security association lifetime: 4608000 kilobytes/3600 seconds
            PFS (Y/N): N
            Transform sets={ esp-tunnel-internet, }
                 Serial0
spoke-1-west#show ip route
Gateway of last resort is 9.1.1.129 to network 0.0.0.0

     9.0.0.0/30 is subnetted, 1 subnets
C        9.1.1.128 is directly connected, Serial0
     10.0.0.0/8 is variably subnetted, 1 subnets
C        10.0.64.0/24 is directly connected, Ethernet0
S*   0.0.0.0/0 [1/0] via 9.1.1.129
```

NOTE   The Cisco IOS product line allows hair-pinning of traffic on the same interfaces. Because the Cisco PIX product line is currently not capable of hair-pinning IPSec traffic on a single interface, a second IPSec-enabled interface is required to hairpin traffic in the PIX.

The proper allocation of addresses within the VPN certainly simplifies configuration complexity. Thus far, we have only considered traffic that stays within the VPN. One of the motivations for building IPSec VPNs over the Internet is to provide both VPN and Internet services over a common infrastructure in order to achieve cost optimization. Next, you'll explore how Internet access is coupled with hub-and-spoke topology.

Internet Connectivity

Internet access is a typical requirement for most sites within a VPN. In a hub-and-spoke scenario it is possible for the remote spoke sites to have Internet access using *split tunneling*. Split tunneling is a method of forcing IPSec protection for certain traffic flows leaving an interface while excluding other traffic flows from IPSec protection (for example, Internet traffic). Many enterprises will not accept this model due to increased exposure to security vulnerabilities.

The most manageable and secure option for offering Internet access to VPN sites is the centralized firewall option in which all traffic to the Internet passes through a firewall at the hub. You saw earlier that the any-to-any provisioning model at the hub provided insufficient information in order to associate traffic to the appropriate spoke. You also have seen that aggregate profiles simplify configuration complexity. In a properly designed network, the largest aggregate route (that is, any source or any destination) may be used to simplify the configuration. In fact, it may be the only way to get traffic to the Internet because the destination addresses on the Internet are not known a priori. If you consider the requirement for each spoke to send traffic for any address to the hub, the inverse property is for the hub to send traffic with any source to the spoke with the associated destination address. You find in this scenario that all of the transit traffic requirements may be represented by a single aggregated IPSec crypto profile. As a result, the crypto map profiles are significantly simplified, as shown in Table 5-3.

Table 5-3   *Crypto Map Profiles for Hubs and Spokes*

Crypto Map Applied	Remote Site	Source
VPN-GW1-WEST	SPOKE-1-WEST	Any -> 10.0.64.0/24
VPN-GW1-WEST	SPOKE-2-WEST	Any -> 10.0.65.0/24
VPN-GW1-WEST	SPOKE-1-EAST	Any -> 10.0.68.0/24
SPOKE-1-WEST	VPN-GW1-WEST	10.0.64.0/24 -> Any
SPOKE-2-WEST	VPN-GW1-WEST	10.0.65.0/24 -> Any
SPOKE-1-EAST	VPN-GW1-WEST	10.0.68.0/24 -> Any

A simple modification to the IPSec proxy profiles on the hub and spoke is all that is required to facilitate Internet access via the hub site. In this example, none of the spokes is allowed to perform split tunneling. Example 5-9 shows the hub configuration listing and Example 5-10 shows the SPOKE-1-WEST configuration modifications.

Example 5-9   *Native IPSec Hub Configuration for Internet Access*

```
ip access-list extended esp-spoke-1-west
 permit ip 0.0.0.0 255.255.255.255 10.0.64.0 0.0.0.255
 !
```

Example 5-10   *Native IPSec Spoke Configuration for Internet Access*

```
ip access-list extended esp-tunnel-list
 permit ip 10.0.64.0 0.0.0.255 0.0.0.0 255.255.255.255
 !
```

Clearly, the transit communication model with Internet access simplifies the IPSec profile for both the hub and spoke site. What we have compromised is the granularity of security control mechanisms for protecting specific flows of traffic between the sites. Usually this is not an issue for enterprise traffic.

Scalability Using the IPSec Connection Model

The IPSec VPN hub-and-spoke model introduces new constraints that the designer may not have encountered with traditional VPNs. The fact that the IPSec profiles effectively act as routing entries may simplify the routing protocols where default routes exist; however, the complexity of the IPSec profiles mitigates the advantage. A large IP VPN with poorly allocated address space may require $O(N^2)$ IPSec configuration profiles at the hub, where N is the number of spokes. The use of aggregate IP address ranges can reduce the number of IPSec configuration entries to O(N) if the designer assigns the appropriate address space to the remote sites. Regardless, the scalability of the hub is critical to the proper functioning of the VPN. The hub must satisfy memory requirements for data structures supporting IKE and IPSec SAs. The hub must also satisfy the additional processing requirements for IKE state management and IPSec data traffic forwarding. The processing constraints will limit the number of spokes supported as well as the volume of transit data. In most cases, hardware-accelerated IPSec data forwarding is required due to the processing requirements associated with encryption.

NOTE   While dynamic routing updates may be used to provide explicit routing where default routes are inappropriate, the routing updates typically also require protection. The IPSec profiles discussed thus far do not address the protection of routing updates where the source and destinations are associated with the IPSec tunnel endpoints. The addition of IPSec profiles protecting routing updates (for example, BGP peers within the VPN) significantly increases the configuration complexity. Also note that current IPSec standards do not address IPSec protection of multicast and broadcast packets typically used with dynamic routing protocols such as OSPF, RIP, and EIGRP.

Aside from IPSec scalability, many other scalability constraints need to be addressed to accommodate the building of large-scale VPN networks. We have emphasized IPSec scalability simply because it is likely to be one of the constraints that the operator will encounter early on. You will find that solving the IPSec scalability constraint will likely reveal another scalability constraint such as queuing, routing, or packet-forwarding constraints. Next, you will look at another IPSec model that presents a completely different scalability model.

GRE Model

The hub-and-spoke architecture built with IPSec-protected GRE tunnels significantly simplifies the VPN design process. The primary difference between the GRE model and the IPSec model is the range of addresses protected by the IPSec crypto profile. In the GRE model, the hub crypto map defines a protection profile for encapsulated data originating from the hub's tunnel source and destined to each spoke's tunnel interface. The primary advantage is that IPSec profiles do not have to reference addresses assigned in the private LAN. All of the private user traffic is encapsulated inside the tunnel that is represented by a single source and a destination address. Likewise, the spoke requires a crypto map that protects the tunnel source and destination address. The simplification of the IPSec profiles may conserve IPSec memory resources if the tunnel hides the non-contiguous private address ranges that do not follow efficient IP address allocation schemes. Figure 5-5 provides the topology for the GRE hub-and-spoke model.

Figure 5-5   *GRE Hub-and-Spoke VPN Topology*

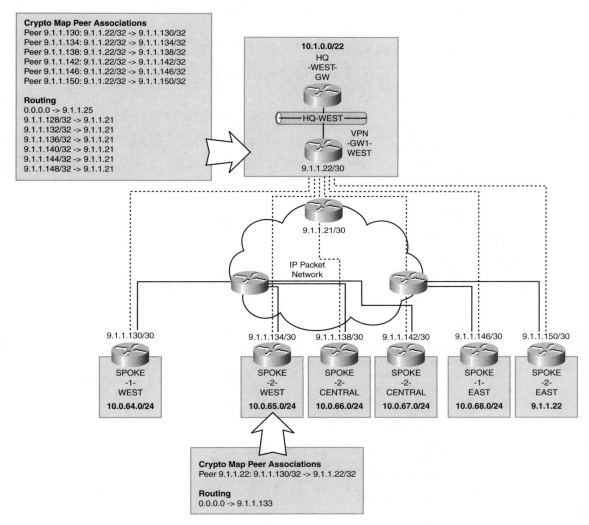

The hub configuration for the hub-and-spoke topology is provided in Example 5-11. Particular emphasis is placed on the modifications to the IPSec proxy profiles. The IPSec access list specifies the protection of traffic from the hub's GRE tunnel IP address (9.1.1.22) to each spoke's GRE tunnel IP address (9.1.1.130, 9.1.1.134, 9.1.1.138, and so on). The protected LAN IP addresses associated with the spokes are explicitly routed into the GRE tunnels. The router encapsulates the packet using the specified GRE tunnel parameters. The GRE-encapsulated packets are subsequently encrypted by IPSec and routed out the serial interface to the backbone.

Typically, we will use transport mode on the IPSec tunnel protection profile such that the GRE-encapsulated IP addresses are visible after encryption.

Example 5-11 *IPSec-protected GRE Hub Configuration Listing*

```
vpn-gw1-west# show running-config
!
! Transform with transport mode using GRE encapsulation instead of IPsec
crypto ipsec transform-set esp-tunnel-internet esp-des esp-md5-hmac
 mode transport
!
! Sequence of crypto maps - one for each spoke
crypto map vpn 10 ipsec-isakmp
 set peer 9.1.1.130
 set transform-set esp-tunnel-internet
 match address gre-spoke-1-west
crypto map vpn 20 ipsec-isakmp
 set peer 9.1.1.134
 set transform-set esp-tunnel-internet
 match address gre-spoke-2-west
crypto map vpn 30 ipsec-isakmp
 set peer 9.1.1.138
 set transform-set esp-tunnel-internet
 match address gre-spoke-1-central
crypto map vpn 40 ipsec-isakmp
 set peer 9.1.1.142
 set transform-set esp-tunnel-internet
 match address gre-spoke-2-central
crypto map vpn 50 ipsec-isakmp
 set peer 9.1.1.146
 set transform-set esp-tunnel-internet
 match address gre-spoke-1-east
crypto map vpn 60 ipsec-isakmp
 set peer 9.1.1.150
 set transform-set esp-tunnel-internet
 match address gre-spoke-2-east
!
! Set of GRE tunnel interfaces - one for each spoke
!
interface Tunnel0
 ip unnumbered Ethernet4/0
 tunnel source 9.1.1.22
 tunnel destination 9.1.1.130
!
interface Tunnel1
 ip unnumbered Ethernet4/0
 tunnel source 9.1.1.22
 tunnel destination 9.1.1.134
!
interface Tunnel2
 ip unnumbered Ethernet4/0
 tunnel source 9.1.1.22
 tunnel destination 9.1.1.138
!
```

Example 5-11   *IPSec-protected GRE Hub Configuration Listing (Continued)*

```
interface Tunnel3
 ip unnumbered Ethernet4/0
 tunnel source 9.1.1.22
 tunnel destination 9.1.1.142
!
interface Tunnel4
 ip unnumbered Ethernet4/0
 tunnel source 9.1.1.22
 tunnel destination 9.1.1.146
!
interface Tunnel5
 ip unnumbered Ethernet4/0
 tunnel source 9.1.1.22
 tunnel destination 9.1.1.150
!
interface Serial1/0:0
 ip address 9.1.1.22 255.255.255.252
 crypto map vpn
!
interface Ethernet4/0
 ip address 10.1.0.1 255.255.255.0
!
! Static route into tunnel for each spoke's protected IP address
ip route 10.0.64.0 255.255.255.0 Tunnel0
ip route 10.0.65.0 255.255.255.0 Tunnel1
ip route 10.0.66.0 255.255.255.0 Tunnel2
ip route 10.0.67.0 255.255.255.0 Tunnel3
ip route 10.0.68.0 255.255.255.0 Tunnel4
ip route 10.0.69.0 255.255.255.0 Tunnel5
ip route 0.0.0.0 0.0.0.0 9.1.1.21
!
! IPsec proxy  profiles protect GRE encapsulated packets from hub to spoke
ip access-list extended gre-spoke-1-central
 permit gre host 9.1.1.22 host 9.1.1.138
ip access-list extended gre-spoke-1-east
 permit gre host 9.1.1.22 host 9.1.1.146
ip access-list extended gre-spoke-1-west
 permit gre host 9.1.1.22 host 9.1.1.130
ip access-list extended gre-spoke-2-central
 permit gre host 9.1.1.22 host 9.1.1.142
ip access-list extended gre-spoke-2-east
 permit gre host 9.1.1.22 host 9.1.1.150
ip access-list extended gre-spoke-2-west
 permit gre host 9.1.1.22 host 9.1.1.134
!
```

NOTE	Notice the configuration in Example 5-11 uses the traditional configuration model for protecting GRE tunnels with IPsec wherein the crypto map configuration is applied to the physical egress interfaces that the GRE tunnel traverses. A newer configuration model was introduced in Chapter 3, "Enhanced IPSec Features," that uses the 'tunnel protection' command syntax. This configuration model can also be applied for all the IPsec over GRE examples in this chapter. This new model requires the crypto map configuration to be applied only to the tunnel interface and not the physical interface. The only caveat of the 'tunnel protection' configuration model is the lack of support for GRE keepalives. Other than this caveat the newer model is a more efficient configuration method and recommended.

The configuration results in a set of crypto maps that protect traffic only between the GRE tunnel endpoints; however, all of the VPN traffic is routed through the tunnels. Therefore, the VPN traffic is always protected while traffic passing outside of the tunnel remains unprotected. Example 5-12 shows the state of the hub configuration.

Example 5-12 *GRE Hub Configuration State*

```
vpn-gw1-west#show crypto map
Crypto Map "vpn" 10 ipsec-isakmp
        Peer = 9.1.1.130
        Extended IP access list gre-spoke-1-west
            access-list gre-spoke-1-west permit gre host 9.1.1.22 host 9.1.1.130
        Current peer: 9.1.1.130
        Security association lifetime: 4608000 kilobytes/3600 seconds
        PFS (Y/N): N
        Transform sets={ esp-tunnel-internet, }

Crypto Map "vpn" 20 ipsec-isakmp
        Peer = 9.1.1.134
        Extended IP access list gre-spoke-2-west
            access-list gre-spoke-2-west permit gre host 9.1.1.22 host 9.1.1.134
        Current peer: 9.1.1.134
        Security association lifetime: 4608000 kilobytes/3600 seconds
        PFS (Y/N): N
        Transform sets={ esp-tunnel-internet, }

Crypto Map "vpn" 30 ipsec-isakmp
        Peer = 9.1.1.138
        Extended IP access list gre-spoke-1-central
            access-list gre-spoke-1-central permit gre host 9.1.1.22 host 9.1.1.138
        Current peer: 9.1.1.138
        Security association lifetime: 4608000 kilobytes/3600 seconds
        PFS (Y/N): N
        Transform sets={ esp-tunnel-internet, }

Crypto Map "vpn" 40 ipsec-isakmp
        Peer = 9.1.1.142
        Extended IP access list gre-spoke-2-central
            access-list gre-spoke-2-central permit gre host 9.1.1.22 host 9.1.1.142
        Current peer: 9.1.1.142
```

Example 5-12 *GRE Hub Configuration State (Continued)*

```
                  Security association lifetime: 4608000 kilobytes/3600 seconds
                  PFS (Y/N): N
                  Transform sets={ esp-tunnel-internet, }

Crypto Map "vpn" 50 ipsec-isakmp
         Peer = 9.1.1.146
         Extended IP access list gre-spoke-1-east
             access-list gre-spoke-1-east permit gre host 9.1.1.22 host 9.1.1.146
         Current peer: 9.1.1.146
         Security association lifetime: 4608000 kilobytes/3600 seconds
         PFS (Y/N): N
         Transform sets={ esp-tunnel-internet, }

Crypto Map "vpn" 60 ipsec-isakmp
         Peer = 9.1.1.150
         Extended IP access list gre-spoke-2-east
             access-list gre-spoke-2-east permit gre host 9.1.1.22 host 9.1.1.150
         Current peer: 9.1.1.150
         Security association lifetime: 4608000 kilobytes/3600 seconds
         PFS (Y/N): N
         Transform sets={ esp-tunnel-internet, }
         Interfaces using crypto map vpn:
                 Serial1/0:0

vpn-gw1-west#show ip route

Gateway of last resort is 9.1.1.21 to network 0.0.0.0

     9.0.0.0/8 is variably subnetted, 3 subnets, 2 masks
C        9.1.1.20/30 is directly connected, Serial1/0:0
     10.0.0.0/8 is variably subnetted, 5 subnets, 2 masks
C        10.1.0.0/24 is directly connected, Ethernet4/0
S        10.0.64.0/24 is directly connected, Tunnel0
S        10.0.65.0/24 is directly connected, Tunnel1
S        10.0.66.0/24 is directly connected, Tunnel2
S        10.0.67.0/24 is directly connected, Tunnel3
S        10.0.68.0/24 is directly connected, Tunnel4
S        10.0.69.0/24 is directly connected, Tunnel5
S*   0.0.0.0/0 [20/0] via 9.1.1.21, 1d01h
```

NOTE   It is critical to note that traffic that is supposed to be routed through a tunnel that is down will be routed out the public interface unencrypted. A common practice is to insert an aggregate static route to a NULL interface for VPN traffic. This drops VPN traffic for an unreachable spoke as opposed to passing it unencrypted to the backbone.

The crypto profile associated with the interface Serial1/0:0 in Example 5-11 protects only the traffic that matches the GRE tunnel profiles specifically protecting the traffic to the spokes. It is important to note that the route forwarding established in Example 5-12 will route any traffic not matching a route to a spoke to the Serial1/0:0 interface. This traffic will not match the crypto profile; therefore, it will not be encrypted. This may be acceptable if the traffic is intended to reach the Internet via this path. If that is not the case, then you will want to prevent traffic from inadvertently leaving the protected network. We can do this by forcing all the traffic that doesn't match a spoke to NULL route, thereby dropping the traffic. You can use the following to prevent traffic destined to undefined 10.0.0.0/8 addresses from leaving the VPN:

```
ip route 10.0.0.0 255.0.0.0 NULL0
```

The reciprocal configuration required of a spoke is provided in Example 5-13. The crypto transform must match the hub (there is no IPSec encapsulation required because GRE encapsulation is used). An important distinction is that you only need to insert a static route for the GRE tunnel endpoint in order to make the tunnel operational. The static route for the hub's protected address space is directed into the GRE tunnel.

Example 5-13 *GRE Spoke Configuration Listing*

```
spoke-2-west#show runring-config
!
crypto isakmp policy 10
 hash md5
 authentication pre-share
 lifetime 3600
crypto isakmp key cisco address 9.1.1.22
crypto isakmp keepalive 10
!
crypto ipsec transform-set esp-tunnel-internet esp-des esp-md5-hmac
 mode transport
!
crypto map vpn 10 ipsec-isakmp
 set peer 9.1.1.22
 set transform-set esp-tunnel-internet
 match address gre-tunnel-list
!
!
interface Ethernet0
 ip address 10.0.65.1 255.255.255.0
!
interface Tunnel0
 ip unnumbered Loopback1
 tunnel source 9.1.1.134
 tunnel destination 9.1.1.22
!
interface Serial0
 ip address 9.1.1.134 255.255.255.252
 crypto map vpn
!

ip route 9.1.1.20 255.255.255.252 9.1.1.133
ip route 10.1.0.0 255.255.255.0 Tunnel0

ip access-list extended gre-tunnel-list
 permit gre host 9.1.1.134 host 9.1.1.22
```

Note from the spoke's configuration state shown in Example 5-14 that only the tunnel will be protected. The only traffic passed to the backbone is the encapsulated traffic that is encrypted. All of the VPN traffic will be forced into the GRE tunnel and unreachable destinations are dropped.

Example 5-14 *GRE Spoke Configuration State*

```
spoke-2-west#show crypto map
Crypto Map "vpn" 10 ipsec-isakmp
        Peer = 9.1.1.22
        Extended IP access list gre-tunnel-list
            access-list gre-tunnel-list permit gre host 9.1.1.134 host 9.1.1.22
        Current peer: 9.1.1.22
        Security association lifetime: 4608000 kilobytes/3600 seconds
        PFS (Y/N): N
        Transform sets={ esp-tunnel-internet, }
        Interfaces using crypto map vpn:
                Serial0
spoke-2-west#show ip route

      9.0.0.0/30 is subnetted, 6 subnets
S        9.1.1.20 [1/0] via 9.1.1.133
C        9.1.1.132 is directly connected, Serial0
      10.0.0.0/24 is subnetted, 3 subnets
S        10.1.0.0 is directly connected, Tunnel0
C        10.0.65.0 is directly connected, Ethernet0
```

Once the tunnels are defined and protected from each spoke to the hub, the routing plane for tunnel connectivity must be established. The tunnel source address may be associated with one of the public interfaces or a publicly addressable loopback interface. If the remote peer's tunnel destination address is not directly connected, the source VPN device will need a route to the tunnel destination. The routes between tunnel endpoints may be learned via dynamic routing on devices between the tunnel endpoints. Alternatively, the VPN devices may have static routes defined to reach the peer's tunnel endpoint.

At a minimum, the peer's encapsulating tunnel address must not be routed into the local tunnel interface. Doing so will create a recursive routing loop that will prevent tunnel establishment. An example of recursive routing is when the destination for a tunnel termination point is routed into the local tunnel interface. Once the tunnel interface is defined and has a viable route to the destination address, the status of the interface will transition to an operational UP state. This is true regardless of the reachability of the peer.

NOTE   A tunnel may provide an UP status, yet fail to pass traffic to the tunnel peer. This may occur when a locally defined static route provides a viable route out of the VPN device but an end-to-end tunnel path does not exist. A viable tunnel path assumes that each router between the tunnel endpoints has routes to these endpoints. In addition, an IPSec security association must be capable of being established for the tunnel. By using GRE keepalives, you can verify that a viable routing path exists and that the IPSec security association is established properly.

With a viable tunnel path, the VPN routing plane may be established through the tunnel. The simplest case is to use static routes into each tunnel interface. The hub must define a static route into the tunnel for each spoke's protected address range. If the spoke's protected address range is not contiguous, multiple static routes may be required. Likewise, each spoke will require a static route to the hub's protected address space. For complex routing scenarios, we may wish to use a dynamic routing protocol within the VPN in order to avoid installing numerous static routes. This is easily accomplished by associating a dynamic routing process with the tunnel interface's assigned address. The tunnel interface may be bound to a LAN interface, a WAN interface, a loopback interface, or may use an assigned IP address. Figure 5-6 shows several options for binding dynamic routing processes to the tunnel interfaces.

NOTE   The tunnel interface's assigned address is not the tunnel interface's encapsulating source address. The tunnel interface may have a unique IP address assigned, use an unnumbered address while binding to another interface, or have no address assigned at all. The objective is to bind the VPN routing process to the tunnel interface's assigned address even if the tunnel is bound to another interface. The choices for tunnel address assignment provide great flexibility in determining which routing process will be invoked for the tunnel.

As a general recommendation, the model shown in Figure 5-6 provides the most flexibility and control. It does require management of additional address subnet ranges on the tunnels that are distinct from the LAN and WAN subnets. These distinct address ranges assigned to the tunnel interfaces allow explicit control of the IGP routing protocol's scope.

A routing process defined on the hub will likely redistribute routes learned from one spoke to another spoke where the hub is defined as the next hop. Perhaps you don't want the spokes to automatically discover routing paths to the other spokes via the hub. In that case, you must consider various methods to avoid or prevent transit routing through the hub. One approach might be to apply static access control lists (ACLs) on the hub to block spoke-to-spoke traffic. This approach becomes quite cumbersome and is prone to configuration errors. A better alternative is to select a routing protocol that allows route filters. Link-state routing protocols (such as OSPF and IS-IS) do not meet this requirement because the routing database must be synchronized on all the nodes. A distance-vector routing protocol such as EIGRP or RIPv2 will suffice. You may install route filters on the hub that only pass IP address ranges associated with the hub to the spokes. Blocking all the spoke routes from being distributed to any other spoke effectively prevents spoke-to-spoke connectivity.

The configuration for the hub remains essentially the same as the static routing scenario except for the dynamic routing process. The Example 5-15 configuration listing for the hub shows how the EIGRP routing process is bound to the Ethernet4/0 interface while the tunnel interface is also bound to the Ethernet4/0 interface. The EIGRP process will establish peers over both the Ethernet4/0 and the tunnel interfaces.

Figure 5-6   *Routing Protocol Binding Options*

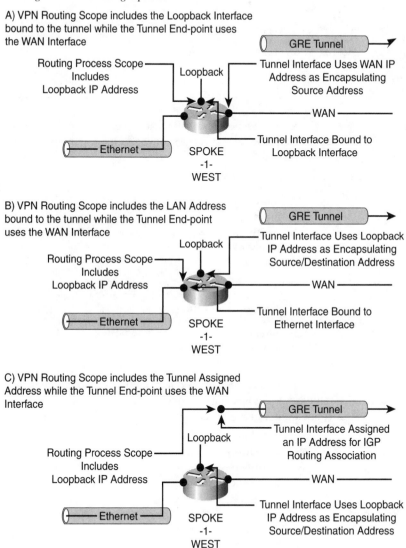

A) VPN Routing Scope includes the Loopback Interface bound to the tunnel while the Tunnel End-point uses the WAN Interface

Routing Process Scope Includes Loopback IP Address

Loopback

GRE Tunnel

Tunnel Interface Uses WAN IP Address as Encapsulating Source Address

WAN

Tunnel Interface Bound to Loopback Interface

Ethernet

SPOKE -1- WEST

B) VPN Routing Scope includes the LAN Address bound to the tunnel while the Tunnel End-point uses the WAN Interface

Loopback

GRE Tunnel

Tunnel Interface Uses Loopback IP Address as Encapsulating Source/Destination Address

Routing Process Scope Includes Loopback IP Address

WAN

Ethernet

Tunnel Interface Bound to Ethernet Interface

SPOKE -1- WEST

C) VPN Routing Scope includes the Tunnel Assigned Address while the Tunnel End-point uses the WAN Interface

GRE Tunnel

Loopback

Tunnel Interface Assigned an IP Address for IGP Routing Association

Routing Process Scope Includes Loopback IP Address

WAN

Ethernet

Tunnel Interface Uses Loopback IP Address as Encapsulating Source/Destination Address

SPOKE -1- WEST

Example 5-15   *GRE Hub Configuration with Dynamic Routing*

```
hostname vpn-gw1-west

interface Ethernet4/0
 ip address 10.1.0.1 255.255.255.0
!
```

continues

Example 5-15 *GRE Hub Configuration with Dynamic Routing (Continued)*

```
interface Tunnel1
 ip unnumbered Ethernet4/0
 tunnel source 9.1.1.22
 tunnel destination 9.1.1.130
!
router eigrp 100
 network 10.1.0.0 0.0.0.255
```

The EIGRP process will establish a neighbor adjacency over each of the tunnel interfaces and dynamically learn the protected IP address ranges for each spoke. Example 5-16 shows the state of the hub router's IP routing table.

Example 5-16 *Hub Configuration State for GRE with Dynamic Routing*

```
vpn-gw1-west#show ip route

     9.0.0.0/8 is variably subnetted, 3 subnets, 2 masks
C       9.1.1.20/30 is directly connected, Serial1/0:0
     10.0.0.0/8 is variably subnetted, 5 subnets, 2 masks
C       10.1.0.0/24 is directly connected, Ethernet4/0
D       10.0.64.0/24 [90/297270016] via 10.0.64.1, 00:40:03, Tunnel1
D       10.0.65.0/24 [90/297370016] via 10.0.65.1, 00:39:53, Tunnel0
D       10.0.64.0/24 [90/297270016] via 10.0.66.1, 00:40:03, Tunnel2
D       10.0.65.0/24 [90/297370016] via 10.0.67.1, 00:39:53, Tunnel3
D       10.0.64.0/24 [90/297270016] via 10.0.68.1, 00:40:03, Tunnel4
D       10.0.65.0/24 [90/297370016] via 10.0.69.1, 00:39:53, Tunnel5
S*   0.0.0.0/0 [20/0] via 9.1.1.21, 1d02h
```

The configuration for the spoke is also modified to establish a dynamic routing process on the tunnel interface. Example 5-17 shows that the EIGRP routing process is bound to the Ethernet0 interface, as is the Tunnel0 interface. This allows the spoke to establish a neighbor relationship with the hub.

Example 5-17 *Spoke Configuration for GRE with Dynamic Routing*

```
hostname spoke-2-west

interface Ethernet0
 ip address 10.0.65.1 255.255.255.0
!
interface Tunnel0
 ip unnumbered Ethernet0
 tunnel source 9.1.1.134
 tunnel destination 9.1.1.22
!
interface Serial0
 ip address 9.1.1.134 255.255.255.252
 crypto map vpn
!
router eigrp 100
 network 10.0.65.0 0.0.0.255
!
```

The configuration establishes an EIGRP neighbor relationship between the spoke and hub. Example 5-18 shows the configuration state of the spoke. Note that the spoke has learned two routes via the Tunnel0 interface—the subnet from the hub site and a second subnet from another spoke that is currently connected to the hub. This example highlights the default paradigm of providing all routes to all VPN sites.

Example 5-18 *Spoke Configuration State for GRE with Dynamic Routing*

```
vpn-gw1-west#show crypto map
Crypto Map "vpn" 10 ipsec-isakmp
        Peer = 9.1.1.22
        Extended IP access list gre-tunnel-list
            access-list gre-tunnel-list permit gre host 9.1.1.134 host 9.1.1.22
        Current peer: 9.1.1.22
        Security association lifetime: 4608000 kilobytes/3600 seconds
        PFS (Y/N): N
        Transform sets={ esp-tunnel-internet, }
        Interfaces using crypto map vpn:
                Serial0
                Tunnel0
vpn-gw1-west#show ip route

     9.0.0.0/30 is subnetted, 6 subnets
S        9.1.1.20 [1/0] via 9.1.1.133
C        9.1.1.132 is directly connected, Serial0
     10.0.0.0/8 is subnetted, 4 subnets
D        10.1.0.0 [90/284472576] via 10.1.0.1, 00:00:05, Tunnel0
D        10.0.64.0 [90/297272576] via 10.1.0.1, 00:48:22, Tunnel0
C        10.0.65.0 is directly connected, Ethernet0
```

Example 5-19 provides a configuration listing that blocks the redistribution of EIGRP routes at the hub router. The hub will still learn all the routes from the spokes; however, the hub will only advertise the 10.1.0.0/16 subnets associated with the hub's protected IP address range.

Example 5-19 *EIGRP Dynamic Routing with Route Blocking*

```
router eigrp 100
 network 10.1.0.0 0.0.0.255
 distribute-list 10 out
!
access-list 10 permit 10.1.0.0 0.0.255.255
```

The route filter blocks all the other spokes' VPN routes such that each spoke knows how to reach only the hosts at the hub site. Example 5-20 shows the new IP routing state of SPOKE-2-WEST.

Example 5-20 *Filtered Routes on the Spoke for GRE with Dynamic Routing*

```
spoke-1-west#show ip route
Gateway of last resort is 0.0.0.0 to network 0.0.0.0

     9.0.0.0/30 is subnetted, 6 subnets
```

continues

Example 5-20 *Filtered Routes on the Spoke for GRE with Dynamic Routing (Continued)*

```
S        9.1.1.20 [1/0] via 9.1.1.133
C        9.1.1.132 is directly connected, Serial0
         10.0.0.0/8 is subnetted, 3 subnets
D           10.1.0.0 [90/284472576] via 10.1.0.1, 00:00:51, Tunnel0
C           10.0.65.0 is directly connected, Loopback1
```

The use of dynamic routing within the GRE tunnels in the hub-and-spoke model changes the IPSec tunnel protection paradigm. The native hub-and-spoke model allows connectivity only between those address ranges that are explicitly defined by the IPSec profiles. In contrast, the use of dynamic routing in GRE tunnels protected by IPSec allows connectivity between all sites unless explicitly prevented.

We have shown that GRE encapsulation with IPSec protection may significantly simplify the VPN design process. The IPSec profiles are much simpler to define because they are associated only with the GRE tunnel endpoints as opposed to the private LAN address space. Unfortunately, you lose the ability to explicitly define IPSec protection models for different traffic types because the crypto profile identifies only the GRE protocol. The advantage is that you can pass any traffic you chose through the tunnel while avoiding changes to the IPSec profile. With the ability to pass routing protocols through the tunnel, you are able to dynamically build the routing paths between the hub and spokes. You have also seen that the connectivity paradigm shifts from connect-if-allowed to connect-unless-blocked when dynamic routing protocols are used through IPSec-protected tunnels. The next section will show how to exploit this capability when we define transit hub-and-spoke architectures using GRE.

Transit Site-to-Site Connectivity

You have already seen that dynamic routing within the GRE tunnels implicitly provides connectivity between any of the VPN sites. Assuming transit traffic may pass through the hub to the other spokes, the choice of routing protocols is expanded to include link-state routing protocols such as OSPF or IS-IS. The IPSec profiles associated with the GRE tunnels remain the same as in the previous example; however, the routing assumptions must be qualified.

First, consider the case in which Internet access is not required. Each spoke will require a route via the hub for all the other spoke's protected address ranges. With the dynamic routing process configured on the spoke and bound to both the private interface and the tunnel assigned address, the protected address range will be propagated to the hub. In addition, any routes learned via this interface may also be propagated to the hub. The hub site will need a routing process that binds to each of the tunnel interface's assigned address. The hub site subsequently relays the routes to other spokes. As a result, all the spokes learn a viable path to the protected addresses on all the other spokes (as well as the hub). The paradigm of allowing all connectivity unless explicitly denied applies in this case. This is true for any address space included in the VPN routing plane; therefore, the designer must use care in associating the routing process with all the interfaces on the VPN device.

In order to avoid recursive routing, tunnel endpoint IP addresses should not be propagated through the VPN routing plane. Usually, this is not a problem because the tunnel endpoint addresses are typically assigned from the public IP address space when the tunnels traverse the Internet. If the tunnel endpoints use private addresses from the same IP address block as the protected addresses, care must be taken to ensure that the tunnel endpoint addresses have a preferred path that does not use the tunnel as the next hop. A separate backbone routing plane with a lower administrative weight may be appropriate to ensure that the physical interfaces are always preferred for routing to remote tunnel endpoints. The backbone routing process can be bound to the public physical interfaces and tunnel endpoint addresses. This is common when traversing the Internet. The backbone routing plane uses BGP, whereas the VPN routing plane might use EIGRP.

Transit Site-to-Site Connectivity with Internet Access

Now to address the requirement of providing Internet access to the spokes. The use of dynamic routing protocols in the VPN tends to break down in this scenario. Although propagating all the Internet routes to a spoke is possible, it may not be the most viable approach because the Internet routing table is quite large and spoke routers typically have limited routing memory. A more appropriate approach is to provide a default route to the spoke via the VPN routing plane. As a result, the spoke will have a path to any address (including other VPN addresses) via the tunnel. The hub will still need to have a path for return traffic to the appropriate spoke site; therefore, a VPN dynamic routing plane may continue to be useful. In the absence of a dynamic VPN routing plane, the use of hub-and-spoke architecture facilitates a fairly simple model in which static routes easily accommodate the connectivity requirements. Again, a key point is that the tunnel endpoints must be routed outside of the VPN routing plane. This presents an interesting scenario for the IPSec VPN built over the Internet where the traditional destination of the default route is to the Internet next hop using the backbone routing plane. In contrast, you must now use the default route in the VPN routing plane. Therefore, you must replace the default route in the backbone routing plane with an explicit route for the remote tunnel endpoint.

In Example 5-21, the EIGRP routing process is bound to the tunnel interfaces; however, doing so only propagates the default route to the spokes. The spokes continue to propagate their respective protected networks to the hub. This allows a host at any spoke to route packets to the hub site where the packets are redirected to the appropriate spoke site.

Example 5-21 *Hub Configuration for GRE with Default Route Propagation*

```
hostname vpn-gw1-west
!
router eigrp 100
! Include the default route in the EIGRP routing process
 redistribute static
 network 10.1.0.0 0.0.0.255
! Propagate only the default route to the spokes
 distribute-list 10 out
```

continues

Example 5-21 *Hub Configuration for GRE with Default Route Propagation (Continued)*

```
 no auto-summary
!
ip route 0.0.0.0 0.0.0.0 9.1.1.21
!
access-list 10 permit 0.0.0.0
```

The routing table for the hub is shown in Example 5-22. Note that the hub learns all of the spoke routes via the tunnels.

Example 5-22 *Hub Default Routing State for GRE*

```
vpn-gw1-west#show ip route

Gateway of last resort is 9.1.1.21 to network 0.0.0.0

     9.0.0.0/8 is variably subnetted, 3 subnets, 2 masks
C       9.1.1.20/30 is directly connected, Serial1/0:0
     10.0.0.0/8 is variably subnetted, 5 subnets, 2 masks
C       10.1.0.0/24 is directly connected, Ethernet4/0
D       10.0.64.0/24 [90/297270016] via 10.0.64.1, 00:06:13, Tunnel1
D       10.0.65.0/24 [90/297372416] via 10.0.65.1, 00:06:16, Tunnel0
S*   0.0.0.0/0 [1/0] via 9.1.1.21
```

The spoke configuration requires only a routing process that is associated with the tunnel interface, as shown in Example 5-23. The spoke will now propagate the routes learned via the Ethernet0 interface to the hub router. Note that the static route for the remote tunnel endpoint (that is, 9.1.1.22) prevents the recursive routing of the tunnel.

Example 5-23 *Spoke Configuration for GRE with Spoke Default Routing*

```
hostname spoke-2-west
!
interface Ethernet0
 ip address 10.0.65.1 255.255.255.0
!
interface Tunnel0
 ip unnumbered Ethernet0
 tunnel source 9.1.1.134
 tunnel destination 9.1.1.22
!
router eigrp 100
 network 10.0.65.0 0.0.0.255
 auto-summary
 no eigrp log-neighbor-changes
!
ip route 9.1.1.20 255.255.255.252 9.1.1.133
```

Example 5-24 shows the routing state of the spoke. The spoke uses the default route learned through the tunnel; however, it has not received any updates from the hub on the other spoke subnets. Any traffic destined to the Internet or other spokes will be directed into the tunnel such that IPSec protection may be applied. Encapsulated traffic destined for the hub tunnel endpoint will be routed outside of the tunnel via the Serial0 interface.

Example 5-24   *Spoke Default Routing State for GRE*

```
spoke-2-west#show ip route

Gateway of last resort is 10.1.0.1 to network 0.0.0.0

     9.0.0.0/30 is subnetted, 6 subnets
S       9.1.1.20 [1/0] via 9.1.1.133
C       9.1.1.132 is directly connected, Serial0
     10.0.0.0/24 is subnetted, 2 subnets
C       10.0.65.0 is directly connected, Ethernet0
D*EX 0.0.0.0/0 [170/284958976] via 10.1.0.1, 00:01:17, Tunnel0
```

The GRE model with transit hub routing provides a very simple method of providing Internet access. In addition, the security model for the spoke is quite simple. The loss of the tunnel (or IPSec connection protecting the tunnel) to the hub removes all external routing paths. The only external path remaining during loss of connectivity is the path to the IPSec peer identity and tunnel endpoint.

Scalability of GRE Hub-and-Spoke Models

The size of the hub-and-spoke VPN may be constrained by the hub's throughput capacity. The hub must serve as a transit routing node for both Internet and spoke-to-spoke connectivity. Spoke-to-spoke traffic must be decrypted and re-encrypted. This transit traffic doubles the crypto hardware's processing requirements. The hardware encryption capability is usually a gating factor when large packets are sent, because they must pass through the encryption engine twice. Smaller packets typically overwhelm the processing power on the CPU before the crypto hardware's capacity is exhausted. Ironically, when no split tunneling is used at the spoke, Internet traffic initiated from the spoke is encrypted between the hub and spoke while it passes in the clear from the Internet to the hub site. Introducing split tunneling at the spoke eliminates the Internet transit traffic load at the hub; however, it increases the complexity of security.

The complexity of IPSec profiles is significantly simplified with the GRE tunneling model. We have shown that GRE tunnels aggregate multiple IP flows (as well as other protocols) into a single IP address pair represented by the tunnel. The IPSec proxy statements are required only to identify the tunnel endpoints as opposed to all the sources and destinations of traffic flowing through the tunnel. As a result, the flow consolidation reduces the number of IPSec SAs. This is particularly useful where the VPN uses non-contiguous IP address ranges that cannot be represented as address aggregates. The number of IKE SAs remains the same as in the native IPSec tunnel model because each spoke still requires the control connection to the hub. The complexity of provisioning is minimized through the aggregation of flows into a single pair of IPSec SAs and one IKE SA.

The scalability of IKE is still a concern at the hub because every spoke will require some form of IKE state synchronization. In the absence of IKE state management, we introduce the potential for stale IPSec SAs where the SA resides in the security association database, but the remote peer is no longer viable. A stale IPSec SA can be reclaimed when an incoming IKE request matches the SA's proxy statement. Therefore, the IKE state management may be eliminated if a bi-directional link-state management function is used on the GRE tunnel. Two potential link-state management functions are the GRE keepalive and dynamic routing. The advantage of using GRE keepalives or dynamic routing exchanges via the tunnels is that the packets used to exchange state validate not only the tunnel state, but the IPSec SA state. The use of dynamic routing does increase the hub's computational requirements with little value in the simple hub-and-spoke model. The size of the VPN may be limited due to the number of dynamic routing adjacencies the hub can sustain. In addition, dynamic routing forces IKE initialization from the hub to all the spokes as soon as viable routes exist for the tunnel endpoints. This places a heavy IKE computational burden on the hub especially at startup or reboot. You will see the true value of dynamic routing when redundancy is explored in Chapter 6, "Designing Fault-Tolerant IPSec VPNs."

In summary, the hub-and-spoke VPN built with IPSec-protected GRE tunnels is very popular. The topology simplifies IPSec configuration while providing the ability to transport multiple protocols. The scalability of the VPN architecture is usually constrained by the capabilities of the hub. The hub scalability limits include packet processing rates, security associations, routing neighbor adjacencies, link-state management functions, and configuration memory constraints. Also, note that the point-to-point GRE tunnels require knowledge of the tunnel endpoints at the time of configuration. This makes the GRE model difficult to use on access environments in which IP addresses are dynamically assigned by the service provider. The next section provides dynamic client connection alternatives for the hub-and-spoke model that may simplify the configuration while addressing some of the constraints identified in site-to-site architectures.

Remote Access Client Connection Model

In this model, the spokes are remote access clients connecting to a hub site. The remote client connection to the hub typically occurs over the public Internet, which means the client IP address could be any publicly routable address in the Internet; therefore, the hub must allow incoming IPSec connections from any IP address that is not known in advance to the hub. This is different from the site-to-site model in which each spoke IPSec tunnel endpoint is known in advance and is statically configured on the hub.

NOTE   The IPSec profiles configured at the hub, or referred to by the hub, define the range of protected addresses for the client. The range might limit access to specific networks at the hub site or allow access to the Internet via the hub. Likewise, the hub may exclude protection of specific IP address ranges (that is, split tunneling) such that traffic directed to these sites does not get encrypted and directed to the hub. One of the most commonly excluded addresses is the local subnet to which the client is connected. This feature allows the client to use local resources such as printers and file servers while providing IPSec encryption for all remote services and Internet services.

One of the principle advantages of the client connection model is that hub configuration is dramatically simplified. Additionally, the VPN is automatically built with each incoming client connection. Next, you'll explore how this simple creation of a hub-and-spoke VPN can accommodate multiple hosts on a remote client connection.

Easy VPN (EzVPN) Client Mode

The client mode works well in a telecommuter situation in which the remote client is just one device that originates the IPSec connection. You saw in the previous section how the client mode simplifies the configuration at the hub dramatically by consolidating the security policy at the hub (or by having the hub refer to a database for security policy). Given the advantage of the client mode, it is worthwhile to extend this model to a site-to-site connection. The EzVPN client mode does just that! In this model, the remote client (instead of being a single PC initiating the IPSec connection) is a router that operates in EzVPN mode with multiple hosts behind the router. From the perspective of the hub, the incoming connection looks like it originated from a single software client. The hub leverages all of the previously defined authentication and authorization models defined in Chapter 3, "Enhanced IPSec Features," whereas the remote site emulates a software client.

Let's look at the process of connection establishment in this model. Recall from the previous section that the hub assigns a single IP address to the client during the authorization phase. The obvious question in the EzVPN model is how multiple hosts at the remote site can use a single assigned IP address. The EzVPN solution addresses this through the use of a technique known as Port Address Translation (PAT). Figure 5-7 shows a typical EzVPN deployment scenario.

Figure 5-7 shows an EzVPN-capable router with hosts behind it while IP connectivity is assumed to be available between the remote router and the hub site. In this model, the EzVPN router is also serving as a DHCP server for all the hosts behind it. All the remote hosts obtain their private IP addresses using DHCP. Now, when a host behind the EzVPN router needs to send traffic to a host on the hub site, the remote host forwards the packet to the EzVPN router that is the default gateway for this host. Once the packet arrives into the EzVPN router, routing configuration on this node determines that this traffic is destined out of the protected interface, and initiates an IPSec session to the hub. It establishes an IPSec connection to the hub and receives an assigned private address. The IKE SA establishes an IPSec proxy profile that protects traffic from the assigned IP address to the hub site addresses. The host source IP address is mapped (using Port Address Translation) to the address assigned by the hub to the EzVPN router. In addition to mapping the source IP address, the original source port address is mapped to a unique port address in order to avoid conflict with other hosts. As a result, the host is represented to the hub as a unique data flow from the assigned IP address and unique source port address. For return traffic to the host, the process is reversed such that traffic destined to the remote site's protected IP address and uniquely assigned port is mapped back to the originating host's IP address and original port.

Figure 5-7 *EzVPN Client Mode Connectivity*

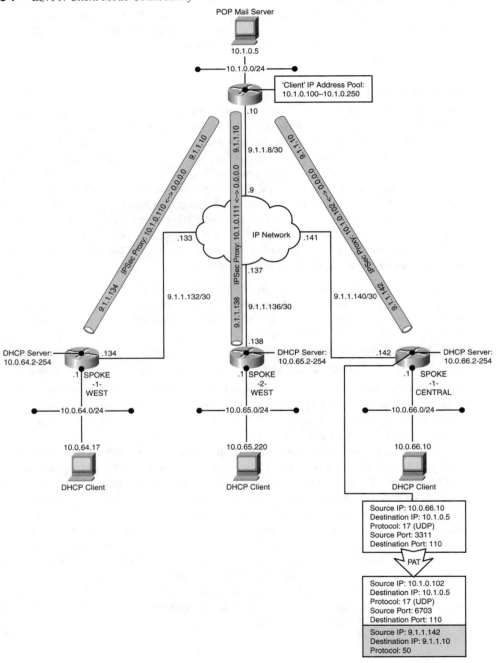

Now that the IPSec session is established between the remote site EzVPN router and the hub, additional application flows may originate from the same host or other hosts at the remote site. Each unique flow (source IP, destination IP, protocol, source port, and destination port) may connect to hub resources with each flow dynamically assigned a unique source port on the remote router's protected IP address. The PAT process makes each flow unique. All of these flows will use the original IPSec SA pair; therefore, the number of IPSec connections is minimized on the hub site. The configuration and routing state supporting the client mode IPSec connectivity model is shown in the following examples.

Example 5-25 provides a configuration example of an IOS router allowing incoming IPSec connections from dynamically assigned spoke addresses. The hub does enforce two phases of authentication in the same manner that a software client is required to supply a group name and password as well as a username and password.

Example 5-25 *Hub Configuration for Client Mode EzVPN Connectivity*

```
vpn-gw1-west#show running-config
!
hostname vpn-gw1-west
!
aaa new-model
!
!
aaa authentication login user-auth local
aaa authorization network group-auth local
!
! User authentication database
username cisco password 0 cisco123
username client-mode password 0 cisco123
!
crypto isakmp policy 3
 encr 3des
 authentication pre-share
 group 2
!
crypto isakmp keepalive 60 5
!
! IPSec Group Attributes
crypto isakmp client configuration group client-mode
 key cisco123
 domain cisco.com
 pool client-mode-pool
 idletime 3600
!
crypto ipsec transform-set client-transform esp-3des esp-md5-hmac
!
! Dynamic crypto map used for clients with Reverse Route Injection
crypto dynamic-map dyn-map 10
 set transform-set client-transform
 reverse-route
!
!  Crypto map authentication and authorization methods defined
```

continues

Example 5-25 *Hub Configuration for Client Mode EzVPN Connectivity (Continued)*

```
crypto map clientmap client authentication list user-auth
crypto map clientmap isakmp authorization list group-auth
crypto map clientmap client configuration address respond
crypto map clientmap 10 ipsec-isakmp dynamic dyn-map
!
! Assigned address pool for software and Client Mode connections
ip local pool client-mode-pool 10.1.0.100 10.1.0.110
ip route 0.0.0.0 0.0.0.0 9.1.1.9
```

Example 5-26 shows the SPOKE-1-CENTRAL EzVPN client that provides a DHCP server for the locally connected hosts within the 10.0.66.0/24 address range. The egress interface is specified for default routes and IPSec protection using EzVPN. Note that the EzVPN mode is specified as client mode. Only the groupname and password is provided in this example; the username and password is requested via the CLI during IKE initialization and authentication.

Example 5-26 *Spoke Configuration for Client Mode EzVPN Connectivity*

```
spoke-1-central#show running-config
!
ip dhcp excluded-address 10.0.66.1
!
ip dhcp pool private
   import all
   network 10.0.66.0 255.255.255.0
   default-router 10.0.66.1
   lease infinite
!
crypto ipsec client ezvpn remote
 group client-mode key cisco123
 mode client
 peer 9.1.1.10
!
interface Ethernet0
 ip address 10.0.66.1 255.255.255.0
 hold-queue 100 out
!
interface Ethernet1
 ip address 9.1.1.142 255.255.255.252
 crypto ipsec client ezvpn remote
!
ip route 0.0.0.0 0.0.0.0 9.1.1.141
!
```

The crypto maps established between the hub and spoke are provided in Examples 5-27 and 5-28. Emphasis is placed on the IPSec proxy profiles that protect traffic from the assigned EzVPN IP address (for example, 10.1.0.102 on SPOKE-1-CENTRAL) to the hub's protected address range. In this example, all traffic is protected including traffic destined for the Internet.

Example 5-27 *Hub Crypto State for an EzVPN Client–Connected Spoke*

```
vpn-gw1-west#show crypto ipsec sa

interface: Serial1/0
    Crypto map tag: clientmap, local addr. 9.1.1.10

    local  ident (addr/mask/prot/port): (0.0.0.0/0.0.0.0/0/0)
    remote ident (addr/mask/prot/port): (10.1.0.102/255.255.255.255/0/0)
    current_peer: 9.1.1.142
      PERMIT, flags={}
     #pkts encaps: 5, #pkts encrypt: 5, #pkts digest 5
     #pkts decaps: 5, #pkts decrypt: 5, #pkts verify 5
     #pkts compressed: 0, #pkts decompressed: 0
     #pkts not compressed: 0, #pkts compr. failed: 0, #pkts decompress failed: 0
     #pkts no sa (send) 0, #pkts invalid sa (rcv) 0
     #pkts encaps failed (send) 0, #pkts decaps failed (rcv) 0
     #pkts invalid prot (recv) 0, #pkts verify failed: 0
     #pkts invalid identity (recv) 0, #pkts invalid len (rcv) 0
     #pkts replay rollover (send): 0, #pkts replay rollover (rcv) 0
     ##pkts replay failed (rcv): 0
     #pkts internal err (send): 0, #pkts internal err (recv) 0

      local crypto endpt.: 9.1.1.10, remote crypto endpt.: 9.1.1.142
      path mtu 4470, media mtu 4470
      current outbound spi: 12978441
…
vpn-gw1-west#show crypto map

Crypto Map "clientmap" 10 ipsec-isakmp
        Dynamic map template tag: dyn-map

Crypto Map "clientmap" 20 ipsec-isakmp
        Peer = 9.1.1.142
        Extended IP access list
             access-list  permit ip any host 10.1.0.102
             dynamic (created from dynamic map dyn-map/10)
        Current peer: 9.1.1.142
        Security association lifetime: 4608000 kilobytes/3600 seconds
        PFS (Y/N): N
        Transform sets={ client-transform, }
        Reverse Route Injection Enabled
        Interfaces using crypto map clientmap:
                Serial1/0
```

Example 5-28 *Spoke IPSec SA State for an EzVPN Client Connection*

```
spoke-1-central#show crypto ipsec sa

interface: Ethernet1
    Crypto map tag: Ethernet1-head-0, local addr. 9.1.1.142

    local  ident (addr/mask/prot/port): (10.1.0.102/255.255.255.255/0/0)
```

continues

Example 5-28 *Spoke IPSec SA State for an EzVPN Client Connection*

```
  remote ident (addr/mask/prot/port): (0.0.0.0/0.0.0.0/0/0)
  current_peer: 9.1.1.10
    PERMIT, flags={origin_is_acl,}
   #pkts encaps: 5, #pkts encrypt: 5, #pkts digest 5
   #pkts decaps: 5, #pkts decrypt: 5, #pkts verify 5
   #pkts compressed: 0, #pkts decompressed: 0
   #pkts not compressed: 0, #pkts compr. failed: 0, #pkts decompress failed: 0
   #send errors 0, #recv errors 0

    local crypto endpt.: 9.1.1.142, remote crypto endpt.: 9.1.1.10
    path mtu 1500, media mtu 1500
    current outbound spi: 6C697758
  ...
```

The client-connected EzVPN spoke will maintain a translation for each and every unique flow. Note in Example 5-29 that each ICMP Echo packet represents unique flow from 10.0.66.1 to 10.1.0.2. A stream of packets from a TCP or UDP traffic flow would only require a single translation. Each translation is created dynamically as packets leave the spoke site destined for the hub; therefore, connections originating from the hub (or other spokes) cannot reach hosts behind this spoke.

Example 5-29 *PAT Mapping for an EzVPN Client–Connected Spoke*

```
spoke-1-central#show ip nat translations
Pro Inside global      Inside local      Outside local      Outside global
icmp 10.1.0.102:2607   10.0.66.1:2607    10.1.0.2:2607      10.1.0.2:2607
icmp 10.1.0.102:2608   10.0.66.1:2608    10.1.0.2:2608      10.1.0.2:2608
icmp 10.1.0.102:2609   10.0.66.1:2609    10.1.0.2:2609      10.1.0.2:2609
icmp 10.1.0.102:2610   10.0.66.1:2610    10.1.0.2:2610      10.1.0.2:2610
icmp 10.1.0.102:2611   10.0.66.1:2611    10.1.0.2:2611      10.1.0.2:2611
```

An obvious drawback to the client mode is the limitation that sessions cannot be initiated from other sites to a host on a remote site. Sessions initiated to a host at a remote site will have a destination port that is not valid on the remote site EzVPN router, and the traffic will be dropped. As a result, the Client Extension Mode is not appropriate for VPN topologies in which servers are located at the remote sites.

NOTE   Servers may reside at the remote site; however, they would only be accessible to hosts at that remote site. An architectural model that fulfills this requirement is one in which the remote site server caches data from the hub site. In this connection model, the remote site server must initiate the connection to the hub site server and synchronize data using a single flow.

Despite the limitations of the Client Extension Mode, it is still quite useful in a number of VPN architectures. It is particularly helpful for small remote sites where almost all the network resources reside at the hub site. You have seen how the client connection model simplifies the configuration of the hub by dynamically allowing incoming connections. We have augmented this model with the Client Extension Mode enabling multiple remote hosts to use a single IPSec connection from the remote site to the hub. Doing so improves the hub's scalability by reducing the number of IPSec connections. Unfortunately, the dynamic source port allocation and Port Address Translation prevents a number of applications from functioning properly. Next, you'll explore modifications to the Client Extension Mode to accommodate flow establishment in both directions.

EzVPN Network Extension Mode

The Network Extension Mode modifies the Client Mode such that a range of protected IP addresses is statically assigned to the remote site router as opposed to a single IP address. The remote site may continue to use a dynamically assigned public IP address. Therefore, the hub must accept incoming IPSec connections from any IP address. The Network Extension Mode deviates from the previous routing models in which the protected IP address is assigned by the hub. Because the IP address is pre-assigned at the remote site, the hub must install a route for this remote IP address range when the remote site is connected. The hub's route to the remote site's protected address range can't be pre-configured. The hub will only learn the appropriate remote site termination point when the IPSec connection is established. During the IKE establishment phase, the protected address range is inserted in the hub routing table using Reverse Route Injection. The hub may propagate the dynamically inserted route to other routers in order to build a viable return path. Figure 5-8 shows the topology that is dynamically built when using Network Extension Mode.

The pre-assigned address range allows each host to have a unique IP address. Having a unique IP address for each remote host eliminates the requirement to dynamically map-source ports on flows from the remote hosts. With PAT removed from the process, sessions may be initiated to the remote host's well-known application ports, provided a route exists to the site. Recall that the route is dynamically created in the hub using Reverse Route Injection during the IPSec establishment.

Slight modifications are required to the configurations provided in Client Extension Mode. The hub must provide Reverse Route Injection for a remote site's protected subnet in order to establish a return path for packets destined to that spoke's hosts while the spoke must specify the use of Network Extension Mode in order to avoid receiving a dynamically assigned IP address from the hub. Examples 5-30 and 5-31 provide the configuration modifications required on the hub and spoke, respectively.

Figure 5-8 *Hub-and-Spoke VPN with Network Extension Mode*

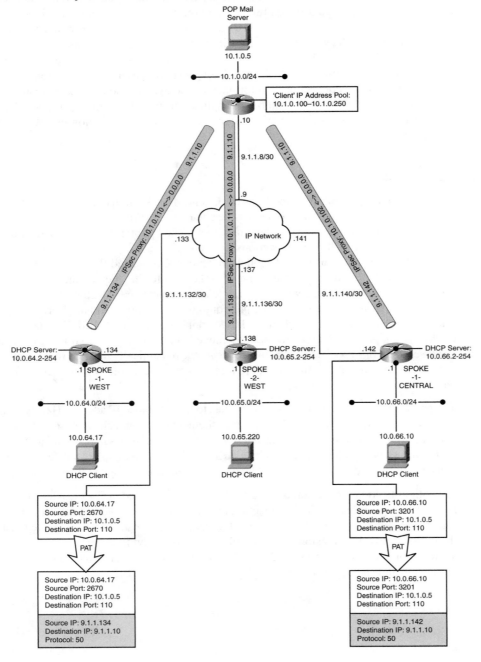

Example 5-30 *Hub Configuration Supporting Network Extension Mode*

```
vpn-gw1-west#show running-config
!
aaa new-model
!
aaa authentication login user-auth local
aaa authorization network group-auth local
!
! User authentication database
username cisco password 0 cisco123
username client-mode password 0 cisco123
!
crypto isakmp policy 3
 encr 3des
 authentication pre-share
 group 2
!
crypto isakmp keepalive 60 5
!
! IPSec Group Attributes (no IP address pool required)
crypto isakmp client configuration group client-mode
 key cisco123
 domain cisco.com
 idletime 3600
!
crypto ipsec transform-set client-transform esp-3des esp-md5-hmac
!
! Dynamic crypto map used for clients with Reverse Route Injection
crypto dynamic-map dyn-map 10
 set transform-set client-transform
 reverse-route
!
!  Crypto map authentication and authorization methods defined
crypto map clientmap client authentication list user-auth
crypto map clientmap isakmp authorization list group-auth
crypto map clientmap client configuration address respond
crypto map clientmap 10 ipsec-isakmp dynamic dyn-map
!
ip route 0.0.0.0 0.0.0.0 9.1.1.9
```

Example 5-31 *Spoke Configuration Requesting Network Extension Mode*

```
spoke-1-central#show running-config
!
crypto ipsec client ezvpn remote
 group client-mode key cisco123
 mode network-extension
 peer 9.1.1.10
!
interface Ethernet0
 ip address 10.0.66.1 255.255.255.0
 hold-queue 100 out
```

continues

Example 5-31 *Spoke Configuration Requesting Network Extension Mode (Continued)*

```
!
interface Ethernet1
 ip address 9.1.1.142 255.255.255.248
 crypto ipsec client ezvpn remote
!
ip route 0.0.0.0 0.0.0.0 9.1.1.141
```

NOTE   Well-known ports are used for specific services on hosts and routers. Incoming connections must use these well-known ports in order to obtain service. As an example, an SMTP mail server uses the well-known TCP port of 25. Some services, such as VoIP, signal the port address in the call control messages. Modification of the source port through PAT will interfere with the end-to-end connection model and will likely prevent the establishment of the calls. Since Network Extension Mode does not modify the VoIP terminal's IP address and port, IP telephony through IPSec VPNs may be simplified. Also note that remote IP telephony terminals may register with a server at the hub site such that the EzVPN connection is always established.

Example 5-32 provides the hub's crypto map and routing state for SPOKE-1-CENTRAL in which emphasis is placed on the IPSec proxy and the static route. The IPSec proxy provides protection for traffic initiated from any remote host assigned a private address by the EzVPN router to any host at the hub site. The static route is dynamically inserted in the hub's routing for the duration of the IPSec connection.

Example 5-32 *Hub Crypto Map State for Network Extension Mode*

```
vpn-gw1-west#show crypto map

Crypto Map "clientmap" 10 ipsec-isakmp
        Dynamic map template tag: dyn-map

Crypto Map "clientmap" 20 ipsec-isakmp
        Peer = 9.1.1.142
        Extended IP access list
            access-list  permit ip any 10.0.66.0 0.0.0.255
            dynamic (created from dynamic map dyn-map/10)
        Current peer: 9.1.1.194
        Security association lifetime: 4608000 kilobytes/3600 seconds
        PFS (Y/N): N
        Transform sets={ client-transform, }
        Reverse Route Injection Enabled
        Interfaces using crypto map clientmap:
                Serial1/0

vpn-gw1-west#show ip route

Gateway of last resort is 9.1.1.9 to network 0.0.0.0
```

Example 5-32 *Hub Crypto Map State for Network Extension Mode (Continued)*

```
      9.0.0.0/30 is subnetted, 1 subnets
C        9.1.1.8 is directly connected, Serial1/0
      10.0.0.0/8 is subnetted, 2 subnets
C        10.1.0.0 is directly connected, FastEthernet0/1
S        10.0.66.0 [1/0] via 0.0.0.0, Serial1/0
S*    0.0.0.0/0 [20/0] via 9.1.1.9, 3w2d
```

Unfortunately, an IPSec connection cannot be initiated from the hub site to the remote site because the remote site's public IP address may not be known a priori. The hub-and-spoke VPN can be dynamically built if each remote site router maintains an IPSec connection to the hub. A simple persistent connection initiated from a remote server to a server at the hub site will sustain the IPSec. Although the IPSec connection may expire, the remote server's persistent connection will likely use a frequent polling mechanism to verify the state of the hub server. The polling mechanism will immediately reestablish the IPSec session, enabling access to the other servers at the remote site.

Scalability of Client Connectivity Models

You have seen how the client connectivity models enable the dynamic creation of a simple hub-and-spoke VPN, greatly simplifying the configuration requirements at both the hub and spoke. In addition, aggregating each site's route requirements into a single IPSec proxy statement minimizes the number of IPSec sessions. We initially provided a framework for building a hub-and-spoke VPN using the software client mode connection model. The client mode enabled connection capabilities for multiple clients at the remote site by embedding the client connection model in the remote site router. Finally, we enhanced the model with Network Extension Mode. The VPN is still dynamically built while using statically assigned private addresses for each of the sites. The elimination of Port Address Translation enables many more services on the VPN than otherwise. The Network Extension Mode leverages all of the scalability attributes of a client-connected model while providing the look and feel of a more traditional hub-and-spoke VPN.

The client connection model provides a reasonably scalable hub-and-spoke network. The number of simultaneously connected remote sites determines the scalability requirements of the hub in terms of IPSec SAs and IKE SAs. The use of Reverse Route Injection eliminates the requirement for establishing a private routing protocol connection between the hub and its spokes. Therefore, the hub is no longer burdened with maintaining routing state. The hub site may continue to use IKE dead peer detection or keepalive in order to validate the IPSec state for each of its connected remotes. The most common scalability constraint incurred by the hub is the volume of data passing through the device as transit traffic. The hub site must route traffic from each of the spokes and mostly likely will provide transit access to the Internet.

Most network traffic demands are driven by client–server connections that tend to be hub-and-spoke in nature. New peer-to-peer applications are slowly changing that paradigm. As these traffic demands increase, the spoke-to-spoke transit traffic passing through the hub becomes a performance constraint. Next, you'll explore how full-mesh architecture addresses this connectivity requirement.

Full-Mesh Architectures

The *full-mesh architecture* establishes a direct IPSec connection between every site in the VPN. Effectively, every IPSec router in the VPN must serve as a hub for its site. A hub's scalability constraints described in the previous sections still apply. The motivation for creating full-mesh VPN should be based on actual traffic demands requiring traffic between any site to any other site in the VPN. Assuming the traffic demands warrant the creation of a full-mesh IPSec VPN, we can consider several connectivity models that enable direct connections between the sites.

Native IPSec Connectivity Model

The simplest full-mesh connection model uses a simple IPSec connection between each site. Each IPSec connection requires a unique proxy statement that protects traffic between a specific set of VPN peers. If we assume that there are N routers terminating IPSec connections in the VPN, then each site will require a minimum of N-1 IPSec proxy statements. The IPSec connections may or may not be persistent; however, they must be defined in order to direct traffic to the appropriate remote VPN node. The total number of IPSec connections can be modeled as N(N-1)/2. Because an IPSec connection requires a proxy statement defined at each end, there are N(N-1) IPSec proxy statements defined in the VPN. Figure 5-9 shows the topology that is built with an IPSec full-mesh configured.

The full-mesh IPSec VPN router configuration looks equivalent to a hub node in a hub-and-spoke IPSec VPN. The configuration for VPN-GW1-WEST shown originally in the Example 5-1 hub-and-spoke configuration remains the same; however, there is no need for transit traffic protection. The SPOKE-1-WEST configuration shown in Example 5-3 is modified to accommodate direct IPSec connections between each of the other sites. The modified configuration is shown in Example 5-33.

Figure 5-9 *IPSec Tunnels for a Full-Mesh Topology*

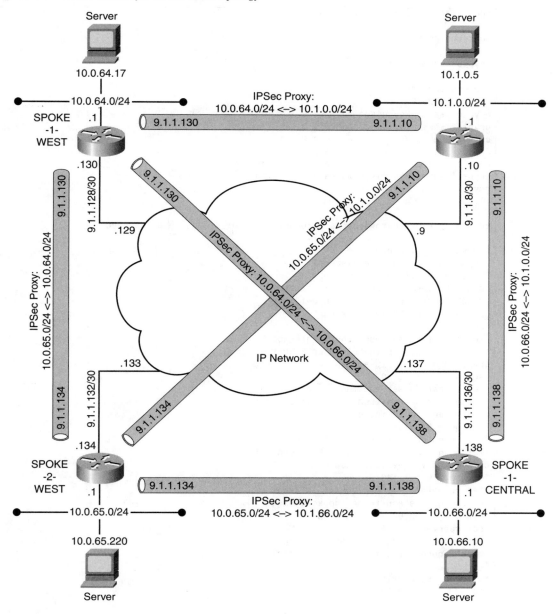

Example 5-33 *Native IPSec Full-Mesh Spoke Configuration*

```
spoke-1-west #show running-config
!
hostname spoke-1-west
!
crypto isakmp policy 10
 hash md5
 authentication pre-share
 lifetime 3600
crypto isakmp key cisco address 9.1.1.10
crypto isakmp key cisco address 9.1.1.134
crypto isakmp key cisco address 9.1.1.138
crypto isakmp key cisco address 9.1.1.142
crypto isakmp key cisco address 9.1.1.146
crypto isakmp key cisco address 9.1.1.150
crypto isakmp keepalive 10
!
!
crypto ipsec transform-set esp-tunnel-internet esp-des esp-md5-hmac
!
! Crypto map for hub site peer
crypto map vpn 10 ipsec-isakmp
 set peer 9.1.1.10
 set transform-set esp-tunnel-internet
 match address esp-tunnel-vpn-gw1-west
crypto map vpn 20 ipsec-isakmp
 set peer 9.1.1.134
 set transform-set esp-tunnel-internet
 match address esp-tunnel-spoke-2-west
crypto map vpn 30 ipsec-isakmp
 set peer 9.1.1.138
 set transform-set esp-tunnel-internet
 match address esp-tunnel-spoke-1-central
crypto map vpn 40 ipsec-isakmp
 set peer 9.1.1.142
 set transform-set esp-tunnel-internet
 match address esp-tunnel-spoke-2-central
crypto map vpn 50 ipsec-isakmp
 set peer 9.1.1.146
 set transform-set esp-tunnel-internet
 match address esp-tunnel-spoke-1-east
crypto map vpn 60 ipsec-isakmp
 set peer 9.1.1.150
 set transform-set esp-tunnel-internet
 match address esp-tunnel-spoke-2-east
!
interface Ethernet0
 ip address 10.0.64.1 255.255.255.0
!
interface Serial0
 ip address 9.1.1.130 255.255.255.252
 crypto map vpn
```

Example 5-33 *Native IPSec Full-Mesh Spoke Configuration (Continued)*

```
!
! default route to the backbone
ip route 0.0.0.0 0.0.0.0 9.1.1.129
!
! Protected address ranges from spoke to hub
ip access-list extended esp-tunnel-vpn-gw1-west
 permit ip 10.0.64.0 0.0.0.255 10.1.0.0 0.0.0.255
ip access-list extended esp-tunnel-spoke-2-west
 permit ip 10.0.64.0 0.0.0.255 10.0.65.0 0.0.0.255
ip access-list extended esp-tunnel-spoke-1-central
 permit ip 10.0.64.0 0.0.0.255 10.0.66.0 0.0.0.255
ip access-list extended esp-tunnel-spoke-2-central
 permit ip 10.0.64.0 0.0.0.255 10.0.67.0 0.0.0.255
ip access-list extended esp-tunnel-spoke-1-east
 permit ip 10.0.64.0 0.0.0.255 10.0.68.0 0.0.0.255
ip access-list extended esp-tunnel-spoke-2-east
 permit ip 10.0.64.0 0.0.0.255 10.0.69.0 0.0.0.255
end
```

As the size of the VPN increases, the configuration complexity increases with $O(N^2)$. The full-mesh VPN gets even more interesting when one or more of the sites have a non-contiguous IP address range. A non-contiguous IP address range at one site requires a unique IPSec proxy statement defined between that site and all of the others, further adding to the complexity of the configuration. Each non-contiguous IP address range in the network effectively creates an additional site in the full mesh. This may be modeled as $N(N-1)/2 + M(N-1)$ connections, where *M* represents the total number of non-contiguous IP address ranges in the VPN. Figure 5-10 highlights the new IPSec topology map with the addition of a non-contiguous IP address range at the hub site. Note that all the other sites require additional IPSec proxy statements to accommodate the non-contiguous IP address range.

Figure 5-10 *Non-contiguous IP Address Ranges on Full-Mesh Topology*

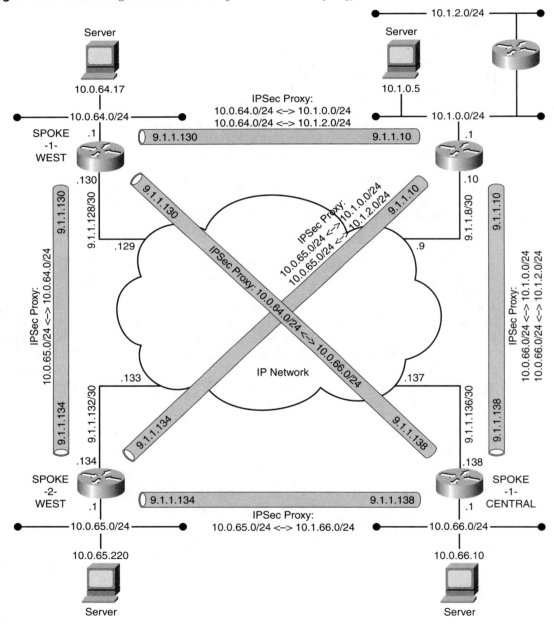

Thus far, we have addressed only the requirement for IPSec proxy statements, and have not addressed routing requirements. The task is simplified if you assume that the each of the sites uses a default route to the backbone. This is typically the case when building the VPN over the Internet. You may recall from the section regarding building hub-and-spoke VPNs that the IPSec proxy statement effectively replaces the routing functions as packets leave the router. As long as the backbone maintains proper routing paths between the IPSec endpoints, the backbone topology may be arbitrarily defined.

Internet access using this model can be achieved with either split tunneling or by directing all unknown destinations to a designated site in the VPN. Most enterprises avoid providing direct Internet access from each site in order to minimize the number of security exposure points. The enterprise will usually designate one site as the Internet access site where firewalls protect the entire VPN. Effectively, the Internet access site becomes a preferred hub in the full-mesh VPN for any unknown destination. Figure 5-11 shows the full-mesh IPSec VPN with a default hub for Internet traffic.

In this scenario, traffic flows originating and terminating within the VPN potentially match two IPSec proxy statements—the explicit one defined for intranet traffic and the generic one defined for Internet traffic. Obviously, the intranet profile should take priority over the Internet profile. If the priority is reversed, the VPN will operate as a hub-and-spoke, thereby negating the benefits of the site-to-site IPSec profiles. The priority of the proxy statements is determined by the order of the crypto map instances. Referring back to Example 5-33, we note that the IPSec proxy configuration on SPOKE-1-WEST explicitly defines the protection of specific subnets protected by remote peers. The configuration does not address protection of Internet-destined traffic that is not associated with any of the peers; therefore, Internet traffic is not protected by the IPSec crypto proxy statements.

The previous configuration for the spoke routers requires the addition of a default crypto map as the last in the sequence. Example 5-34 highlights the modifications required. The last crypto map serves as a crypto map of last resort, forcing Internet-bound traffic to the "hub" router in the full-mesh VPN. Note also that the more specific crypto map for the "hub" router's protected address can be removed because it is redundant with the protection of all Internet traffic that is to transit the hub. The hub's protected address range is in the aggregate range of the Internet. The hub router must still serve as a transit router for Internet traffic as shown previously in Example 5-9.

Figure 5-11 *Full-Mesh IPSec VPN with Default Internet Hub*

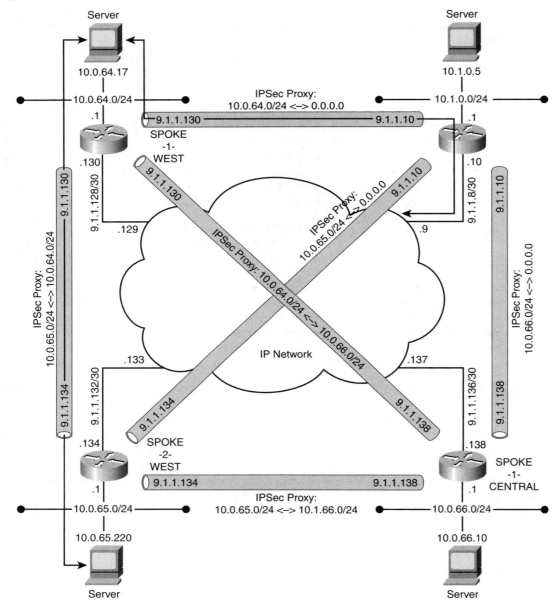

Example 5-34 *Native IPSec Full-Mesh Spoke Configuration with Default*

```
spoke-1-west #show running-config
!
hostname spoke-1-west
!
crypto isakmp policy 10
 hash md5
 authentication pre-share
 lifetime 3600
crypto isakmp key cisco address 9.1.1.10
crypto isakmp key cisco address 9.1.1.134
crypto isakmp key cisco address 9.1.1.138

crypto isakmp keepalive 10
!
!
crypto ipsec transform-set esp-tunnel-internet esp-des esp-md5-hmac
!
! IPsec Proxy sequence 10 removed for hub site.  Refer to default below
crypto map vpn 20 ipsec-isakmp
 set peer 9.1.1.134
 set transform-set esp-tunnel-internet
 match address esp-tunnel-spoke-2-west
crypto map vpn 30 ipsec-isakmp
 set peer 9.1.1.138
 set transform-set esp-tunnel-internet
 match address esp-tunnel-spoke-1-central
! IPsec Proxy default for spoke-to-hub including Internet
crypto map vpn 70 ipsec-isakmp
 set peer 9.1.1.10
 set transform-set esp-tunnel-internet
 match address esp-tunnel-internet
!
interface Ethernet0
 ip address 10.0.64.1 255.255.255.0
!
interface Serial0
 ip address 9.1.1.130 255.255.255.252
 crypto map vpn
!
! default route to the backbone
ip route 0.0.0.0 0.0.0.0 9.1.1.129
!
! Protected address ranges from spoke to spoke
ip access-list extended esp-tunnel-spoke-2-west
 permit ip 10.0.64.0 0.0.0.255 10.0.65.0 0.0.0.255
ip access-list extended esp-tunnel-spoke-1-central
 permit ip 10.0.64.0 0.0.0.255 10.0.66.0 0.0.0.255
! Protected address range from spoke to hub including Internet
ip access-list extended esp-tunnel-internet
 permit ip 10.0.64.0 0.0.0.255 0.0.0.0 255.255.255.255
end
```

The full-mesh VPN is a highly desirable architecture when a large amount of traffic must be sent from any given site to all the other sites. Applications such as VoIP might drive this requirement even when the call control is located at a single site in the VPN. The bearer traffic for VoIP will want to follow the shortest path between two sites. With a full-mesh IPSec VPN, the VoIP-bearer traffic may avoid passing through a hub site where the traffic must be decrypted and subsequently re-encrypted. Another application that requires any-to-any connectivity is IP multicast. Unfortunately, the earlier implementations of IPSec were not designed to handle point-to-multiple traffic peers; therefore, this architecture does not handle multicast streams in the VPN.

In summary, the full-mesh IPSec VPN does allow site-to-site traffic to pass directly between the sites without having to traverse the hub. The advantages of any-to-any connectivity are offset by the additional configuration complexity required to build the full-mesh IPSec proxy statements. In addition, the improper assignment of IP address ranges will further complicate the configuration. We have also introduced additional scalability constraints in the VPN devices because every site must effectively become a hub for its protected address range. Every site must handle the maximum potential number of IKE and IPSec SAs necessary to reach every other site's protected address space. A site with fewer simultaneous traffic demands to every other site might be able to use a less scalable device. This assumption is based on the premise that IKE and IPSec SAs are instantiated only when there are active traffic demands between the two peers.

Some IPSec equipment such as the Cisco VPN 3000 Series devices activate IKE and IPSec SAs once configured in the router. In contrast, the Cisco IOS based devices establish IKE and IPSec SAs only when traffic flows match the IPSec profiles. The tradeoff between the two models is a delay during tunnel establishment versus a permanently allocated resource for idle IPSec tunnels. The IOS devices must negotiate IKE and IPSec SAs prior to passing traffic between the sites. The VPN 3000 devices pre-negotiate the LAN-to-LAN SAs such that traffic may pass immediately through the IPSec tunnel. Clearly, the permanently established full-mesh of IPSec SAs creates a scalability constraint for platforms with limited memory.

There are many trade-offs that the network architect must consider when building the full-mesh VPN. In this chapter, you've seen a few of the more critical design elements. One of the most challenging aspects of full-mesh VPNs built with IPSec is managing the IPSec proxy statements as the VPN evolves. As new sites or IP subnets are added, all of the other sites must be configured to accommodate the address ranges and IPSec termination points. The next section explores the use of GRE to simplify some of the configuration aspects of the full-mesh IPSec VPN.

GRE Model

As you saw demonstrated in the hub-and-spoke architecture, IPSec-protected GRE tunnels simplify the IPSec proxy statements by aggregating traffic flows into a single source/destination IP address pair. The same principles apply to the full-mesh model in which IPSec protects GRE. Even IP multicast and non-IP routing protocols may leverage the IPSec-protected GRE tunnel. As the size of the VPN grows, the configuration complexity still increases as $O(N^2)$; however, non-contiguous IP address ranges do not impact the IPSec proxy statements. The number of IPSec connections is bounded by $N(N-1)/2$. The configuration complexity is moved to the IP routing at each site. The protected IP address ranges are simply routed into the tunnels. In the absence of a dynamic routing protocol operating through the VPN tunnels, the number of static routes required is modeled as $N(N-1) + M(N-1)$, where N is the number of sites in the VPN and M is number of non-contiguous IP address ranges at any site. The full-mesh VPN using static routes over IPSec-protected GRE tunnels is twice as complex as the native IPSec tunnel model because all the adjacencies must be configured in both the routing plane and the IPSec peer statements. You can simplify the routing configuration by applying a dynamic routing protocol over the GRE tunnels.

Now, to consider the impact of a dynamic routing plane through the GRE tunnels. The introduction of dynamic routing through the GRE tunnels minimizes the configuration complexity by eliminating the static routes. Assuming the routing protocol is capable of dynamically building routing adjacencies through the tunnels (for example, EIGRP, OSPF, and RIPv2), the only configuration needed is configuring the IPSec connections for the GRE tunnel endpoints and applying the routing protocol to the tunnel interface. Figure 5-13 shows how the routing is modified based on the association of a routing protocol to the tunnel interfaces.

Figure 5-12 *Full-Mesh GRE with Static Routes*

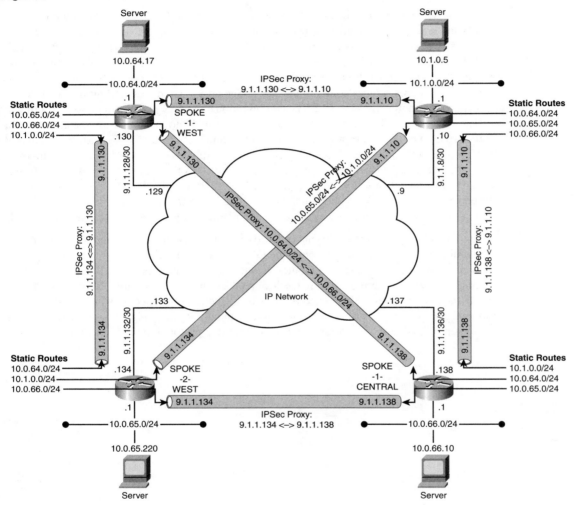

Figure 5-13   *Full-Mesh GRE with Dynamic Routing*

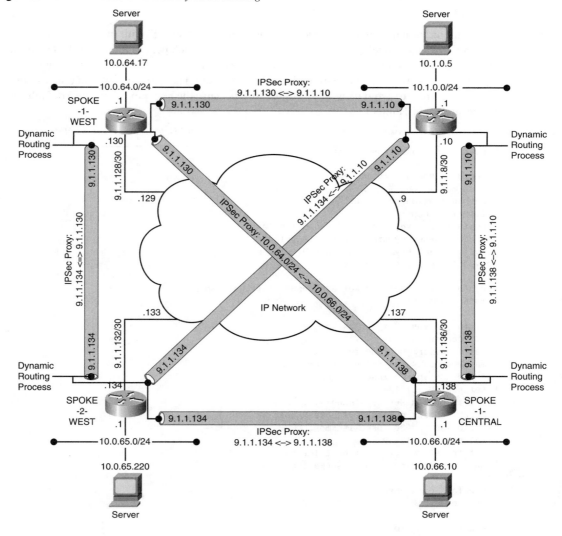

Figure 5-13 highlights the fact that an IGP routing process will have to evaluate many potential paths when building the routing topology. Each router in the full-mesh VPN must build a shortest path tree that includes every path available between every router in the VPN. Of course, almost all of these paths are discarded because the router eventually converges on the path that is directly established between the two routers. In all likelihood, the loss of a direct path between two routers means that the remote peer is off the network and all the other potential paths are invalid as well. The full-mesh IGP topology places an extreme load on small VPN routers due to the computational complexity.

The configuration listing in Example 5-35 shows how the "spoke" with full-mesh connectivity requires a unique tunnel, crypto map, and access list for each peer in the network. The route process is bound to the entire set of tunnel interfaces such that protected addresses are dynamically propagated and learned through the tunnels. The explicit route statements are required in order to avoid recursive routing loops because the hub will propagate a default route to the spoke via Tunnel0.

Example 5-35 *Full-Mesh GRE Spoke Configuration with Dynamic Routing and Default Route via the Hub*

```
spoke-1-west#show running-config
!
crypto isakmp policy 10
 hash md5
 authentication pre-share
 lifetime 3600
crypto isakmp key cisco address 9.1.1.10
crypto isakmp key cisco address 9.1.1.134
crypto isakmp key cisco address 9.1.1.138
crypto isakmp keepalive 10
!
crypto ipsec transform-set esp-tunnel-internet esp-des esp-md5-hmac
 mode transport
!
crypto map vpn 10 ipsec-isakmp
 set peer 9.1.1.10
 set transform-set esp-tunnel-internet
 match address gre-tunnel-vpn-gw1-east
crypto map vpn 20 ipsec-isakmp
 set peer 9.1.1.134
 set transform-set esp-tunnel-internet
 match address gre-tunnel-spoke-2-west
crypto map vpn 30 ipsec-isakmp
 set peer 9.1.1.138
 set transform-set esp-tunnel-internet
 match address gre-tunnel-spoke-1-central
!
interface Ethernet0
 ip address 10.0.64.1 255.255.255.0
!
interface Tunnel0
 ip unnumbered Ethernet0
 tunnel source 9.1.1.130
 tunnel destination 9.1.1.10
 crypto map vpn
interface Tunnel1
 ip unnumbered Ethernet0
 tunnel source 9.1.1.130
 tunnel destination 9.1.1.134
 crypto map vpn
interface Tunnel2
```

Example 5-35 *Full-Mesh GRE Spoke Configuration with Dynamic Routing and Default Route via the Hub (Continued)*

```
 ip unnumbered Ethernet0
 tunnel source 9.1.1.130
 tunnel destination 9.1.1.138
 crypto map vpn
!
interface Serial0
 ip address 9.1.1.130 255.255.255.252
 crypto map vpn
!
router eigrp 100
 network 10.0.64.0 0.0.0.255
!
ip route 9.1.1.10 255.255.255.252 9.1.1.129
ip route 9.1.1.132 255.255.255.252 9.1.1.129
ip route 9.1.1.136 255.255.255.252 9.1.1.129
!
ip access-list extended gre-tunnel-vpn-gw1-east
 permit gre host 9.1.1.130 host 9.1.1.10
ip access-list extended gre-tunnel-spoke-2-west
 permit gre host 9.1.1.130 host 9.1.1.134
ip access-list extended gre-tunnel-spoke-1-central
 permit gre host 9.1.1.130 host 9.1.1.138
```

The simplification of this configuration does not come without a cost. With dynamic routing through the tunnels, the routing adjacencies and IPSec SAs are always established. This requires every site to have its entire set of configured IPSec SAs active. In addition, the routing adjacencies require state management that places additional processing burdens on the processor. These routing design constraints are similar to those incurred when implementing a full-mesh VPN using a classic FR/ATM network. The number of routing and IPSec adjacencies that any given site can simultaneously maintain provides an upper bound for the size of the VPN. The route calculation functions are fairly processor intensive, especially given the number of shortest path trees that a router must evaluate. Dynamic routing protocols such as EIGRP and OSPF provide a rapid means of convergence and fault detection. A large full-mesh network with link-state routing protocols is sensitive to IPSec failures. An excessively large number of routers and paths may extend the initialization or convergence time, making the network unusable. Extreme caution is advised when designing a full-mesh network that approaches one of the router's maximum limits (for example, IKE, IPSec, routing adjacencies, or interfaces).

The full-mesh IPSec-protected GRE network does support Internet access with or without split tunneling. Split tunneling allows the IPSec tunnel endpoints to use the default route to the backbone whereas the private addresses are propagated using dynamic routing over the GRE tunnels. A design that does not use split tunneling requires propagation of the default route from the designated Internet access router. Other routers that receive the default route through the GRE tunnel will need a more explicit path for their IPSec peer IP address that does not use the GRE tunnel in order to avoid recursive routing.

The next chapter presents methods for building more scalable IPSec networks that take advantage of dynamic routing topology. It is evident at this point that the persistent full-mesh of IGP neighbor establishment should be avoided. Likewise, you will have to address the routing protocols limitations with the breadth and depth of the shortest path tree calculations in order for the system to scale to hundreds or thousands of sites.

Summary

One of the most challenging aspects of designing an IPSec VPN is choosing an appropriate architectural model. This chapter has presented a variety of architectural models in order to highlight the advantages and disadvantages of each. When selecting one model over another, network designers must choose among tradeoffs, paying close attention to simplification of the configuration and processing efficiency. The combination of these two attributes enables the design of scalable IPSec VPNs. It is also notable that the architectural models are not necessarily mutually exclusive. A large VPN is likely to have different service requirements when comparing large branch offices to small branch offices. For example, the network architect may elect to use a client connectivity model for small home offices while using hub-and-spoke GRE-protected tunnels for large branch office sites. In fact, these functions may be integrated on a single hub platform. Of course, the aggregate requirements must be met on the integrated platform. Integration of various architectural models on a common platform may be necessary for smaller VPNs. In contrast, dedicating a VPN gateway for each architectural model may be economically justified within a large VPN in order to enable scalability. Now that you have seen how to design large-scale VPNs, reliability of the VPN is of paramount importance. In the next chapter, you'll be introduced to methods for achieving fault tolerance in the architectural models discussed in this chapter.

CHAPTER 6

Designing Fault-Tolerant IPSec VPNs

Chapter 2, "IPSec Overview," and Chapter 3, "Enhanced IPSec Features," presented the fundamental concepts of IPSec. Chapter 5, "IPSec VPN Architectures," covered IPSec VPN architectural models at a conceptual level. In the next few chapters, you will focus on the design aspects of IPSec and begin to apply mechanisms and protocols you have learned in building real-life IPSec VPNs. In this chapter, you will explore mechanisms and architectures for fault-tolerant IPSec VPN design.

Link Fault Tolerance

Because VPN data networks are a critical element of the overall business process, you must ensure that the VPN provides a reliable service to users and their applications. This section focuses on designing fault-tolerant networks. A fault-tolerant VPN is a network that is resilient to changes in the routing paths that may be due to hardware, software, or path failures between the VPN ingress and egress points, including access to the VPN.

One of the primary rules of fault-tolerant network design is that there is no such thing as a cookie-cutter design that can be applied to all networks. You can, however, focus on VPN fault-tolerant design principles, which are dictated by the goals and objectives of the network. In many cases, the design might be more driven by economic factors than technical reasoning. Similarly, the design of fault-tolerant IPSec VPN networks depends on what faults the VPN needs to be able to withstand. Let's start by looking at the types of faults that can happen in an IPSec VPN, and look at how to design a VPN that is tolerant to these failures.

You know from previous chapters that IPSec uses a peer-to-peer model that assumes the peers are reachable via an IP path provided by the network connecting the two peers. Figure 6-1 shows a basic IPSec VPN connecting two sites.

Figure 6-1 *IPSec Peer Relationship*

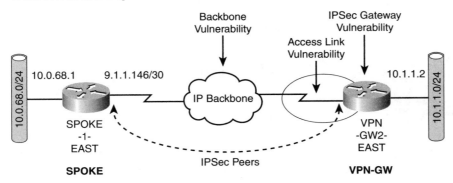

The model in the figure shows which of the components of the IPSec VPN are susceptible to failures and examines mechanisms to design fault-tolerant VPNs. From a fault-tolerance perspective, the IPSec VPN can be broken down into the following components:

- The backbone IP network, connecting the sites of the VPN
- Access link—The link that connects the IPSec gateway to the IP backbone
- The IPSec gateway itself

Backbone Network Fault Tolerance

The backbone network, connecting the sites of an IPSec VPN, can be the public Internet, a private Layer 2 network, or a single service provider IP network. This network may be owned and operated by an organization other than the owner of the IPSec VPN. It is usually built to be fault tolerant to link and IP routing failures within the network. IPSec protocols simply use this backbone for transport and inherently use the IP packet-routing functions provided by this network. In many cases, the IPsec VPN designers have no control over the backbone IP fault tolerance capabilities. We will focus our attention on those components where we can affect fault tolerance – the VPN gateways.

NOTE   Because an entire book can be written on the fault-tolerant design principles of this backbone and it is not the subject of this book, the design rules and mechanisms to be used in the backbone are not covered here. If you are interested in learning more about this topic, you may wish to reference books published on this subject, including *Fault-Tolerant IP and MPLS Networks*, by Iftekhar Hussain (Cisco Press, 2004)

Access Link Fault Tolerance

Figure 6-1 showed the access link terminating directly on the IPSec gateway. Note that this is a conceptual representation, and it may not look like this in a real network. Figure 6-2 shows one common physical representation of a site.

Figure 6-2   *Typical IPSec VPN Site ConnectivityI*

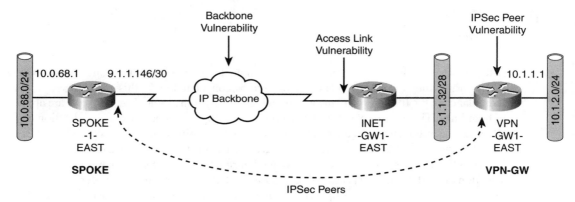

In this figure, the access link from the backbone terminates on an IP gateway (INET-GW1-EAST) router that connects the site to the backbone. The IPSec gateway (VPN-GW1-EAST) that terminates IPSec from the remote site is a physically separate entity that is responsible for the IPSec functions. In this model, the INET-GW1-EAST router is the general-purpose gateway router to the site; connectivity to this site is obviously broken if the access link between the INET-GW router and the backbone goes down. One simple mechanism to protect from this type of failure is adding a second access link from the INET-GW to the backbone. In addition to this simple scheme, there are many more ways to make this design fault tolerant to link and node failures of the INET-GW. This is a generic IP network design issue—as IPSec designers, we won't dwell on this element. The INET-GW, just like the backbone network, simply provides IP transport to the IPSec gateway. For all discussions in this chapter, we will use the conceptual representation of the IPSec VPN shown in Figure 6-1.

So far, we have discussed what we will not cover in this chapter; now, let's explore components that we will address with respect to IPSec fault-tolerant design. From an IPSec point of view, the chapter will cover two points of failure to provide a fault-tolerant IPSec VPN site. The first point of failure is the access link that terminates on the IPSec gateway (VPN-GW1-WEST). The second point of failure is the gateway itself, and the chapter addresses the VPN-GW1-WEST gateway failure in the peer redundancy section. This section, focuses on designing the site to withstand access link failures.

The most obvious solution to the access link failure is shown in Figure 6-3. Adding a second link to terminate on VPN-GW1-WEST and enabling both links for IPSec certainly improves the fault tolerance.

Figure 6-3 *Redundant IPSec Access Links*

Although the solution is, conceptually, quite simple, there are some interesting "twists" in the IPSec forwarding and control plane that need to be considered make this work. IPSec redundancy in the forwarding plane will be achieved only if the same IPSec policies are applied to both links. The control plane (IKE) is a bit more complicated because the application of IPSec on the redundant links creates two possible IKE identities for VPN-GW1-WEST. Recall from Chapter 2, "IPSec Overview," that the IKE process establishes IPSec connectivity and validates the peer based on the identity provided during the initial IKE exchange. Therefore, the selection of an IKE identity is critical in building an IKE relationship with a peer. The designer may choose to create either multiple IKE identities or a single IKE identity. In the next sections, we explore the implications of choosing either of these identity models.

Multiple IKE Identities

You know, from previous chapters, that the IKE identity of an initiator is derived from the source IP address in the initial IKE message. The initiator knows the IKE identity of its peer from the "set peer" configuration. In Figure 6-3, the VPN-GW1-WEST has two access links enabled for IPSec, and either of these access link IP addresses can be configured on SPOKE-1-WEST as the IKE identity of the VPN-GW1-WEST using the set peer command. In the multiple IKE identity model, both access link IP addresses are configured on SPOKE-1-WEST as IKE identities of VPN-GW1-WEST. When SPOKE-1-WEST initiates IKE negotiation, the first peer IP address is used by IKE and becomes VPN-GW1-WEST's IKE identity for this peer. If this IKE SA times out during the negotiation, the second IP address becomes the IKE identity of the VPN-GW1-WEST.

Example 6-1 shows the configuration of the IPSec peers in Figure 6-3.

Example 6-1 *IPSec Peer with Multiple IKE Identities*

```
VPN-GW1-WEST
crypto isakmp policy 10
 hash md5
 authentication pre-share
crypto isakmp key cisco address 9.1.1.130
crypto isakmp keepalive 60
!
crypto ipsec transform-set esp-tunnel esp-des esp-md5-hmac
```

Example 6-1   *IPSec Peer with Multiple IKE Identities (Continued)*

```
!
crypto map vpn 10 ipsec-isakmp
 set peer 9.1.1.130
 set transform-set esp-tunnel
 match address esp-tunnel-list
!
interface Serial1/0:0
 ip address 9.1.1.22 255.255.255.252
 crypto map vpn
!
interface Serial1/1:0
 ip address 9.1.1.26 255.255.255.252
 crypto map vpn
!
!
ip access-list extended esp-tunnel-list
 permit ip 10.0.0.0 0.255.255.255 10.0.64.0 0.0.0.255
```
```
SPOKE-1-WEST
crypto isakmp policy 10
 hash md5
 authentication pre-share
crypto isakmp key cisco address 9.1.1.22
crypto isakmp key cisco address 9.1.1.26
crypto isakmp keepalive 60
!
crypto ipsec transform-set esp-tunnel esp-des esp-md5-hmac
!
crypto map vpn 10 ipsec-isakmp
 set peer 9.1.1.26
 set peer 9.1.1.22
 set transform-set esp-tunnel
 match address esp-tunnel-list
!
interface Ethernet0
 ip address 10.0.64.1 255.255.255.0
!
interface Serial0
 ip address 9.1.1.130 255.255.255.252
 crypto map vpn
!
!
ip access-list extended esp-tunnel-list
 permit ip 10.0.64.0 0.0.0.255 10.0.0.0 0.255.255.255
```

Note the two set peer statements on SPOKE-1-WEST's crypto map configuration. The order of the set peer statements on the spoke is important, because it is the order of the statements that determines which IKE identity will be used by the spoke for the first IKE initialization. Step through the process of the peer establishment and see how IKE SAs and IPSec SAs are set up in this model; for this example, assume the IKE is initiated by SPOKE-1-WEST to VPN-GW1-WEST.

1 Interesting traffic that matches the IPSec policy on SPOKE-1-WEST triggers an IKE connection toward VPN-GW1-WEST.

2 The IKE message in step 1 uses the IP address from the first set peer statement on SPOKE-1-WEST (9.1.1.26) as the IKE identity of VPN-GW1-WEST. The IKE message is destined to this IP address with a source address of the serial0 interface IP address (9.1.1.130).

3 The IKE packet is received by VPN-GW1-WEST and passed on for IKE processing.

4 The IKE response packet is built by VPN-GW1-WEST and is sent to the source IP address of the original IKE message (serial Serial0 IP address of SPOKE-1-WEST).

5 The IKE response is received by the spoke and processed.

Recall from Chapter 2, "IPSec Overview," that this completes phase, 1 of IKE and creates the IKE SAs on both peers. IKE phase 2 follows this phase and IPSec SAs are built on both the peers. So far, so good! Next, you'll see how IP routing configuration on VPN-GW1-WEST can add some interesting twists in the data plane.

It's possible that IP routing configuration on VPN-GW1-WEST is such that the access link used to send packets to SPOKE-1-WEST is not the same as the access link on which packets arrive from SPOKE-1-WEST to VPN-GW1-WEST. This is known as asymmetric routing, and it is not uncommon in a multi-path configuration. Let's see what effect asymmetric routing has on IPSec.

IKE phase 1 is unaffected by asymmetric routing. IKE phase 2 establishes the IPSec SAs between peers and binds them to the interface that matches the IKE identity. As an example, assume that SPOKE-1-WEST initiates IKE to VPN-GW1-WEST's serial1/1:0 IP address (9.1.1.26). Example 6-2 shows how the IKE and IPSec SAs look on VPN-GW1-WEST after IKE negotiation is complete between the two peers.

Example 6-2 *IKE and IPSec SA State for Distinct IKE Identities*

```
VPN-GW1-WEST IKE Status
Vpn-gw1-west# show crypto isakmp sa
dst              src              state           conn-id    slot
9.1.1.130        9.1.1.26         QM_IDLE              2        0


VPN-GW1-WEST IPSec Status
Vpn-gw1-west# show crypto ipsec sa

interface: Serial1/0:0
   Crypto map tag: vpn, local addr. 9.1.1.22

   local  ident (addr/mask/prot/port): (10.0.0.0/255.0.0.0/0/0)
   remote ident (addr/mask/prot/port): (10.0.64.0/255.255.255.0/0/0)
   current_peer: 9.1.1.130
     PERMIT, flags={origin_is_acl,}
    #pkts encaps: 0, #pkts encrypt: 0, #pkts digest 0
    #pkts decaps: , #pkts decrypt: 0, #pkts verify 0
```

Example 6-2   *IKE and IPSec SA State for Distinct IKE Identities (Continued)*

```
       #pkts compressed: 0, #pkts decompressed: 0
       #pkts not compressed: 0, #pkts compr. failed: 0, #pkts decompress failed: 0
       #send errors 0, #recv errors 0

        local crypto endpt.: 9.1.1.22, remote crypto endpt.: 9.1.1.130
        path mtu 1500, media mtu 1500
        current outbound spi: 0

        inbound esp sas:

        inbound ah sas:

        inbound pcp sas:

        outbound esp sas:

        outbound ah sas:

        outbound pcp sas:


interface: Serial1/1:0
    Crypto map tag: vpn, local addr. 9.1.1.26

    local  ident (addr/mask/prot/port): (10.0.0.0/255.0.0.0/0/0)
    remote ident (addr/mask/prot/port): (10.0.64.0/255.255.255.0/0/0)
    current_peer: 9.1.1.130
      PERMIT, flags={origin_is_acl,}
     #pkts encaps: 4, #pkts encrypt: 4, #pkts digest 4
     #pkts decaps: 4, #pkts decrypt: 4, #pkts verify 4
     #pkts compressed: 0, #pkts decompressed: 0
     #pkts not compressed: 0, #pkts compr. failed: 0, #pkts decompress failed: 0
     #send errors 6, #recv errors 0

      local crypto endpt.: 9.1.1.26, remote crypto endpt.: 9.1.1.130
      path mtu 1500, media mtu 1500
      current outbound spi: 8711A91

      inbound esp sas:
       spi: 0x4DC4EC6(81546950)
         transform: esp-des esp-md5-hmac ,
         in use settings ={Tunnel, }
         slot: 0, conn id: 2029, flow_id: 1, crypto map: vpn
         sa timing: remaining key lifetime (k/sec): (4607999/3117)
         IV size: 8 bytes
         replay detection support: Y

      inbound ah sas:

      inbound pcp sas:
```

continues

Example 6-2   *IKE and IPSec SA State for Distinct IKE Identities (Continued)*

```
outbound esp sas:
 spi: 0x8711A91(141630097)
   transform: esp-des esp-md5-hmac ,
   in use settings ={Tunnel, }
   slot: 0, conn id: 2030, flow_id: 2, crypto map: vpn
   sa timing: remaining key lifetime (k/sec): (4607999/3108)
   IV size: 8 bytes
   replay detection support: Y

outbound ah sas:

outbound pcp sas:
```

You see that the IPSec SA on VPN-GW1-WEST is bound to the Serial1/1:0 interface. You can derive this information from the output due to the fact that both the inbound and outbound SAs only exist on serial1/1:0.

Now, you see what happens in the forwarding plane. Remember, IP routing is asymmetric here, which means packets from SPOKE-1-WEST to VPN-GW1-WEST arrive on serial1/1:0, but packets from VPN-GW1-WEST to SPOKE-1-WEST will take interface Serial1/0:0. You know that the IPSec SAs on VPN-GW1-WEST are bound to serial1/1:0, therefore IPSec traffic traveling inbound to the gateway will be fine, but you have a problem for outbound traffic from VPN-GW1-WEST to SPOKE-1-WEST: There is no IPSec SA on serial1/0:0. Actually, things are not all that bad because there is a crypto-map on serial1/0:0 that has the same policy as the one on Serial1/1:0. Recall from Chapter 2, "IPSec Overview," that interesting traffic out of an interface will trigger IKE negotiation. As a result of this IKE negotiation, a new set of IKE and IPSec SAs, is initiated from VPN-GW1-WEST to SPOKE-1-WEST.

The spoke processes this new IKE SA and replaces IPSec SAs for this crypto map. This means that the spoke may have multiple IKE identities for the same VPN-GW. All this extra IKE and IPSec SA creation obviously means more memory usage on the peers, which is not desirable. Figure 6-4 illustrates this scenario.

Figure 6-4   *Asymmetric IKE Peering due to Fault-Tolerant Configuration*

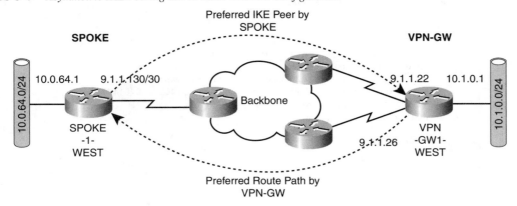

Figure 6-5   *Sequence of IKE Initialization for Asymmetric Routing*

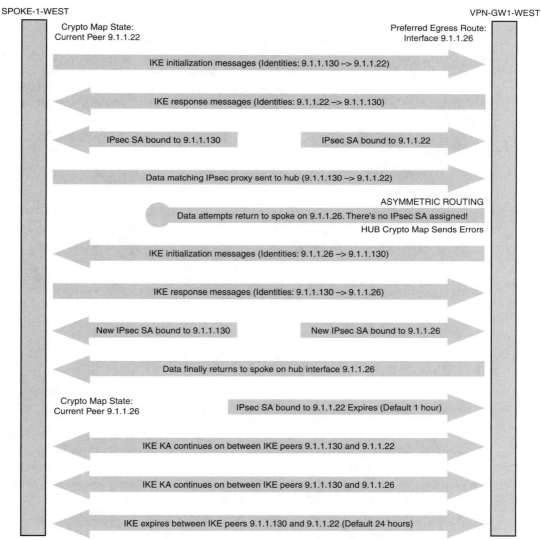

Even if there is no asymmetric routing and the primary link on the VPN-GW fails (assuming the remote peer detects three missing IKE keepalive messages), the remote peer initiates another IKE and IPSec SA with the VPN-GW, and the original IKE and IPSec SA associated with Serial 1/1:0 still remain in the VPN-GW1-WEST SADB until they time out. Therefore, this transient memory usage must be taken into account even without asymmetric routing in the multiple IKE identity model.

Multiple IKE Identities Associated with Dial Backup

Dial backup solutions introduce a slight modification to the previous scenario. Note in Figure 6-3 that the access link on the VPN-GW is protected, whereas the access link on the spoke is not protected. Dial backup solutions are a special case of multiple IKE identities in which both ends have unique IKE identities. Of course, the underlying premise is that the spoke can detect a failure in the primary path to the VPN-GW. There are many ways to do this (for example, use dialer watch on the spoke to detect local interface failure or watch for route removal due to primary path failure). Figure 6-6 shows the topology in which dial backup is used to provide access link redundancy.

Figure 6-6 *Multiple IKE Identities Using Dial Backup*

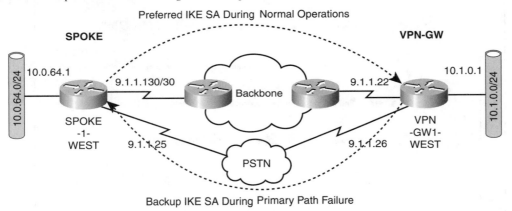

NOTE   Using dialer watch to monitor the availability of a local interface does not allow the spoke to detect the failure of the access link at the VPN-GW. If the access link fails, the spoke will persistently retry an IPSec connection via the backbone. Various methods exist for validating the primary path through the backbone. Examples include using BGP between the hub and spoke, building GRE over IPSec with an IGP routing protocol, or using an IPSec-aware probe on the spoke to monitor the viability of the backbone path. Upon detection of backbone path failure, the spoke transitions to the dial backup interface.

The important thing to remember is that the failure of the primary path causes the spoke to invoke a temporary backup connection via the PSTN (Public Switched Telephone Network) to the VPN-GW. Note from Figure 6-5 that the spoke and the VPN-GW have unique IP addresses on these dialer interfaces; hence, there are multiple IKE identities on both the spoke and VPN-GW.

One of the more important abilities when designing access link redundancy using dial backup is knowing when to tear down the backup link. IPSec will attempt to keep the dial backup link active with IKE keepalives (or the equivalent if GRE over IPSec is used over the dial backup interface). Because the cost of dial backup services can be quite high, the designer should be very careful to design a failback solution to avoid using the dial backup path more than necessary. Again, the same mechanisms used for primary path failure detection may be used to reset the conditions at the spoke such that the dial backup interface is no longer preferred.

Single IKE Identity

As the name suggests, in this model the VPN-GW is identified by all of its peers with a single IKE identity which is achieved by using a loopback address on the VPN-GW as the source IP address for IKE exchange messages.

NOTE   Any interface with an IPv4 address may be used as an IKE identity. The loopback interface is commonly chosen because it is always in an active state, whereas other interfaces are dependent upon the state of the media connection.

Figure 6-7 demonstrates the topology with the single IKE identity defined by a loopback interface.

Figure 6-7   *IPSec Gateway with a Single IKE Identity*

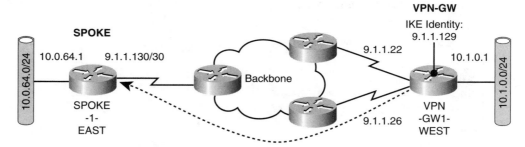

Figure 6-7 shows that a single IKE identity associated with the loopback interface (9.1.1.129) may be used for an IKE security association over either interface 9.1.1.22 or 9.1.1.26. Although a single IKE SA is shared by the interfaces, unique IPSec SAs must be established for the respective interfaces.

The biggest advantages of this scheme are:

* Establishment of a single IKE connection with a given peer saves resources on the VPN-GW and makes troubleshooting easier. A common IKE SA will exist between the peers regardless of which interface is used. This minimizes instability during failover periods by reusing the existing IKE SA.

* Decoupling of the IKE connection from the state of the access link that terminates IPSec expedites the transition of the IPSec SA to an alternate interface. The IKE connection may be tied to the loopback interface whose state never goes down. In that case, IKE phase 1 does not need to be reestablished during failover periods.

Example 6-3 shows the hub VPN-GW1-WEST and the remote peer SPOKE-1-WEST. The configuration is essentially the same as the multiple IKE model except for the use of the loopback address.

Example 6-3   *IPSec Gateway with a Single IKE Identity*

```
VPN-GW1-WEST
crypto isakmp policy 10
 hash md5
 authentication pre-share
crypto isakmp key cisco address 9.1.1.14
!
crypto ipsec transform-set esp-tunnel esp-des esp-md5-hmac
!
crypto map vpn local-address Loopback0
crypto map vpn 10 ipsec-isakmp
 set peer 9.1.1.130
 set transform-set esp-tunnel
 match address esp-tunnel-list
!
interface Loopback0
 ip address 9.1.1.49 255.255.255.252
!
interface Ethernet4/0
 ip address 10.1.0.1 255.255.255.0
!
interface Serial1/0:0
 ip address 9.1.1.22 255.255.255.252
 crypto map vpn
!
interface Serial1/1:0
 ip address 9.1.1.26 255.255.255.252
 crypto map vpn
!
router bgp 100
 no synchronization
 network 9.1.1.48 mask 255.255.255.252
 neighbor 9.1.1.21 remote-as 50
 neighbor 9.1.1.25 remote-as 50
!
ip access-list extended esp-tunnel-list
 permit ip 10.0.0.0 0.255.255.255 10.0.64.0 0.0.0.255
SPOKE-1-WEST
crypto isakmp policy 10
 hash md5
 authentication pre-share
crypto isakmp key cisco address 9.1.1.49
!
crypto ipsec transform-set esp-tunnel esp-des esp-md5-hmac
!
crypto map vpn 10 ipsec-isakmp
 set peer 9.1.1.49
 set transform-set esp-tunnel
```

Example 6-3 *IPSec Gateway with a Single IKE Identity (Continued)*

```
 match address esp-tunnel-list
!
interface Ethernet0
 ip address 10.0.64.1 255.255.255.0
!
interface Serial0
 ip address 9.1.1.130 255.255.255.252
 crypto map vpn
!
!
ip access-list extended esp-tunnel-list
 permit ip 10.0.64.0 0.0.0.255 10.0.0.0 0.255.255.255
```

In this configuration, both access links advertise IP reachability of the loopback interface on the VPN-GW. In the event of failure of one of the access links, the loopback is still reachable from VPN-GW's peers. The redundant link will maintain the established IKE and IPSec security associations.

On the VPN-GW, both access links have the same crypto map configuration as in the multiple IKE model. Cisco IOS IPSec implementation causes an interesting and useful effect in this model. IOS mirrors all the IPSec SAs on both the access links, even if they were originally set up on one of the access links. In the given example, if IP routing dictates that the path to and from a remote peer to the VPN-GW's loopback is via Serial 1/1:0, the IPSec SAs that are created will be replicated on all access links where the crypto map is applied. In the multiple IKE model, the IKE and IPSec SAs are associated only on the interface where IKE packets arrived in the VPN-GW from the spoke. In the scenario of a failed primary access link, IPSec SAs need not be negotiated with the remote peer; they pre-exist. The IKE SA in this model is also not renegotiated if one of the access links goes down because the loopback (IKE identity of the VPN-GW) never goes down.

Example 6-4 shows the IKE and IPSec SAs on VPN-GW1-WEST. The inbound and outbound secure parameter indices (SPIs) of both serial interfaces are identical. This demonstrates that encrypted packets arriving on either interface may be decrypted with the existing IPSec SA rather than requiring the reestablishment of a new IPSec on the alternate interface.

Example 6-4 *VPN-GW1-WEST Crypto State*

```
Vpn-gw1-west# show crypto ipsec sa map vpn

interface: Serial1/0:0
    Crypto map tag: vpn, local addr. 9.1.1.49

   local  ident (addr/mask/prot/port): (10.0.0.0/255.0.0.0/0/0)
   remote ident (addr/mask/prot/port): (10.0.64.0/255.255.255.0/0/0)
   current_peer: 9.1.1.130
     PERMIT, flags={origin_is_acl,}
    #pkts encaps: 7, #pkts encrypt: 7, #pkts digest 7
```

continues

Example 6-4   *VPN-GW1-WEST Crypto State (Continued)*

```
       #pkts decaps: 7, #pkts decrypt: 7, #pkts verify 7
       #pkts compressed: 0, #pkts decompressed: 0
       #pkts not compressed: 0, #pkts compr. failed: 0, #pkts decompress failed: 0
       #send errors 0, #recv errors 0

        local crypto endpt.: 9.1.1.49, remote crypto endpt.: 9.1.1.130
        path mtu 1500, media mtu 1500
        current outbound spi: 178108C4

        inbound esp sas:
         spi: 0x9393CB47(2475936583)
            transform: esp-des esp-md5-hmac ,
            in use settings ={Tunnel, }
            slot: 0, conn id: 2029, flow_id: 1, crypto map: vpn
            sa timing: remaining key lifetime (k/sec): (4607997/3105)
            IV size: 8 bytes
            replay detection support: Y

        inbound ah sas:

        inbound pcp sas:

        outbound esp sas:
         spi: 0x178108C4(394332356)
            transform: esp-des esp-md5-hmac ,
            in use settings ={Tunnel, }
            slot: 0, conn id: 2030, flow_id: 2, crypto map: vpn
            sa timing: remaining key lifetime (k/sec): (4607998/3096)
            IV size: 8 bytes
            replay detection support: Y

        outbound ah sas:

        outbound pcp sas:


interface: Serial1/1:0
    Crypto map tag: vpn, local addr. 9.1.1.49

    local  ident (addr/mask/prot/port): (10.0.0.0/255.0.0.0/0/0)
    remote ident (addr/mask/prot/port): (10.0.64.0/255.255.255.0/0/0)
    current_peer: 9.1.1.130
      PERMIT, flags={origin_is_acl,}
     #pkts encaps: 7, #pkts encrypt: 7, #pkts digest 7
     #pkts decaps: 7, #pkts decrypt: 7, #pkts verify 7
     #pkts compressed: 0, #pkts decompressed: 0
     #pkts not compressed: 0, #pkts compr. failed: 0, #pkts decompress failed: 0
     #send errors 0, #recv errors 0

       local crypto endpt.: 9.1.1.49, remote crypto endpt.: 9.1.1.130
```

Example 6-4   *VPN-GW1-WEST Crypto State (Continued)*

```
        path mtu 1500, media mtu 1500
        current outbound spi: 178108C4

        inbound esp sas:
         spi: 0x9393CB47(2475936583)
            transform: esp-des esp-md5-hmac ,
            in use settings ={Tunnel, }
            slot: 0, conn id: 2029, flow_id: 1, crypto map: vpn
            sa timing: remaining key lifetime (k/sec): (4607997/3096)
            IV size: 8 bytes
            replay detection support: Y

        inbound ah sas:

        inbound pcp sas:

        outbound esp sas:
         spi: 0x178108C4(394332356)
            transform: esp-des esp-md5-hmac ,
            in use settings ={Tunnel, }
            slot: 0, conn id: 2030, flow_id: 2, crypto map: vpn
            sa timing: remaining key lifetime (k/sec): (4607998/3096)
            IV size: 8 bytes
            replay detection support: Y

        outbound ah sas:

        outbound pcp sas:
```

The IPSec SA is replicated on all of the interfaces where the crypto map is applied and is associated with the IKE. The connection state might be considered stateful across all the interfaces. As a result, the memory and processing resources are conserved. In addition, the end-to-end traffic flow may be restored as fast as the routing protocols converge between the two IPSec peers. Once convergence occurs between the two peers, the IPSec flow using the IKE identities as the IPSec headers is also restored.

CAUTION   If the routing protocol convergence takes longer than the IKE dead peer detection, then the IKE SAs expire and the memory resources allocated to the IPSec SA are removed. Care must be taken to ensure that routing transients don't induce repeated disruptions of the IPSec processes. You accomplish this by tuning the routing protocols between the IPSec peers so they converge faster than IKE detects a dead peer or by extending the dead peer detection interval of IKE such that the routing protocol can converge first.

Single IKE Identity Using Multi-link PPP on the Access Links

A variation of the single IKE identity model can be implemented if the access links that terminate on the IPSec gateway are members of a multi-link PPP bundle (MLPPP). MLPPP allows multiple PPP links terminating on a router to appear as a single logical access link from a Layer 3 perspective; the multiple links may be used to provide link redundancy. Although the primary function of MLPPP is to provide load balancing across the multiple PPP links, a secondary benefit is the resiliency created by the additional links, which can be exploited. When MLPPP is used, individual links in the MLPPP bundle may become active or inactive without changing the state of the MLPPP interface. With IPSec associated with the MLPPP interface as opposed to the individual interfaces in the MLPPP bundle, the IPSec state is decoupled from the state of the individual links in the MLPPP bundle. The use of MLPPP is shown in Figure 6-8.

Figure 6-8 *IPSec Associated with an MLPPP Interface*

In this configuration, the gateway is identified to its peers by a single IP address (the address configured on the multi-link interface) similar to the loopback interface in the single IKE identity model. Example 6-5 shows the configuration of the VPN-GW shown in Figure 6-8.

Example 6-5 *VPN-GW1-WEST Multi-link PPP Bundle*

```
interface Multilink1
 ip address 9.1.1.22 255.255.255.252
 ppp multilink
 no ppp multilink fragmentation
 multilink-group 1
 crypto map vpn
!
interface Serial1/0:0
 encapsulation ppp
 no fair-queue
 ppp multilink
 multilink-group 1
!
interface Serial1/1:0
 encapsulation ppp
 no fair-queue
 ppp multilink
 multilink-group 1
!
```

The loss of a single PPP link in a multi-link bundle on the VPN-GW does not affect end-to-end IP connectivity from the remote peer. The IPSec peer relationship between the remote peer (SPOKE-1-WEST) and the hub (VPN-GW1-WEST) remains active and, more importantly, the IKE and IPSec SAs are not renegotiated. Note also that the IPSec configuration is simplified because the same crypto map is applicable to all the physical and virtual interfaces associated with the link bundle.

Access Link Fault Tolerance Summary

Our focus on fault-tolerant link access models has addressed one of the most common failure elements in a VPN—the access link. A variety of methods has been presented to support the recovery of an access link failure. As each method was presented, the level of resiliency increased because of the inclusion of additional redundancy elements. Adding redundant elements forces the designer to accommodate more complex failure modes, which in turn, forces a compromise between scale, convergence speed, simplicity, and performance. We briefly described scalability constraints such as duplication of IKE and IPSec SAs; convergence is dependent upon the link status state management models such as keepalive messages, link signaling, and resilient routing protocols. Although peer-to-peer recovery mechanisms provide resiliency to link failures, these mechanisms do not address the failure of a peer or the state of prefix reachability beyond a remote peer. The next section explores peer redundancy scenarios that are applicable to IPSec VPNs. We will address the reachability of prefixes beyond a remote peer in subsequent sections.

IPSec Peer Redundancy

In the "Access Link Fault Tolerance" section of this chapter, we discussed fault tolerance to access link failures. Access link redundancy is sufficient as long as the IPSec peer itself does not fail. In this section, you look into fault-tolerance mechanisms to recover from IPSec node failures. Node failures can be unintentionally induced due to hardware or software issues, or intentionally induced for software upgrades or maintenance. Whatever the reason, IPSec nodal failure affects the connectivity to IPSec peers connected to the affected node. To preserve the integrity of the VPN connections, various peer redundancy models are presented and each model's advantages and disadvantages are highlighted. The review begins with the simple peer redundancy model.

Simple Peer Redundancy Model

The simplest technique to protect against IPSec node failure is adding a second node. Figure 6-9 shows this model.

Figure 6-9 *Redundant IPSec Peer Gateways*

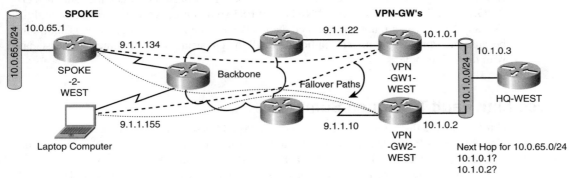

The peer redundancy model depicted in Figure 6-9 shows two VPN-GW peers for the spoke SPOKE-2-WEST. At any given time, only one VPN-GW is active; the other is in standby mode. The VPN gateway that is currently supporting the IPSec processing is active. The standby gateway monitors the active gateway for proper operation; therefore, it has no IPSec state associated with its interfaces. As in the multiple IKE identities model, the order of the set peer configuration statements on the spoke determines the preferred VPN-GW peer. The SPOKE-2-WEST router will first attempt to build an IPSec SA to the VPN-GW1-WEST. Should the spoke's connection attempt fail on this path, the SPOKE-2-WEST router attempts to build an IPSec SA using the same policies to VPN-GW2-WEST.

NOTE   A router with multiple set peer statements caches the peer address that successfully completed the last IPSec connection. Subsequent IPSec connections initiated from this peer use the cached peer as the first attempted peer regardless of the order of set peer statements.

Just as in the access link redundancy model, for this model to work, the IPSec policies and transforms applied using the crypto-map configuration should match on both VPN-GW peers. Example 6-6 shows the configuration of the spoke.

Example 6-6   *SPOKE-2-WEST Ordered Set of Peers for Hub Site Peer Redundancy*

```
crypto isakmp key cisco address 9.1.1.22
crypto isakmp key cisco address 9.1.1.10
crypto isakmp keepalive 10
!
crypto ipsec transform-set esp-tunnel-internet esp-des esp-md5-hmac
!
crypto map vpn 10 ipsec-isakmp
 set peer 9.1.1.22
```

Example 6-6   *SPOKE-2-WEST Ordered Set of Peers for Hub Site Peer Redundancy (Continued)*

```
 set peer 9.1.1.10
 set transform-set esp-tunnel-internet
 match address esp-tunnel-list
!
ip access-list extended esp-tunnel-list
 permit ip 10.0.65.0 0.0.0.255 10.0.0.0 0.255.255.255
 !
```

Because either VPN-GW may serve as the active gateway, an interesting problem must be resolved. Traffic returning to the spoke from the HQ-WEST router must be sent to the active VPN-GW; otherwise, asymmetric routing may occur. Let's review the issues asymmetric IP routing may cause in this model. Asymmetric routing occurs when reachability for prefixes behind the VPN-GWs from the spoke is via VPN-GW1-WEST and reachability for prefixes behind the spoke is via VPN-GW2-WEST. The configuration of the spoke, as shown in the example, will cause IKE to be initiated to the VPN-GW1-WEST (9.1.1.22). The VPN-GW1-WEST responds to the spoke's IKE message, IKE negotiation proceeds, and the IKE establishes IPSec SAs on the spoke and the VPN-GW1-WEST. So far, so good! Now, when data packets are sent from the spoke to the hub, the packets arrive into VPN-GW1-WEST, get decrypted, and are routed into the HQ-WEST router.

Packets returning to the spoke will be directed via VPN-GW2-WEST—but all the IKE and IPSec SAs were previously established on VPN-GW1-WEST! The crypto-map configuration on VPN-GW2-WEST causes it to trigger IKE messages to the spoke. The spoke and VPN-GW2-WEST negotiate a new set of IKE and IPSec SAs. The spoke now has two sets of IKE and IPSec SAs. One associated with VPN-GW1-WEST and another set associated with VPN-GW2-WEST. For traffic returning from the spoke side to the gateway side, the spoke chooses the SA from which it last received packets. If HQ-WEST load balances packets across both VPN-GW1-WEST and VPN-GW2-WEST, packets will alternate using both sets of SAs in both directions. You will look at resolving the asymmetric routing and redundant resource consumption issue in a bit more detail in the section later in this chapter, "Peer Redundancy Using GRE." First, however, you will explore the fault-tolerance aspects of the simple peer redundancy.

Next, you'll see how fault tolerance to a VPN-GW failure works in this model. Assume that the active gateway for the spoke is currently VPN-GW1-WEST and the IKE and IPSec SAs are established between the spoke and the active gateway. Now, if the active gateway has a failure of some sort, the first thing the spoke must do is detect this failure. Failure of the active gateway to respond to three consecutive IKE keepalive messages signals the spoke that the active gateway has failed. Next, the spoke initiates a new set of IKE and IPSec SAs to the secondary gateway. Until the IKE and IPSec SAs are built, all traffic between sites will be lost. Another important point to bear in mind here is that there is no concept of pre-emption in IPSec fault tolerance. In other words, after the failure of VPN-GW1-WEST, the spoke now has IPSec sessions with VPN-GW2-WEST. When VPN-GW1-WEST recovers from a failure, the spoke may not revert back to VPN-GW1-WEST. Instead, the return path is determined by HQ-WEST's decision to route the packet to VPN-GW1-WEST or VPN-GW2-WEST. This means there may potentially be spokes whose current IPSec peer is VPN-GW1-WEST and others whose current active peer is VPN-GW2-WEST.

An interesting point of failure in the simple peer model is the failure of the private Ethernet interface on the active VPN-GW1-WEST. This failure may not be synchronized with the IPSec state because IKE keepalives will continue to be exchanged between the spoke and the active VPN-GW1-WEST. As far as the spoke is concerned, the VPN-GW1-WEST has not failed. Under this condition, all data packets that arrive from the spoke to the gateway will be sent into a black hole after decryption. A simple fix for this is to have redundant Ethernet links on the VPN-GW routers to the HQ-WEST router, an Ethernet link connecting the two VPN-GW routers together, or even better, a redundant link and a redundant HQ-WEST router, as shown in Figure 6-10.

Figure 6-10 *Resiliencies Through Redundant VPN-GW*

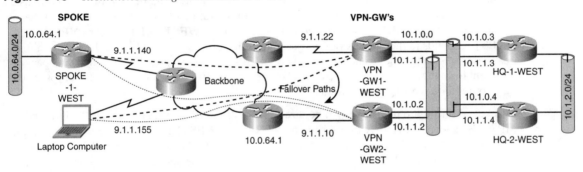

Although the addition of redundant links between the VPN-GWs and HQ router improves the resiliency of the peer redundancy, it does not reconcile the issue of asymmetric routing. Next, you will explore a couple of common methods that resolve the asymmetric routing issue and the IPSec black hole created when the VPN-GW Ethernet interface fails.

The asymmetric routing problem is reconciled fairly easily by routing mechanisms deployed on the VPN-GWs. One commonly used tool for simplifying route management is HSRP/VRRP. The HQ-WEST router may use a default route to a virtual IP address that is shared between the VPN-GWs on the private side. Because the VPN-GW's HSRP and IPSec state may not be synchronized, the same router may not be active for both HSRP and IPSec. The router serving as the active HSRP node may be forced to quickly establish IPSec connections when traffic returns to the spoke such that HSRP and IPSec are synchronized. Synchronization of HSRP and IPSec may occur rather quickly for a few spokes; however, a VPN design supporting hundreds or thousands of spokes may experience a longer delay as the VPN-GW, assuming the active IPSec role must rebuild all of the IKE and IPSec connections simultaneously. If fast recovery is required, this issue limits the scalability of our VPN design. Figure 6-11 demonstrates the use of HSRP on the VPN-GW's private interfaces.

Figure 6-11   *Resilient VPN-GW Routers using HSRP*

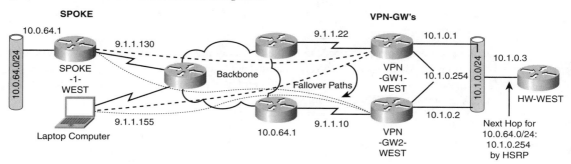

HSRP can be configured with or without pre-emption. Without HSRP pre-emption, the recovery of a preferred VPN-GW router will not force reconvergence. With HSRP pre-emption, the recovery of a preferred VPN-GW router will force reconvergence for all IPSec connections. Forcing pre-emption may cause unnecessary data loss while the preferred VPN-GW attempts to recover it's role as the primary gateway. Unless there is a compelling reason for the preferred gateway to resume control of the active sessions, the designer should not use pre-emption.

NOTE Dynamic IPSec crypto maps implemented on the VPN-GWs do not allow the creation of outbound IPSec SAs because the SPOKE peer identities are unknown. HSRP will not be able to force the synchronization of HSRP-active and IPSec-active VPN-GWs.

A second routing method that resolves the asymmetric routing problem is synchronizing the return routes for the spoke with the active IPSec VPN-GW. The implementation of Reverse Route Injection (RRI) on the VPN-GWs allows the active VPN-GW to propagate the spoke's protected route to the HQ-WEST router. With the return routes and IPSec synchronized on the VPN-GWs, the asymmetric routing problem is solved while improving the stability of the network. Unfortunately, you still have the potential for dropping data at the VPN-GW routers because the failure of the Ethernet interface prevents the VPN-GW from propagating the reverse route to the HQ-WEST router. A simple solution for this problem is to use RRI in conjunction with HSRP. The more specific routes from RRI are propagated to HQ-WEST, and the HSRP (virtual) IP address is used as the default gateway for HQ-WEST. Should the failed Ethernet on VPN-GW1-WEST prevent the reverse routes from propagating to the HQ-WEST router, the HQ-WEST router will direct traffic to the default route that is associated with the active HSRP node, VPN-GW2-WEST. The active HSRP node will force the IPSec state to synchronize such that the VPN-GW2-WEST router becomes the active IPSec peer for the spokes. Unfortunately, you are still subject to data black holes at the VPN-GWs if dynamic crypto maps are used. The next section will demonstrate a viable solution to address the dynamic crypto map scenario.

In summary, the simple IPSec peer redundancy model provides a reasonably efficient method of providing fault tolerance. However, you must add many auxiliary functions such as RRI and HSRP in order to prevent asymmetric routing and black holes. In the next section, you'll find out how to simplify the IPSec configuration and routing management.

Virtual IPSec Peer Redundancy Using HSRP

In the access redundancy section, we presented a method for using a single IKE identity to restore services when one of the VPN-GW's access links failed. A similar single IKE model is also possible for peer redundancy. Figure 6-12 shows the Virtual IPSec Peer Redundancy model.

Figure 6-12   *Virtual IPSec Peer Redundancy*

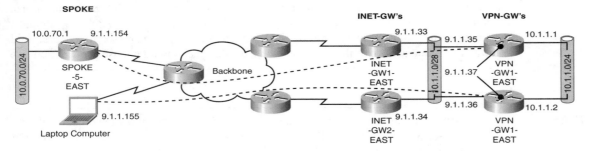

In this model, the VPN-GW peers are on a common public Ethernet using HSRP. The HSRP configuration makes one of the VPN-GW routers active and places the other one in standby at any given time. From an IPSec perspective, the spoke has an IPSec peer relationship with the HSRP virtual IP address owned by the active HSRP router. The advantages of this virtual peer model as compared to the simple peer model are as follows:

- Configuration of the remote peers is simpler. The remote peers now need only one set peer configuration; therefore, the order of the set peer statements is irrelevant.

- HSRP groups can be used to distribute spoke IPSec security associations across redundant peers. Some spokes might use one HSRP group virtual IP address as the peer, whereas other spokes use a second HSRP group virtual IP address as the peer.

- HSRP can track the state of another interface on the VPN-GW (specifically the private Ethernet interface) and decide if the router needs to be active or standby.

- Reverse Route Injection (RRI) can be coupled with HSRP to provide a fault-tolerant IPSec VPN.

The important aspect to the virtual IPSec peer model is that the routing state and the crypto state are synchronized. This minimizes the potential for creating black holes where data is dropped during failures.

Example 6-7 and Example 6-8 show the configurations of the VPN-GW's in this model.

Example 6-7   *VPN-GW1-EAST Configuration*

```
crypto isakmp policy 10
 hash md5
 authentication pre-share
crypto isakmp key cisco address 9.1.1.138
!
!
crypto ipsec transform-set esp-tunnel esp-des esp-md5-hmac
!
crypto map vpn 10 ipsec-isakmp
 set peer 9.1.1.138
 set transform-set esp-tunnel
 match address esp-tunnel-list
!
interface FastEthernet0/0
 ip address 10.1.1.1 255.255.255.0
!
interface FastEthernet0/1
 ip address 9.1.1.35 255.255.255.240
 standby track Fa0/0
 standby 1 priority 100 preempt
 standby 1 ip 9.1.1.37
 crypto map vpn
!
ip access-list extended esp-tunnel-list
 permit ip 10.0.0.0 0.255.255.255 10.0.66.0 0.0.0.255
!
```

Example 6-8   *VPN-GW2-EAST Configuration*

```
crypto isakmp policy 10
 hash md5
 authentication pre-share
crypto isakmp key cisco address 9.1.1.138
!
!
crypto ipsec transform-set esp-tunnel esp-des esp-md5-hmac
!
crypto map vpn 10 ipsec-isakmp
 set peer 9.1.1.138
 set transform-set esp-tunnel
 match address esp-tunnel-list
!
interface Ethernet4/0
 ip address 10.1.1.2 255.255.255.0
!
```

continues

Example 6-8   *VPN-GW2-EAST Configuration*

```
interface Ethernet4/1
 ip address 9.1.1.36 255.255.255.240
 half-duplex
 standby 1 priority 50
 standby track Et4/0
 standby 1 ip 9.1.1.37
 crypto map vpn
!
ip access-list extended esp-tunnel-list
 permit ip 10.0.0.0 0.255.255.255 10.0.66.0 0.0.0.255
!
```

Notice the use of the standby track command, which refers to the private Ethernet interface configuration. With this command, the private interface can be tracked. If this interface goes down on the active VPN-GW, then the other VPN-GW automatically takes over, resulting in no black hole for data traffic. In fact, HSRP standby tracking can be used on both private and public Ethernet interfaces such that return routes and IPSec state may always be synchronized. If HSRP is only used on the public interfaces of the VPN-GWs, then RRI may be used to propagate the spoke's route prefix to the HQ-WEST router. Fortunately, the HSRP implementation on the public interface may track the private interfaces such that traffic does not end up in a black hole when the private Ethernet interfaces fail on the VPN-GWs.

IPSec Stateful Failover

We discussed the IPSec stateful failover mechanism in Chapter 3, "Enhanced IPSec Features." An interesting extension to the virtual IPSec peer model is its ability to provide stateful failover. As was just demonstrated, the configuration of HSRP on the public and private interfaces of both VPN-GWs forces the synchronization of IP routing and IPSec. But, without stateful failover, convergence in a large VPN will take quite some time when the active IPSec gateway fails. The delay is due to the fact that new IKE and IPSec SAs must be established between all the spokes and the new VPN-GW. The critical element that is missing for stateful failover is the exchange of the IKE and IPSec SA information between the redundant peers. Recall that the single IKE identity model for redundant access links allowed the SA information to be replicated on any interface where the crypto map was applied. With stateful failover, a control channel is used to replicate the same SA information to public interfaces of the peer that is serving as the standby HSRP node. The replication of SA information ensures that the standby HSRP router and standby IPSec peer have the necessary information to immediately assume the role of an active HSRP and active IPSec peer. In the stateful failover case, the IKE and IPSec SAs do not need to be reestablished, as described previously when discussing the virtual IPSec peer redundancy model. Figure 6-13 demonstrates the relationship of the routers for stateful failover.

Figure 6-13   *Stateful IPSec Failover Topology*

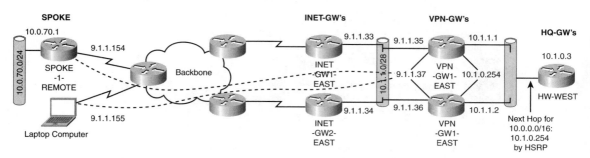

The stateful failover allows VPNs built with the virtual IPSec peer redundancy architecture to scale with minimal configuration complexity. We have eliminated asymmetric routing and black holes and enabled rapid recovery of IKE and IPSec SAs. On the other hand, we have increased the memory requirements on the VPN-GWs because they must manage all the IPSec SAs in the HSRP group even though a router is serving as a standby router. The reason for implementing stateful failover is to improve the convergence interval, which is dependent upon the time required for the standby VPN-GW to detect the loss of active VPN-GW. Once the standby router assumes the active role, the communications path is restored in both directions. Example 6-9 and Example 6-10 show the configuration of the VPN-GW's supporting stateful failover.

Example 6-9   *VPN-GW1-EAST Configuration*

```
!
ssp group 1
 remote 9.1.1.36
 redundancy public-ipsec
!
crypto isakmp policy 1
 authentication pre-share
crypto isakmp key spoke address 9.1.1.154
crypto isakmp ssp 1
!
crypto ipsec transform-set tunnel esp-des esp-sha-hmac
!
crypto map stateful ha replay-interval inbound 1000 outbound 1000
crypto map stateful 10 ipsec-isakmp
 set peer 9.1.1.154
 set transform-set tunnel
 match address remote
!

interface Ethernet2/0
```

continues

Example 6-9 *VPN-GW1-EAST Configuration (Continued)*

```
 ip address 10.1.1.2 255.255.255.0
 standby delay minimum 0 reload 0
 standby 2 track Ethernet2/2
 standby 2 ip 10.1.1.254
 standby 2 timers msec 250 1
 standby 2 preempt
 standby 2 name ipsec-private
 standby 2 track Ethernet2/2
!
interface Ethernet2/2
 ip address 9.1.1.35 255.255.255.240
 standby delay minimum 5 reload 0
 standby ip 9.1.1.37
 standby timers msec 250 1
 standby preempt
 standby name public-ipsec
 standby track Ethernet2/0
 crypto map stateful ssp 1
!
ip access-list extended remote
 permit ip 10.1.1.0 0.0.0.255 10.0.70.0 0.0.0.255
```

Example 6-10 *VPN-GW2-EAST Configuration*

```
!
ssp group 1
 remote 9.1.1.35
 redundancy public-ipsec
!
crypto isakmp policy 1
 authentication pre-share
crypto isakmp key spoke address 9.1.1.154
crypto isakmp ssp 1
!
crypto ipsec transform-set tunnel esp-des esp-sha-hmac
!
crypto map stateful ha replay-interval inbound 1000 outbound 1000
crypto map stateful 10 ipsec-isakmp
 set peer 9.1.1.154
 set transform-set tunnel
 match address remote
!
interface Ethernet1/2
 ip address 10.1.1.1 255.255.255.0
 standby delay minimum 0 reload 0
 standby 2 track Ethernet2/2
 standby 2 ip 10.1.1.254
 standby 2 timers msec 250 1
 standby 2 preempt
 standby 2 name ipsec-private
 standby 2 track Ethernet1/1
!
interface Ethernet1/1
```

Example 6-10 *VPN-GW2-EAST Configuration (Continued)*

```
ip address 9.1.1.36 255.255.255.240
standby delay minimum 5 reload 0
standby ip 9.1.1.37
standby timers msec 250 1
standby preempt
standby name public-ipsec
standby track Ethernet1/2
crypto map stateful ssp 1
!
ip access-list extended remote
 permit ip 10.1.1.0 0.0.0.255 10.0.70.0 0.0.0.255
```

The stateful failover configuration introduces quite a few new elements. You see that the ssp group is defined, which provides information about the node that you must share state with. You see that the crypto maps make reference to the ssp group such that you know which crypto state needs to synchronized with the stateful failover members. Finally, you see that the HSRP elements of the interfaces are augmented with the ssp group such that you know which interfaces need to be monitored for fault detection.

NOTE	Example 6-10 shows the IPSec stateful failover configuration using SSP. An alternate mechanism for IPSec stateful switchover, Stateful Switchover (SSO), was illustrated in Chapter 3, "Enhanced IPSec Features" in Example 3-7. Functionally, both achieve the same result. The SSP mechanism was developed specifically for IPSec stateful failover, whereas the SSO mechanism was developed under the framework of a more generic High Availability infrastructure which is used for providing stateful failover mechanisms for many other protocols in Cisco IOS such as OSPF, BGP, IP, and others in addition to IPSec. SSO is the recommended configuration method for stateful switchover for IPSec.

The configuration for stateful failover associates the control channel by name (that is, public-ipsec) between the redundant nodes to the HSRP profile names. The HSRP synchronizes the state of the necessary interfaces on both the private and public interfaces of the VPN-GW and, finally, the crypto map is associated with the stateful IPSec control channel. The combination of these elements allows the VPN-GW routers to maintain the proper state and provide a stateful virtual IPSec peer for all of the spokes associated with the IKE address.

The virtual IPSec peer redundancy model provides a robust means of fault tolerance. We have demonstrated how the VPN-GWs are able to present a single IPSec peer to the spokes, which simplifies the configuration of the spokes while enabling rapid recovery of failures associated with the VPN-GWs. One of the limitations with the IPSec model is the lack of support for multiple protocols. The next section describes an alternative peer redundancy method that enables robust fault tolerance while enabling multi-protocol support.

One of the more significant disadvantages to using HSRP is that it tracks only local failures (that is, interfaces). HSRP on the VPN-GWs is not able to track the viability of routing paths behind HQ-WEST. We will explore more comprehensive fault-tolerant methods when we associate routing protocols with the crypto state in subsequent sections. In addition, the use of the Gateway Load Balancing Protocol (GLBP) also mitigates the value of the using stateful IPSec failover because the load-balancing function directs traffic to both the active and the standby VPN-GW. The standby VPN gateway is not in a forwarding state, and therefore packets will be dropped on this VPN-GW.

Peer Redundancy Using GRE

Chapter 2, "IPSec Overview," demonstrated that GRE tunnels may be used for site-to-site IPSec tunnels. One of the many advantages of implementing GRE protected by IPSec is the ability to reflect the state of the IPSec connection in the router's routing table. The most common reason to use GRE for site-to-site IPSec connectivity is to provide dynamic routing capabilities between the sites. The routing decisions may be cached in the Cisco Express Forwarding (CEF) table for high-performance routing, tunneling, forwarding, and encryption. For this reason, a significant majority of the enterprise customers use GRE protected by IPSec. We may leverage this capability to provide peer redundancy. This feature can be used to provide IPSec peer redundancy as shown in Figure 6-14.

Figure 6-14 *IPSec Peer Redundancy with GRE Tunnels*

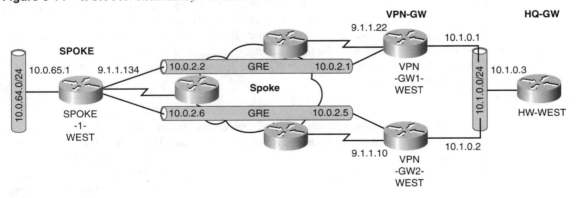

In this example, the SPOKE-2-WEST has two IPSec-protected GRE tunnels—one for each VPN-GW. At both the spoke and the VPN-GWs, IKE and IPSec SAs are created to protect the source and destination of the GRE tunnels. IPSec policies on both the VPN-GWs are configured to match protection policies for their respective GRE tunnel. The IP routing database on the spoke determines which GRE tunnel the traffic should take to reach the prefixes protected by the VPN-GWs. Meanwhile, the VPN-GWs learn of the spoke's protected prefix and then propagate that route to the HQ-WEST router. In most cases, both GRE tunnels from the spoke will be operational all the time, and therefore it does not matter if traffic is routed asymmetrically across the peers.

Fault tolerance, in this model with dynamic routing, is straightforward. IP routing updates validate the GRE paths that require a valid IPSec SA. The routing algorithm calculates the best paths, detects path failure, and reroutes to alternate GRE paths for redundancy. A quick review of the process demonstrates how this will work:

- If a destination at the VPN-GW site is reachable via both the GRE tunnels from the spoke, the spoke uses the best path calculated by the routing process. If both paths are equally weighted, the spoke will send traffic using CEF load balancing across both GRE tunnels.

- If one of the VPN-GWs goes down, then the dynamic routing protocol will update the reachability information for these prefixes via the corresponding GRE tunnel. All traffic destined to the VPN-GW destination prefix would take the second available GRE path. The most significant advantage for this model is that no IKE and IPSec SAs need to be negotiated across the alternate path as they are already present and validated by the routing protocols, thus helping convergence.

- By default, the GRE tunnel interface does not verify reachability of the remote GRE tunnel endpoint. Dynamic routing protocols serve to validate the path and reflect the viability of the path in the routing database.

- If dynamic routing is not used and one of the VPN-GW peers goes down, then traffic will be sent into a GRE tunnel with no viable endpoint. GRE keepalives may be configured in such instances to validate reachability of the GRE tunnel endpoint and assist in the process of convergence.

Example 6-11 and Example 6-12 show the configurations for the redundant pair of VPN-GWs, whereas Example 6-13 shows the configuration for the SPOKE.

Example 6-11 *VPN-GW1-WEST Configuration with GRE Tunnel*

```
crypto isakmp policy 10
 hash md5
 authentication pre-share
 lifetime 3600
crypto isakmp key cisco address 9.1.1.134
crypto ipsec transform-set esp-tunnel-internet esp-des esp-md5-hmac
!
crypto map vpn 10 ipsec-isakmp
 set peer 9.1.1.134
 set transform-set esp-tunnel-internet
 match address gre-tunnel-list
!
interface Tunnel0
 ip address 10.0.2.1 255.255.255.252
 tunnel source 9.1.1.22
 tunnel destination 9.1.1.134
 crypto map vpn
!
interface Serial1/0:0
 ip address 9.1.1.22 255.255.255.252
 crypto map vpn
!
interface Ethernet4/0
```

Example 6-11   *VPN-GW1-WEST Configuration with GRE Tunnel*

```
ip address 10.1.0.1 255.255.255.0
!
router eigrp 100
 network 10.1.0.0 0.0.0.255
 network 10.0.2.0 0.0.0.255
 no auto-summary
!
ip access-list extended gre-tunnel-list
 permit gre host 9.1.1.22 host 9.1.1.134
```

Example 6-12   *VPN-GW2-WEST Configuration with GRE Tunnel*

```
crypto isakmp policy 10
 hash md5
 authentication pre-share
 lifetime 3600
crypto isakmp key cisco address 9.1.1.134
crypto ipsec transform-set esp-tunnel-internet esp-des esp-md5-hmac
!
crypto map vpn 10 ipsec-isakmp
 set peer 9.1.1.134
 set transform-set esp-tunnel-internet
 match address gre-tunnel-list
!
interface Tunnel0
 ip address 10.0.2.5 255.255.255.252
 tunnel source 9.1.1.10
 tunnel destination 9.1.1.134
 crypto map vpn
!
interface Serial1/0
 ip address 9.1.1.10 255.255.255.252
 crypto map vpn
!
interface Ethernet4/0
 ip address 10.1.0.2 255.255.255.0
!
router eigrp 100
 network 10.1.0.0 0.0.0.255
 network 10.0.2.0 0.0.0.255
 no auto-summary
!
ip access-list extended gre-tunnel-list
 permit gre host 9.1.1.10 host 9.1.1.134
```

NOTE   The assignment of an IP address to the tunnel interface is critical for the propagation of routes. In the example provided, the tunnel's IP address assignment references the private Ethernet interface that is within the scope of addresses covered by the EIGRP routing process. Therefore, routing updates would be directed into the GRE tunnel. Alternately, the tunnel interface's IP address may be anchored to a loopback interface or to the public interface. In many cases, anchoring the tunnel to a loopback interface provides much more control and reliability over route distribution because the routing process is not associated with either the private or public interfaces.

NOTE   The requirement to apply the crypto map to both tunnel and physical interfaces in the configuration was removed in IOS versions 12.2(13)T, 12(3)M, and 12(3)T. Subsequent releases only require configuring the crypto map on the physical interfaces.

Example 6-13   *SPOKE-2-WEST with GRE Tunnels to Redundant GRE Peers*

```
crypto isakmp policy 10
 hash md5
 authentication pre-share
 lifetime 3600
crypto isakmp key cisco address 9.1.1.22
crypto isakmp key cisco address 9.1.1.10
!
crypto ipsec transform-set esp-tunnel-internet esp-des esp-md5-hmac
!
crypto map vpn 10 ipsec-isakmp
 set peer 9.1.1.22
 set transform-set esp-tunnel-internet
 match address gre-tunnel-list
crypto map vpn 20 ipsec-isakmp
 set peer 9.1.1.10
 set transform-set esp-tunnel-internet
 match address gre-tunnel-list2
!
interface Tunnel0
 ip address 10.0.2.2 255.255.255.252
 tunnel source 9.1.1.134
 tunnel destination 9.1.1.22
 crypto map vpn
!
interface Tunnel1
 ip address 10.0.2.6 255.255.255.252
 tunnel source 9.1.1.134
 tunnel destination 9.1.1.10
 crypto map vpn
!
interface FastEthernet0
 ip address 10.0.65.1 255.255.255.0
!
interface Serial0
 no ip address
 ip address 9.1.1.134 255.255.255.252
 crypto map vpn
!
router eigrp 100
 network 10.0.65.0 0.0.0.255
 network 10.0.2.0 0.0.0.255
 no auto-summary
!
ip access-list extended gre-tunnel-list
 permit gre host 9.1.1.134 host 9.1.1.22
ip access-list extended gre-tunnel-list2
 permit gre host 9.1.1.134 host 9.1.1.10
```

The configuration for the spoke with redundant GRE peers highlights the fact that a unique IKE and IPSec SA is defined for each tunnel within the context of a single crypto map. The same will be true for a hub with hundreds of spokes attached. That is, the hub will have a unique sequence number for each spoke attached to the hub.

The support for dynamic routing on GRE tunnels allows you design highly fault-tolerant IPSec-protected VPNs. Many features of the routing protocols may be leveraged to optimize traffic flows, convergence intervals, and fault detection. Of course, all this flexibility does not come for free. The IPSec gateway has to deal with routing protocol scalability limitations in addition to IPSec. This is especially true at the hub of a hub-and-spoke architecture.

In addition, you find that the routing processes may create additional demands on the IPSec processing functions. The most important aspect is the simultaneous creation and persistence of multiple IPSec sessions when routing updates are broadcast into the GRE tunnels. When the VPN-GW routers become viable endpoints, all the spokes will attempt to restore their GRE tunnels and IPSec SAs. Likewise, the VPN-GW will attempt to restore a GRE tunnel to each of its spokes. This process places a tremendous burden on the VPN-GW during periods of transition; therefore, scalability becomes a critical design factor. Nevertheless, the IPSec-protected GRE model is the most commonly deployed architecture due to its robustness, simplicity, and versatility. Remember that this model is only for site-to-site IPSec fault tolerance; remote access clients do not support GRE.

Virtual IPSec Peer Redundancy Using SLB

You have already seen a virtual IPSec peer redundancy model using HSRP in a previous section in this chapter. One of the disadvantages of the HSRP model is that, at any given time, only one of the VPN-GWs is an active IPSec peer. In this section, we will discuss an alternate scheme for virtual IPSec peer redundancy using the IOS Server Load Balancing feature (SLB).

The concept behind this model is to load balance the incoming IPSec connections from the spokes or remote access clients across a farm of VPN-GWs. The spokes are only aware of a virtual IP address that represents the VPN-GW farm defined on the SLB. The load-balancing device (or SLB feature) distributes IPSec requests across the farm and, in the case of failure, the VPN-GWs are transparently removed from operation. There are different load-balancing algorithms that can be used to distribute VPN traffic, from a simple round robin up to more sophisticated algorithms, based on the concurrent number of connections, server load, and weight.

Server Load Balancing Concepts

As noted in the previous section, IOS SLB is an IOS feature that provides IP server load balancing. Using this feature, you can define a virtual VPN-GW that represents a cluster of real gateways known as a gateway farm. In this environment, the clients initiate IKE requests to the IP address of the virtual VPN-GW. When a client or a spoke initiates a connection, the IOS SLB function chooses a real gateway for the connection from among the gateways using the same virtual address. Which gateway is selected also depends on the configured load-balancing algorithm. SLB provides two load-balancing algorithms:

- **Weighted round robin**—This algorithm assigns a weight (n) to each gateway. SLB assigns new incoming connections to any given real gateway n times before the next gateway is chosen.

- **Weighted least connections**—This algorithm specifies that the next real gateway chosen from a gateway farm for a new connection is the one with the fewest active connections. Each real VPN-GW is assigned a weight; the gateway with the fewest connections is based on the number of active connections on each gateway and on the relative capacity of each gateway. The capacity of a given real gateway is calculated as the assigned weight of that gateway divided by the sum of the assigned weights of all of the real gateways associated with that virtual server, or $n1/(n1+n2+n3...)$.

Either algorithm can be used for choosing a real VPN-GW for each new connection request that arrives at the IOS SLB for IPSec termination. IOS SLB automatically detects failure of a real VPN-GW using pings and increments a failure counter for that gateway. If a gateway's failure counter exceeds a configurable faildetect *failure threshold*, the gateway is considered *out of service* and is removed from the list of active real gateways.

IOS SLB also allows configuration of *maximum connections* for a real VPN-GW. If the maximum number of connections is reached for a VPN-GW, IOS SLB automatically switches all further connection requests to other real VPN-GWs until the connection number drops below the specified limit.

One more key concept for SLB that is used for the IPSec fault-tolerant design is that of *sticky connections.* This concept assigns new connections from a client IP address or subnet to the *same* real VPN-GW as were previous connections from that address or subnet.

IPSec Peer Redundancy Using SLB

This section examines how the SLB concepts can be applied to the IPSec peer redundancy model. Figure 6-15 illustrates this model.

Figure 6-15 *Architecture for Load-Balanced IPSec Connections*

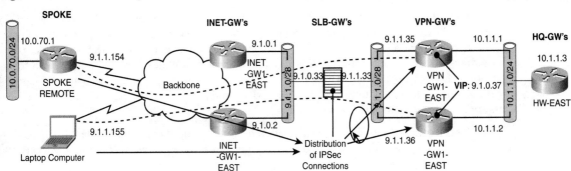

The two VPN-GWs in this model are connected to a Catalyst 6500 switch with an MSFC card running IOS that supports SLB functionality. The two VPN-GWs constitute the gateway farm and share a single IKE identity, which is the virtual IP address on the SLB. Example 6-14 shows the configuration of the SLB device and the VPN-GWs.

Example 6-14 *Configuration of the Server Load Balancer*

```
Current configuration : 7178 bytes
!
version 12.1
service timestamps debug uptime
service timestamps log uptime
no service password-encryption
!
hostname slb-east
!
boot system flash sup-bootflash:c6sup22-jk2o3sv-mz.121-11b.E1.bin
enable password lab
!
redundancy
 main-cpu
   auto-sync standard
!
vlan 1
!
vlan 10    --- vlan to the inet-gw
!
vlan 11    --- vlan to the vpn-gws
!
!
no ip domain-lookup
!
ip slb probe SERVER-PROBE ping
 interval 30
 faildetect 3
!
```

Example 6-14 *Configuration of the Server Load Balancer (Continued)*

```
ip slb serverfarm IPSEC
 failaction purge
 probe SERVER-PROBE
 !
 real 9.1.1.35
  weight 1
  maxconns 5000
  inservice
 !
 real 9.1.1.36
  weight 1
  maxconns 5000
  inservice
 !

ip slb vserver IPSEC-ESP
 virtual 9.1.0.37 esp
 serverfarm IPSEC
 sticky 6000 group 1
 idle 3650
 inservice
!
ip slb vserver IPSEC-ISAKMP
 virtual 9.1.0.37 udp isakmp
 serverfarm IPSEC
 sticky 6000 group 1
 idle 3650
 inservice
 !
 !
 !
interface FastEthernet3/1
 description to VPN-gateway
 duplex full
 speed 100
 switchport
 switchport access vlan 10
 !
interface FastEthernet3/5
 description to vpn-gw1-east
 no ip address
 duplex full
 speed 100
 switchport
 switchport access vlan 11
 !
interface FastEthernet3/6
 description to vpn-gw2-east
 no ip address
 duplex full
 speed 100
```

continues

Example 6-14 *Configuration of the Server Load Balancer (Continued)*

```
 switchport
 switchport access vlan 11
!
!
interface Vlan1
 no ip address
!
interface Vlan10
 ip address 9.1.0.33 255.255.255.0
!
interface Vlan11
 ip address 9.1.1.33 255.255.255.0
!
router ospf 1
 log-adjacency-changes
 network 9.1.0.0 0.0.0.255 area 0


slb-east#show ip slb realserver

real                    farm name         weight  state          conns
-----------------------------------------------------------------------
9.1.1.35                IPSEC             1       OPERATIONAL    2
9.1.1.36                IPSEC             1       OPERATIONAL    2ECE

ILB-1#show ip slb conn

vserver         prot client                  real            state      nat
--------------------------------------------------------------------------------
IPSEC-ESP       ESP  9.1.1.155:0            9.1.1.35        ESTAB      none
IPSEC-ISAKMP    UDP  9.1.1.155:500         9.1.1.35        ESTAB      none
IPSEC-ESP       ESP  9.1.1.154:0            9.1.1.36        ESTAB      none
IPSEC-ISAKMP    UDP  9.1.1.154:500         9.1.1.36        ESTAB      none

ILB-1#show ip slb vservers

slb vserver     prot  virtual           state          conns
----------------------------------------------------------------
IPSEC-ESP       ESP   9.1.0.37/32:0     OPERATIONAL    0
IPSEC-ISAKMP    UDP   9.1.0.37/32:500   OPERATIONAL    0
vpn-gw1-east#
crypto isakmp policy 1
 encr 3des
 authentication pre-share
 group 2
cryto isakmp key cisco 9.1.1.154 255.255.255.255 no-xauth
crypto isakmp keepalive 300 5

crypto isakmp client configuration group cisco
 key coke123
 dns 15.15.15.15
```

Example 6-14 *Configuration of the Server Load Balancer (Continued)*

```
 wins 16.16.16.16
 domain cisco.com
 pool cisco

crypto ipsec transform-set esp-tunnel-internet esp-3des esp-sha-hmac
 !
crypto dynamic-map cisco 10
 set transform-set esp-tunnel-internet
 reverse-route
 !
crypto map crypmap local-address Loopback0
crypto map crypmap 2 ipsec-isakmp dynamic cisco
 !
 !
interface Loopback0    ---- this address configured is same as the  virtual server
  address
 ip address 9.1.0.37 255.255.255.255

 !
interface FastEthernet0/0
 description to public  ip address 9.1.1.35 255.255.255.0
 crypto map crypmap
 !
interface FastEthernet0/1
 description to corporate
 ip address 10.1.1.1 255.255.255.0
 !
 !
router ospf 10
log-adjacency-changes
network 10.1.1.0 0.0.0.255 area 0
redistribute static subnets
default-information originate
 !
ip route 0.0.0.0 0.0.0.0 9.1.1.33
```

NOTE   The configuration of all the VPN-GWs behind the SLB will look exactly the same, except for the real and private IP addresses.

NOTE   Static crypto maps should not used on the VPN-GWs with set peer statements because the SLB function operates only on connections initiated from the spokes and clients. The dynamic crypto map will eliminate a significant configuration burden. The VPN-GWs must use dynamic crypto maps in order to receive IPSec connections from unknown remote peers.

Notice that the configuration of the SLB has two instances of the slb vserver command, one for IKE traffic and another for encapsulating security payload (ESP) traffic. It is important to bind both these vservers together to avoid asymmetric IKE and IPSec paths. In other words, we don't want IKE negotiation to happen with a VPN-GW1-EAST while IPSec traffic termination is directed to a separate VPN-GW2-EAST. The concept of sticky connections binds these together. A couple of other important aspects of this model are:

- An extra VPN-GW in the gateway farm provides for redundancy. A failure of one VPN-GW in the gateway farm requires the load to be redistributed entirely among the remaining servers.

- The max connections parameter on the SLB should take into account both IKE and IPSec connections; for example, if a real VPN-GW can terminate 1000 IPSec tunnels, the maxconnections should be configured as 2000 (1000 IKE SA and 1000 incoming IPSec SA).

The spoke configuration uses the virtual IP address as the IKE identity of the gateway farm. When the spoke sends an IKE message to this virtual IP address, the SLB receives the IKE traffic and routes it to one of the real VPN-GWs based on the load-balancing algorithm configured on the SLB. For the message to terminate and be processed at the real VPN-GW, the SLB virtual IP address must be configured on the real VPN-GW. A loopback interface is typically used for this purpose. All the real VPN-GWs in the gateway farm should be configured with the same virtual IP address because the IKE and IPSec traffic for an IPSec session could potentially terminate on any VPN-GW. This overlapping IP address scheme violates general IP network design principles, and care should be taken to not advertise this IP address in the rest of the network.

Cisco VPN 3000 Clustering for Peer Redundancy

The Cisco VPN 3000 Concentrator supports a peer redundancy model that conceptually works just like the SLB scheme discussed previously. The VPN 3000 model of peer redundancy is known as clustering. This model is shown in Figure 6-16 and is implemented by grouping together logically, into a virtual cluster, two or more VPN 3000 Concentrators on the same private LAN-to-LAN network, private subnet, and public subnet. A virtual cluster is a set of Concentrators that all serve the same group of users. The remote clients are unaware of the fact that multiple Concentrators exist, because they connect to a virtual representation of the set of Concentrators.

Figure 6-16   *IPSec Clustering for Peer Redundancy*

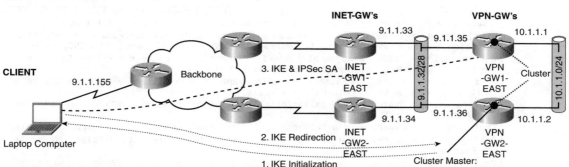

All devices in the virtual cluster carry session loads. One device in the virtual cluster, the virtual cluster master, is responsible for directing incoming calls to the other devices, which are called secondary devices. The virtual cluster master monitors all the devices in the cluster and keeps track of how busy each one is, distributing the session load accordingly. The role of virtual cluster master is not tied to a physical device; it can shift among devices. For example, if the current virtual cluster master fails, one of the secondary devices in the cluster takes over that role and immediately becomes the new virtual cluster master.

NOTE   VPN clustering works only with Cisco VPN clients. It does not work for site-to-site connections.

The virtual cluster appears, to outside clients, as a single virtual cluster IP address. This IP address is not tied to a specific physical device—it belongs to the current virtual cluster master, and is, therefore, considered virtual. A VPN client attempting to establish a connection will connect first to this virtual cluster IP address. The virtual cluster master then returns the public IP address of an available, and least loaded, host in the cluster. In a second transaction (transparent to the user), the client connects directly to that host. In this way, the virtual cluster master directs traffic evenly and efficiently across resources. Example 6-15 shows the configuration of the VPN 3000 for clustering.

Example 6-15 *VPN 3000 Configuration for Clustering*

```
Configuration > Interface Configuration > Configure Ethernet #2 (Public) > Interface
  Setting > Enable using Static IP Addressing > Enter IP Address = 9.1.1.35
Configuration > Interface Configuration > Configure Ethernet #2 (Public) > Interface
  Setting > Enable using Static IP Addressing > Enter Subnet Mask = 255.255.255.240
Configuration > Policy Management > Traffic Management > Filters > Assign Rules to a
  Filter > Add a Rule to this Filter (Public) > VCA In
Configuration > Policy Management > Traffic Management > Filters > Assign Rules to a
  Filter > Add a Rule to this Filter (Public) > VCA Out
Configuration > System > Load Balancing > Cluster Configuration > VPN Virtual Cluster
  IP Address = 9.1.1.37
Configuration > System > Load Balancing > Cluster Configuration > Encryption = Enabled
Configuration > System > Load Balancing > Cluster Configuration > Load-Balancing Enable
  = Enable
Configuration > System > Load Balancing > Cluster Configuration > IPSec Shared Secret
  = cisco123
Configuration > System > Load Balancing > Device Configuration > Enable/Disable Load
  Balancing = Enable
Configuration > System > Load Balancing > Device Configuration > Device Priority = 10
```

If a VPN 3000 in the cluster fails, the client may close the IPSec session state and immediately reconnect to the virtual cluster IP address. The virtual cluster master then directs these connections to another active device in the cluster. Should the virtual cluster master fail, a secondary device in the cluster automatically takes over as the new virtual session master. Even if several devices in the cluster fail, users can continue to connect to the cluster as long as any one device in the cluster is up and available.

Peer Redundancy Summary

This section highlighted several peer redundancy models, emphasizing the advantages as well as the disadvantages for the various models. In particular, IPSec peer redundancy may be more appropriate for client-initiated connections. The deficiencies in the route management and the complex proxy statements limit the utility of native IPSec models for site-to-site connections. Conversely, we have demonstrated that the GRE peer redundancy model is more appropriate for static environments such as site-to-site connections in which complex routing adjacencies may be required between the two IPSec peers. In all cases, the state management of the IPSec security associations may affect the performance and scalability of the redundancy model.

Intra-Chassis IPSec VPN Services Redundancy

Thus far, we have discussed redundancy based on external attributes of the VPN router—that is, link redundancy and peer redundancy. Designers must also consider scenarios in which internal redundancy improves the reliability of the IPSec services. There are two options to consider:

- Stateless Failover
- Stateful Failover

Stateless IPSec Redundancy

The stateless failover model assumes that the state of the encryption processes is not synchronized across redundant hardware within the chassis. Designers are forced in that case to use an active/standby redundancy model, in which the standby hardware assumes the identity of the active hardware when the active hardware fails. Unfortunately, the standby hardware has no knowledge of the existing IPSec sessions; therefore, sites and clients with established IPSec sessions to the VPN router will be terminated. Subsequently, the remote sites and clients must reinitialize their connection to the VPN router. Effectively, the standby encryption hardware is equivalent to the redundant peer model described in the previous section.

The impact of a stateless failover varies based on the types of IPSec connections and the applications. For remote office sites, the peers may detect the loss of the active encryption hardware and reconnect to the standby hardware. Note that the remote hosts retain their originally assigned IP addresses and the applications may periodically check for the reestablishment of end-to-end communications. The impact may be minimized if the fault detection and connection reestablishment is successful before the application's timeout due to loss of end-to-end connectivity. In contrast, remote client applications will likely be terminated because the reestablishment of an IPSec connection to a standby encryption process will inevitably lead to the assignment of a new IP address for client connections. In this case, the standby encryption hardware provides marginal value.

Stateful IPSec Redundancy

Now, let's look at the stateful failover scenario. The stateful failover scenario may use an active/active model or an active/standby model; however, the state of IPSec connections is always synchronized. The primary difference between the active/active and active/standby model is that the active/active model leverages some form of load balancing that may occur, whereas active/standby keeps the standby encryption hardware idle at all times.

When designing an active/active redundancy model, network architects must ensure that the cumulative load of the active/active encryption hardware does not exceed 100 percent; it is advisable to keep it less than 70 percent as a reasonable design principle. Assuming perfect load balancing, the two encryption engines would each sustain approximately 35 percent of the total load. If one of the encryption engines fails, then the redundant engine would service the cumulative load of 70 percent.

The active/standby stateful failover model assumes that the active encryption hardware will sustain all IPSec connections until failure occurs. At that point, the standby encryption hardware sustains all of the IPSec connections. Obviously, the standby encryption hardware must have similar or better capabilities or it will have a negative impact on performance. The primary advantage of using the stateful failover model is that all the IPSec sessions are synchronized between the two IPSec encryption engines. The platform detects the hardware failure or removal and immediately transfers responsibility for the IPSec connections to the standby encryption hardware. The advantage is that remote sites and clients do not need to renegotiate

IPSec state, and therefore the recovery period is much shorter. More importantly, remote IPSec clients retain their previously assigned IP address and thus are able to sustain their end-to-end application connections. The trade-off with the stateful IPSec failover is that a reliable control channel must be sustained between the two encryption engines because each IPSec session keeps tracks of anti-replay sequence numbers, counters, and timers. Not only must the state of the IPSec encryptions be synchronized, but any auxiliary functions that are tightly coupled with the encryption engine may also need to be synchronized, such as IP routing state and MAC adjacencies.

Summary

In this chapter, you looked at various IPSec fault-tolerant models that illustrate how to recover from access link failures and node failures. The assessment of each model highlighted the pros and cons of each model. The combination of redundancy and large-scale VPNs creates additional design constraints that must be addressed; the next two chapters address the scalability issues of these models in greater detail.

CHAPTER 7

Auto-Configuration Architectures for Site-to-Site IPSec VPNs

In Chapter 5, "IPSec VPN Architectures," you saw various IPSec VPN architectural models. The IPSec VPN configuration can become quite complex with any architecture, especially as the number of IPSec endpoints becomes significantly large. In this chapter, you will examine mechanisms to alleviate the configuration complexity of a large-scale IPSec VPN. The principle advantage of these mechanisms is the dynamic creation of the IPSec security associations without requiring pre-defined IPSec proxy profiles. This attribute is particularly important when building large full-, partial-, or temporal-mesh topologies. In this chapter, you will explore two mechanisms used to automate the configuration of IPSec VPNs

- Tunnel Endpoint Discovery (TED)
- Dynamic Multipoint VPN (DMVPN)

The TED model enables the establishment of native IPSec tunnel connections across an IP cloud while the DMVPN model leverages the IPSec transport of multi-protocol GRE packets. In the next sections, you'll take a closer look at the two models.

IPSec Tunnel Endpoint Discovery

Traditional IPSec VPN configuration on a Cisco IOS router requires the static configuration of the IPSec peer endpoints via crypto maps. As the name suggests, Tunnel Endpoint Discovery (TED) allows for an IPSec peer to dynamically discover the corresponding IPSec peers. The TED model provides a scalable approach to dynamically building IPSec VPNs based on standard routing protocols. The benefits of using TED include the following:

- Simplified crypto configuration
- Dynamic crypto maps eliminating a priori peer configuration
- IPSec protection built on demand

With TED, the initiating router dynamically determines an IPSec peer for secure IPSec communications. To configure a large, fully meshed network without TED, each peer must have static crypto maps to every other peer in the network. For example, if there are 100 peers in a large, fully meshed network, each router needs 99 static crypto maps, one for each of its peers. With TED, only a single dynamic crypto map with TED enabled is needed because the other peers are discovered dynamically. Thus, static crypto maps do not have to be configured for each peer, which significantly simplifies the configuration.

Principles of TED

Let's take a look at the operation of TED using the network topology described in Figure 7-1. The TED mechanism uses the inherent routing topology of the network to discover tunnel endpoints for prefixes that need to be protected. This means that the protected source and destination IP prefixes must be routable in the backbone between the two IPSec endpoints. The sequence outlined in the following steps is necessary to discover the remote peer endpoints and policies associated with each endpoint:

Figure 7-1   *IPSec Tunnel Endpoint Discovery Topology*

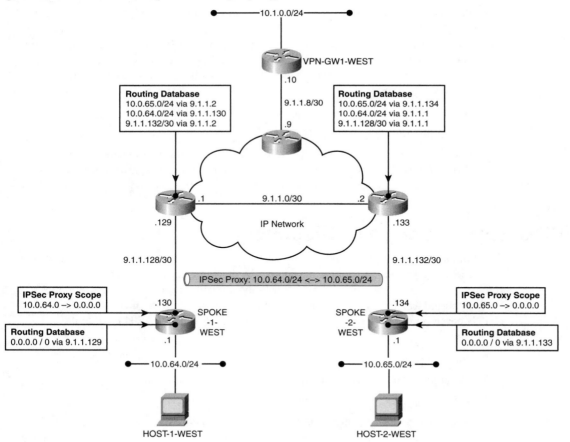

1   In this example, HOST-1-WEST sends an IP packet destined to HOST-2-WEST. Assume also that IP reachability information is available in all the routers shown in the figure for all destination subnets. The IP packet is routed to SPOKE-1-WEST where TED is configured on the egress interface destined to HOST-2-WEST. IPSec policy configured on SPOKE-1-WEST identifies that the packet destined to HOST-2-WEST needs to be encrypted, but there is no SA (security association) associated with this.

2   SPOKE-1-WEST sends a TED probe with a source address of HOST-1-WEST and a destination address of HOST-2-WEST. The TED probe is an IKE message with UDP source and destination port 500. The probe has the following payloads:

— Vendor payload—Cisco vendor ID

— ID Endpoint Payload—ID, encoded as IP address (SPOKE-1-WEST's IP address)

— ID Proxy Payload—The proxy address (HOST-1-WEST's subnet derived from the IPSec proxy configured)

3   The TED probe is intercepted by SPOKE-2-WEST. The TED probe is an IPSec packet that matches the crypto proxy policy defined by an ACL on SPOKE-2-WEST. The intercepting router knows the packet should have been encrypted based on its IPSec policy; however, it also knows that TED is configured. As a result, the router evaluates the packet and determines that it is a probe packet that conforms to the IPSec proxy policies designed to protect the hosts behind SPOKE-2-WEST. SPOKE-2-WEST determines that the flow from HOST-1-WEST to HOST-2-WEST should be protected. The SPOKE-2-WEST then sends a TED reply. The TED response has the SPOKE-2-WEST's IKE identity and the IP subnet that is associated with the IPSec proxy protecting the HOST-2-WEST.

NOTE   An IPSec proxy policy that matches only TCP traffic will not intercept the TED probes based on protocol type UDP and port 500. If your intent is to protect only TCP traffic between the hosts, then an additional entry is required in the crypto ACL in order to match the UDP TED probes.

4   When SPOKE-1-WEST receives the TED response, it reads the ID payloads to get the peer's (SPOKE-2-WEST's) IKE identity IP address, and the peer's half of the IPSec proxy.

5   SPOKE-1-WEST initiates IKE to SPOKE-2-WEST and follows the usual IKE exchange to establish the IKE and IPSec SAs between the peers.

The sequence of events described in the previous numbered list emphasizes the discovery process of TED between two IPSec gateways. Figure 7-2 shows where the Tunnel Endpoint

Discovery process occurs relative to the traditional routing updates, IKE initialization, and IPSec data transfer.

Figure 7-2 *IPSec Tunnel Endpoint Discovery Process*

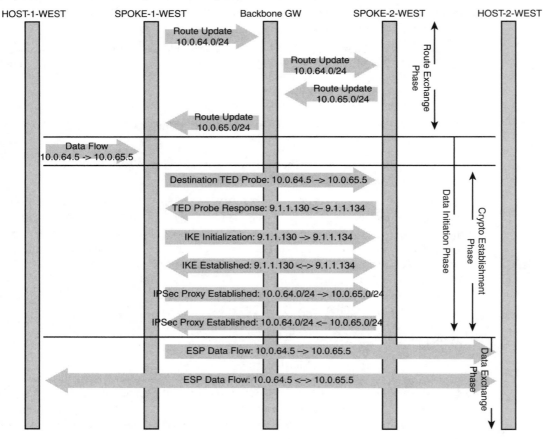

Limitations with TED

Although TED reduces configuration complexity and enables dynamic discovery of IKE endpoints in large-scale IPSec VPN deployments, it has several limitations.

The most critical limitation with the TED mechanism is the assumption that routing information for every protected subnet behind each VPN gateway is available in every routing node between the IPSec endpoints. As you learned in previous chapters. One of the biggest motivations for an IPSec VPN is the cost savings reaped by building a VPN over a public network such as the Internet. Typically, the private protected subnets use private addresses

(RFC 1918) that are not reachable over a public network. If an IPSec VPN is deployed using private addresses that are not routable across the public network, TED cannot be used because the probe and response packets rely on end-to-end reachability of the source and destination hosts in the private subnets. In IPSec deployments without this limitation (for example, in MPLS/VPN or Frame Relay networks), TED can be quite useful in reducing the configuration complexity.

Some other limitations with TED are:

- The crypto proxy configurations must adequately represent the address space (both source and destination) that will be protected; therefore, that address space must be known in advance.

- The destination may be represented as "all" routes while the source must represent the address space that the VPN gateway is protecting.

- Because the peer is not known at the time of configuration, key management must also be addressed. One option is to use a pre-shared key that is consistent across all VPN gateways in the network. The other alternative is to use a PKI system to dynamically create the key material between the peers.

NOTE   The creation of IPSec SAs requires the presence of viable VPN routes throughout the network, including the backbone. The TED proxy profiles must not include protection of the VPN routing updates to backbone routers between the IPSec gateways because these backbone routers must be able to process the routing updates. Most routing protocols, such as OSPF or EIGRP, use a multicast or broadcast address to establish adjacencies and send routing updates; these addresses are typically excluded from the IPSec proxy policy. Therefore, inadvertent encryption of the routing protocol between the TED end-point and the next-hop gateway is usually not an issue. Special care must be taken when BGP is used as it relies on unicast to establish neighbor adjacencies.

TED Configuration and State

Figure 7-2 highlighted the establishment of a direct IPSec relationship between SPOKE-1-WEST and SPOKE-2-WEST using TED. The listing in Example 7-1 shows the necessary configuration elements.

Example 7-1   *SPOKE-1-WEST Configuration for TED*

```
spoke-1-west#show running-config

!
crypto isakmp policy 10
 authentication pre-share
crypto isakmp key cisco address 0.0.0.0 0.0.0.0
crypto isakmp keepalive 10
```

continues

Example 7-1 *SPOKE-1-WEST Configuration for TED (Continued)*

```
!
crypto ipsec transform-set ted-transform esp-des esp-md5-hmac
!
crypto dynamic-map ted-map 10
 set transform-set ted-transform
 match address ted
!
!
crypto map tedtag 10 ipsec-isakmp dynamic ted-map discover
!
interface FastEthernet0/0
 ip address 10.0.64.1 255.255.255.0
 duplex half
 speed 100
!
interface Serial1/0:0
 ip address 9.1.1.130 255.255.255.252
 crypto map tedtag
!
ip route 0.0.0.0 0.0.0.0 9.1.1.129
!
ip access-list extended ted
 permit ip 10.0.64.0 0.0.0.255 10.0.0.0 0.255.255.255
!
```

Note that the TED configuration does not require the configuration of each IPSec peer relationship. The IPSec SA is dynamically established after traffic matches the IPSec proxy on the backbone uplink interface. Let's assume that the traffic is initiated from the host (10.0.64.5), behind SPOKE-1-WEST, to the host (10.0.65.5), behind SPOKE-2-WEST. The backbone routing protocol must create a path for the destination that forwards the traffic over the interface where IPSec protection is applied. The IP route table listing in Example 7-2 shows that the route process will forward the traffic over the serial interface where the crypto map is applied.

Example 7-2 *Routing State for SPOKE-1-WEST*

```
Spoke-1-west#show ip route

     9.0.0.0/8 is variably subnetted, 1 subnets, 1 masks
C       9.1.1.128/30 is directly connected, Serial1/0:0
     10.0.0.0/8 is variably subnetted, 1 subnets, 1 masks
C       10.0.64.0/24 is directly connected, FastEthernet0/0
S*   0.0.0.0/0 [1/0] via 9.1.1.129
```

You can see that the routing table will force traffic destined to 10.0.65.0 out the serial interface where the crypto map is applied. Example 7-3 shows the crypto map state on the serial interface before and after the establishment of SAs between the VPN gateways.

Example 7-3   *Spoke IPSec Security Association*

```
spoke-1-west#show crypto map
Crypto Map "tedtag" 10 ipsec-isakmp
          Dynamic map template tag: ted-map
          Discover enabled
          Serial1/0:0

… After IPSec Establishment …

spoke-1-west#show crypto map
Crypto Map "tedtag" 10 ipsec-isakmp
          Dynamic map template tag: ted-map
          Discover enabled


Crypto Map "tedtag" 20 ipsec-isakmp
          Peer = 9.1.1.134
          Extended IP access list
              access-list  permit ip 10.0.64.0 0.0.0.255 10.0.65.0 0.0.0.255
              dynamic (created from dynamic map ted-map/10)
          Current peer: 9.1.1.134
          Security association lifetime: 4608000 kilobytes/3600 seconds
          PFS (Y/N): N
          Transform sets={ ted-transform, }
          Interfaces using crypto map tedtag:
          Serial1/0:0
```

The recipient node of the TED request (SPOKE-2-WEST) establishes a corresponding IPSec proxy state such that return traffic will be directed to the appropriate initiating router. Recall that SPOKE-2-WEST has an aggregate IPSec proxy defined as 10.0.65.0 -> 0.0.0.0. If this aggregate were used solely for SPOKE-1-WEST, any traffic leaving SPOKE-2-WEST would have to be directed solely to SPOKE-1-WEST. Clearly, that is not the goal, as each spoke should be able to pass traffic to any number of peers. The originating IKE connection specifies that SPOKE-1-WEST is only providing protection for the subnet 10.0.64.0/24; therefore, SPOKE-2-WEST installs only a subset of its IPSec proxy (that is, 10.0.65.0/24 -> 10.0.64.0/24). This restriction allows any subsequent request from a different peer to establish the appropriate IPSec proxy statement that does not overlap with the IPSec proxy established between SPOKE-1-WEST and SPOKE-2-WEST. The listing in Example 7-4 shows the crypto IPSec SA on SPOKE-1-WEST after the establishment of the IPSec SA. Note the explicit IPSec proxy profile defined between SPOKE-1-WEST and SPOKE-2-WEST.

NOTE The IPSec proxy established between two TED endpoints is the logical intersection between the two proxies defined at either end. The initiator has a proxy profile that includes protection of many more remote addresses than the receiver protects. Likewise, the receiver has a proxy profile that includes protection of many more sources than the receiver protects. Typically, the receiver's IPSec proxy policy must be an inverse superset of the initiator's proxy policy in order to accept the proposal. TED allows the receiver to accept the initiator's IPSec proxy policy despite the fact that it is a superset of the receiver's IPSec proxy policy. The receiver's TED process reconciles the discrepancy between the two IPSec proxy policies by identifying a non-mutually exclusive IPSec proxy policy that is a subset of both the initiator's and the receiver's IPSec proxy policy.

Example 7-4   *TED Recipient IPSec Crypto State*

```
spoke-1-west#show crypto ipsec sa

interface: Serial1/0:0
    Crypto map tag: tedtag, local addr. 9.1.1.130

   local  ident (addr/mask/prot/port): (10.0.64.0/255.255.255.0/0/0)
   remote ident (addr/mask/prot/port): (10.0.65.0/255.255.255.0/0/0)
   current_peer: 9.1.1.134
     PERMIT, flags={}
    #pkts encaps: 4, #pkts encrypt: 4, #pkts digest 4
    #pkts decaps: 4, #pkts decrypt: 4, #pkts verify 4
    #pkts compressed: 0, #pkts decompressed: 0
    #pkts not compressed: 0, #pkts compr. failed: 0, #pkts decompress failed: 0
    #send errors 0, #recv errors 0

     local crypto endpt.: 9.1.1.130, remote crypto endpt.: 9.1.1.134
     path mtu 1500, media mtu 1500
     current outbound spi: 17339A3B

    inbound esp sas:
     spi: 0x52B2154D(1387402573)
       transform: esp-des esp-md5-hmac ,
       in use settings ={Tunnel, }
       slot: 0, conn id: 2000, flow_id: 1, crypto map: tedtag
       sa timing: remaining key lifetime (k/sec): (4607998/3489)
       IV size: 8 bytes
       replay detection support: Y

    inbound ah sas:

    inbound pcp sas:

    outbound esp sas:
     spi: 0x17339A3B(389257787)
       transform: esp-des esp-md5-hmac ,
```

Example 7-4 *TED Recipient IPSec Crypto State (Continued)*

```
        in use settings ={Tunnel, }
        slot: 0, conn id: 2001, flow_id: 2, crypto map: tedtag
        sa timing: remaining key lifetime (k/sec): (4607999/3489)
        IV size: 8 bytes
        replay detection support: Y

    outbound ah sas:

    outbound pcp sas:
```

We note that the existence of multiple connections from unique peers requires the instantiation of a unique IPSec proxy for each peer. Over time, each peer will dynamically build IPSec state for traffic flows that match a full mesh. With minimal configuration, the TED method is able essentially to provide fully meshed network connectivity. The TED solution is also able to conserve resources, as you will establish IPSec SAs only between gateways that sustain user data traffic flows. In addition, the IPSec SAs may expire after a period of inactivity, thereby preserving memory in the security association database. Next, you'll investigate what happens when the routing state of the backbone network changes such that the IPSec state is no longer valid.

TED Fault Tolerance

The establishment of TED IPSec SAs clearly makes use of the current state of the backbone routing topology. Note that an interesting situation may occur when routing topology changes. There are two cases that should be considered: routing topology changes between the IPSec endpoints and routing topology changes around the IPSec endpoints. The TED process uses IPSec tunnel mode to encapsulate the protected traffic; therefore, the encrypted traffic uses the IPSec VPN gateway encapsulating addresses to route the packets across the backbone.

In the first scenario (that is, backbone topology change), the IPSec-encapsulated packets will simply follow an alternate path to reach the same IPSec peer endpoint. Assuming the convergence interval of the backbone is short enough, the IPSec IKE process will not detect the loss of the peer, and the IPSec session state will be sustained. A more interesting situation occurs when the backbone routing topology changes such that optimal path to the destination host is no longer through the same VPN gateway. If an alternate remote peer router advertises the protected address space, the originating router will continue to send data using the existing crypto SPI (security parameter index) to the original remote peer router. The alternate router will not receive the packets because it has no crypto state and is not the remote peer defined by the tunneling header. Only when return packets from the remote site invoke a probe packet from the alternate remote VPN gateway, is it possible for the responding host's packets to return to the initiating host. Let's take a look at the topology described in Figure 7-3.

Figure 7-3   *Redundant TED Peer Recovery*

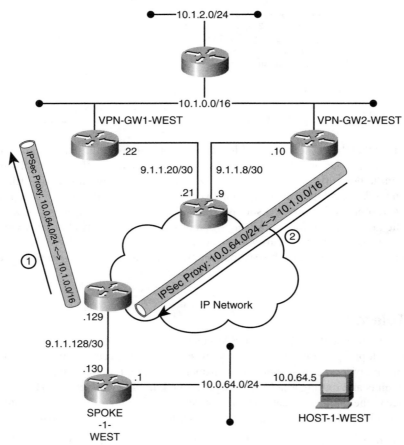

Assume that the primary path to the subnet 10.1.2.0/24 from the backbone network is via VPN-GW1-WEST. When HOST-1-WEST needs to establish a connection to a host on 10.1.2.0/24, SPOKE-1-WEST initiates a TED probe to target the host on 10.1.2.0/24. The TED probe follows the primary route to VPN-GW1-WEST. The VPN-GW1-WEST subsequently responds to SPOKE-1-WEST indicating that an IPSec proxy should be established between the two gateways protecting traffic between 10.0.64.0/24 and 10.1.0.0/16. Once the IPSec SA is established, SPOKE-1-WEST encapsulates the packets using the designated identities (9.1.1.130 <-> 9.1.1.22). If a routing change occurs such that the backbone now routes packets to 10.1.2.0/24 to VPN-GW2-WEST, you have an interesting dilemma. For traffic leaving SPOKE-1-WEST, there may be no routing change. Therefore, SPOKE-1-WEST may continue to direct packets from 10.1.2.0 to VPN-GW1-WEST. If the LAN interface of VPN-GW1-WEST is down, the packets will be dropped for lack of a viable path to the destination host.

NOTE	The remote peer receiving the packet may decrypt the packet and may have discovered an alternate route to the destination via the backbone (that is, forwarding the packet back out the same interface from which it came); however, the IPSec policy on this remote peer does not provide protection for packets sourced from addresses other than those on its associated LAN.

Only when return traffic from the 10.1.2.0/24 subnet forces VPN-GW2-WEST to issue a TED probe to SPOKE-1-WEST does SPOKE-1-WEST realize a new IPSec SA is being requested. SPOKE-1-WEST may now respond to VPN-GW2-WEST with the appropriate IPSec proxy information such that the two gateways may establish a replacement IPSec SA.

Clearly, there are scenarios in which traffic flows may be interrupted while routing gateways try to determine a more appropriate TED path. The scenario described previously is typically rectified quickly because clients and servers with persistent connections (such as TCP connections) will periodically retry the connection before closing the session. Application connection retries in both directions force the discovery of a new TED path. In scenarios in which clients do not maintain persistent TCP connections to the servers (for example, HTTP, POP3, SMTP, and others), the servers never initiate connections to the clients. Scenarios using applications such as these will lead to long periods of lost connectivity. If the remote peer is still accessible but the hosts behind the peer are inaccessible, the TED state can lead to a persistent "black hole," in which packets are persistently dropped. The situation is only rectified when IKE expires and the initiator establishes a new IKE session. This will lead to the discovery of the alternate peer and will restore the data path between the hosts.

In summary, TED is a reasonable method for dynamically establishing partial- and full-mesh IPSec topologies. It significantly simplifies configuration and allows for redundant topologies with a reasonably quick convergence interval. The one major limitation of TED is that the protected subnet address ranges must be routable in the backbone between the IPSec endpoints, a situation that is not feasible when the protected subnets are private IP networks that are not routable across public networks such as the Internet. Dynamic Multipoint VPN (DMVPN), discussed in the next section, addresses other limitations of TED.

Dynamic Multipoint VPN

One of the major motivations for building IPSec VPNs is their ability to have sites of an enterprise connected to each other over the public Internet. You studied various IPSec VPN architectures in Chapter 5, "IPSec VPN Architectures," and saw that, for large VPNs with hundreds of sites, a full-mesh IPSec architecture has serious scaling limitations. Next-best alternatives to the full-mesh model are hub-and-spoke or partial-mesh models, as long as traffic patterns between sites are well known in advance. Given that the Internet has become ubiquitous, many large enterprises are building IPSec VPNs over the public Internet and have growing demands for dynamic spoke-to-spoke communication. For such enterprises, it would be desirable to establish direct spoke-to-spoke connectivity over IPSec on demand rather than transit the hub. This connectivity is exactly what DMVPN enables.

The DMVPN model provides a scalable configuration for a dynamic-mesh VPN based on the premise that the only relationships configured are those between the hub and spokes. The DMVPN architecture dynamically establishes a routable path via a GRE over IPSec connection between any two members in the DMVPN subnet. The destination prefixes and their next hops are discovered through traditional routing protocols while GRE tunnel endpoints are dynamically discovered and the IPSec protection policy of the tunnels is inferred from the tunnel source and tunnel destination. DMVPN uses a combination of a Multipoint GRE (mGRE) interface and Next Hop Resolution Protocol (NHRP) to achieve its objectives. The topology shown in Figure 7-4 describes DMVPN.

Figure 7-4   *DMVPN Network Topology*

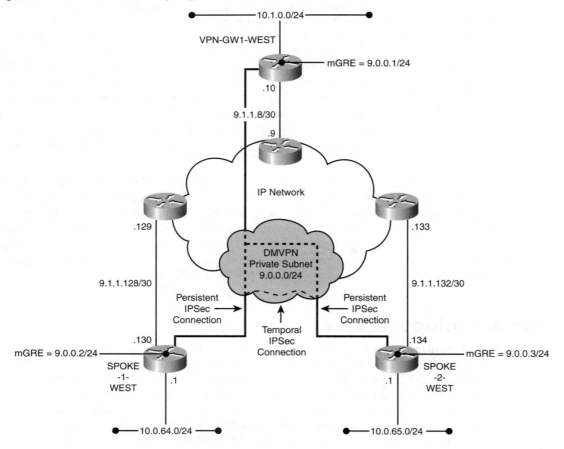

DMVPN introduces several new functional components that you must review in order to understand the process of connection establishment. The three key functional components are as follows:

- Multipoint GRE interfaces
- Next Hop Resolution Protocol
- IPSec Proxy Instantiation

The next few sections present the characteristics for each of these functional components, and describe their value. Then, we illustrate how the functional components work together to create a scalable VPN.

Multipoint GRE Interfaces

Chapter 5, "IPSec VPN Architectures," discussed the GRE model for hub-and-spoke IPSec VPNs and conveyed that the hub site uses statically defined point-to-point GRE tunnel interfaces for each spoke. This requirement of a unique GRE tunnel interface on the hub for each spoke limits the scalability of this model. Each tunnel interface in Cisco IOS consumes a data struc-ture known as an Interface Descriptor Block (IDB), which limits the scalability of this model. Another limitation of the traditional GRE model is that the IP address of the GRE tunnel endpoint on the spokes needs to be known in advance and this is a problem for spokes that use a dynamic address allocation from the backbone provider. Multipoint GRE (mGRE) solves both these problems.

As the name suggests, mGRE is a point-to-multipoint interface, in which a single tunnel interface can terminate all the GRE tunnels from all the spokes. This efficiency eliminates a great deal of configuration complexity and memory resource allocation. Second, it allows incoming GRE tunnel connections from any peer, including those with dynamically assigned tunnel addresses. The single multipoint tunnel interface dramatically simplifies the config-uration of the hub in a hub-and-spoke VPN whereas a low-end platform may now participate in a temporal full-mesh topology. For the moment, we'll ignore the IPSec protection requirement in order to highlight the GRE configuration aspects. The listing in Example 7-5 shows the traditional GRE model in which a unique point-to-point GRE interface configuration is required on the hub to establish connections for the spokes. Contrast this configuration with the listing in Example 7-6, where the mGRE tunnel interface is used.

Example 7-5   *Hub Site with Point-to-Point GRE Interfaces*

```
interface Tunnel0
 ip address 9.0.0.1 255.255.255.252
 no ip redirects
 ip mtu 1420
 ip ospf metric 10
 ip ospf priority 2
 delay 1000
 tunnel source Serial0/0
 tunnel destination 9.1.1.130
```

continues

Example 7-5 *Hub Site with Point-to-Point GRE Interfaces (Continued)*

```
interface Tunnel1
 ip address 9.0.0.5 255.255.255.252
 no ip redirects
 ip mtu 1420
 ip ospf metric 20
 ip ospf priority 2
 delay 1000
 tunnel source Serial0/0
 tunnel destination 9.1.1.134
```

Example 7-6 *Hub Site with Multipoint GRE Interface*

```
interface Tunnel0
 ip address 9.0.0.1 255.255.255.0
 no ip redirects
 ip mtu 1420
 ip ospf network broadcast
 ip ospf priority 2

 delay 1000
 tunnel source Serial0/0
 tunnel mode gre multipoint
```

Notice that the hub configuration in Example 7-6 uses a single mGRE interface, thereby eliminating the replication of the tunnel interface configuration in the hub for each spoke. Clearly, the multipoint GRE interface configuration is much more scalable for provisioning, which is particularly valuable when the size of the hub-and-spoke VPN is very large. The mGRE interface consumes a single IDB, which conserves interface memory structures and interface process management on the hub.

The use of a multipoint interface does create a dilemma, however. Notice in Example 7-5 that each tunnel interface on the hub is configured with a tunnel source and tunnel destination IP address; these addresses are routable between the GRE endpoints. In contrast, notice in Example 7-6, which uses the mGRE interface on the hub, that a tunnel source address is configured under the mGRE interface but there is no tunnel destination address. Therefore, a mechanism to identify the remote peer's tunnel endpoint address is required with this scheme. This address resolution is performed by the Next Hop Resolution Protocol (NHRP). The fact that DMVPN does not need to know the remote tunnel endpoint IP address in advance is a compelling advantage for building site-to-site hub-and-spoke VPNs in which the spoke's IP address is dynamically assigned. Dynamic IP address assignment is commonly used in dial, DSL, and cable access networks.

A second important point of contrast between the two configurations is the association of a private subnet with the GRE interface. With a point-to-point GRE model, each tunnel may have a unique IP subnet defined. A unique tunnel subnet allows more granular control over the routing processes that are assigned to each tunnel. In Example 7.6, we might associate different Open Shortest Path First (OSPF) cost metrics with each tunnel interface. In practice, the Multipoint GRE interface is associated with a large subnet. The Multipoint GRE interface does not provide a simple means of differentiating routes received from various spokes connected to this subnet because the routing metric used to reach any remote peer is based on the local mGRE interface's assigned metric. To influence the path taken (that is, to determine which peer will be used for prefixes with the same destination), the operator must create route maps or routing filter lists that must be associated with specific peers or prefixes in order to influence the metrics for routes received.

Recall that a GRE interface has two local addresses—the GRE tunnel's interface source IP address, used for routing in the public backbone, and the GRE tunnel's assigned private IP address used for routing in the private and protected network. If the GRE tunnel's source address is associated with an egress interfaces that uses a dynamically assigned IP address, then the GRE tunnel source IP address will also use the dynamically assigned IP address. Example 7-7 shows a tunnel interface bound to an egress interface in which the egress interface uses dynamically allocated IP addresses.

Example 7-7   *GRE Interface with Logical Interface Sources*

```
interface Serial0
ip address negotiated
 encapsulation ppp

interface Tunnel0
 ip address 9.0.0.1 255.255.255.0
 no ip redirects
 ip mtu 1416
 delay 1000
 tunnel source Serial0
 tunnel mode gre multipoint
 tunnel key 999
```

Dynamic routing updates advertised from the GRE interface will reference the Multipoint GRE interface's assigned private IP address as the next hop. These routing updates may be propagated to the hub router where the spoke's private subnet is inserted in the hub router's route table with the spoke's private GRE interface IP address as the next hop. But how does the hub know which IP encapsulation header to use for packets destined to the private IP destination associated with that particular spoke? The hub has the route prefix and the GRE next hop, but it isn't able to discern the public IP address associated with the spoke's Multipoint GRE interface. To address this situation, the hub's adjacency database must locate the remote peer's public IP address that is associated with that spoke's assigned GRE tunnel IP address. To enable this, you must resolve the GRE tunnel private next-hop address to a publicly routable destination address. You can do this by using the Next Hop Resolution Protocol.

Next Hop Resolution Protocol

In the DMVPN model, each spoke has a protected IP address space that is not initially known by any other router in the VPN. First, you must provide a means of informing all the other spokes (and the hub) of the subnets that each spoke protects. Assuming that the hub router will have a permanent public IP address (that is, an IKE identity), then each of the spokes may be pre-configured to connect to the hub at boot time. The spokes may then initiate a connection to the hub, register with the hub, and inform the hub of the address space that each spoke protects. The objective of the routing process is to inform the hub and all the spokes of the private routable prefixes and the associated spoke's Multipoint GRE (mGRE) interface for each prefix.

NOTE	The two typical routing models used within enterprises are the distance vector routing algorithms (such as RIP and EIGRP) and link state routing algorithms (such as OSPF and ISIS). Distance vector routing protocols require the specification of no split-horizon in order for the updates to be redistributed back to the Multipoint GRE interface at the hub from which the updates arrived. Link state routing protocols will automatically reflect the appropriate next hop within the subnet.

NOTE	Typically, OSPF would be configured in a point–multipoint mode on the mGRE interface. The DMVPN cloud must be treated as a broadcast environment such that the spokes install routes to the destination prefixes via the appropriate spokes. The use of OSPF in a point–multipoint mode causes host routes to be installed on the spokes with the next hop defined as the hub. The insertion of hub address as the next-hop for the other spoke's prefix obviously negates the point of building the DMVPN network topology.

The routing updates provide the hub and each spoke with the appropriate next-hop address for the mGRE interface associated with each prefix. Figure 7-5 shows the logical multipoint subnet and the associated routing database.

You can see from Figure 7-5 that the hub routing database refers only to a remote spoke's configured mGRE interface as the next hop for a given prefix. The Routing Information Base next-hop entry is not the dynamically assigned public IP address of the spoke. You need a mechanism to resolve the remote spoke's mGRE interface to the remote spoke's public IP address in order to establish an IKE security association. The Next Hop Resolution Protocol (NHRP) established between the hub and spoke will play a role in this adjacency reconciliation.

Figure 7-5   *Dynamic Multipoint VPN Tunnel Subnet*

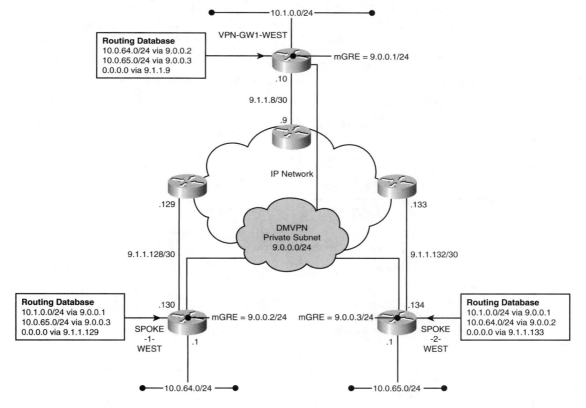

The NHRP protocol established between the spoke and the hub provides the necessary "glue" to associate a spoke's public IP address with its configured private mGRE interface address. When the spoke initiates a connection to the hub, it registers with the hub via NHRP. The registration process at the hub binds the spoke's mGRE interface to that spoke's dynamically assigned public IP address. The hub now has an adjacency database for the all the active spokes in the entire DMVPN. This information is not broadcast to the active spokes; however, the spokes recognize that the hub serves as the adjacency database. Next, we'll illustrate how NHRP works with an example.

Assume that SPOKE-1-WEST needs to establish a connection to another spoke, such as SPOKE-2-WEST. The originating spoke (SPOKE-1-WEST) knows that SPOKE-2-WEST's private route prefix exists (in this case, it is 10.0.65.0/24) and also knows the remote spoke's mGRE address as the next hop (in this case, 9.0.0.3). SPOKE-1-WEST does not know SPOKE-2-WEST's public IP address (which is 9.1.1.134). In order to gain this information, SPOKE-1-WEST queries the hub for the tunnel endpoint adjacency information. The hub will respond with the appropriate public IP address associated with SPOKE-2-WEST's mGRE next hop.

Figure 7-6 shows the sequence of events necessary to establish the connections between the spokes and the hub of the DMVPN cloud. When the hub-and-spoke topology is established, the routing processes are able to inform the spokes of all the accessible prefixes behind the other spokes. Figure 7-7 shows the information exchange process necessary for the spokes to establish a bidirectional tunnel with another spoke.

Figure 7-6 *NHRP Exchange and Route Resolution Process for Hub-and-Spoke Topology Establishment*

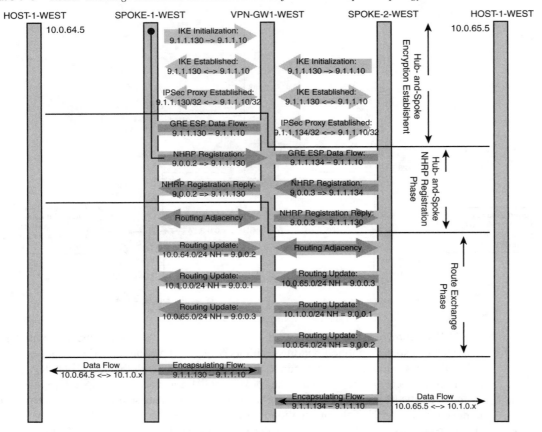

Figure 7-7 *NHRP Exchange and Route Resolution for Spoke-to-Spoke Connection Establishment*

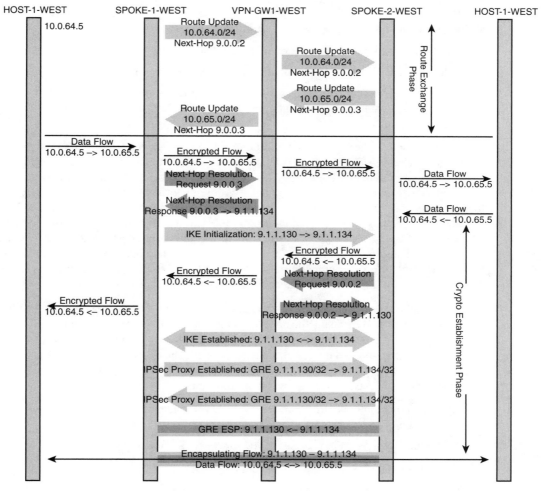

The originating spoke (that is, SPOKE-1-WEST) now has sufficient information to dynamically create a GRE tunnel instance to the remote spoke. The GRE tunnel instance will build an IP header with the tunnel source defined as the local spoke's public IP address (9.1.1.130) and the tunnel destination defined as the remote spoke's public IP address (9.1.1.134). Both of these addresses are routable on the IP backbone whereas the mGRE interface address may be a private address or non-routable address. You now have a viable tunnel path directly between the spokes, although you never defined an IPSec proxy for this instantiated point-to-point tunnel. Next, you'll explore the protection process of the instantiated GRE tunnel.

Dynamic IPSec Proxy Instantiation

The IPSec protection of GRE tunnels defined in previous chapters requires two fundamental attributes that were known prior to configuring the peer relationship:

- An IPSec proxy profile associated with each GRE tunnel
- A peer's IKE identity associated with the tunnel's IPSec proxy profile

The DMVPN architecture allows spokes to have dynamically assigned public addresses. Therefore, spokes cannot have preconfigured IPSec proxy profiles or IKE identities for spoke-to-spoke connections.

In previous chapters, the IPSec proxy profile matched the GRE tunnel header's IP source and destination address. A DMVPN with dynamic address assignment at the spokes precludes the ability to pre-configure the IPSec proxy. Therefore, Cisco developed an automatic IPSec proxy profile instantiation process for GRE tunnels. With IPSec protection of GRE tunnels, it is safe to assume that IPSec must protect the IP addresses encapsulating the GRE header. The NHRP reconciliation process provides the initiating spoke with the relevant tunnel destination IP address. The IPSec proxy profile is dynamically instantiated to protect the GRE packets sourced from the locally assigned public IP address and the remote's assigned public IP address. Any traffic routed into this GRE tunnel instance matches the IPSec proxy profile; therefore, IPSec protection is initiated for the instantiated point-to-point tunnel between the spokes.

The second dilemma arises because a key is needed to establish a relationship with the remote spoke's IKE identity. Here again, the initiating spoke cannot have a remote spoke's IKE identity and key configured a priori. However, by applying the same assumptions used in creating the IPSec proxy profile, the initiating spoke may assume that the destination IP address in the GRE tunnel is also the IKE identity of the peer. The initiating spoke must now associate a key with the inferred IKE identity. You have several options here:

- Pre-configure a unique pre-shared key for each IKE identity (if every IKE peer is known at the time of configuration)
- Pre-configure a globally pre-shared key for every IKE identity
- Implement a public key infrastructure

As noted, the first option is not viable when the spokes use dynamically assigned public IP addresses. A unique pre-shared key can only be configured where the peer's IKE identity is known. Clearly, this is not the case when spokes use dynamic public IP address assignments. The second option is to use the same pre-shared key across all the VPN gateways in the network where the IKE identity of the all the remote peers is specified as 0.0.0.0. The real IKE identity for a peer is instantiated by the NHRP routing proxy database (that is, the IKE identity is assumed to be the same as the remote GRE tunnel endpoint). This may be a satisfactory approach for some customers; however, the process of changing the pre-shared key may pose an interesting challenge if there are problems during the transition to a new pre-shared key. Assuming all the devices are accessible simultaneously, the pre-shared key could be changed on all the devices, and the transition period would be minimal. Unfortunately, most network management teams loathe a "flag day," on which all the devices must change at essentially the same time. Making global changes to a network in a short period of time is prone to error and makes recovery especially difficult. Doing so becomes especially troubling for large IPSec VPNs where DMVPN is implemented precisely to support scalability. The third option is to use digital certificates. The PKI option is certainly the most robust method; however, it is also the most complex. Nevertheless, PKI is the recommended method of securing the IKE establishment.

Establishing a Dynamic Multipoint VPN

Now that you have seen the three new fundamental functions in a DMVPN (mGRE interfaces, NHRP, and automatic IPSec), you will step through the process of multipoint VPN establishment. A typical VPN uses a hub site router as the central point of route control for an enterprise. The DMVPN architecture requires high availability of the hub site and uses a permanent IP address for IPSec connections. Most large VPN networks leverage redundant hub sites. DMVPN is certainly capable of leveraging the fault-tolerant models described in Chapter 6 "Designing Fault-Tolerant IPSec VPNs." For the purpose of this example, you will focus on a single hub router (VPN-GW1-WEST) in which you step through the basic building blocks for configuring the DMVPN and the subsequent traffic-driven events that initiate establishment of the full-mesh connectivity. Example 7-8 shows the hub's configuration associated with the following configuration elements:

- Establish the hub router with a static public IP interface
- Establish the hub router with the mGRE interface that references the public IP interface
- Enforce IPSec protection of the GRE interface
- Allow incoming IKE connections from any device protecting GRE
- Establish a dynamic routing protocol on the mGRE interface
- Establish the NHRP server process on the mGRE interface

Example 7-8   *Single Hub DMVPN Configuration*

```
vpn-gw1-west#show running-config
hostname "vpn-gw1-west"
!
crypto isakmp policy 1
 authentication pre-share
crypto isakmp key dmvpn address 0.0.0.0 0.0.0.0
!
crypto ipsec transform-set dmvpn-trans esp-des esp-md5-hmac
!
crypto ipsec profile dmvpn-profile
 set transform-set dmvpn-trans
!
! Multi-point GRE interface in DMVPN Private Overlay Cloud
```

continues

Example 7-8   *Single Hub DMVPN Configuration (Continued)*

```
! NHRP Server Config for Spoke clients
! OSPF Process associated with DMVPN Private Overlay Cloud
! Multi-point GRE header uses IP address in backbone routing domain
! Multi-point GRE header is used to build dynamic IPSec proxy
!
interface Tunnel0
 ip address 9.0.0.1 255.255.255.0
 ip mtu 1416
! NHRP authentication password used by the spokes to build an NHRP adjacency
 ip nhrp authentication nhrp-pwd
! Map multicast forwarding to any new dynamically created NHRP adjacencies
 ip nhrp map multicast dynamic
! Unique descriptor for the NHRP in this particular DMVPN cloud
 ip nhrp network-id 1
! Hold the NHRP state for 300 seconds before destroying the adjacency due to idle timer
expiration
 ip nhrp holdtime 300
 ip ospf network broadcast
 ip ospf priority 2
 ip ospf mtu-ignore
 tunnel source Serial0/0
 tunnel mode gre multipoint
 tunnel key 999
 tunnel protection ipsec profile dmvpn-profile
!
! Static IP Address in Backbone Routing Domain
interface Serial0/0
 ip address 9.1.1.10 255.255.255.252
!
! Private interface on protected subnet
interface Ethernet0/1
 ip address 10.1.0.1 255.255.255.0
!
! Routing process associated with private subnets and DMVPN cloud
router ospf 1
 router-id 10.1.0.1
 network 9.0.0.0 0.0.0.255 area 0
 network 10.0.0.0 0.0.0.255 area 0
!
ip route 0.0.0.0 0.0.0.0 9.1.1.9
```

Note from the configuration in Example 7-8 that the hub has no defined relationships with any spokes. The NHRP server process is ready to receive dynamic NHRP client associations. Likewise, the mGRE interface has no defined spoke destinations and, lastly, the IPSec proxies are undefined.

At this point, the hub is ready to receive spoke connections. Example 7-9 focuses on a remote site router (SPOKE-1-WEST) and shows the spoke configuration associated with the following configuration elements:

- Establish the spoke router with a dynamically assigned public interface or a permanent IP address
- Establish a mGRE interface on the spoke router that references the public IP address
- Enforce IPSec protection of the spoke's mGRE interface
- Allow incoming IKE connections from any device protecting GRE
- Establish a dynamic routing protocol on the mGRE interface referencing the hub as the route target
- Establish NHRP configuration on the mGRE interface referencing the hub as the NHRP server

Example 7-9 *Single Hub DMVPN Spoke Configuration*

```
spoke-1-west# show running-config
hostname "spoke-1-west "
!
crypto isakmp policy 1
 authentication pre-share
crypto isakmp key dmvpn address 0.0.0.0 0.0.0.0
!
!
crypto ipsec transform-set dmvpn-trans esp-des esp-md5-hmac
!
crypto ipsec profile dmvpn-profile
 set transform-set dmvpn-trans
!
! Multi-point GRE interface in DMVPN Private Overlay Cloud
! NHRP Client Config for Hub Server
! OSPF Process associated with DMVPN Private Overlay Cloud
! Multi-point GRE header uses IP address in backbone routing domain
! Multi-point GRE header is used to build dynamic IPSec proxy
!
interface Tunnel0
 ip address 9.0.0.2 255.255.255.0
 no ip redirects
 ip mtu 1416
 ip nhrp authentication nhrp-pwd
 ip nhrp map 9.0.0.1 9.1.1.10
 ip nhrp map multicast 9.1.1.10
 ip nhrp network-id 1
 ip nhrp holdtime 300
 ip nhrp nhs 9.0.0.1
 ip ospf network broadcast
 ip ospf priority 0
 ip ospf mtu-ignore
 tunnel source Serial0/0
 tunnel mode gre multipoint
 tunnel key 999
 tunnel protection ipsec profile dmvpn-profile
!
```

continues

Example 7-9   *Single Hub DMVPN Spoke Configuration (Continued)*

```
interface Serial0/0
 ip address 9.1.1.130 255.255.255.252
!
interface Ethernet0/1
 ip address 10.0.64.1 255.255.255.0
!
router ospf 1
 router-id 10.0.64.1
 log-adjacency-changes
 network 9.0.0.0 0.0.0.255 area 0
 network 9.1.0.0 0.0.0.255 area 0
 network 10.0.64.0 0.0.0.255 area 0
!
ip classless
ip route 0.0.0.0 0.0.0.0 9.1.1.129
!
!
```

Note in Example 7-9 that the NHRP client is statically configured to map the hub's NHRP private address in the DMVPN overlay cloud to the hub's backbone-facing public address.

At this point, the VPN configuration is complete. There are two phases to VPN establishment. The first phase establishes IPSec tunnels from all the spokes to the hub; these tunnels are persistent. The second phase begins when on-demand spoke-to-spoke IPSec tunnels are established with DMVPN, triggered by spoke-to-spoke traffic. Figure 7-8 shows the two phases of the topology that occur during the VPN establishment.

The sequence of events for the first phase is as follows:

1 The spoke router (SPOKE-1-WEST) is connected to the backbone IP infrastructure and an IP address is assigned to the public interface.

2 The NHRP configuration on the spoke's tunnel interface attempts to establish a connection through the GRE tunnel to the hub. Note that the hub's IP address is pre-configured on the spoke. The mGRE tunnel interface encapsulates the NHRP client request with the hub as the destination.

3 IPSec configuration on the spoke triggers IKE from the spoke to the hub based on a GRE connection request from the spoke to the hub site (the hub's IKE identity is inferred from the GRE tunnel endpoints).

4 At the completion of the IKE and IPSec process, an IPSec protected GRE tunnel is established between the spoke and hub.

5 The spoke's NHRP client registration with the hub's NHRP server creates an entry in the hub's NHRP database for the mapping of the client's mGRE tunnel address to its dynamically assigned public IP address.

6 Routing protocol configuration on the spoke provides the reachability information for protected subnets behind the spoke to the hub.

7 The hub advertises reachability of a spoke's protected subnets to other spokes. Note that when a hub advertises the subnets from one spoke to the other, the next hop for these routes is *not* that hub, but rather is the spoke that originated these subnets.

Figure 7-8   *DMVPN Connection Establishment*

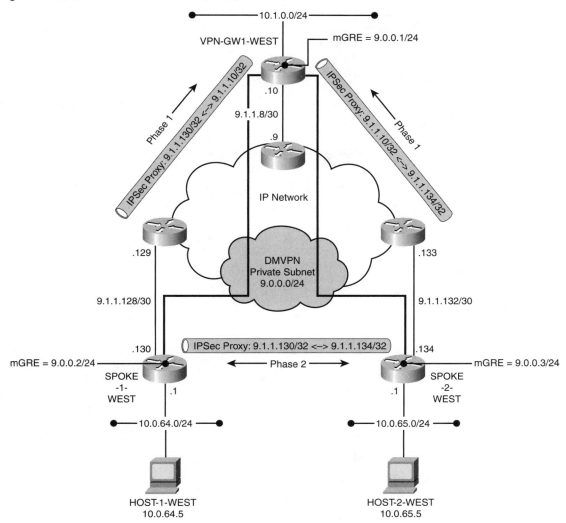

The process between the spoke and the hub of NHRP registration, IPSec tunnel establishment, and advertisement of the subnets are performed by all spokes in the DMVPN. Upon completion of this phase, all spokes have a persistent IPSec tunnel established with the hub, and dynamic routing has advertised reachability for all protected subnets to the hub and all spokes. Note that there is no pre-configured IPSec tunnel configuration defined between the spokes.

Next, you will look at the state of the hub-and-spoke router prior to sending data between the spokes. The VPN-GW1-WEST router has two IPSec sessions established that protect instantiated GRE tunnels to the SPOKE-1-WEST and SPOKE-2-WEST. We also see that the VPN-GW1-WEST has two NHRP clients registered that correspond to the spokes' public backbone interfaces. Lastly, the OSPF routing updates from the spokes have provided the appropriate GRE next hop. Example 7-10 shows the IPSec state of the hub VPN-GW1-WEST, Example 7-11 shows the NHRP state, and Example 7-12 shows the OSPF state.

Example 7-10 *Hub State for IPSec in DMVPN*

```
vpn-gw1-west#show crypto map
Crypto Map "Tunnel0-head-0" 1 ipsec-isakmp
        Profile name: dmvpn-profile
        Security association lifetime: 4608000 kilobytes/3600 seconds
        PFS (Y/N): N
        Transform sets={
                dmvpn-trans,
        }

Crypto Map "Tunnel0-head-0" 2 ipsec-isakmp
        Map is a PROFILE INSTANCE.
        Peer = 9.1.1.130
        Extended IP access list
            access-list  permit gre host 9.1.1.10 host 9.1.1.130
        Current peer: 9.1.1.130
        Security association lifetime: 4608000 kilobytes/3600 seconds
        PFS (Y/N): N
        Transform sets={
                dmvpn-trans,
        }

Crypto Map "Tunnel0-head-0" 3 ipsec-isakmp
        Map is a PROFILE INSTANCE.
        Peer = 9.1.1.134
        Extended IP access list
            access-list  permit gre host 9.1.1.10 host 9.1.1.134
        Current peer: 9.1.1.134
        Security association lifetime: 4608000 kilobytes/3600 seconds
        PFS (Y/N): N
        Transform sets={
                dmvpn-trans,
        }
        Interfaces using crypto map Tunnel0-head-0:
                Tunnel0
```

Example 7-11 *Hub State for NHRP in DMVPN*

```
vpn-gw1-west#show ip nhrp
9.0.0.2/32 via 9.0.0.2, Tunnel0 created 00:58:30, expire 00:04:32
  Type: dynamic, Flags: authoritative unique registered
  NBMA address: 9.1.1.130
9.0.0.3/32 via 9.0.0.3, Tunnel0 created 00:16:03, expire 00:03:52
  Type: dynamic, Flags: authoritative unique registered
  NBMA address: 9.1.1.134
```

Example 7-12 *OSPF State for Hub's Neighbor Adjacency*

```
vpn-gw1-west#show ip ospf neighbor

Neighbor ID     Pri   State          Dead Time   Address      Interface
10.0.65.1       0     FULL/DROTHER   00:00:36    9.0.0.3      Tunnel0
10.0.64.1       0     FULL/DROTHER   00:00:36    9.0.0.2      Tunnel0
vpn-gw1-west# show ip route

     9.0.0.0/8 is variably subnetted, 3 subnets, 2 masks
C       9.1.1.8/30 is directly connected, Serial0/0
C       9.0.0.0/24 is directly connected, Tunnel0
     10.0.0.0/8 is variably subnetted, 6 subnets, 2 masks
C       10.1.0.0/24 is directly connected, Ethernet0/1
O       10.0.64.0/24 [110/11] via 9.0.0.2, 00:14:59, Tunnel0
O       10.0.65.0/24 [110/11] via 9.0.0.3, 00:15:00, Tunnel0
S       0.0.0.0 [1/0] via 9.1.1.9
```

Most importantly, we see that the hub (VPN-GW1-WEST) has the necessary information to link the spoke routes (10.0.64.0, 10.0.65.0) to the appropriate GRE next-hop address (9.0.0.2, 9.0.0.3) and the GRE next-hop address to the backbone interface address (9.1.1.130, 9.1.1.134).

A quick look at the SPOKE-1-WEST state shows that it has established a single IPSec connection to the hub, registered as an NHRP client, and provided a routing update. Example 7-13 shows the IPSec state of SPOKE-1-WEST, Example 7-14 shows the NHRP state, and Example 7-15 shows the OSPF state.

Example 7-13 *Spoke State for IPSec in DMVPN*

```
spoke-1-west# show crypto map
Crypto Map "Tunnel0-head-0" 1 ipsec-isakmp
        Profile name: dmvpn-profile
        Security association lifetime: 4608000 kilobytes/3600 seconds
        PFS (Y/N): N
        Transform sets={
                dmvpn-trans,
        }

Crypto Map "Tunnel0-head-0" 2 ipsec-isakmp
        Map is a PROFILE INSTANCE.
        Peer = 9.1.1.10
        Extended IP access list
```

continues

Example 7-13 *Spoke State for IPSec in DMVPN (Continued)*

```
              access-list  permit gre host 9.1.1.130 host 9.1.1.10
          Current peer: 9.1.1.10
          Security association lifetime: 4608000 kilobytes/3600 seconds
          PFS (Y/N): N
          Transform sets={
                  dmvpn-trans,
          }
          Interfaces using crypto map Tunnel0-head-0:
                  Tunnel0
```

Example 7-14 *Spoke State for NHRP in DMVPN*

```
spoke-1-west#show ip nhrp
9.0.0.1/32 via 9.0.0.1, Tunnel0 created 01:00:34, never expire
  Type: static, Flags: authoritative used
  NBMA address: 9.1.1.10
```

Example 7-15 *Spoke State for OSPF in DMVPN*

```
spoke-1-west#show ip ospf neighbor

Neighbor ID     Pri    State          Dead Time    Address       Interface
10.0.0.1          2    FULL/DR        00:00:32     9.0.0.1       Tunnel0

spoke-1-west#show ip route

     9.0.0.0/8 is variably subnetted, 3 subnets, 2 masks
C        9.0.0.0/24 is directly connected, Tunnel0
C        9.1.1.128/30 is directly connected, Serial0/0
     10.0.0.0/8 is variably subnetted, 6 subnets, 2 masks
O        10.0.0.0/24 [110/11] via 9.0.0.1, 00:59:50, Tunnel0
C        10.0.64.0/24 is directly connected, Ethernet0/1
O        10.0.65.0/24 [110/11] via 9.0.0.3, 00:59:52, Tunnel0
S        0.0.0.0 [1/0] via 9.1.1.129
```

The important element to note in the SPOKE-1-WEST state is that the protected subnet 10.0.65.0 is accessible via a next hop of 9.0.0.3, in which Tunnel0 is a member of the 9.0.0.0 subnet. In addition, the Next Hop Server (NHS, 9.0.0.1) for the network 9.0.0.0 is accessible via 9.1.1.10. The spoke has sufficient information to resolve a route to SPOKE-2-WEST's protected prefix.

With the completion of phase 1, all communication between the hub and spoke takes place over the persistent IPSec tunnels. Next, assume that a spoke has traffic destined for another spoke. DMVPN can dynamically build an IPSec tunnel between the spokes to achieve direct spoke-to-spoke communication as follows:

1   A host on the protected subnet of SPOKE-1-WEST needs to establish a connection to a host on the protected subnet of SPOKE-2-WEST. An IP packet is directed from HOST-1-WEST to HOST-2-WEST.

2 Phase 1 populated the routing table on SPOKE-1-WEST for SPOKE-2-WEST's protected subnet via a next hop of SPOKE-2-WEST's tunnel IP address. But SPOKE-1-WEST does not have the public IP address of SPOKE-2-WEST. This mapping is available in the NHRP database of the hub (VPN-GW1-WEST), and therefore, SPOKE-1-WEST sends an NHRP request to VPN-GW1-WEST to resolve SPOKE-2-WEST's public IP address.

3 While SPOKE-1-WEST is waiting for the NHRP response from VPN-GW1-WEST, it forwards the packet destined to SPOKE-2-WEST's protected subnet via the hub (VPN-GW1-WEST). All spoke-to-spoke traffic via the hub will be decrypted and re-encrypted at the hub while waiting for the spoke-to-spoke tunnel to be established. Note that the encryption and decryption at the hub calls for extra processing overhead for the hub and induces latency for spoke-to-spoke traffic, and thus, may not be suitable for certain applications, such as voice.

4 VPN-GW1-WEST forwards the packets it receives from SPOKE-1-WEST and routes them to SPOKE-2-WEST.

5 Meanwhile, VPN-GW1-WEST responds to the NHRP resolution request and informs SPOKE-1-WEST that a direct NHRP mapping exists between SPOKE-1-WEST and SPOKE-2-WEST using the publicly assigned IP address of SPOKE-2-WEST.

6 The SPOKE-1-WEST installs the NHRP mapping from 9.0.0.3 -> 9.1.1.134, which triggers IKE/IPSec to SPOKE-2-WEST. While the IKE/IPSec negotiation is not complete, all data to SPOKE-2-WEST will continue to transit via VPN-GW1-WEST.

7 Upon completion of the IKE and IPSec establishment, packets from HOST-1-WEST to HOST-2-WEST use the direct IPSec-protected GRE tunnel between SPOKE-1-WEST and SPOKE-2-WEST.

We have now established a bidirectional IPSec connection between the spokes. The IPSec proxy is protecting a dynamically established GRE tunnel between the spokes' mGRE interfaces. Note that SPOKE-2-WEST has not resolved a reverse path. The first response packet from HOST-2-WEST to HOST-1-WEST will initiate a similar process in the reverse direction. In this case, the IPSec SA already exists and only the route proxy resolution is necessary. The establishment of the dynamic point-to-point GRE tunnel between the spokes will use the existing IPSec SA.

Next, you will contrast the state of SPOKE-1-WEST after it has established a direct connection to SPOKE-2-WEST. Example 7-16 shows the IPSec state.

Example 7-16 *Spoke State for IPSec DMVPN with Direct Connection*

```
show crypto map
Crypto Map "Tunnel0-head-0" 1 ipsec-isakmp
        Profile name: dmvpn-profile
        Security association lifetime: 4608000 kilobytes/3600 seconds
        PFS (Y/N): N
        Transform sets={
                dmvpn-trans,
```

continues

Example 7-16 *Spoke State for IPSec DMVPN with Direct Connection (Continued)*

```
        }

Crypto Map "Tunnel0-head-0" 2 ipsec-isakmp
        Map is a PROFILE INSTANCE.
        Peer = 9.1.1.10
        Extended IP access list
            access-list  permit gre host 9.1.1.130 host 9.1.1.10
        Current peer: 9.1.1.10
        Security association lifetime: 4608000 kilobytes/3600 seconds
        PFS (Y/N): N
        Transform sets={
                dmvpn-trans,
        }

Crypto Map "Tunnel0-head-0" 3 ipsec-isakmp
        Map is a PROFILE INSTANCE.
        Peer = 9.1.1.134
        Extended IP access list
            access-list  permit gre host 9.1.1.130 host 9.1.1.134
        Current peer: 9.1.1.134
        Security association lifetime: 4608000 kilobytes/3600 seconds
        PFS (Y/N): N
        Transform sets={
                dmvpn-trans,
        }
        Interfaces using crypto map Tunnel0-head-0:
                Tunnel0
```

Note that a crypto map tunnel instance number 3 has been created with IPSec protection
between the two spokes. The crypto map and tunnel instance are temporary in nature and will
expire after the lifetime interval has passed. So how does the SPOKE-1-WEST know to tunnel
a packet destined 10.0.65.0 with the appropriate GRE/IP header? During the NHRP resolution
and tunnel establishment phase, the Cisco Express Forwarding (CEF) forwarding and
adjacency entries are updated such that the appropriate encapsulation is applied to the packet.
Example 7-17 shows the CEF forwarding state for the route prefix 10.0.65.0 and tunnel to
9.0.0.3 in addition to the adjacency table for the tunnel.

Example 7-17 *CEF State for DMVPN Tunnel*

```
spoke-1-west#show ip cef tunnel 0 detail
Adjacency Table has 4 adjacencies
9.0.0.0/24, version 25, epoch 0, attached, connected
0 packets, 0 bytes
  via Tunnel0, 0 dependencies
    valid glean adjacency
9.0.0.1/32, version 14, epoch 0
0 packets, 0 bytes
  via 9.0.0.1, Tunnel0, 0 dependencies
    next hop 9.0.0.1, Tunnel0
    valid adjacency
```

Example 7-17 *CEF State for DMVPN Tunnel (Continued)*

```
9.0.0.3/32, version 30, epoch 0, connected
0 packets, 0 bytes
  via 9.0.0.3, Tunnel0, 0 dependencies
    next hop 9.0.0.3, Tunnel0
    valid adjacency
10.1.0.0/24, version 27, epoch 0
0 packets, 0 bytes
  via 9.0.0.1, Tunnel0, 0 dependencies
    next hop 9.0.0.1, Tunnel0
    valid adjacency
10.0.65.0/24, version 28, epoch 0
0 packets, 0 bytes
  via 9.0.0.3, Tunnel0, 0 dependencies
    next hop 9.0.0.3, Tunnel0
    valid adjacency

spoke-1-west# show adjacency tunnel 0 detail
Protocol Interface                Address
IP       Tunnel0                  9.0.0.1(5)
                                  0 packets, 0 bytes
                                  4500000000000000FF2FA74109010182
                                  0901010A20000800000003E7
; BOLD HEX = 9.1.1.10
                                  TED          never
                                  Epoch: 0
IP       Tunnel0                  9.0.0.3(5)
                                  0 packets, 0 bytes
                                  4500000000000000FF2FA6C509010182
                                  0901018620000800000003E7
; BOLD HEX = 9.1.1.134
                                  TED          never
                                  Epoch: 0
```

You see from the CEF table that 10.0.65.0 is bound to the next hop (9.0.0.3) and that it has a valid adjacency. The adjacency table shows that the GRE/IP encapsulating header for the destination 9.0.0.3 has a source of 0x09010182 (9.1.1.130) and destination of 0x0901086 (9.1.1.134). Both of these addresses are routable within the backbone and are included in the IPSec proxy statement.

With all the machinery in place (GRE, NHRP, IPSec, and CEF), it is possible to dynamically build a full-mesh IPSec-connected network while provisioning only a single hub-and-spoke topology. The DMVPN mechanism has dramatically simplified the provisioning model while allowing the any-to-any capabilities of IP network to be exploited. Clearly, the solution allows for a very scalable network architecture. With scalability, however, comes the need to address resiliency. Next, you will examine the methods needed to increase fault tolerance in the DMVPN network.

DMVPN Architectural Redundancy

The DMVPN architecture supports two redundancy models. One model uses redundant hubs within the single mGRE subnet. The other uses separate mGRE subnets. A single DMVPN subnet is subject to the limitations of a single routing protocol in the mGRE subnet. In contrast, the dual DMVPN model allows flexibility in the assignment of unique routing protocols and cost metrics on two distinct DMVPN subnets. Figure 7-9 and Figure 7-10 highlight the differences between the two models.

Figure 7-9 *Dual Hub, Single Subnet DMVPN Redundancy*

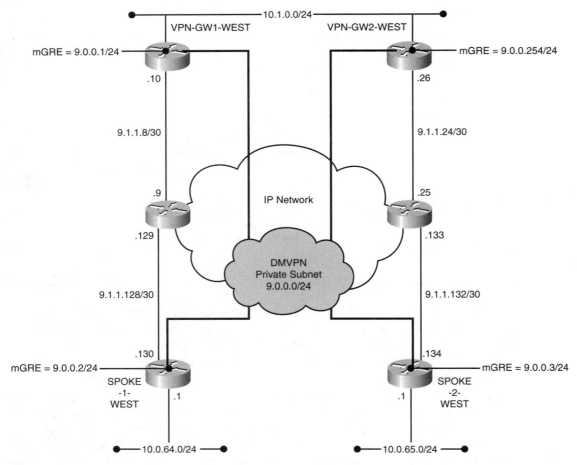

The DMVPN cloud serves as an overlay network in which all the hubs and spokes appear directly connected in a common subnet. In this model, the spokes are all NHRP clients to both hub routers, and the secondary hub router is a client to the primary hub router. The primary hub router should have a routing priority or metric defined such that it serves as the primary transit point. The loss of the primary hub router allows the routing to gracefully failover to the secondary hub router.

In contrast to the single DMVPN cloud, the dual DMVPN cloud uses distinct interfaces on the hubs and spokes to maintain connectivity in two overlay subnets.

Figure 7-10   *Dual Hub, Dual Subnet DMVPN Redundancy*

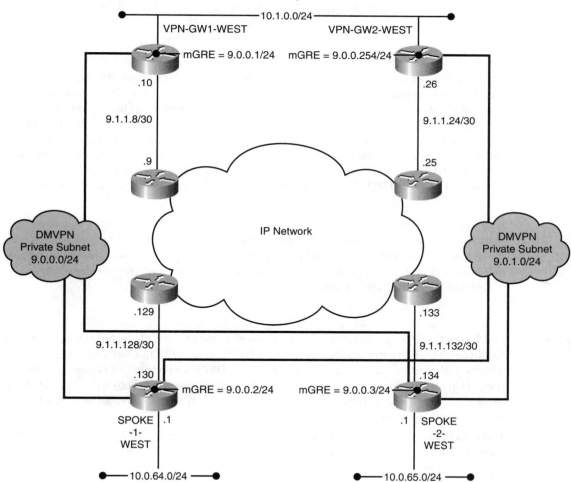

NOTE   The most significant limitation of the dual subnet DMVPN model is the requirement to use an IP address with a unique IKE identity on the spoke for each mGRE interface. The unique IKE identity addresses allow IKE to associate the IPSec SA from a DMVPN cloud with the spoke's appropriate mGRE interface. The IKE identities might be associated with separate logical backbone interfaces. Alternately, the IKE identity might also be a loopback interface associated with the appropriate DMVPN cloud.

The requirement to provide a unique IKE identity for each DMVPN cloud was relaxed in Cisco IOS 12.3(4.2).

Let's now turn our attention to the dual hub, single DMVPN subnet model. The DMVPN model uses an IP subnet that is common to all the Multipoint GRE interfaces of the spokes and the designated hub. Each router's Multipoint GRE interface is a member of the common subnet. In previous examples, we designated a single hub for the subnet and all of the spokes registered with the hub. If the hub fails, the entire DMVPN state will be ruined because the hub acts as the routing proxy point. Although the IPSec SAs may not immediately expire, the routing integrity is disrupted. Clearly, redundancy is needed. Redundancy is easily accomplished by defining a secondary hub in the DMVPN cloud. Figure 7-11 shows the relationship between the routers in a dual hub-and-spoke DMVPN.

Each spoke may register with the Next Hop Server (NHS) on both the primary and secondary hubs such that an alternate route proxy point is established. A failure of the primary hub forces the secondary hub to serve as the DMVPN cloud's route proxy server. Note that the secondary hub is a client of the NHS on the primary hub. The routing protocol should naturally synchronize with the active NHS processes.

NOTE   OSPF uses the priority setting for selecting the designated router (DR) such that the router with the highest OSPF priority will be elected the DR. The primary NHS should have the highest priority, followed by the secondary NHS, and so on. OSPF supports only a primary designated router (DR) and backup designated router (BDR); therefore, only two hubs will be viable at any given time. The spokes should never be selected as a DR; therefore, the spoke router's OSPF process should have a priority of zero.

Distance vector routing protocols such as EIGRP and RIP must use interface metrics to influence the selection of the primary router.

Figure 7-11   *Dual Hub-and-Spoke DMVPN Architecture*

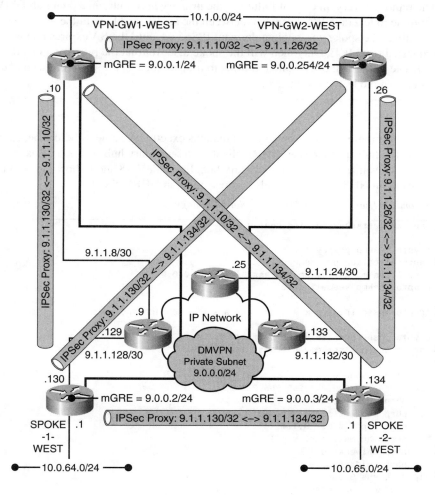

When a spoke is unable to connect to the primary hub router's NHS, the NHRP client connections from the spokes will timeout. The spokes will then seek to resolve routes through the secondary hub's NHS. The hold timer for the NHRP client process will determine the convergence interval before new connections can be established using the secondary hub's NHS as the route proxy.

Note that existing connections between spokes are retained because their IKE and IPSec SAs do not expire and the resolved addresses for the spokes are consistent on the secondary hub. The recovery process is essentially the same as the initial establishment of the DMVPN network. Once connectivity is restored to primary hub, all the spokes attempt to register with the primary hub, and subsequently, use the primary hub's routing database for route resolution.

NOTE   The rapid recovery, in case of failure of the primary hub router in a dual hub DMVPN, may continue to leverage IKE keepalive between the spokes and hub. In the absence of IKE keepalive, the spoke will retain a dormant IPSec SA until the SA expires and new keys are requested from IKE. Only then will the spoke discover that the primary hub's IPSec state was lost. The spoke will use dynamic routing to transition packet flows to the secondary hub much faster than the IKE convergence.

The configuration for the primary hub remains exactly the same as before because the secondary hub appears as an NHRP client. The secondary hub serves both as an NHS for the spokes as well as a client to the primary hub. Example 7-18 shows how the secondary hub serves as an NHS server while also representing an NHRP client.

Example 7-18   *Secondary Hub in a Single DMVPN Subnet Topology*

```
vpn-gw2-west#show running-config
!
crypto isakmp policy 1
 authentication pre-share
crypto isakmp key dmvpn address 0.0.0.0 0.0.0.0
crypto isakmp keepalive 10
!
crypto ipsec transform-set dmvpn-trans esp-des esp-md5-hmac
!
crypto ipsec profile dmvpn-profile
 set transform-set dmvpn-trans
!
interface Tunnel0
 ip address 9.0.0.254 255.255.255.0
 ip nhrp authentication nhrp-pwd
 ip nhrp map multicast dynamic
 ip nhrp map 9.0.0.1 9.1.1.10
 ip nhrp map multicast 9.1.1.10
 ip nhrp network-id 1
 ip nhrp holdtime 300
 ip nhrp nhs 9.0.0.1
 ip ospf network broadcast
 ip ospf cost 15
 ip ospf priority 1
 ip ospf mtu-ignore
 tunnel source Serial0/0
 tunnel mode gre multipoint
 tunnel key 999
 tunnel protection ipsec profile dmvpn-profile
!
interface Serial0/0
 ip address 9.1.1.26 255.255.255.252
!
interface Ethernet0/1
 ip address 10.1.0.2 255.255.255.0
```

Example 7-18 *Secondary Hub in a Single DMVPN Subnet Topology (Continued)*

```
!
router ospf 1
 router-id 10.1.0.2
 network 9.0.0.0 0.0.0.255 area 0
 network 10.1.0.0 0.0.0.255 area 0
 default-information originate
!
ip route 0.0.0.0 0.0.0.0 9.1.1.25
!
```

The listing shows that the secondary hub, VPN-GW2-WEST, uses VPN-GW1-WEST as the primary NHS while also accepting incoming NHRP requests. Note that the OSPF priority is configured as a lower value than the primary hub, but configured as a higher value than the spokes. This ensures that the spokes use the primary hub's routing database as the designated router. Should the primary hub fail, the secondary hub will transition from the OSPF backup designated router to the OSPF designated router. Example 7-19 shows the configuration listing for the spoke that is dual homed to the primary and secondary hubs.

Example 7-19 *Spoke Configuration in a Dual Hub, Single DMVPN Topology*

```
spoke-2-west# show running-config
!
crypto isakmp policy 1
 authentication pre-share
crypto isakmp key dmvpn address 0.0.0.0 0.0.0.0
crypto isakmp keepalive 10
!
!
crypto ipsec transform-set dmvpn-trans esp-des esp-md5-hmac
!
crypto ipsec profile dmvpn-profile
 set transform-set dmvpn-trans
!
!
!

!
interface Tunnel0
 ip address 9.0.0.3 255.255.255.0
 ip mtu 1416
 ip nhrp authentication nhrp-pwd
 ip nhrp map 9.0.0.1 9.1.1.10
 ip nhrp map multicast 9.1.1.10
 ip nhrp map 9.0.0.254 9.1.1.26
 ip nhrp map multicast 9.1.1.26
 ip nhrp network-id 1
 ip nhrp holdtime 300
 ip nhrp nhs 9.0.0.1
 ip nhrp nhs 9.0.0.254
 ip ospf network broadcast
```

continues

Example 7-19 *Spoke Configuration in a Dual Hub, Single DMVPN Topology (Continued)*

```
ip ospf priority 0
ip ospf mtu-ignore
delay 1000
tunnel source Serial0/0
tunnel mode gre multipoint
tunnel key 999
tunnel protection ipsec profile dmvpn-profile
!
interface Serial0/0
 ip address 9.1.1.134 255.255.255.252
 no fair-queue
!
interface Ethernet0/1
 ip address 10.0.65.1 255.255.255.0
 half-duplex
 no keepalive
!
router ospf 1
 router-id 10.0.65.1
 log-adjacency-changes
 network 9.0.0.0 0.0.0.255 area 0
 network 10.0.65.0 0.0.0.255 area 0
!
ip route 9.1.1.10 255.255.255.255 9.1.1.133
ip route 9.1.1.26 255.255.255.255 9.1.1.133
```

A couple of key issues to note in the spoke configuration: There are two NHS servers specified. There is no priority in the order of the NHS servers, and the spoke will establish IPSec-protected GRE connections to both VPN gateways VPN-GW1-WEST and VPN-GW2-WEST. The priority of one server over the other is determined by the OSPF routing priority. The spoke should never serve as the designated or backup designated router; therefore, its OSPF priority is set to zero.

DMVPN Model Summary

As in the TED model, the benefits of DMVPN are not achieved without some constraints necessary to make the solution functional. The VPN gateways serving as a route database proxy must have statically assigned public IP addresses. Usually this is not a problem because the route proxy function is typically implemented on the enterprise hub routers. With the hub router's proxy IP address known at the time of spoke configuration, the spokes are able to register with the hub route proxy and establish routing adjacencies. Essentially, a persistent hub-and-spoke network is dynamically established. The route proxy provides reference information about all of the VPN routes and the VPN gateways protecting each IP address block. The reference information allows every registered VPN gateway to establish a direct IPSec-protected GRE tunnel to any other VPN gateway without having a statically configured GRE tunnel and IPSec peer relationship defined.

Summary

We provided two viable means of building auto-configuration IPSec VPNs using dynamic IPSec connection models. In both methods, the configuration complexity is dramatically simplified while temporarily establishing IPSec connections for specific data flows. The models conserve IPSec resources that may be critical in low-end routers where full-mesh networks are required. The spoke-to-spoke IPSec SAs are established only when direct traffic flows are present and may use dynamically assigned backbone interfaces. Once the traffic flows are present, the IPSec proxies are automatically instantiated based on traffic flow requirements. All of these attributes enable the IPSec VPN to scale to very large network topologies.

You learned that there are limitations with both of the auto-configuration models —particularly with key management. However, DMVPN has some significant advantages. Particularly, the DMVPN leverages the mGRE encapsulation process to allow private address to traverse public IP networks. In addition, the mGRE interface supports multicast traffic. The multicast-capable mGRE interface enables IPSec protection of routing protocols and also allows other multicast routing processes to function on the IPSec VPN.

Clearly, the DMVPN model facilitates the creation of a robust IPSec VPN that scales to large networks while conserving resources in low-end routers that do not require permanent IPSec connections to all members of the VPN. You also saw that the DMVPN model can significantly simplify the configuration of the basic hub-and-spoke configuration. Even if there is no requirement for spoke-to-spoke traffic, the DMVPN is quite useful for operational simplification. DMVPN does support spokes with dynamical public addresses because the NHRP process provides a means of reconciling the private to public address for each spoke registered with the NHRP server.

You have observed several ways in which constraints come into play when designing large networks, especially in the areas of provisioning, peer termination scalability, and fault tolerance. The next chapter addresses many of the scalability and performance limitations that dominate the design criteria when building large IPSec VPNs.

CHAPTER 8

IPSec and Application Interoperability

One of the primary motivations for deploying an IPSec VPN is financial cost savings, yet deploying an IPSec VPN may affect the interoperability of other applications, such as voice and video. Therefore, there is an operational cost to deploying IPSec. Although previous chapters demonstrated many methods for simplifying IPSec VPNs, they did not address the opportunity costs that impact deployment of voice and video over the VPN.

In this chapter, you examine the challenges with deploying voice and video applications on an IPSec VPN, and explore techniques to overcome those challenges. Given that voice and video are typically real-time applications, the network's performance must be carefully engineered to meet the application requirements. It is critical to note that real-time and delay-sensitive applications require consistent performance from the network infrastructure. In fact, variability in network performance may make the application completely dysfunctional.

Capacity management is one of the most basic tenets of network engineering. Applications, such as circuit-switched telephony, have well-defined bandwidth requirements per call. The migration of circuit-switched telephony to packet-based telephony introduces a whole new genre of capacity engineering principles. The statistical nature of a packet network requires more granular quality of service (QoS) mechanisms to ensure that voice (real-time) and video (pseudo real-time) packets receive the proper capacity at each routing node in the network.

NOTE   Voice-over IP fundamentals are beyond the scope of this book. To learn more about the fundamentals of packet voice and QoS requirements associated with real-time applications, you may refer to *Voice over IP Fundamentals* (Cisco Press, 2000) or *Voice-Enabling the Data Network: H.323, MGCP, SIP, QoS, SLAs, and Security* (Cisco Press, 2002).

One thing is clear: IPSec complicates the capacity management task for enabling real-time applications. To begin, you explore some of the nuances of enabling QoS on IPSec VPNs in order to assess the impact to applications such as packet voice and video.

QoS-Enabled IPSec VPNs

The growing availability of IP networks has fueled tremendous momentum towards convergence of voice, video, and data onto a single infrastructure—all based on IP. Among the obstacles network engineers face when trying to combine voice, video, and data onto one network is that different types of traffic require different levels of service from the network. The answer to deploying these services over IP networks is to use the various IP QoS mechanisms to condition traffic streams based on the type of service that each requires. Although a complete description of IP QoS mechanisms is beyond the scope of this book, in this section you will be presented with an overview of IP QoS mechanisms and will focus on the specific challenges of deploying these mechanisms over IPSec.

Overview of IP QoS Mechanisms

IP QoS mechanisms can be classified into two broad categories:

- Packet classification
- Congestion management

Packet classification, or coloring of packets, is a means of classifying packets into traffic classes so that the IP network can offer differentiated services based on traffic classes. In an IP network, packets may be classified on a flow basis by the five IP protocol attributes—that is, the 5-tuple: source IP address, destination IP address, IP protocol field, source ports, and destination ports. Although an IP network could apply QoS on an individual flow basis, this mechanism is not very scalable as the number of flows can be very large. The generally accepted best practice is to categorize the packets into traffic classes based on their flow parameters and mark the IP precedence or Differentiated Services Code Point (DSCP) field of a packet based on its traffic class. Once the packets are classified as priority voice/video traffic, congestion management or avoidance mechanisms such as Class-Based Weighted Fair Queuing (CBWFQ), Low-Latency Queuing (LLQ), or Weighted Random Early Discard (WRED) can be applied to the packets. These mechanisms allow the network to treat priority applications with consistency, thereby fulfilling their network requirements.

Figure 8-1 shows the typical IP QoS process flow.

Figure 8-1   *QoS Process Flow*

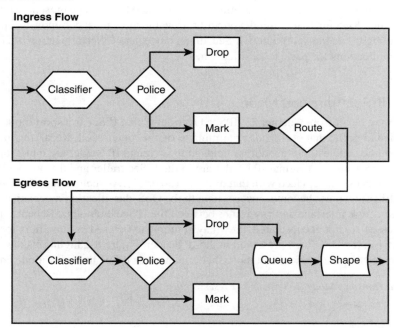

IPSec Implications for Classification

The classification of IP packets on the 5-tuple described previously is easily accomplished on unencrypted traffic, although IPSec presents a challenge to packet classification. As you saw in Chapter 2, "IPSec Overview," IPSec headers may mask the original IP packet header information such as protocol identifiers and source and destination port numbers. We know that the IPSec process will encapsulate the original IP header (tunnel mode) with a new IP header or add an IPSec header behind the original IP header (transport mode). In the process, the protocol identifiers and port numbers are replaced with IPSec protocols and ports. ESP uses the IP protocol ID of 50, and AH uses 51. The IKE protocol uses IP protocol ID 17 (that is, UDP) with port number 500. Finally, IPsec Network Address Translation–Transparency (NAT-T) also uses UDP encapsulation with port number 4500 as a means to provide IPsec establishment through NAT gateways. The only remaining QoS attributes available following encryption are the DSCP bits identified in the IKE, ESP, NAT-T, or AH IP header.

Note that the IPSec standard specifies the automatic preservation of the DSCP bits in the original IP packet. As such, the original IP header's DSCP must be present in the IPSec packet's IP header. Keeping that in mind, you will review the three most common encapsulation models including IPSec transport mode, IPSec tunnel mode, and IPSec protection of GRE, and explore the implications for packet classification.

QoS Applied to IPSec Transport Mode

You may recall from Chapter 2, "IPSec Overview," that IPSec transport mode is typically applied to traffic that originates or terminates on the router itself. Recall that in transport mode the source and destination address fields in the original IP header are intact, but the protocol identifiers from the original IP header are in the IPSec trailer and the protocol identifier in the original packet is replaced with that of IPSec (50 or 51). As such, access to the original protocol identifier and ports becomes inaccessible to the QoS classification mechanisms applied on the IPSec egress interface and any router between the IPSec endpoints. Because the original IP addresses are not encapsulated, they may continue to be used as classifiers for IP QoS. Likewise, the DSCP are preserved in the IP header. Figure 8-2 highlights the typical QoS attributes that are masked and those that remain after IPSec transport mode encapsulation.

Figure 8-2   *IPSec Transport Mode QoS Attribute Preservation*

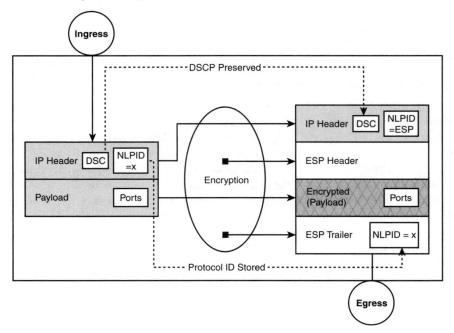

QoS Applied to IPSec Tunnel Mode

In contrast to IPSec transport mode, you learned that with the IPSec tunnel mode, the original IP packet is encapsulated with a new IP header; therefore, all of the original QoS attributes in the IP header (that is, the IP addresses, protocols, and ports) are lost, with the exception of DSCP, which must be copied into the encapsulating IPSec header. None of these lost attributes can be used for classification by the router on the IPSec egress interface or any router between the IPSec endpoints. Figure 8-3 highlights the typical QoS attributes that are masked and those that remain after IPSec tunnel mode encapsulation. Note also the disposition of the protocol identifier (Proto ID) from the original packet to the encrypted packet.

IPSec Transport Mode - QoS Attribute Preservation of GRE Tunnels

With IPSec-protected GRE, the original IP packet is first encapsulated during the GRE process. Of course, similar to the IPSec tunnel mode, the entire original IP packet is encapsulated, hiding the original QoS attributes (addresses, protocols, and ports). The new GRE IP header should copy the DSCP field; however, the protocol will change to protocol ID 47 and the IP addresses will be specified by the GRE encapsulation process. Next, the GRE IP packet must pass through the IPSec encapsulation process defined previously. Clearly, the IPSec process will only be able to preserve the QoS attributes specified in the GRE IP header (that is, addresses and DSCP for transport mode, DSCP for tunnel mode, and GRE protocol ID if qos pre-classify is used). Figure 8-4 highlights the protocol attributes typically used for QoS, and shows those that are encrypted or hidden as well as those that remain accessible to QoS processing after IPSec transport mode encapsulation of GRE tunnels.

Figure 8-3 *IPSec Tunnel Mode QoS Attribute Preservation*

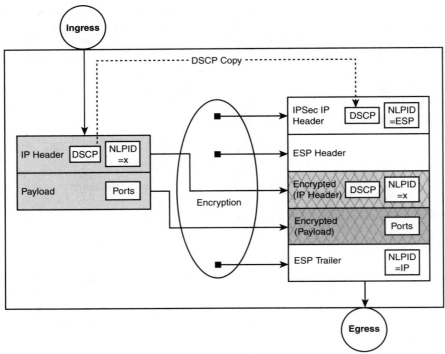

NOTE	Note that qos pre-classify may be applied to the tunnel interface as well. Doing so allows the original IP packet's attributes to be available for subsequent crypto and QoS processing. These attributes are only available to the processes on the encrypting gateway. Any QoS functions between the encrypting and decrypting gateways will not have access to this information; therefore, it's imperative that the DSCP be marked appropriately for consistent application of QoS tools.

Figure 8-4   *IPSec Transport Mode QoS Attribute Preservation of GRE*

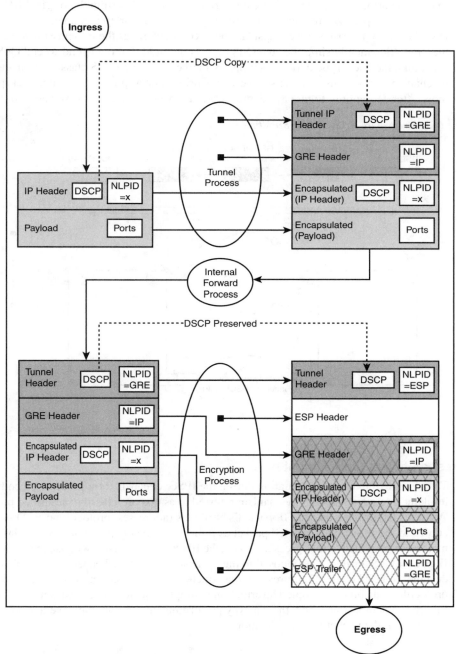

Transitive QoS Applied to IPSec

In this scenario, the only persistent QoS attribute is the DSCP from the original IP header. Again, this emphasizes the importance of classifying and marking an unencrypted packet's DSCP prior to incurring any encapsulation (GRE or IPSec) as the pre-classification and marking dramatically simplifies the QoS models required to provide end-to-end QoS. Assuming the unencrypted traffic is properly marked, the same QoS classification and queuing mechanisms may be used in the sub-networks prior to encryption, those after encryption, and those after decryption. Figure 8-5 demonstrates the value of the transitive nature of the DSCP.

Figure 8-5 *Transitive Nature of DSCP in IPSec VPNs*

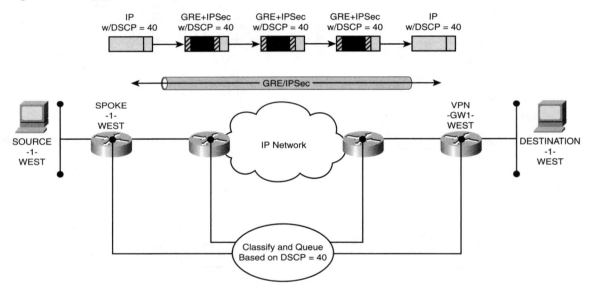

Internal Preservation of QoS Attributes

To reconcile the loss of information during the IPSec encapsulation process, Cisco has implemented a special QoS mechanism referred to as qos pre-classify (described previously). With this feature, the original IP packet's attributes (addresses, protocol, ports, DSCP) are copied to the IPSec-encapsulated packet as it moves to the egress queue. When classification methods are applied to the egress interface, the IP QoS mechanisms will use the copied original IP packet QoS attributes as opposed to the encapsulating IPSec header. This model allows the designer to build queue structures that may queue packets based on the original addresses, protocols, and ports. The copied information is simply discarded as the packet leaves the router. Figure 8-6 demonstrates how the gateway performing encryption may leverage additional attributes of the packet for classification.

Figure 8-6   *Classification Capabilities with QoS Pre-Classify*

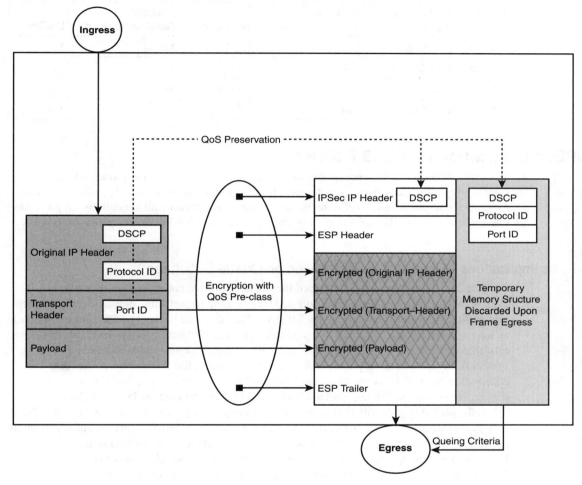

Of course, any interim router processing the packet between the two IPSec endpoints will not have access to the same QoS attributes as the encrypting gateway. All the interim routers will still have access to the DSCP bits in the IPSec encapsulated packet which were copied from the original IP packet and preserved. Therefore, it is a best practice to set the DSCP bits as close to the original host as possible. Doing so allows a consistent packet classification end-to-end.

Table 8-1 highlights the parameters that are preserved by the encryption and encapsulation processes. Although some of the attributes used for QoS are available on the encrypting router, the only attribute that is consistently available between the encrypting and decrypting routers is the set of DSCP values.

Table 8-1 *Preservation of QoS Attributes After Encryption*

Attribute Preservation After Encryption	Source/ Destination IP	Protocol	Source/ Destination Port	DSCP
IPSec transport mode	Yes	No	No	Yes
IPSec tunnel mode	No	No	No	Yes
IPSec-protected GRE	No	No	No	Yes
IPSec-protected UDP	No	No	No	Yes

IPSec Implications on QoS Policies

The introduction of IPSec encryption (or IPSec protection of GRE encapsulation) may significantly affect the queuing model used to provide quality of service. It is worthwhile to focus on the implications of IPSec on queue structures and bandwidth allocations. Of particular interest is the size of the packets as they go through the encryption or encapsulation processes.

IPSec Implications of Packet Size Distribution on Queue Structures

Chapter 2, "IPSec Overview," described the impact of IPSec encapsulation on the MTU. It is evident that the process of encapsulating and fragmenting packets may dramatically change the probability distribution for various packet sizes. The observed packet size distribution used on an unencrypted FR interface may be quite different on an IPSec-protected interface; therefore, careful consideration must be given to buffer allocations assigned to class queues as well as system buffers. As an example, assume a simplified data traffic flow with a packet size distribution ratio of 4-7-4 for 40-, 512-, and 1500-byte packets, respectively. If we pass this packet stream into an IPSec-protected GRE tunnel where the GRE MTU is specified as 1400 bytes, the packet size distribution will change due to packet fragmentation to a ratio of 4-7-4-4 with packet sizes of 40, 512, 100, and 1400 bytes, respectively. Note that the frequency of small packets (those less than 104 bytes applicable to the system's small buffers) is doubled. Likewise, the class queue structure and buffers allocated to each class may need to be adapted from the default 64 packets to handle the modified packet distribution.

IPSec Implications of Packet Size on Queue Bandwidth Assignments

Another interesting challenge with IPSec encapsulation is the assignment of bandwidth parameters associated with QoS policies applied to interfaces. Obviously, the encapsulation overhead of IPSec and GRE will increase the number of bits per second that must pass through an interface. A common error made by designers is to assess gateway QoS requirements based on the application's bandwidth (that is, VoIP bearer bit rates), but fail to consider the additional bandwidth that encryption and encapsulation add to the flows at the encrypting router. The issue is particularly relevant on low-speed interfaces and traffic flows with a high concentration of small packets.

The appropriate solution to this problem is to set the QoS bandwidth allocation to a value higher than the actual application bandwidth requirements such that the post-encrypted flow approaches the actual bandwidth assigned to the application's queue. Again, the traffic application's expected packet size distribution profile is necessary to estimate the percentage of overhead required on a particular interface. A low-speed interface will be much more susceptible to congestion; hence, the ramifications of IPSec on QoS are much more severe on low-speed interfaces. Likewise, traffic flows dominated by VoIP will incur a large percentage of overhead due to the small packet size of VoIP frames. Now, you'll explore some of the intricacies of running VoIP flows through IPSec VPN connections.

VoIP Application Requirements for IPSec VPN Networks

It is becoming increasingly important for enterprises that build IPSec VPNs to deliver voice services over the VPN. Voice over IP in itself brings unique challenges; adding IPSec complicates this further. The most critical network characteristics that need to be considered for a successful voice over IP deployment are delay, jitter, availability, and packet loss.

Delay Implications

The generally accepted International Telecommunication Union (ITU) value for one-way delay is considered to be 150msec. In a circuit-switched paradigm, this requirement is easily achieved except for in the most extreme cases such as satellite relays. A packet-switched network may push the delay for a packet flow well over 150msec. In fact, it's not uncommon for a congested IP network to experience delays exceeding 1 or 2 seconds. End-to-end packet delay can be attributed to delays due to switching, queuing, serialization, or propagation.

Switching is the function of receiving an IP packet and making a decision regarding which output interface to *switch* the packet to. In most modern IP routers, the switching delay for IP packets is a few micro or nanoseconds, and therefore almost a non-issue. Note, however, that because IPSec does increase switching delay, it may be important to consider when dealing with applications like voice—especially when IPSec encryption and decryption is done in software. For applications such as voice that have a stringent budget on end-to-end delay, the use of hardware-assisted encryption and decryption is recommended. Hardware-assisted encryption and decryption will minimize encryption delays mitigating the impact to the end-to-end voice delay budget. Nevertheless, the hardware-accelerated encryption/decryption processes do add several milliseconds to the delay, which must be considered in the delay budget.

Once the switching decision has been made, the packet is queued for transmission out a physical link. At this point, it is possible to have queuing delay. On an interface that is not very busy or not congested, queuing delay may not be very significant and the default FIFO queuing scheme will suffice. Queuing delay becomes very significant when traffic bursts egress the outbound interface, making the interface congested and thereby causing outbound queues to build up. A priority queuing mechanism such as Low-Latency Queuing (LLQ) should be applied to voice traffic to protect from queuing delays. Typically, voice packets are classified into the priority queue based on DSCP bits in the IP header. As mentioned previously, the original IP packet's DSCP bits are copied into the IPSec IP header; therefore, classification and priority queuing of voice traffic can be performed at the encrypting end of the IPSec tunnel endpoint without a problem. Of course, implementing LLQ of voice traffic end-to-end along each hop is recommended.

All the queuing mechanisms are applied to packets queued on the outbound interface. At the head end of the IPSec tunnel (where packets that match the IPSec policy are encrypted), the encryption engine may only have a first-in, first-out (FIFO) queue. The encryption engine with a FIFO queue will not distinguish between the data and voice packets. It is possible for a low priority data flow to congest the encryption engine. Although queue management on the outbound interface uses LLQ to handle voice, it is negated by the FIFO queue in the encryption engine. Cisco IOS version 12.2(15)T introduced a new feature that adds LLQ at the crypto engine. There is no configuration required to enable this feature; it is enabled by the QoS service on the output interface. This feature is available only with the hardware encryption engine and not with software encryption—another reason to use hardware-assisted encryption for voice over IPSec. Note that it is still possible to congest the LLQ on the encryption engine. Certain applications (for example, multicast and routing updates in GRE tunnels) will present a flood of replicated traffic to the crypto engine. If this traffic is high-priority and queued on the crypto engines LLQ, then congestion may occur, causing loss.

Once the packet is queued for transmission on the output link, serialization delay comes into the picture. All circuits have a common characteristic known as serialization delay, which represents the time it takes some unit of data to be serialized onto the circuit. The delay is directly related to the length of the packet, the bandwidth of the circuit, and the framing technology employed. For instance, the serialization delay for sending a 1500-byte HDLC-encapsulated packet on a 45Mbps circuit will be:

(1504 bytes * 8 bits/byte) / 44040192 bits/sec = .27 ms

Serialization delay at low-speed links can contribute significantly to the end-to-end voice delay budget. Voice-over-IP packets are much smaller in size than a 1500-byte data packet. For example, on a 56Kbps leased line link where voice and data traffic coexist, a voice packet may be enqueued to transmit just when a 1500-byte data packet starts transmission (that is, serialization) over the link. Now, there's a problem. The delay-sensitive voice packet will have to wait 214 msec before being transmitted due to the serialization delay for the 1500-byte packet. Fragmenting these large data packets into smaller ones and interleaving voice packets among the fragments reduces the delay and jitter. The Cisco IOS feature Link Fragmentation and Interleaving (LFI) can be configured to do this fragmentation.

NOTE	LFI is required only on slow-speed interfaces. The recommendation is to use this feature on interfaces whose bandwidth is less than 768kbps.

Alternatively, you may apply a much smaller MTU on GRE tunnel interfaces such that you induce host fragmentation where possible and fragment IP packets prior to encryption, accordingly.

The last delay attribute is called propagation delay. This is simply the time between the completion of data transmission at the application sender and data reception at the other end by the application receiver. This attribute is going to be dictated by the length of the medium and speed of signal propagation in that medium.

Jitter Implications

Jitter is the variance in the arrival interval of a stream of packets. Clearly, a VoIP encoder will generate a constant stream of voice-encoded packets with a defined constant interval between successive packets. Once these packets traverse the packet-switched network, the delays mentioned previously create variability in the arrival interval of the VoIP packets. To accommodate the jitter, a jitter buffer is used to collect the VoIP packets with a minimally induced delay. This allows the voice decoder to continuously play out the voice stream with no drops.

Typically, the jitter buffer will be adaptive with the induced delay starting at a default value such as 20msec. The jitter buffer will attempt to reduce the induced delay if the network demonstrates consistent packet inter-arrival times or increase the induced delay to perhaps 50msec if the network experiences severe congestion and jitter. Scheduling voice packets into the priority queues through the network minimizes the jitter experienced by VoIP packets as they traverse the network. The IPSec encryption and decryption process may induce a negligible amount of jitter; therefore, designers rely on the continuity of the DSCP before, during, and after the encryption/decryption processes at the two endpoints in order to minimize the jitter induced by the network. Typically, a well-managed backbone network will demonstrate no more than 2msec of jitter and may approach jitter values as low as 100usec.

CAUTION	Platforms that use software encryption and decryption may induce significant jitter due the non-linear encryption processing requirements for large versus small packets. Hardware-accelerated encryption and decryption should be considered mandatory for VoIP services.

Loss Implications

An extensive amount of research on VoIP's sensitivity to loss has demonstrated that packet loss exceeding one percent of the VoIP data stream will be apparent to end users. It is apparent that the network must preserve the VoIP stream, especially in congested points in the network such as access links. The use of priority queuing on VoIP-encrypted packets allows the VoIP packets to pass through the congested links with minimal loss. Generally, voice and data packets will be passing between two crypto gateways using the same security association. The voice packets are typically identified by a DSCP setting of Explicit Forwarding (EF) while data packets will use one of the Assured Forwarding (AF) DSCP settings. The queue systems that come into play after encryption between the crypto gateways will use the DSCP values to prioritize the voice packets ahead of the data packets.

The ramification of scheduling VoIP packets ahead of other data packets in the same IPSec SA is that the sequence of packets arriving at the decryption device is out of order. By default, IPSec will use a 64-packet anti-replay window to detect packets that are potentially replay attacks. We'll assume the crypto gateway has received crypto packet with sequence number N. The gateway will now accept any valid crypto packet with a sequence number between N-64 and N. Packets that arrive with a sequence number less than the N-64 violate the anti-replay window. Such packets are assumed to be replay attacks by IPSec and are dropped. With a substantial volume of VoIP-encrypted traffic passing through a congested interface, we mitigate packet delay of the voice streams while inducing latency or loss in the other data streams that use the same IPSec SA. If the encrypted data packets of an SA are sufficiently delayed relative to the voice packets, the data packets may violate the anti-replay window while the voice packets are accepted.

Mitigating Anti-replay Loss in Combined Voice/Data Flows

There are two means of mitigating the loss to data streams in a combined voice/data encrypted flow. First, the link capacity may be increased, or more bandwidth may be made available to the data packets in the combined voice/data flow. The additional schedule time available to the data flow decreases the probability of a data packet being delayed beyond the 64-packet window. The second alternative is to increase the anti-replay window. Preliminary testing of this feature indicates that an anti-replay window of 1000 packets is sufficient to mitigate frame loss due to anti-replay violations.

Mitigating Anti-replay Loss in Separate Voice/Data Flows

An alternative to the combined voice/data flow is to create two IPSec proxy policies that specifically put voice into one IPSec SA and place data in a second IPSec SA. The intermediate queuing systems that delay the data packets and forward the voice packets do not change the order of voice or data packets with respect to their individual IPSec SA anti-replay sequence. This approach is acceptable for native IPSec encryption processes; however, this is less feasible in GRE-tunneled scenarios. The native IPSec proxy may select unique IPSec SAs by referring to the QoS attributes of the original packet. The use of IPSec-protected GRE performs GRE encapsulation prior to presenting the encapsulated data to the IPSec encryption processes. The GRE packet has no criteria available to distinguish between the VoIP and data because the original IP addresses, protocol, and ports are hidden. The IPSec proxy cannot use the DSCP values as criteria for creating unique IPSec SAs. The GRE encapsulation process typically uses the same IP source address, destination address, and protocol ID for all encrypted flows between the gateways. The result is the establishment of a single IPSec SA.

The only way to avoid this is to use the parallel GRE tunnels with unique source and destination tunnel endpoints that correlate with unique IPSec proxy statements. The unique tunnel source or destination IP addresses allow IPSec to establish distinct voice and data IPSec SAs for VoIP and data flows, respectively.

Engineering Best Practices for Voice and IPSec

Most network architects find that combining voice and data flows into a single IPSec SA is preferred over splitting voice and data into separate IPSec SAs. The combined voice and data flow saves on the number of IPSec SAs deployed, which improves network scalability. In addition, the routing of voice and data into separate IPSec-protected GRE SA streams becomes quite complicated. Likewise, maintaining distinct IPSec proxies for voice and data streams becomes quite an onerous provisioning task. In general, it's best to traffic engineer the links such that prioritized VoIP traffic will not exhaust the queuing resources or eliminate scheduling time for the data queues.

By using VoIP traffic engineering best practices (that is, by limiting voice streams to less than 33% of the link bandwidth) and ensuring that the combined voice/data flow does not exceed 70% of link utilization, the combined flow of VoIP and data rarely experiences anti-replay loss. Should the operator continue to experience loss due to anti-replay violations, the recommendation is to increase the anti-replay window. A typical voice stream will generate roughly 50 packets per second (that is, 20msec voice-sampling interval). Increasing the anti-replay window from 64 packets to 1000 packets has minimal impact on the security risk of the system. The anti-replay time interval for a single voice flow increases from 1.28 seconds (64 packets divided by 50 packets per second) to 20 seconds (1000 packets divided by 50 packets per second), assuming no other traffic is passing through the IPSec SA which is rarely the case. The IPSec SA is usually carrying a variety of traffic types at a packet-forwarding rate that makes the anti-replay interval short enough to mitigate all but the most determined attacker.

IPSec VPN Architectural Considerations for VoIP

You saw in Chapter 5, "IPSec VPN Architectures," various topological options for the deployment of IPSec VPNs. The previous section defined various implications of running voice applications in IPSec. The large-scale introduction of voice applications on a network has serious ramifications for the viability of designing, building, and managing IPSec VPNs. In this section, we will explore the impact of accommodating VoIP in the various VPN architectures.

Decoupled VoIP and Data Architectures

First, you should consider whether VoIP must be encrypted at all. From a routing perspective, it is much easier to treat all VoIP traffic as high priority data traffic over a single routing topology. The converged voice and data topology must simply handle the traffic classes appropriately through the queuing mechanisms discussed previously. Many organizations are evolving their VoIP communication systems to use end-to-end bearer encryption based on Secure Real Time Protocol (SRTP). In this case, encryption of VoIP traffic with IPSec is redundant. Some organizations have chosen to exclude SRTP VoIP traffic from the IPSec topology. There are two common methods for achieving this architecture.

The first method uses IPSec proxy policies that exclude VoIP traffic. Recall that the IPSec tunneling methods essentially direct encrypted traffic to the peer gateway. Routing decisions in the backbone for data traffic will be based on the IPSec tunnel addresses, whereas routing decisions for VoIP traffic will be based on the bearer endpoint addresses. Essentially, there are two routing topologies and traffic matrices—one for voice flows and the other for data. Figure 8-7 shows the disjointed VoIP and data topologies.

Figure 8-7   *Decoupled IPSec VoIP and Data Topologies*

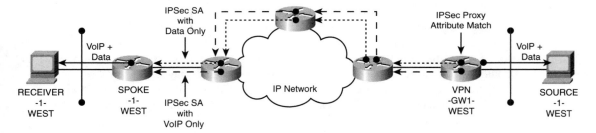

The second method uses an explicitly defined overlay topology using GRE tunnels. Essentially, a VoIP GRE overlay topology is built in which the GRE tunnel addresses are excluded from the IPSec policy. A separate data GRE topology is built in which the GRE tunnel addresses are included in the IPSec policy. Now we can use Policy Based Routing (PBR) in the VPN gateway to route the VoIP streams into the unencrypted GRE topology while routing the data streams into the encrypted GRE topology. The VoIP bearers and data streams from end users typically use the same source and destination IP address space; therefore, the PBR must vector the appropriate packets into the disjoint VoIP and data tunnel overlay topologies using protocol and port identifiers.

NOTE	The whole point of VoIP is to leverage voice and data services in a synergistic manner. Although it is possible to use a distinct VoIP endpoint address space, doing so typically defeats one of the primary motivations for using VoIP technologies—integrated voice and data applications.

Figure 8-8 shows how the two GRE topologies are defined and where the PBR functions are applied.

Figure 8-8   *Decoupled IPSec-protected GRE Data and GRE VoIP Topology*

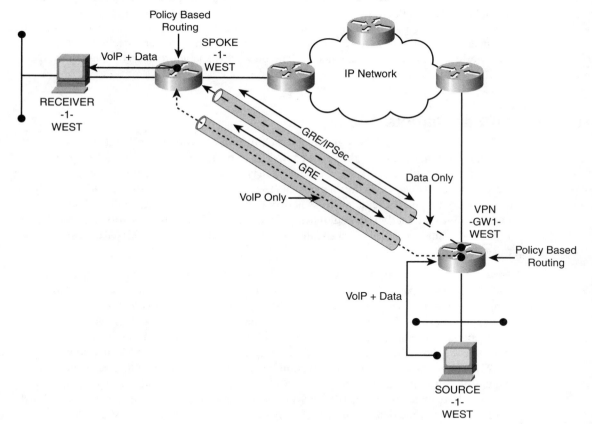

NOTE   The IPSec proxy configured on the VPN gateways must be able to distinguish between the data GRE tunnel and the VoIP GRE tunnel. Because there are no source or destination ports and the protocol ID is always the same, the IPSec proxy must use a unique IP address on one of tunnel endpoints. Generally, it is easiest to configure two GRE tunnel endpoints on the hub—one that is used for data tunnels and one that is used for VoIP tunnels. Doing so allows the IPSec proxy on both the hub and spoke to uniquely identify the data GRE tunnels.

The explicit VoIP exclusion techniques (for example, PBR or IPSec proxy) usually become unwieldy in large VPN topologies. It is also difficult to accommodate fault-tolerant architectures using the static configuration techniques. As a result, most customers elect to use a convergent topology for voice and data to simplify their network architecture, traffic engineering, and fault-tolerance models. Therefore, this chapter focuses on these convergent VoIP and data architectures.

VoIP over IPSec Remote Access

In the ideal scenario, designers are able to architect the network according to a known set of design constraints. Provided the service provider or backbone operator has adequately characterized the IP network (for example, it may be Multi-Service CPN certified), designing the VoIP topology and QoS control mechanisms is relatively straightforward. Unfortunately, the same cannot be said for remote access networks in which multiple providers are involved and QoS attributes are rarely honored, much less preserved. Clearly, the network between the two IPSec endpoints (the IPSec client and the Concentrator) must be characterized as best-effort and treated as such.

Nevertheless, you can mitigate certain problems by controlling the flow of traffic at the IPSec endpoints. One aspect where VoIP call characteristics can be improved is through traffic-shaping techniques. We must assume that the IP path between the two IPSec endpoints has no support for QoS. One critical piece of information is the maximum bandwidth available. For example, a remote access user may have a DSL circuit with a maximum of 640kbps downstream and 384kbps upstream. We can improve our packet loss performance by shaping our VoIP and data stream into the maximum bandwidth available such that we avoid loss. Naturally, you want the VoIP stream to have the highest chance of success. By shaping the combined stream to not exceed 640kbps downstream and 384kbps upstream and prioritizing the VoIP stream over the data stream (preferably prior to encryption), you preclude the low bandwidth remote access network link from indiscriminately discarding voice or data. Figure 8-9 demonstrates the optimal shaping, queuing, and scheduling of the VoIP and IPSec flow on a remote access link.

Figure 8-9   *Low-Loss Shaped Encrypted Flow on Constrained Bandwidth*

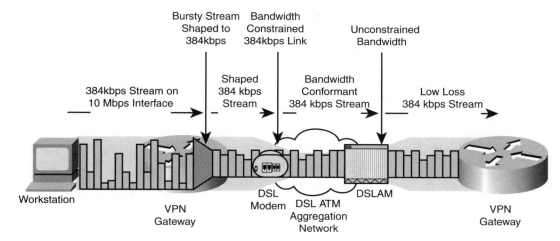

VoIP over IPSec-Protected GRE Architectures

Site-to-site architectures for an IPSec VPN commonly use GRE tunnels protected by IPSec. Applying QoS policies to a tunnel interface that is an abstract interface can be challenging, as it is possible that the encrypted packet flow may be switched out to a high-speed or low-speed link. Obviously, you can assign a queue structure to any of the VPN gateway's physical interfaces, allowing the queues to be defined relative to the physical bandwidth. The tunnel interface QoS structure has no adaptive knowledge of which interface is actually in use; therefore, a hierarchical queue structure is required with explicit bandwidth statements in order to use shaping or bandwidth percentage-based queue structures.

Of course, the bandwidth applied to the tunnel interface may not match the physical interface that the tunnel uses to reach the peer. The principle advantage of applying QoS to the tunnel interface is that the packet order for a set of streams to the same peer is defined, scheduled, and queued prior to encryption. Reordering packets on entry into the tunnel interface forces the VoIP traffic to precede the data traffic upon leaving the VPN gateway. Once the data is encrypted, intermediate nodes between the VPN gateways may reorder packets of the tunnel when congestion occurs; therefore, anti-replay drops may still be a factor. This is a principle disadvantage of IPSec over GRE. There is a single IPSec SA defined for the aggregate set of streams in the GRE tunnel. One effective way to mitigate the anti-replay drops is to set the bandwidth of the GRE tunnel's queue structure to the slowest link between the tunnel peers. Example 8-1 shows a configuration model in which the QoS mechanism uses a parent policy to shape the traffic according to the slowest link while prioritizing the VoIP ahead of the data traffic.

Example 8-1 *Hierarchical Shaping of VoIP and Data Prior to Encryption*

```
spoke-2-west# show configuration
 ...
policy-map vpn
  class control
    bandwidth percent 5
  class mmoip
    priority percent 30
  class data
    bandwidth percent 63
 ...
policy-map gre-qos
  class shape-t1
    shape average 1464000
    service-policy vpn
 ...
class-map match-all shape-t1
  match any
class-map match-all data
  match ip precedence 0  1  2  3
class-map match-all control
  match ip precedence 6  7
class-map match-all mmoip
  match ip precedence 4  5
 ...
interface Tunnel1
 ip address 9.0.0.2 255.255.255.252
 ip pim sparse-mode
 service-policy output gre-qos
 tunnel source 9.1.1.134
 tunnel destination 9.1.1.10
 tunnel protection ipsec profile spoke-2-west
 ...
end
```

You see that we have two service policies: vpn and gre-qos. The gre-qos service policy is applied to the tunnel interface such that any traffic entering the tunnel conforms to the average bandwidth rate of 1.46Mbps (assuming that the constrained bandwidth available to this site is consistent with a T1). With the traffic shaped to fit inside a T1, we prioritize our VPN traffic such that MultiMedia over IP (mmoip) is scheduled first and set to not exceed 30% of the shaped capacity. We have also guaranteed control traffic, or routing protocols, 5% of the bandwidth with data traffic essentially obtaining the rest. Also, note that we have selected the precedence bits (a component of the DSCP) as the matching criteria. Next, you'll see the implications of QoS when applied to the IPSec architecture.

VoIP Hub-and-Spoke Architecture

As you saw in Chapter 5, "IPsec VPN Architectures," the hub-and-spoke topology is one of the most widely deployed IPSec VPN architectures. In this topology, all spoke-to-spoke communication (including VoIP) transits via the hub. The introduction of a hub transit point to the VoIP bearer stream needs to be accounted for in the traffic engineering and voice delay budget. Having spoke-to-spoke VoIP traffic hair-pinning through the IPSec hub, wherein the hub has to decrypt the VoIP traffic it receives from the spoke and encrypt the traffic again to the spoke the traffic is destined to, may significantly impact the performance of the network. First, the packet size distribution will be radically altered through the IPSec VPN connections. The substantial increase in forwarding requirements for the increased percentage of small packets may consume an inordinate amount of packet processing resources on the IPSec VPN hub. Second, the underlying IP network queue schedulers must be altered to accommodate the traffic engineering of the transient IPSec-protected VoIP stream. Figure 8-10 shows the implications for these two fundamental changes in the network architecture.

Figure 8-10   *Transient VoIP Traffic through IPSec VPN Hubs*

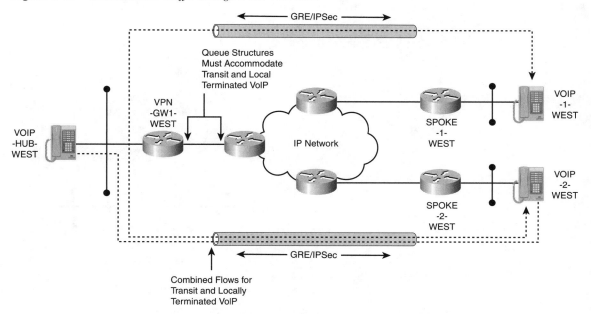

The introduction of redundant hubs in the topology further complicates the traffic engineering challenge. One obvious alternative to the hub-and-spoke architecture is to build a full-mesh architecture. Of course, eliminating the transient decryption, routing, and encryption through a hub doesn't come for free. Chapter 6, "Designing Fault-Tolerant IPSec VPNs," outlined the provisioning and operational costs associated with building a full-mesh IPSec VPN. The trade-off between optimal traffic engineering and IPSec configuration complexity will likely be driven by the probability of VoIP calls being established between branch sites. The complexity of the full-mesh IPSec VPN may not be justified if the percentage of site-to-site calls is rather low. As a result, most enterprises chose to use a hub-and-spoke topology for all communications.

VoIP over DMVPN Architecture

An alternative to the static full mesh is the DMVPN architecture. The main advantages of the DMVPN architecture are reduced configuration complexity and the ability to build temporary direct spoke-to-spoke connections on demand. The feasibility of using a temporal full mesh may be mitigated by the delay associated with the IKE and IPSec SA establishment between spokes. The transaction delay for establishing the IPSec SA is substantial. Assuming the VoIP call-control follows a different path than the bearer path, you are likely to run into a delayed talk interval following the completion of call setup, but prior to completion of the IPSec SA that carries the bearer.

Figure 8-11 *Post-dial Delayed Bearer with VoIP over IPSec*

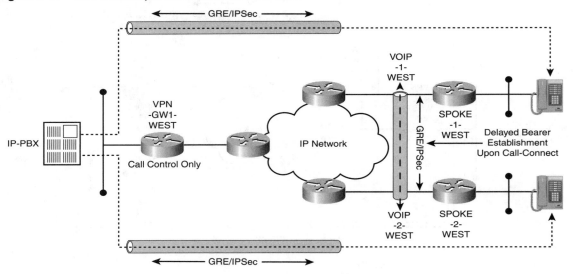

The only way to mitigate the delayed talk interval is to either reduce the IPSec SA establishment intervals through accelerated IKE and IPSec SA establishment, temporarily route the bearer through the hub, or induce post-dial delay.

VoIP Bearer Path Optimization with DMVPN

The DMVPN architecture allows spoke-to-spoke traffic to transit via the hub while waiting for the spoke-to-spoke IPSec process to complete. Doing so avoids the post-dial-delay and dead-talk interval following a call-connect by allowing the traffic to transit the hub. Once the IPSec session is established directly between the spokes, the VoIP flow will transition to direct connection following a more expeditious route. The drawback to this solution is that the jitter buffers in the VoIP endpoints are synchronized with the delay associated with traffic transiting the hub. The completion of the shorter IPSec/GRE path causes VoIP traffic to arrive early at both receivers. The VoIP jitter buffers must advance the play out, causing a glitch in the audio. Fortunately, this scenario only occurs when a VoIP call is causing the spoke-to-spoke connection establishment. If the spoke-to-spoke connection exists prior to call-connect, then the VoIP bearer will take the shortest path at the time of call-connect.

VoIP Bearer Path Synchronization with DMVPN

The alternative to transitioning VoIP bearers from the non-optimal path to the optimal path is to force the VoIP to take the optimal path during the call-connection establishment. Post-dial delay may be induced by waiting for an RSVP path reservation to complete via the encrypted bearer path. The RSVP processes kick off the establishment of the IPSec SA prior to allowing the call-connect. The RSVP RESV message requires the direct spoke-to-spoke connection to be established prior to proceeding with the subsequent stages of call-connect. By the time an operator initiates a discussion, the IPSec spoke-to-spoke connection has already been established. This discussion highlights the importance of synchronizing the VoIP call-control and bearer paths with the IPSec VPN topology.

NOTE   At this time, the Cisco IOS Multipoint GRE interfaces do not allow per-peer QoS policies. The QoS policy associated with the mGRE interface must take into account the aggregate bandwidth required for all sites connected to the mGRE interface.

VoIP Traffic Engineering Summary

You have seen it demonstrated that designing VoIP to operate within an IPSec VPN is certainly possible by accounting for the anomalies created by the IPSec connection model. The usual VoIP bandwidth and delay attributes must be considered while also accommodating IPSec VPN topology, anti-replay windows, and IPSec overhead.

Multicast over IPSec VPNs

Applications that use IP multicast are becoming increasingly important to many enterprises. They range from file and software updates, to video broadcasts, to multi-party conferencing and many other applications. In this section, you will explore how IPSec VPN handles multicast. Multicast applications typically rely on a combination of unicast routing protocols and multicast routing protocols. The current IPSec standards (for example, RFC 2401 through 2410) do not support IP multicast over native IPSec tunnels, although extensive research is in progress in the IETF under the auspices of the MSEC working group for Multicast Security.

As of this writing, the only choices available are for carrying multicast traffic over an IPSec VPN. The first is to use virtual IPSec interfaces with an IPSec proxy of SOURCE: ANY, DESTINATION: ANY. This approach requires each virtual IPSec interface to have an explicitly defined peer. The second approach is to use tunnels between VPN sites and use IPSec to encrypt the tunnel. Cisco currently leverages the IPSec protection of GRE tunnels to accommodate multicast; however, a forthcoming interface model using a virtual IPSec interface will effectively achieve the same goal. As you saw in Chapter 2, "IPSec Overview," IPSec protection of GRE between the VPN sites performs encapsulation in GRE that results in a unicast frame. The multicast traffic between sites is merely payload for the GRE tunnel that is protected by IPSec. The multicast processes are associated with the tunnel interfaces and hidden from the underlying IPSec processes.

Multicast over IPSec-protected GRE

The most common reason for deploying IPSec VPNs over GRE tunnels is to support dynamic routing protocols between sites of the VPN that use IP multicast such as EIGRP and OSPF. Most multicast applications are essentially point-to-multipoint where there is a single source and many receivers. Clearly, the hub-and-spoke network architecture shown in Figure 8-12 will serve this application well, assuming that the source of the multicast traffic is co-located with the hub.

The configuration of multicast on hub-and-spoke topology is shown in Example 8-2. The configuration of a basic multicast capability on IOS is rather simple. It is important to understand that most multicast protocols rely upon the router's existing routing topology forwarding information base (FIB) derived from protocols such as IGP and BGP. Multicast protocols such Protocol Independent Multicast (PIM) use the FIB to determine where to send multicast join messages based on Reverse Path Forwarding (RPF), which is the shortest path back to the source. First, you'll need to enable multicast globally on the router, then you'll need to enable multicast on each of the eligible interfaces (that is, GRE tunnel interfaces). In this case, simply enable multicast on the tunnel interfaces at the hub-and-spoke VPN gateways. PIM sparse mode (PIM-SM) has been configured on the GRE tunnel interface in our example. PIM dense mode (PIM-DM) could also be used as the multicast adjacency protocol, but it is not recommended because dense mode will send multicast traffic to a site irrespective of whether the site has receivers.

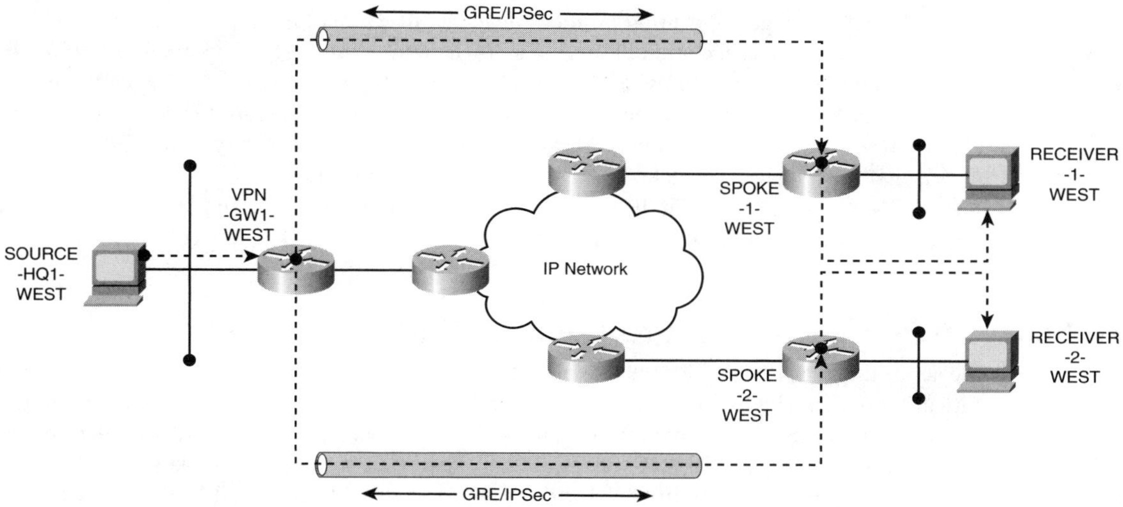

Figure 8-12   *Multicast over IPSec-encrypted GRE tunnels*

Example 8-2   *Multicast Configuration on GRE/IPSec Spoke*

```
vpn-gw1-west#show run interface Tunnel 1
interface Tunnel1
 description Tunnel to spoke-1-west
 ip address 10.2.2.1 255.255.255.252
 ip pim sparse-mode
 tunnel source 9.1.1.10
 tunnel destination 9.1.1.22
 tunnel protection ipsec profile gre
vpn-gw1-west#show run interface Tunnel 2
interface Tunnel2
 description Tunnel to spoke-2-west
 ip address 10.2.2.5 255.255.255.252
 ip pim sparse-mode
 tunnel source 9.1.1.10
 tunnel destination 9.1.1.138
 tunnel protection ipsec profile gre
vpn-gw1-west# show run interface FastEthernet0/1
interface FastEthernet0/1
 description VPN RP interface
 ip address 10.1.1.1 255.255.255.0
 ip pim sparse-dense-mode
```

In this configuration, the hub's Ethernet interface (10.1.1.1) has been designated as the rendezvous point (RP) for the Multicast VPN.

The topology assumes the hub router does the multicast replication. This places a significant burden on the hub router as it must perform IPSec protection, GRE encapsulation/ decapsulation, manage the routing protocol on each GRE tunnel interface, and replicate multicast frames across each tunnel serving a downstream multicast receiver. The combination of these functions typically limits the scalability of the network due to processing constraints at the hub. In order to alleviate the burden of replicating and forwarding multicast streams on the VPN hub, some VPN architectures leverage the spoke-to-spoke topology of the GRE/IPSec tunnels in order to conserve packet processing resources at the hub site. Assume that a full-mesh IPSec VPN is justified between the potential multicast application participants. In that case, we would build a full-mesh IP tunneled network where each IP tunnel is encrypted with IPSec.

Multicast on Full-Mesh Point-to-Point GRE/IPSec Tunnels

The set of full-mesh IP tunnels may be established in one of two ways. The first approach is to statically build an IP/GRE tunnel between each VPN gateway serving a multicast endpoint. A statically configured IPSec proxy builds an SA that encrypts the associated IPSec/GRE tunnel. The GRE/IPSec tunnels will establish an IPSec connection between the spokes only if there is data that must pass over the tunnel. Some designers may be tempted to build GRE/IPSec tunnels with static routing and no keepalives between the spokes in order to minimize the number of active GRE/IPSec connections on each spoke. However, once you configure multicast on the GRE tunnel interface, the multicast processes attempt to find peers capable of multicast adjacencies. Adjacencies are built by multicasting Hello messages on each multicast-enabled interface to identify potential peers as described in RFC 2362. Once the peers are established, an adjacency is sustained by periodic Hello messages. Figure 8-13 provides an example in which the network architecture leverages spoke-to-spoke use of GRE/IPSec tunnels to mitigate the transient traffic at the hub site.

The multicast adjacency process sustains every GRE/IPSec tunnel to validate that link as a viable path. If resource conservation was a primary concern at any of the GRE/IPSec nodes, then the multicast Hello protocol just violated that assumption because every possible GRE/ IPSec path is established. The PIM-SM avoids sending multicast streams until receiving explicit joins whereas the PIM-DM multicast processes prune back the multicast flows to the minimal distribution tree required. Nevertheless, both dense- and sparse-mode multicast use multicast Hello packets to sustain neighbors.

Figure 8-13   *Multicast Implications for Temporal GRE/IPSec Full Mesh*

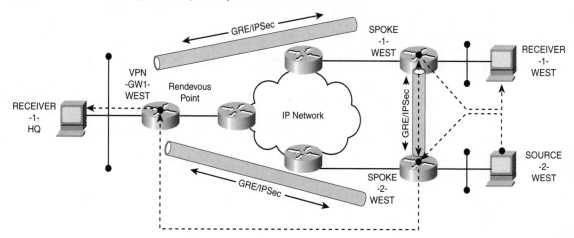

The requirement to build a static GRE/IPSec tunnel for each potential multicast peer obviously limits the scalability of the architecture. Every spoke must participate in PIM Hello exchanges with every other spoke; therefore, every GRE/IPSec tunnel will be active in order to maintain the PIM adjacencies. Scalability is further constrained by the fact that each spoke must establish its multicast peers simultaneously upon booting. Obviously, we need to find more efficient topologies for multicast.

In this scenario, the configuration of multicast on the GRE tunnel interfaces forces the establishment of all the GRE/IPSec tunnels. Each spoke has assumed the role of a "hub" in this persistent full mesh. Perhaps the spoke has sufficient resources to manage the persistent full mesh; however, that is rarely the case as the VPN becomes sufficiently large. If you look at the state of a spoke before and after the application of multicast routing, you can see that all of the GRE/IPSec tunnels transition to an active state. Example 8-3 shows the configuration of the spoke used in the GRE/IPSec full mesh with the addition of multicast routing.

Example 8-3   *Spoke GRE/IPSec Temporal Full Mesh*

```
spoke-1-west#show run interface tunnel 1
interface Tunnel1
 description Tunnel to vpn-gw1-west
 ip address 10.2.2.2 255.255.255.252
 ip pim sparse-mode
 tunnel source 9.1.1.22
 tunnel destination 9.1.1.10
tunnel protection ipsec profile dmvpn

spoke-1-west#show run interface tunnel 2
interface Tunnel2
 ip address 10.2.2.9 255.255.255.252
 ip pim sparse-mode
 tunnel source 9.1.1.22
 tunnel destination 9.1.1.138
tunnel protection ipsec profile dmvpn

spoke-1-west#show run ¦ include ip route
 ! Default route to the backbone
 ip route 0.0.0.0 0.0.0.0 9.1.1.21
 ! Generic route for VPN via Hub
 ip route 10.0.0.0 255.0.0.0 10.2.2.1
 ! Explicit route for VPN Subnet at spoke-2-west
 ip route 10.0.66.0 255.255.255.0 10.2.2.10
```

Example 8-4 shows the state of the GRE/IPSec tunnels once the multicast is applied.

Example 8-4   *Spoke GRE/IPSec and Multicast State on Temporal Full Mesh*

```
spoke-1-west#show ip pim neighbor
PIM Neighbor Table
Neighbor          Interface             Uptime/Expires     Ver   DR
Address                                                          Prio/Mode
10.2.2.1          Tunnel1               07:35:34/00:01:43 v2    1 / S
10.2.2.10         Tunnel2               07:27:24/00:01:30 v2    1 / S
spoke-1-west#show crypto isakmp sa
dst              src             state         conn-id slot
9.1.1.22         9.1.1.138       QM_IDLE            27    0
9.1.1.10         9.1.1.22        QM_IDLE            19    0
```

You can see that the entire set of GRE tunnels will be active in order to pass multicast Hello packets. The example shows that Tunnel2 between SPOKE-1-WEST and SPOKE-2-WEST will remain active because the PIM process refreshes the neighbor adjacency every 30 seconds. The multicast process assesses every possible path to determine a path's relevance to each potential multicast source. This places a tremendous burden on the CPE, especially in large full-mesh networks.

DMVPN and Multicast

The full-mesh GRE/IPSec architecture obviously has serious constraints when applied in large networks. Recall from Chapter 7, "Auto-Configuration Architectures for Site-to-Site IPSec VPNs," that the DMVPN architecture was designed to accommodate resource-constrained spokes in large temporal full-mesh networks. Next, you'll consider the implications of applying the multicast process on the mGRE interface used in the DMVPN architecture.

At this point, you know that the GRE tunnels are capable of carrying multicast traffic such as OSPF and EIGRP routing protocols. When OSPF and EIGRP processes are assigned to the mGRE interface in DMVPN, you need to prevent the establishment of tunnels to all the spokes. Note that the configuration of the tunnel interface maps multicast traffic to the hub. Example 8-5 highlights the fact that the Next Hop Resolution Protocol (NHRP) will map any multicast traffic towards the NHRP server.

Example 8-5   *Multicast Mapping on DMVPN Multipoint Interfaces*

```
!
interface Tunnel0
 ip address 10.2.0.2 255.255.255.0
 no ip redirects
 ip mtu 1400
 ip pim sparse-mode
 ip nhrp authentication cisco
 ip nhrp map multicast 9.1.1.10
 ip nhrp map 10.2.0.1 9.1.1.10
 ip nhrp network-id 100
 ip nhrp holdtime 300
 ip nhrp nhs 9.1.1.10
 ip nhrp nhs 10.2.0.1
 ip ospf network broadcast
 ip ospf priority 0
 delay 1000
 tunnel source Serial1/0:0
 tunnel mode gre multipoint
 tunnel key 100
 tunnel protection ipsec profile dmvpn
end
```

The PIM process assigned to the multipoint interface uses multicast Hello packets to build the PIM adjacency. The multicast Hello is only directed to the hub; therefore, the spoke-to-spoke PIM adjacency is not established. The only time the spoke-to-spoke GRE tunnel is initiated is when unicast packets are sent. The architecture appears to be a temporal full mesh for unicast flows and a hub-and-spoke architecture for multicast flows. Figure 8-14 shows the flow topology for both multicast and unicast traffic in the DMVPN network.

Figure 8-14 *Multicast and Unicast Flow over a DMVPN Topology*

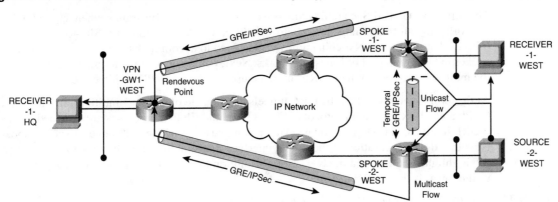

Unfortunately, the dynamic establishment of spoke-to-spoke GRE/IPSec tunnels cannot be leveraged for multicast traffic. Nevertheless, the architecture scales reasonably well for large networks unless the hub is heavily burdened with multicast replication. Typically, multicast sources (for example, content servers) will reside at the hub site anyway; therefore, the multicast replication at the hub site is unavoidable. Of course, the hub will be burdened with routing adjacencies and IPSec peers in addition to the multicast replication.

Fortunately, the number of GRE/IPSec connections is minimized at the spoke. We do find at least one exception to this paradigm. When a spoke serves a multicast source, the receivers at the other spokes will force their spoke gateways to join the multicast tree using a unicast PIM Join message. This message will be sent directly between the spokes, forcing the establishment of the spoke-to-spoke GRE/IPSec connection. The spoke receiving the PIM Join for the multicast source will be able to forward multicast frames only into the multipoint tunnel that subsequently directs the multicast frames to the hub. From a scalability perspective, the spoke servicing a multicast source must be prepared for incoming GRE/IPSec connections from any spoke hosting a receiver of the multicast group. If the receivers are waiting for the multicast source, the spoke hosting the source is likely to receive simultaneous PIM Joins from many spokes hosting receivers. Effectively, the spoke becomes a GRE/IPSec hub for the multicast source and must be prepared to handle the simultaneous initialization of many incoming GRE/IPSec connections. Filtering PIM-SM joins to all sites except the hub prevents the simultaneous initiation of GRE/IPSec connections to a spoke hosting a multicast source. Because the multicast packets are forwarded only to the VPN hub site, the spoke is not burdened with multicast packet replication.

Multicast Group Security

The previous sections addressed methods of "hiding" the multicast from the native IPSec processing through tunnels and virtual IPSec interfaces. The IETF has issued RFC 3740, "The Multicast Group Security Architecture," as the reference for establishing native multicast security. The new architecture establishes the notion of a Group Security Association (GSA) that is valid among all the peers that belong to the same group. The GSA eliminates the necessity of establishing a full mesh of peer-to-peer relationships (tunnels, IKE, and IPSec SA) between the potential multicast source and destinations. The development of native multicast encryption methods will alleviate the requirement to "hide" the multicast frames from the encryption processes.

NOTE   The introduction of a GSA does not necessarily preclude the use of an IPSec SA at the same time. In fact, a GSA is a concept that includes all of the SAs for a group, which may include IPSec SAs.

The group security model is based on the premise that a source cannot know the intended recipient a priori. The potential sources and receivers must identify themselves as members of a group. Members of the same group are afforded a common level of trust such that they may exchange data between themselves. Next, you'll examine how the members of a group are identified.

Group Security Key Management

Each member of a security group is provided a set of credentials that allow the member to authenticate its right to join the group. To enable this process, a common reference point is needed, where all the members may convene. The Group Domain of Interpretation (GDOI) protocol (RFC 3547) defines the means for allowing a group member to authenticate with a Group Controller/Key Server (GCKS). Once authenticated and authorized by the GCKS, the group member establishes a secure communication channel in order to exchange policy and key material with the GCKS. The GCKS may provide a common key for the group member in order for the member to encrypt and decrypt data from any of the other group members. Likewise, the GCKS may re-key or revoke keys from members in order to control the validity of group members. In GDOI, the secure communication channel established between group members and the GCKS reuses IKE phase 1. Recall from Chapter 2 that IKE Phase 2 is used to establish the point-to-point IPSec SAs. The GDOI protocol replaces the IKE phase 2 process in order to accommodate the secure distribution of group keys. Figure 8-15 highlights the network architecture associated with the GCKS and the group members.

Figure 8-15 *Group Key Management Architecture*

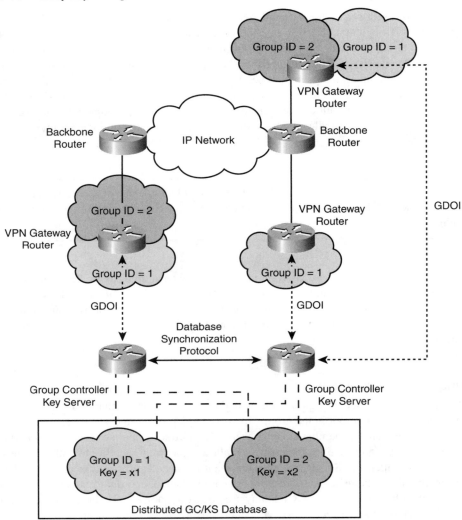

We now have the infrastructure in place to identify group members and distribute key material to the appropriate group members.

Group Security Association

The key management infrastructure allows members to synchronously receive and process traffic flows with a common key. All the members will receive the same key for traffic associated with the group identifier; therefore, any member may encrypt data using the key (and decrypt the traffic using the same key).

You must now determine the appropriate key to use to encrypt traffic. The encrypting router must associate a multicast group (or range of multicast groups) with a group key. The multicast traffic is encrypted using a group key distributed as part of the Group Security Association (GSA). The encapsulating security payload provides confidentiality for the original IP packet and payload while the IP source address and multicast group address are preserved in the outer IP header. Figure 8-16 shows the packet structure of the multicast security encrypted packet.

Figure 8-16   *Multicast Security Payload*

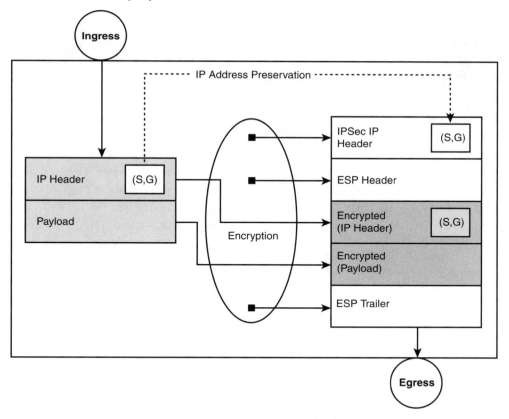

As the packet traverses the multicast-enabled IP core network, the packet may replicate according to the multicast distribution tree (MDT) built using traditional multicast protocols such as PIM. The encrypted packet arrives at the decrypting router, which recognizes the GSA.

The decrypting router may use a criterion set to associate the appropriate group key using the most specific match as follows:

Security Parameter Index, Destination, Source
Security Parameter Index, Destination
Security Parameter Index

At this point, decryption and decapsulation occurs, and the multicast packet continues on the MDT in the clear. Figure 8-17 shows the topological association of two GSAs among various group members.

Figure 8-17 *Multicast GSA Data Plane Association*

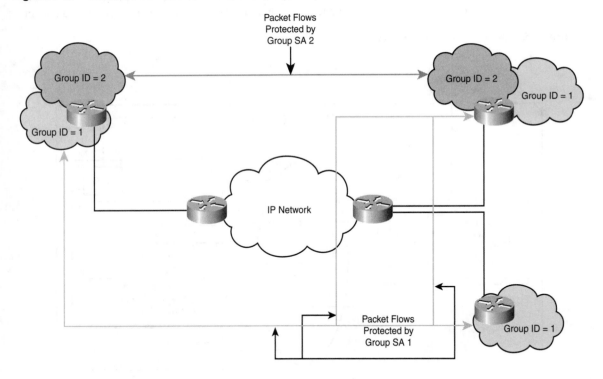

Multicast Group Security Summary

The multicast security model enables a much more efficient method for distributing encrypted multicast traffic by leveraging the multicast replication of the core IP network. The encrypting gateway is responsible for encrypting the multicast traffic and forwarding it to the core; it is no longer responsible for replication of the multicast packet to every receiving VPN gateway. The group security association allows any valid member of the group to encrypt or decrypt traffic such that the number of security associations is minimized on the VPN gateways. Keep in mind that the group security association doesn't mitigate the need for IPSec SAs to accommodate unicast traffic flows. The primary motivation for using multicast security is to provide an efficient means of encrypting and replicating encrypted multicast traffic.

Multicast Encryption Summary

Our analysis of multicast encryption has shown that the overlay tunnel topologies have a significant impact on the creation of the multicast distribution trees. The peer-to-peer nature of IPSec fundamentally conflicts with the communication paradigm induced by multicast. The IETF's effort to improve the relationship between multicast and encryption methods has led to the establishment of a group security model that is fundamentally different from the peer-to-peer model used by IPSec. Research on how to improve the relationship between unicast and multicast security continues using a common security infrastructure.

Summary

In this chapter, you have seen it demonstrated that the IPSec peer-to-peer model has a significant impact on the support of enhanced applications such as VoIP and multicast. Also highlighted was the impact that encryption has on the QoS models used to prioritize these enhanced applications. Specifically, the use of the IP DSCP or precedence values was emphasized as the common denominator for queuing before encryption, between encryption peers, and after encryption. It is critical to use a consistent QoS classification model in the convergence of voice and data streams on a common IPSec topology. Fortunately, the IPSec peer model readily accommodates the point-to-point nature of VoIP communications. In contrast, the multicast communication paradigm does not conform to the IPSec peer model. Network architects must analyze the organization's application communication requirements and business requirements to select the appropriate IPSec paradigm and topology. In doing so, a number of trade-offs are made with regard to optimal topology, traffic management, capacity planning, and provisioning complexity. Many enterprises are turning to service provider solutions such as MPLS/VPN services in order to optimize their application deployment models, capacity planning, and traffic engineering. The final chapter steps through the relationship of IPSec VPN solutions in conjunction with other network-based VPN solutions such as MPLS VPNs.

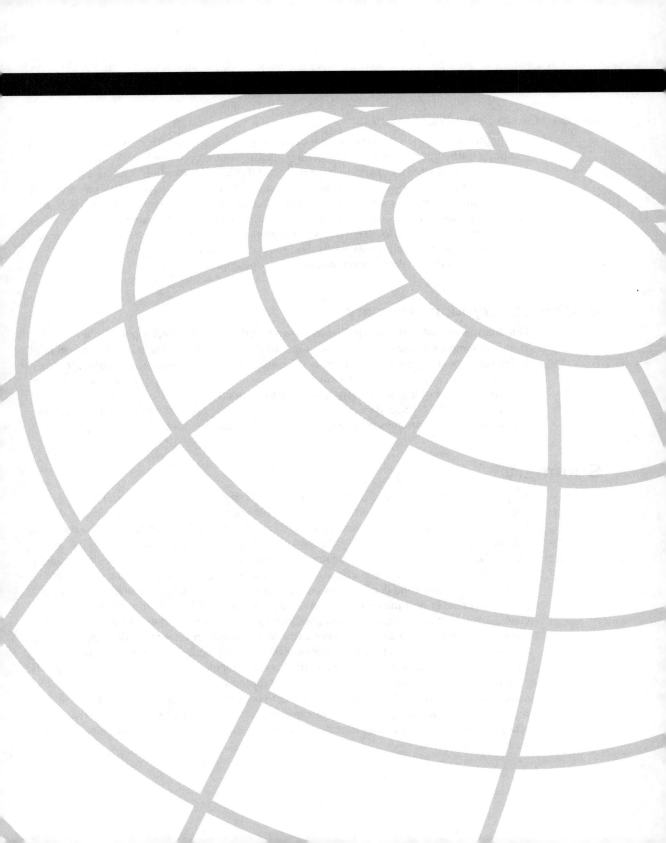

CHAPTER 9

Network-Based IPSec VPNs

In previous chapters, you reviewed IPSec VPN fundamentals and design principles in depth. This chapter explores a new type of VPN service known as the network-based VPN.

Fundamentals of Network-Based VPNs

In a customer edge (CE) VPN or CE-based VPN that uses IPSec, all VPN configuration, encapsulation, and decapsulation is performed by the CEs. The provider network that provides connectivity to the CEs is simply providing a transport service to the CEs and is oblivious of the VPN configuration. In a network or provider edge–based VPN, all VPN configuration, encapsulation, and decapsulation is performed at the provider edge (PE); the CEs in this case are oblivious of the VPN configuration. Figure 9-1 shows a popular PE-based VPN defined in RFC 2547 using Multiprotocol Label Switching (MPLS).

Figure 9-1 *PE-based MPLS VPN Using RFC 2547*

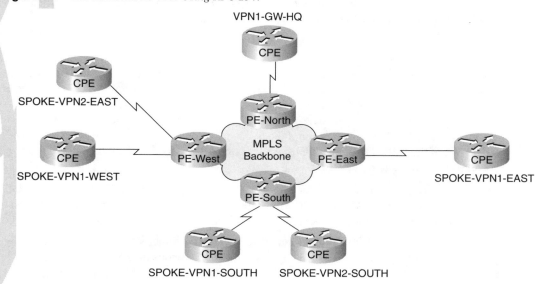

All the tunneling of CE-CE traffic in the MPLS VPN shown in Figure 9-1 is performed by the PE routers at the edge of the service provider network. MPLS VPNs have several advantages over the traditional overlay CE-based IPSec VPNs. Some salient advantages of PE-based VPNs over CE-based VPNs are as follows:

- **Increased scalability**—To connect *N* sites of an IPSec VPN for any-to-any connectivity, each CE will need (*N-1*) tunnels to every other CE. This means that every CE has to be able to deal with this scalability requirement, thereby increasing the cost of the CEs at sites where such a large CE may not be required. In contrast, the same any-to-any connectivity can be established between CEs of an MPLS VPN with a single connection from a CE to the PE. Also, the encapsulation and decapsulation is performed by the PE routers, thereby reducing the cost of the CE by not requiring expensive hardware encryption at the CE.

- **Greatly simplified configuration**—Every time a new site is added to a CE-based IPSec VPN, the configuration has to be changed in (N-1) sites for any-to-any connectivity. In an MPLS-VPN, only the configuration of the PE and the attached CE is changed; none of the remote CEs or remote PEs is affected. In other words, configuration complexity of MPLS-based VPNs is O(1) compared to O(n) for IPSec-based VPNs. This means that it is operationally easier and more economical for a service provider to provision an MPLS-based VPN.

NOTE	One could argue that DMVPN (see Chapter 7, "Auto-Configuration Architectures for Site-to-Site IPSec VPNs") reduces configuration complexity, negating this advantage for MPLS VPN. But DMVPN also requires a dynamic routing protocol such as OSPF in the overlay tunnels, which has limitations as the number of sites of the VPN grows very large.

One of the primary limitations of MPLS VPN architecture is the requirement for each CE to have physical connectivity at Layer 2 to its corresponding PE. Now, imagine a service provider that is offering an MPLS VPN service to its customers. In this scenario, assume that one customer has five sites that need to be connected over the VPN and that the service provider has a point of presence (POP) in only four of the five locations—which means only four of the sites can be part of the VPN. The following list presents the options available for the service provider to connect the fifth site to the VPN:

- **Option 1**—The service provider can extend its backbone network and build a new POP in the new location. Although the most obvious solution, this option is usually not cost effective for the service provider and in some cases is simply not viable.

- **Option 2**—The service provider may backhaul the customer's traffic across other providers using leased lines. This option is the next obvious option, but is also cost prohibitive, has long installation lead times, and may be subject to frequent outages.

- **Option 3**—Connect the fifth site to the VPN via IPSec tunnels over the public Internet to every other site. However, there are several disadvantages of this option:

  — Each site of this VPN now requires a CE that is IPSec-capable.

  — IPSec requires (public) reachability to each CE endpoint. If the IPSec tunnels to each site have to traverse the Internet, all the CEs at the sites need IP reachability over the Internet, which might not be possible.

  — Every site is exposed to the Internet and may require more security protection mechanisms.

- **Option 4**—Build an IPSec tunnel from the remote CE to the service provider PE and map the IPSec tunnel into the appropriate MPLS VPN at the PE. This option is called the Network Based IPSec VPN solution, which is the subject of this chapter. Figure 9-2 illustrates this option. This would be a secure and cost-effective option.

Figure 9-2   *Network-Based IPSec VPN*

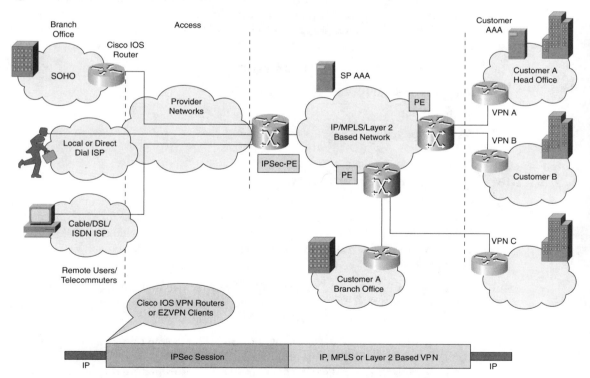

There are several advantages of the Network Based IPSec VPN architecture:

- The PE and CE need only IP connectivity; no dedicated Layer 2 connection is required.
- Connectivity to the four original sites is retained via the MPLS VPN and no additional configuration is needed on the sites to connect the fifth site to the VPN.
- Optimal routing from site to site is possible without a full-mesh configuration.
- Secure connectivity for the new "off net" site. This is important because traffic from this site routinely transits the public Internet.

The rest of this chapter is dedicated to this architecture and presents the configuration and design of network-based VPNs.

The Network-Based IPSec Solution: IOS Features

You have seen conceptually how a network-based IPSec VPN solution enables service providers to expand their VPN portfolio with secure off-net remote access and remote site-to-site services. This section focuses on understanding IOS features that are key to implementing this solution.

The following three key features will be discussed:

- Virtual Routing and Forwarding (VRF) tables
- Crypto keyrings
- ISAKMP profiles

The Virtual Routing and Forwarding Table

The notion of a VRF table was defined in RFC 2547 for MPLS VPNs. As the name suggests, a VRF is a unique routing and forwarding table per VPN. A given PE router may be connected to sites from different VPNs and hence may have multiple VRFs. To provide per-VPN routing segregation and avoid accidentally forwarding packets from one VPN to another, VRFs are kept on the PE routers.

A CE connected to a PE is associated with a VPN by explicit configuration of the VRF on the PE interface connecting the CE. The association between a given VRF and its attached set of interfaces or subinterfaces is determined by explicit configuration.

When a packet arrives from a CE, the routing or forwarding lookup for the destination is performed in the associated VRF table ensuring packets are only forwarded to destinations in the VRF. The VRF itself is populated by learning IPv4 routes from the CE by typical routing protocols such as OSPF, eBGP, static, RIPv2, and EIGRP. The PE advertises the routes learned from the CE to all other PEs via multiprotocol extensions to BGP (MP-BGP). The routes advertised by the PE via MP-BGP are known as VPNv4 routes. A couple of key attributes that are tagged to the VPNv4 routes in MP-BGP are the route target (RT) and the route distinguisher (RD).

The RD enables overlapping address pools between VPNs or VRFs, whereas the RT determines the distribution of the routes into the remote PE's VRF. Both attributes are manually configured.

Crypto Keyrings

You learned in previous chapters that when you configure IPSec, you must configure the Internet Security Association and Key Management Protocol (ISAKMP) policies. If the authentication scheme used is a pre-shared key, then you have to configure the corresponding key for each IPSec endpoint. In the traditional IPSec model, all the IPSec terminations are for connectivity into a single IPSec VPN, whereas in the network-based IPSec model you need to terminate IPSec tunnels belonging to different VPNs on the same IPSec aggregator. This means you need a mechanism to demarcate the keys of different VPNs, which is exactly what *crypto keyrings* are about.

With crypto keyrings, each VPN has its own unique keyring. Example 9-1 shows crypto keyrings for two different VPNs. A crypto keyring is in use if it is attached to one or more ISAKMP profiles. A crypto keyring cannot be deleted while it is in use by one of the profiles.

Example 9-1   *Crypto Keyring Configuration*

```
crypto keyring vpn1
  description keys for vpn1
  pre-shared-key address 9.1.1.145 key vpn1aes
crypto keyring vpn2
  description keys for vpn2
  pre-shared-key address 9.1.1.149 key vpn2ikev2
```

If the VRF keyword is not specified in the **crypto keyring** command, the keyring is bound to the global VRF (global routing table). When a VRF keyword is used in the command, the keyring is associated with the front-door VRF (FVRF). Example 9-2 shows keyring vpn1 bound to front-door VRF vpn1. The concepts of FVRF and inside VRF (IVRF) will be explained in the "Operation of Network-Based IPSec VPNs" section, later in this chapter.

Example 9-2   *Crypto Keyring with FVRF Association*

```
crypto keyring vpn1 vrf vpn1
description keys for vpn1
pre-shared-key address 9.1.1.145 key vpn1aes
```

ISAKMP Profiles

An ISAKMP profile can be viewed as a placeholder for holding phase 1 and phase 1.5 (x-auth/mode-cfg) configuration applicable to an aggregation of peers. The ISAKMP profile selected for a specific peer during Internet Key Exchange (IKE) negotiation can be identified by using one of the following:

- Phase 1 IKE identity. The identities could be of type IP Address, FQDN, USER-FQDN, DN, and ID_KEY_ID.
- Matching fields in the certificate forwarded by the peer during authentication.

NOTE It is important to note that the isakmp profile does not specify ISAKMP policy. Policy is still defined globally because ISAKMP policy selection has to be done prior to knowing the ISAKMP profile when Main Mode is used.

After the identity is matched and IKE phase 1 is complete, the IPsec user or branch site is bound to the appropriate VRF configured on the ISAKMP profile.

Example 9-3 shows the ISAKMP profile configuration with match identity statements using IP address, FQDN, USER_FQDN, and ID_KEY_ID, respectively. As you saw in Chapter 4, "IPSec Authentication and Authorization Models," ID_KEY_ID is the groupname for Cisco Unity clients. You can also see that in the case of remote access, you can configure all the AAA attributes within the ISAKMP profile, as shown in Example 9-3.

Example 9-3 *ISAKMP Profile Configuration*

```
crypto isakmp profile vpn1
 vrf vpn1 description IVRF
 keyring vpn1
 match identity address 9.1.1.145 255.255.255.255
 match identity hostname domain vpn1.com
 accounting vpn
!
crypto isakmp profile vpn1-ra
  vrf vpn1
  match identity user-fqdn user@vpn1.com
  match identity group vpn1group
  client authentication list vpn
  isakmp authorization list vpn
  client configuration address respond
  accounting vpn
```

If the FVRF interface is in a VRF (not in global), then you must make sure there is a configuration that has the match identity statement with the VRF option, as shown in Example 9-4.

Example 9-4 *Configuration Showing FVRF Association with Match Identity for Site-to-Site IPSec VPNs*

```
crypto isakmp profile vpn2
 vrf vpn2
 keyring vpn2
 match identity address 9.1.1.149 255.255.255.255 vrf vpn2
 accounting vpn
```

If the match criteria for the selection of the ISAKMP profile is based on certificates, then define the corresponding certificate map and assign that map to the match certificate, as shown in Example 9-5.

Example 9-5   *Use of Certificates to Bind to a Profile and VRF*

```
crypto isakmp profile vpn1-ra
  vrf vpn1
  ca trustpoint vpn1
  match certificate foo
  client configuration group vpn1group
  client authentication list vpn
  isakmp authorization list vpn
  client configuration address respond
  accounting vpn
!
crypto ca certificate map foo
  subject-name co ou=EAST
  subject-name co o=VPN1
```

The main reason for using certificate matching is for cases in which the assignment of an ISAKMP profile cannot depend solely on the identity sent by the peer, and the intent is to be much more granular. For telecommuter clients wherein the group information cannot be retrieved from the certificate, you can assign a group to the clients.

NOTE   The ISAKMP profile must specify at least one "match" subcommand. An ISAKMP profile is regarded as incomplete without a **match** statement, and any traffic that matches a crypto map to which such a profile is attached will be dropped.

Any number of **match** statements can be specified in a single ISAKMP profile. The **match** statements should be used with care. An incoming identity will be matched in accordance with the following rules:

If the identity is of type IP address, the keyring and the **match** statement will be used. No two profiles should include the same match identity address and a common keyring. For identities of type ID_FQDN, or ID_USER_FQDN, the longest match will be chosen as the correct match.

Operation of Network-Based IPSec VPNs

Now that you have an understanding of the key features in IOS for network-based IPSec VPNs, you are ready to examine the operation of this solution. One of the primary motivations for a network-based IPSec VPN is to extend the service provider's footprint over the public *Internet.* There are several options a service provider has to provide this extension. One could make each PE router IPSec capable; another would be to have a set of dedicated IPSec PEs that is primarily used for this service. The latter is generally the more common approach given the financial considerations and the fact that not all PEs are IPSec capable.

There are two deployment scenarios to offer this solution—one of them uses a single IP address on the PE reachable from the Internet for terminating IPSec tunnels of multiple VPNs and the second one uses a unique IP address per VPN on the terminating PE.

A Single IP Address on the PE

In an MPLS VPN, separation of a CE belonging to a particular VPN is made by explicitly configuring the PE-CE link on the PE to the appropriate VRF. Forwarding decisions for all traffic that is received from the CE are made by referencing the VRF that the PE-CE interface is configured with.

With an understanding of how MPLS VPNs operate, an obvious solution to extend reachability of the CEs across the Internet is to have a dedicated interface facing the Internet explicitly configured in a VRF and terminating IPSec tunnels from the corresponding CEs across the Internet into its VRF interface. Although this solution works, it requires a unique IP address or sub-interface per VRF that is reachable from the Internet.

A more elegant solution would be to use a single IP address for terminating the *off-net* IPSec tunnels, but this presents some interesting challenges. One issue is that a mechanism is needed to somehow separate the CEs belonging to different VPNs and map the traffic to the appropriate VRF.

The operation of mapping the IPSec tunnels into the appropriate VRFs involves several concepts mentioned earlier in this chapter and explained in the following section. One of these concepts is the concept of a front-door VRF (FVRF) and an inside VRF (IVRF).

Front-Door and Inside VRF

Each IPSec tunnel is associated with two VRF domains. The outer IP header of the tunnel-mode IPSec encapsulated packet belongs to the FVRF, whereas the inner IP header is associated with the VPNs private IVRF. Figure 9-3 illustrates the concept of a FVRF and an IVRF. The FVRF pertains to the VRF that the encrypted packet itself is in. The FVRF is commonly on a global VRF. In this example, in which all the IPSec tunnels terminate on a single IP address on the PE facing the Internet, the global interface facing the Internet is considered to be in the FVRF. The IVRF is used for post-decryption forwarding lookups for IPSec traffic terminating on the aggregation PE.

In this example, where all the IPSec tunnels terminate on a single IP address on the PE, the FVRF is the same and is set to the VRF configured on the Internet-facing interface. Traffic arriving from remote CEs that is associated with the IVRF is done during IKE negotiation using ISAKMP profiles.

Figure 9-3 *Conceptual Representation of FVRF and IVRF*

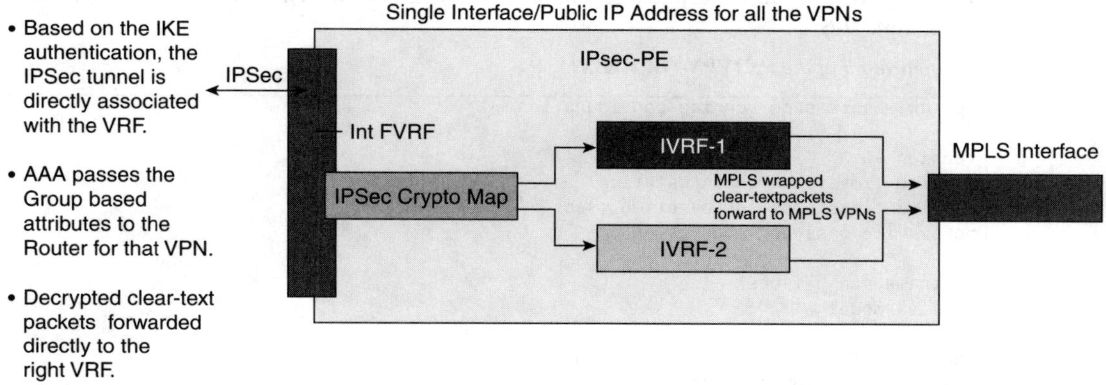

Single Interface/Public IP Address for all the VPNs
• Based on the IKE authentication, the IPSec tunnel is directly associated with the VRF.
• AAA passes the Group based attributes to the Router for that VPN.
• Decrypted clear-text packets forwarded directly to the right VRF.
IPSec
IPsec-PE
Int FVRF
IVRF-1
IPSec Crypto Map
MPLS wrapped clear-textpackets forward to MPLS VPNs
IVRF-2
MPLS Interface

Configuration and Packet Flow

Now that you have a conceptual understanding of FVRF and IVRF, this section will explore the configuration details and packet flow for the deployment scenario of a single IP address on the PE. The single IP address is used for terminating IPSec tunnels from remote sites and telecommuters that belong to multiple VPNs. Figure 9-4 illustrates this scenario.

Figure 9-4 *Single IP Addressing on PE/IPSec aggregator Terminating IPSec Tunnels from the Internet*

AAA
Enterprise AAA Server
CPE
vpn1-qw-hq
PE-North
CPE
SPOKE-VPN1-EAST
CPE
SPOKE-VPN2-EAST
EZVPN
EZVPN-VPN1-EAST
PC
EZVPN-VPN2-EAST
Internet
IGW
Internet Gateway
IPsec VPN
IPsec VPN
IPsec VPN
IPsec VPN
IPsec-PE
VPN-GW1-EAST
MPLS Backbone
PE-South
AAA
SP-AAA-Server
CA
Certifcate Authority Server
CPE
SPOKE-VPN1-SOUTH
CPE
SPOKE-VPN1-EAST

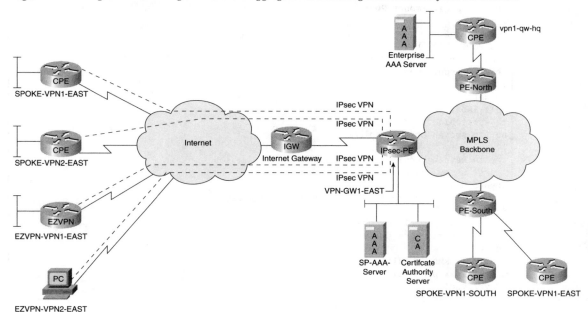

The complete configuration of the PE router terminating the IPSec tunnels from remote CE sites belonging to multiple VPNs and telecommuters (also known as remote access clients) is shown in Example 9-6.

Example 9-6   *Configuration of the PE (VPN-GW1-EAST)*

```
vpn-gw1-east# show running-configuration

version 12.3
service timestamps debug datetime
service timestamps log datetime msec
no service password-encryption
!
hostname vpn-gw1-east
aaa new-model
!
aaa authentication login vpn1 group radius
aaa authorization network vpn1 group radius
aaa accounting update periodic 5
aaa accounting network vpn start-stop group radius
aaa session-id common
ip subnet-zero
!
!
!
!
ip vrf vpn1
 rd 200:1
 route-target export 200:1
 route-target import 200:1
!
ip vrf vpn2
 rd 201:1
 route-target export 201:1
 route-target import 201:1
!
ip cef
mpls label protocol ldp
tag-switching ip default-route
no ftp-server write-enable
!
crypto keyring vpn1
  pre-shared-key address 9.1.1.146 key vpn1aes
crypto keyring vpn2
  pre-shared-key address 9.1.1.150 key vpn2ikev2
!
crypto isakmp policy 1
 authentication pre-share
 group 2
crypto isakmp keepalive 10 10
crypto isakmp profile vpn1
    vrf vpn1
    keyring vpn1
```

Example 9-6   *Configuration of the PE (VPN-GW1-EAST) (Continued)*

```
     match identity address 9.1.1.146 255.255.255.255
crypto isakmp profile vpn1-ra
   vrf vpn1
   match identity group vpn1group
   client authentication list vpn
   isakmp authorization list vpn
   client configuration address respond
   accounting vpn
crypto isakmp profile vpn2
   vrf vpn2
   keyring vpn2
   match identity address 9.1.1.150 255.255.255.255
!
!
crypto ipsec transform-set vpn1 esp-3des esp-sha-hmac
crypto ipsec transform-set vpn2 esp-3des esp-md5-hmac
!
crypto dynamic-map dynamic 1
 set transform-set vpn1
 set isakmp-profile vpn1-ra
 reverse-route remote-peer 9.1.1.33
!
crypto map vpn 1 ipsec-isakmp
set peer 9.1.1.146
set transform-set vpn1
set isakmp-profile vpn1
reverse-route remote-peer address 9.1.1.33
match address 101

crypto map vpn 2 ipsec-isakmp
set peer 9.1.1.150
set transform-set vpn2
set isakmp-profile vpn2
reverse-route remote-peer address 9.1.1.33
match address 102

crypto map vpn 3 ipsec-isakmp dynamic dynamic
!
interface Loopback0
 ip address 9.2.1.100 255.255.255.255
!
interface FastEthernet0/0
 ip address 9.1.1.35 255.255.255.248
 duplex full
 crypto map vpn
!
interface FastEthernet2/0
 ip address 100.1.1.147 255.255.255.0
 duplex full
!
interface FastEthernet4/0
```

Example 9-6 *Configuration of the PE (VPN-GW1-EAST) (Continued)*

```
 ip address 9.2.1.1 255.255.255.252
 duplex full
 tag-switching ip
!
 router ospf 1
 log-adjacency-changes
 network 9.2.1.0 0.0.0.3 area 0
 network 9.2.1.100 0.0.0.0 area 0
!
router bgp 1001
 no synchronization
 bgp log-neighbor-changes
 neighbor 153.1.1.1 remote-as 1001
 neighbor 153.1.1.1 update-source Loopback0
 no auto-summary
 !
 address-family vpnv4
 neighbor 153.1.1.1 activate
 neighbor 153.1.1.1 send-community extended
 exit-address-family
 !
 address-family ipv4 vrf vpn2
 redistribute connected
 redistribute static
 no auto-summary
 no synchronization
 exit-address-family
 !
 address-family ipv4 vrf vpn1
 redistribute connected
 redistribute static
 no auto-summary
 no synchronization
 exit-address-family
!
ip local pool vpn1pool 10.254.245.1 10.254.254.254 group vpn1group
ip classless
ip route 0.0.0.0 0.0.0.0 9.1.1.33
access-list 100 permit ip 10.0.1.0 0.0.0.255 any
access-list 101 permit ip 10.0.1.0 0.0.0.255 any
no ip http server
no ip http secure-server
!
radius-server host 100.1.1.4 auth-port 1645 acct-port 1646
radius-server key cisco
radius-server vsa send accounting
!
end

vpn-gw1-east#
```

We'll parse the configuration on the PE/IPSec aggregator shown in Example 9-6 to illustrate how the association of the inner IP header of the IPSec packet to the IVRF takes place. In this example, the MPLS-PE at the edge of the service provider network is also the IPSec aggregator. We will divide the PE configuration in Example 9-6 into three parts:

- The first part is the generic MPLS-VPN configuration.
- The second part of the configuration is relevant to the termination of the IPSec tunnel from a remote-site CE.
- The third part is relevant to the IPSec tunnel termination from a remote access client or a telecommuter.

Generic MPLS VPN Configuration on the PE

Example 9-7 shows the parts of the configuration that are relevant to the generic MPLS VPN configuration of the PE router.

Example 9-7   *MPLS VPN Relevant Configuration on the PE*

```
ip vrf vpn1
 rd 200:1
 route-target export 200:1
 route-target import 200:1
!
ip vrf vpn2
 rd 201:1
 route-target export 201:1
 route-target import 201:1
!
mpls label protocol ldp
!
interface FastEthernet0/0
 ip address 9.1.1.35 255.255.255.248
 duplex full
 crypto map vpn
!
interface FastEthernet4/0
 ip address 9.2.1.1 255.255.255.252
 duplex full
 tag-switching ip
!
router ospf 1
 log-adjacency-changes
 redistribute static subnets
 network 9.2.1.0 0.0.0.3 area 0
 network 9.2.1.100 0.0.0.0 area 0
!
router bgp 1001
 no synchronization
 bgp log-neighbor-changes
 neighbor 153.1.1.1 remote-as 1001
 neighbor 153.1.1.1 update-source Loopback0
```

Example 9-7 *MPLS VPN Relevant Configuration on the PE (Continued)*

```
no auto-summary
 !
 address-family vpnv4
 neighbor 153.1.1.1 activate
 neighbor 153.1.1.1 send-community extended
 exit-address-family
 !
 address-family ipv4 vrf vpn2
 redistribute connected
 redistribute static
 no auto-summary
 no synchronization
 exit-address-family
 !
 address-family ipv4 vrf vpn1
 redistribute connected
 redistribute static
 no auto-summary
 no synchronization
 exit-address-family
 !
```

In this example, note that there are no PE-CE interfaces explicitly configured in a VRF. The IP address that is reachable from the Internet is 9.1.1.35, configured on the physical interface FastEthernet 0/0. This interface is logically in the front-door VRF on which a crypto map is also configured. In other words, the FVRF is the global routing table. There are two IVRFs configured: VPN1 and VPN2. The rest of the MPLS VPN configuration is basic MPLS VPN configuration (configuration of MP-BGP, RD, and RT), which is outside of the scope of this discussion.

Mapping an IPSec Tunnel from a Site into IVRF at the PE

This section will present the configuration relevant to map the IPSec tunnel from the remote site into an IVRF and explain the packet flow for this mapping.

Before looking at the PE config for the IPSec termination, review Example 9-8, which shows the relevant portions of configuration of the CE router at the branch site.

Example 9-8 *Configuration of the CE (SPOKE-VPN1-EAST)*

```
spoke-vpn1-east#show running-config

hostname spoke-vpn1-east
!
crypto isakmp policy 1
 authentication pre-share
 group 2
crypto isakmp key vpn1aes address 9.1.1.35
crypto isakmp keepalive 10 10
 !
```

Example 9-8   *Configuration of the CE (SPOKE-VPN1-EAST) (Continued)*

```
crypto ipsec transform-set test esp-3des esp-sha-hmac
!
crypto map vpn 1 ipsec-isakmp
 set peer 9.1.1.35
 set transform-set test
 match address 100
!
interface Serial0/0
 ip address 9.1.1.146 255.255.255.252
 crypto map vpn
!
interface Ethernet0/1
 ip address 10.0.68.1 255.255.255.0
 half-duplex
 no keepalive
!
ip classless
ip route 0.0.0.0 0.0.0.0 9.1.1.145
!
access-list 100 permit ip 10.0.68.0 0.0.0.255 any
!
```

Notice that the configuration of the CE router in Example 9-8 is no different than a typical IPSec site router. The IPSec peer address is set to the IP address of the PE (9.1.1.35). The crypto configuration on the serial0/0 interface will trigger IKE and IPSec for packets that match the policy defined in access list 100.

Next, you'll take a step-by-step look at how the IPSec tunnel initiated by the CE router is mapped into the IVRF VPN1 that the CE belongs to. Refer to Figure 9-4 for this discussion, in which it is assumed that the traffic originates from the SPOKE-VPN1-EAST's subnet 10.0.68.0 destined to the remote subnet 10.1.1.0 on PE2. Note that in this discussion, the terms CE and SPOKE-VPN1-EAST are used interchangeably, as well as the terms PE and VPN-GW1-EAST.

Step 1   Inserting traffic that matches IPSec policy on the CE (SPOKE-VPN1-EAST) will trigger IKE negotiation to start establishing an IPSec tunnel with its IPSec peer 9.1.1.35 (VPN-GW1-EAST).

Step 2   The IKE packet from the CE is received on VPN-GW1-EAST's FastEthernet0/0 interface.

Step 2.1   After the IKE packet from the CE is received at the PE via FastEthernet0/0 interface, the crypto configuration on the interface triggers IKE Phase 1 processing. Example 9-9 shows the relevant portions of the configuration from VPN-GW1-EAST and the debug output for this step.

Example 9-9   *Configuration Snippet and Debug from VPN-GW1-EAST for IKE Processing*

```
interface FastEthernet0/0
 description FVRF
 ip address 9.1.1.35 255.255.255.248
 duplex full
 random-detect
```

Example 9-9 *Configuration Snippet and Debug from VPN-GW1-EAST for IKE Processing (Continued)*

```
crypto map vpn

vpn-gw1-east# debug crypto isakmp sa
*Jan  5 19:27:48: ISAKMP (0:0): received packet from 9.1.1.146 dport 500 sport 500
*Jan  5 19:27:48: ISAKMP: local port 500, remote port 500
*Jan  5 19:27:48: ISAKMP:(0:3:SW:1):Input = IKE_MESG_FROM_PEER, IKE_MM_EXCH
*Jan  5 19:27:48: ISAKMP:(0:3:SW:1):Old State = IKE_READY  New State = IKE_R_MM1
```

Step 2.2 As you saw in Chapter 2, "IPSec Overview," IKE Main Mode processing consists of six messages between the initiator and the responder. In this scenario, we won't go through all six messages; the debug output clearly shows the sequence of the messages and the IKE state changes.

One of the first checks in IKE Phase 1 is to see if there is a key associated with the source address of the IKE packet (9.1.1.146). If there is a key for the IKE peer, Main Mode negotiation will continue. The configuration portion for this check and the debug output is shown in Example 9-10.

Example 9-10 *Configuration Snippet and Debug Output from VPN-GW1-EAST for Step 2.2*

```
crypto keyring vpn1
  pre-shared-key address 9.1.1.146 key vpn1aes

*Jan  5 19:27:48: ISAKMP: Looking for a matching key for 9.1.1.146 in default
*Jan  5 19:27:48: ISAKMP: Looking for a matching key for 9.1.1.146 in vpn1 : success
*Jan  5 19:27:48: ISAKMP:(0:3:SW:1):found peer pre-shared key matching 9.1.1.146
*Jan  5 19:27:48: ISAKMP:(0:3:SW:1): local preshared key found
```

Step 2.3 IKE Main Mode processing of messages three and four is no different than typical IKE Main Mode processing, so we'll skip the explanation for these messages.

Step 3 In the fifth message exchange of IKE Main Mode, the identification payload is checked for the IKE Phase 1 identity and the associated keyring. When this check is passed, the ISAKMP profile in turn associates the CE to an IVRF. In this example, the match is for the CE's IP address (9.1.1.146) that will associate all encrypted packets from this source IP address to the IVRF VPN1, as shown in Example 9-11.

Example 9-11 *Configuration and Debug Output for Step 3*

```
crypto isakmp profile vpn1
 vrf vpn1
keyring vpn1
 match identity address 9.1.1.146 255.255.255.255

vpn-gw1-east# debug crypto isakmp sa *Jan  5 19:27:48: ISAKMP:(0:3:SW:1):Old State =
  IKE_R_MM4  New State = IKE_R_MM5
*Jan  5 19:27:48: ISAKMP:(0:3:SW:1): processing ID payload. message ID = 0
```

Example 9-11 *Configuration and Debug Output for Step 3 (Continued)*

```
*Jan  5 19:27:48: ISAKMP (0:134217731): ID payload
          next-payload : 8
          type         : 1
          address      : 9.1.1.146
          protocol     : 17
          port         : 0
          length       : 12
*Jan  5 19:27:48: ISAKMP:(0:3:SW:1):: peer matches vpn1 profile
*Jan  5 19:27:48: ISAKMP: Looking for a matching key for 9.1.1.146 in default
*Jan  5 19:27:48: ISAKMP: Looking for a matching key for 9.1.1.146 in vpn1 : suc
cess
*Jan  5 19:27:48: ISAKMP:(0:3:SW:1):Found ADDRESS key in keyring vpn1
*Jan  5 19:27:48: ISAKMP:(0:3:SW:1): processing HASH payload. message ID = 01
spi 0, message ID = 0, sa = 6509F278
*Jan  5 19:27:48: ISAKMP:(0:3:SW:1):SA authentication status:
*Jan  5 19:27:48: ISAKMP:(0:3:SW:1):     authenticated
*Jan  5 19:27:48: ISAKMP:(0:3:SW:1):SA has been authenticated with 9.1.1.146
*Jan  5 19:27:48: ISAKMP: Trying to insert a peer 9.1.1.35/9.1.1.146/500/, and inserted
  successfully.
```

The entire debug output with all six messages of the IKE Main Mode processing between the
CE and the PE is shown in Example 9-12.

Example 9-12 *Debug Output for Main Mode IKE Between CE and PE*

```
vpn-gw1-east# debug crypto isakmp sa
*Jan  5 19:27:48: ISAKMP (0:0): received packet from 9.1.1.146 dport 500 sport 500
*Jan  5 19:27:48: ISAKMP: local port 500, remote port 500
*Jan  5 19:27:48: ISAKMP:(0:3:SW:1):Input = IKE_MESG_FROM_PEER, IKE_MM_EXCH
*Jan  5 19:27:48: ISAKMP:(0:3:SW:1):Old State = IKE_READY  New State = IKE_R_MM1
*Jan  5 19:27:48: ISAKMP:(0:3:SW:1): processing SA payload. message ID = 0
*Jan  5 19:27:48: ISAKMP:(0:3:SW:1): processing vendor id payload
*Jan  5 19:27:48: ISAKMP:(0:3:SW:1): vendor ID seems Unity/DPD but major 157 mis
match
*Jan  5 19:27:48: ISAKMP:(0:3:SW:1): vendor ID is NAT-T v3
*Jan  5 19:27:48: ISAKMP:(0:3:SW:1): processing vendor id payload
*Jan  5 19:27:48: ISAKMP:(0:3:SW:1): vendor ID seems Unity/DPD but major 123 mis
match
*Jan  5 19:27:48: ISAKMP:(0:3:SW:1): vendor ID is NAT-T v2
*Jan  5 19:27:48: ISAKMP: Looking for a matching key for 9.1.1.146 in default
*Jan  5 19:27:48: ISAKMP: Looking for a matching key for 9.1.1.146 in vpn1 : success
*Jan  5 19:27:48: ISAKMP:(0:3:SW:1):found peer pre-shared key matching 9.1.1.146
*Jan  5 19:27:48: ISAKMP:(0:3:SW:1): local preshared key found
*Jan  5 19:27:48: ISAKMP:(0:3:SW:1):Checking ISAKMP transform 1 against priority 1
  policy
*Jan  5 19:27:48: ISAKMP:      encryption DES-CBC
*Jan  5 19:27:48: ISAKMP:      hash SHA
*Jan  5 19:27:48: ISAKMP:      default group 2
*Jan  5 19:27:48: ISAKMP:      auth pre-share
*Jan  5 19:27:48: ISAKMP:      life type in seconds
*Jan  5 19:27:48: ISAKMP:      life duration (VPI) of  0x0 0x1 0x51 0x80
*Jan  5 19:27:48: ISAKMP:(0:3:SW:1):atts are acceptable. Next payload is 3
```

Example 9-12 *Debug Output for Main Mode IKE Between CE and PE (Continued)*

```
*Jan  5 19:27:48: ISAKMP:(0:3:SW:1): constructed NAT-T vendor-03 ID
*Jan  5 19:27:48: ISAKMP:(0:3:SW:1): sending packet to 9.1.1.146 my_port 500 peer_port
  500 (R) MM_SA_SETUP
*Jan  5 19:27:48: ISAKMP:(0:3:SW:1):Old State = IKE_R_MM1  New State = IKE_R_MM2
*Jan  5 19:27:48: ISAKMP (0:134217731): received packet from 9.1.1.146 dport 500sport
  500 Global (R) MM_SA_SETUP
*Jan  5 19:27:48: ISAKMP:(0:3:SW:1):Input = IKE_MESG_FROM_PEER, IKE_MM_EXCH
*Jan  5 19:27:48: ISAKMP:(0:3:SW:1):Old State = IKE_R_MM2  New State = IKE_R_MM3
*Jan  5 19:27:48: ISAKMP:(0:3:SW:1): processing KE payload. message ID = 0
*Jan  5 19:27:48: ISAKMP:(0:3:SW:1): processing NONCE payload. message ID = 0
*Jan  5 19:27:48: ISAKMP: Looking for a matching key for 9.1.1.146 in default
*Jan  5 19:27:48: ISAKMP:(0:3:SW:1):SKEYID state generated
*Jan  5 19:27:48: ISAKMP:(0:3:SW:1): processing vendor id payload
*Jan  5 19:27:48: ISAKMP:(0:3:SW:1): vendor ID is Unity
*Jan  5 19:27:48: ISAKMP:(0:3:SW:1): processing vendor id payload
*Jan  5 19:27:48: ISAKMP:(0:3:SW:1): vendor ID is DPD
*Jan  5 19:27:48: ISAKMP:(0:3:SW:1): processing vendor id payload
*Jan  5 19:27:48: ISAKMP:(0:3:SW:1): speaking to another IOS box!
*Jan  5 19:27:48: ISAKMP:received payload type 17
*Jan  5 19:27:48: ISAKMP:received payload type 17
*Jan  5 19:27:48: ISAKMP:(0:3:SW:1):Input = IKE_MESG_INTERNAL, IKE_PROCESS_MAIN_MODE
*Jan  5 19:27:48: ISAKMP:(0:3:SW:1):Old State = IKE_R_MM3  New State = IKE_R_MM3
*Jan 5 19:27:48: ISAKMP:(0:3:SW:1): sending packet to 9.1.1.146 my_port 500 peer_port
  500 (R) MM_KEY_EXCH
*Jan  5 19:27:48: ISAKMP:(0:3:SW:1):Input = IKE_MESG_INTERNAL, IKE_PROCESS_COMPLETE
*Jan  5 19:27:48: ISAKMP:(0:3:SW:1):Old State = IKE_R_MM3  New State = IKE_R_MM4
*Jan  5 19:27:48: ISAKMP (0:134217731): received packet from 9.1.1.146 dport 500sport
  500 Global (R) MM_KEY_EXCH
*Jan  5 19:27:48: ISAKMP:(0:3:SW:1):Input = IKE_MESG_FROM_PEER, IKE_MM_EXCH
*Jan  5 19:27:48: ISAKMP:(0:3:SW:1):Old State = IKE_R_MM4  New State = IKE_R_MM5
*Jan  5 19:27:48: ISAKMP:(0:3:SW:1): processing ID payload. message ID = 0
*Jan  5 19:27:48: ISAKMP (0:134217731): ID payload
        next-payload : 8
        type         : 1
        address      : 9.1.1.146
        protocol     : 17
        port         : 0
        length       : 12
*Jan  5 19:27:48: ISAKMP:(0:3:SW:1):: peer matches vpn1 profile
*Jan  5 19:27:48: ISAKMP: Looking for a matching key for 9.1.1.146 in default
*Jan  5 19:27:48: ISAKMP: Looking for a matching key for 9.1.1.146 in vpn1 : suc
cess
*Jan  5 19:27:48: ISAKMP:(0:3:SW:1):Found ADDRESS key in keyring vpn1
*Jan  5 19:27:48: ISAKMP:(0:3:SW:1): processing HASH payload. message ID = 01
spi 0, message ID = 0, sa = 6509F278
*Jan  5 19:27:48: ISAKMP:(0:3:SW:1):SA authentication status:
*Jan  5 19:27:48: ISAKMP:(0:3:SW:1):     authenticated
*Jan  5 19:27:48: ISAKMP:(0:3:SW:1):SA has been authenticated with 9.1.1.146
*Jan 5 19:27:48: ISAKMP: Trying to insert a peer 9.1.1.35/9.1.1.146/500/, and inserted
  successfully.
```

Output from Example 9-13 shows that IKE SAs are successfully established and mapped to the IVRF.

Example 9-13 *IKE SAs Established at the PE*

```
vpn-gw1-east#show cry isa sa det
Codes: C - IKE configuration mode, D - Dead Peer Detection
       K - Keepalives, N - NAT-traversal
       X - IKE Extended Authentication
       psk - Preshared key, rsig - RSA signature
       renc - RSA encryption

C-id Local       Remote          I-VRF    Encr Hash Auth DH Lifetime Cap
3    9.1.1.35    9.1.1.146       vpn1     des  sha  psk  2  23:53:32 D
```

Step 4 After Step 3 is complete and the VRF association is completed for the CE, Quick Mode—also known as IKE Phase 2 negotiation—establishes the IPSec SAs in the IVRF. Example 9-14 shows the debug and show output for the establishment of the IPSec SAs.

Example 9-14 *Debugs of Quick Mode Exchange Between VPN-GW1-EAST and SPOKE-VPN1-EAST*

```
vpn-gw1-east# debug crypto ipsec sa
*Jan  5 19:27:49: IPSEC(validate_proposal_request): proposal part #1,
  (key eng. msg.) INBOUND local= 9.1.1.35, remote= 9.1.1.146,
    local_proxy= 0.0.0.0/0.0.0.0/0/0 (type=4),
    remote_proxy= 10.0.68.0/255.255.255.0/0/0 (type=4),
    protocol= ESP, transform= esp-3des esp-sha-hmac ,
    lifedur= 0s and 0kb,
    spi= 0x0(0), conn_id= 0, keysize= 0, flags= 0x2
*Jan  5 19:27:49: IPSEC(kei_proxy): head = vpn, map->ivrf = vpn1, kei->ivrf = vpn1
*Jan  5 19:27:49: ISAKMP:(0:3:SW:1): Creating IPSec SAs
*Jan  5 19:27:49:            inbound SA from 9.1.1.146 to 9.1.1.35 (f/i)   0/ 1(proxy
  10.0.68.0 to 0.0.0.0)
*Jan  5 19:27:49:            has spi 0x26C9B2C9 and conn_id 2000 and flags
*Jan  5 19:27:49:            lifetime of 3600 seconds
*Jan  5 19:27:49:            lifetime of 4608000 kilobytes
*Jan  5 19:27:49:            has client flags 0x0
*Jan  5 19:27:49:            outbound SA from 9.1.1.35 to 9.1.1.146 (f/i) 0/1(proxy 0.0.0.0
  to 10.0.68.0)
*Jan  5 19:27:49:            has spi 0xD6B17A4B and conn_id 2001 and flags
*Jan  5 19:27:49:            lifetime of 3600 seconds
*Jan  5 19:27:49:            lifetime of 4608000 kilobytes
*Jan  5 19:27:49:            has client flags 0x0
*Jan  5 19:27:49.105: %CRYPTO-5-SESSION_STATUS: Crypto tunnel is UP  .  Peer
  9.1.1.146:500        Id: 9.1.1.146

vpn-gw1-east#show cry ipsec sa

interface: FastEthernet0/0
    Crypto map tag: vpn, local addr. 9.1.1.35

  protected vrf: vpn1
```

Example 9-14 *Debugs of Quick Mode Exchange Between VPN-GW1-EAST and SPOKE-VPN1-EAST (Continued)*

```
local  ident (addr/mask/prot/port): (0.0.0.0/0.0.0.0/0/0)
remote ident (addr/mask/prot/port): (10.0.68.0/255.255.255.0/0/0)
current_peer: 9.1.1.146:500
  PERMIT, flags={origin_is_acl,}
#pkts encaps: 18, #pkts encrypt: 18, #pkts digest: 18
#pkts decaps: 18, #pkts decrypt: 18, #pkts verify: 18
#pkts compressed: 0, #pkts decompressed: 0
#pkts not compressed: 0, #pkts compr. failed: 0
#pkts not decompressed: 0, #pkts decompress failed: 0
#send errors 0, #recv errors 0

 local crypto endpt.: 9.1.1.35, remote crypto endpt.: 9.1.1.146
 path mtu 1500, media mtu 1500
 current outbound spi: D6B17A4B

 inbound esp sas:
  spi: 0x26C9B2C9(650752713)
    transform: esp-3des esp-sha-hmac ,
    in use settings ={Tunnel, }
    slot: 0, conn id: 2000, flow_id: 1, crypto map: vpn
    crypto engine type: Software, engine_id: 1
    sa timing: remaining key lifetime (k/sec): (4474313/3483)
    ike_cookies: EDBF1C2F EDAF2452 038F7139 17D8D460
    IV size: 8 bytes
    replay detection support: Y

 inbound ah sas:

 inbound pcp sas:

 outbound esp sas:
  spi: 0xD6B17A4B(3601955403)
    transform: esp-3des esp-sha-hmac ,
    in use settings ={Tunnel, }
    slot: 0, conn id: 2001, flow_id: 2, crypto map: vpn
    crypto engine type: Software, engine_id: 1
    sa timing: remaining key lifetime (k/sec): (4474313/3483)
    ike_cookies: EDBF1C2F EDAF2452 038F7139 17D8D460
    IV size: 8 bytes
    replay detection support: Y

 outbound ah sas:

 outbound pcp sas:
```

Step 5 Reverse Route Injections (RRI) configured on the static crypto map injects a static route for the CE's protected subnet (10.0.68.0) in VRF VPN1's routing table. Example 9-15 shows the configuration and the route injected by reverse route.

Example 9-15 *Route Injected by Reverse Route within the VRF on VPN-GW1-EAST*

```
crypto map vpn 1 ipsec-isakmp
set peer 9.1.1.146
set transform-set vpn1
set isakmp-profile vpn1
reverse-route remote-peer address 9.1.1.33
match address 101


vpn-gw1-east#show ip  route vrf vpn1

Routing Table: vpn1
Codes: C - connected, S - static, R - RIP, M - mobile, B - BGP
       D - EIGRP, EX - EIGRP external, O - OSPF, IA - OSPF inter area
       N1 - OSPF NSSA external type 1, N2 - OSPF NSSA external type 2
       E1 - OSPF external type 1, E2 - OSPF external type 2
       i - IS-IS, su - IS-IS summary, L1 - IS-IS level-1, L2 - IS-IS level-2
       ia - IS-IS inter area, * - candidate default, U - per-user static route
       o - ODR, P - periodic downloaded static route

Gateway of last resort is not set

     9.0.0.0/32 is subnetted, 1 subnets
S       9.1.1.146 [1/0] via 9.1.1.33
     10.0.0.0/24 is subnetted, 2 subnets
B       10.1.1.0 [200/0] via 153.1.1.1, 3d02h
S       10.0.68.0 [1/0] via 9.1.1.146
```

Notice, the routing table entry for the CE's private subnet is reachable via 9.1.1.146, which is the CE's IP address reachable from the Internet. But how do packets that are destined from the PE in the IVRF on the PE get forwarded? Notice the static route installed in the VRF VPN1 for 9.1.1.146 that is reachable via 9.1.1.33. The 9.1.1.33 address is the IP address of the Internet gateway connected to this PE in the FVRF, which is fa0/0 in this example. CEF will pre-compute this recursion for the CE subnet's reachability, as shown in Example 9-16.

Example 9-16 *Output of CEF for Route Injected by Reverse Route*

```
vpn-gw1-east#show ip  cef vrf vpn1 10.0.68.0
10.0.68.0/24, version 6, epoch 0, cached adjacency 9.1.1.33
0 packets, 0 bytes
  tag information set
    local tag: 528
  via 9.1.1.146, 0 dependencies, recursive
    next hop 9.1.1.33, FastEthernet0/0 via 0.0.0.0/0
    valid cached adjacency
    tag rewrite with Fa0/0, 9.1.1.33, tags imposed: {}
```

Step 6   The SPOKE-VPN1-EAST's subnet 10.0.68.0 is advertised to all other PEs
by redistributing this route into MP-BGP. Redistribution of the static routes
into BGP from VRF VPN1 advertises the CE subnet 10.0.68.0 to all other

PE's via MP-BGP (normal MPLS-VPN operation). Similarly, the route to the 10.1.1.0 subnet behind PE2 is also learned by the VPN-GW1-EAST. Example 9-17 shows this.

Example 9-17 *Routes Learned via MP-BGP from Remote-PE on VPN-GW1-EAST*

```
vpn-gw1-east#show ip bgp v v  vpn1
BGP table version is 10, local router ID is 9.2.1.100
Status codes: s suppressed, d damped, h history, * valid, > best, i - internal,
              r RIB-failure, S Stale
Origin codes: i - IGP, e - EGP, ? - incomplete

   Network          Next Hop            Metric LocPrf Weight Path
Route Distinguisher: 200:1 (default for vrf vpn1)
*  9.1.1.146/32     9.1.1.33                 0          32768 ?
*> 10.0.68.0/24     9.1.1.146                0          32768 ?
*>i10.1.1.0/24      153.1.1.1                0    100       0 ?

vpn-gw1-east#show ip cef vrf vpn1 10.1.1.0
10.1.1.0/24, version 21, epoch 0, cached adjacency 9.2.1.2
0 packets, 0 bytes
  tag information set
    local tag: VPN-route-head
    fast tag rewrite with Fa4/0, 9.2.1.2, tags imposed: {702 498}
  via 153.1.1.1, 0 dependencies, recursive
    next hop 9.2.1.2, FastEthernet4/0 via 153.1.1.1/32
    valid cached adjacency
    tag rewrite with Fa4/0, 9.2.1.2, tags imposed: {702 498}
```

Step 7 After ISAKMP SAs and IPSec SAs are established, traffic arriving from the CE can be decrypted and, in the return path, encrypted from the PE to the CE. For packets' ingress into the PE, the IPSec packet will be destined to the PE's FVRF IP address where the crypto map is applied.

A lookup in the IPSec security association database (SADB) table based on the 3-tuple of outer destination address, protocol, and SPI value, and the right security association (SA) is found in order to decrypt the packet. Once the packet is decrypted, it is mapped to the inside VRF-ID associated with the IPSec SA, as this association was made during IPSec SA establishment (**show crypto ipsec sa**). This means that once the packet is decrypted, the inside IP address destination lookup is done in the context of the IVRF. In this example, if traffic is destined to 10.1.1.0 subnet, the forwarding lookup for this subnet is done in the VRF VPN1.

Step 8 The forwarding lookup for 10.1.1.0 in VRF VPN1 is a success and, as per CEF entry for this subnet, MPLS labels are prepended to the IP packet and switched along the MPLS Label Switch Path (LSP) to the far-end PE2.

Step 9 At the far-end PE, the MPLS VPNv4 label is popped and the IP packet is forwarded to the subnet 10.1.1.0.

Step 10 On the return path, MPLS label imposition at the far-end PE gets the packet back to the IPSec aggregator PE (VPN-GW1-EAST). The VPN label (528, in this example) inserted by the far-end PE associates the packet with an outgoing interface of FastEthernet0/0 on VPN-GW1-EAST. Example 9-18 shows this.

Example 9-18 *CEF and LFIB Information for the Route Injected by Reverse Route*

```
vpn-gw1-east#show ip  cef vrf vpn1 10.0.68.0
10.0.68.0/24, version 6, epoch 0, cached adjacency 9.1.1.33
0 packets, 0 bytes
  tag information set
    local tag: 528
  via 9.1.1.146, 0 dependencies, recursive
    next hop 9.1.1.33, FastEthernet0/0 via 0.0.0.0/0
    valid cached adjacency
    tag rewrite with Fa0/0, 9.1.1.33, tags imposed: {}

vpn-gw1-east#show mpls forwarding-table vrf vpn1
Local  Outgoing    Prefix           Bytes tag  Outgoing    Next Hop
tag    tag or VC   or Tunnel Id     switched   interface
528    Untagged    10.0.68.0/24[V]  0          Fa0/0       9.1.1.33
```

Step 11 Once the MPLS label is popped, the packet is switched out the outgoing interface (fa0/0)—except in this case there is a crypto map on the outgoing interface. The encryption context for the outbound packet is determined by the combination of the IVRF and the 5-tuple value, which is source address, destination address, source port, destination port, and protocol. After the packet is encrypted and the appropriate tunnel header is added, the encrypted packet is routed once more. This time the route lookup table that is used is that of the FVRF-ID of the encrypting SA.

This concludes the packet processing for a branch site connecting to a PE over IPSec and mapping the site into an MPLS VPN.

Mapping an IPSec Tunnel from a Telecommuter into an IVRF at the PE

The general operation of mapping a remote telecommuter into an MPLS VPN is essentially the same as that of a branch site with the key difference being the "match" criteria for the ISAKMP profile. Matches based on the IP address will not work for the telecommuter scenario because the IP address of the telecommuter may not be known in advance. Alternate mechanisms need to be used to make the VRF association.

If the VPN client is using Aggressive Mode or EzVPN, the groupname configured on the clients is used as the ID_KEY_ID. Based on the groupname, the key and attributes are downloaded locally from the PE or from a radius server and are used to map the VPN client to a VRF. In this section, you'll take a step-by-step look at the packet flow for this case. Refer to Figure 9-4 for this discussion.

Step 1   IPSec policy configuration on the VPN client on the telecommuter triggers IKE packet destined to the IPSec PE (VPN-GW1-EAST).

Step 2   The IKE packet from the CE is received on VPN-GW1-EAST's FastEthernet0/0 interface.

Step 2.1   Crypto configuration on the interface triggers IKE phase 1 processing. The relevant portions of the configuration from VPN-GW1-EAST and the debug output for this step are shown in Example 9-19.

Example 9-19   *Configuration Snippet and Debug Output for Aggressive Mode IKE*

```
interface FastEthernet0/0
 description FVRF
 ip address 9.1.1.35 255.255.255.248
 duplex full
 random-detect
crypto map vpn

00:13:32: ISAKMP (0:0): received packet from 9.1.1.154 dport 500 sport 500 Global (N)
 NEW SA
```

Step 2.2   As you saw in Chapter 2, "IPSec Overview," IKE Aggressive Mode processing consists of three messages between the initiator and the responder. We won't go through all the messages; the debug output clearly shows the sequence of the messages and the IKE state changes.

One of the first steps in Aggressive Mode by the responder (VPN-GW1-EAST) is to check if there is an ID _KEY_ID in the identification payload which, in this example, is the groupname configured on the client (vpn1group). The groupname associates the client to the ISAKMP profile, which in turn maps the AAA options and points to the radius server to be used for downloading the keys for authenticating message two and three of Aggressive Mode. Example 9-20 shows the debug ouput for this step.

Example 9-20   *Debug Output for Aggressive Mode IKE—Step 2.2*

```
vpn-gw1-east# debug crypto isakmp sa
00:13:32: ISAKMP (0:0): ID payload
        next-payload : 13
        type         : 11
        group id     : vpn1group
        protocol     : 17
        port         : 0
        length       : 12
00:13:32: ISAKMP:(0:0:N/A:0):: peer matches vpn1-ra profile

aaa authentication login vpn group radius
aaa authorization network vpn group radius
```

Example 9-20 *Debug Output for Aggressive Mode IKE—Step 2.2 (Continued)*

```
crypto isakmp profile vpn1-ra
  vrf vpn1
  match identity group vpn1group
  client authentication list vpn
  isakmp authorization list vpn
  client configuration address respond
  accounting vpn

radius-server host 100.1.1.4 auth-port 1645 acct-port 1646
radius-server key cisco
```

Step 2.3 After this check passes, the key is downloaded from a RADIUS server and processing of Aggressive Mode's second and third message continues.

Step 3 At the end of Step 2.3, IKE SAs are established and the ISAKMP profile is known from Step 2.2, which associates the client with the appropriate IVRF. X-AUTH and MODE-CFG processing is complete at the end of this step, as shown in Example 9-21.

Example 9-21 *Association of the Client with IVRF—Step 3*

```
vpn-gw1-east#sh crypto isakmp sa detail
Codes: C - IKE configuration mode, D - Dead Peer Detection
       K - Keepalives, N - NAT-traversal
       X - IKE Extended Authentication
       psk - Preshared key, rsig - RSA signature
       renc - RSA encryption

C-id  Local         Remote       I-VRF    Status  Encr Hash Auth DH Lifetime    Cap.
1     9.1.1.35      9.1.1.154    vpn1     ACTIVE  3des sha       2  23:51:08    CDX
```

Step 4 IKE Phase 2 (also known as Quick Mode) processing starts for IPSec SA establishment. Example 9-22 shows the relevant configuration and debug output.

Example 9-22 *Relevant Configuration and Debug Output for IPSec SA establishment—Step 4*

```
crypto ipsec transform-set vpn1 esp-3des esp-sha-hmac
!
crypto dynamic-map dynamic 1
 set transform-set vpn1
 set isakmp-profile vpn1-ra
 reverse-route remote-peer 9.1.1.33
!
crypto map vpn 3 ipsec-isakmp dynamic dynamic

vpn-gw1-east#show cry ipsec sa

interface: FastEthernet0/0
```

Example 9-22 *Relevant Configuration and Debug Output for IPSec SA establishment—Step 4 (Continued)*

```
         Crypto map tag: vpn-map, local addr 9.1.1.35

     protected vrf: vpn1
     local  ident (addr/mask/prot/port): (0.0.0.0/0.0.0.0/0/0)
     remote ident (addr/mask/prot/port): (10.254.254.201/255.255.255.255/0/0)
     current_peer 9.1.1.154 port 500
       PERMIT, flags={}
      #pkts encaps: 0, #pkts encrypt: 0, #pkts digest: 0
      #pkts decaps: 0, #pkts decrypt: 0, #pkts verify: 0
      #pkts compressed: 0, #pkts decompressed: 0
      #pkts not compressed: 0, #pkts compr. failed: 0
      #pkts not decompressed: 0, #pkts decompress failed: 0
      #send errors 0, #recv errors 0

       local crypto endpt.: 9.1.1.35, remote crypto endpt.: 9.1.1.154
       path mtu 1500, ip mtu 1500
       current outbound spi: 0xD046BD03(3494296835)

       inbound esp sas:
        spi: 0xA5C427BD(2781095869)
          transform: esp-3des esp-sha-hmac ,
          in use settings ={Tunnel, }
          conn id: 3001, flow_id: SW:1, crypto map: vpn-map
          sa timing: remaining key lifetime (k/sec): (4415994/3562)
          IV size: 8 bytes
          replay detection support: Y
          Status: ACTIVE

       inbound ah sas:

       inbound pcp sas:

       outbound esp sas:
        spi: 0xD046BD03(3494296835)
          transform: esp-3des esp-sha-hmac ,
          in use settings ={Tunnel, }
          conn id: 3002, flow_id: SW:2, crypto map: vpn-map
          sa timing: remaining key lifetime (k/sec): (4415994/3560)
          IV size: 8 bytes
          replay detection support: Y
          Status: ACTIVE

       outbound ah sas:

       outbound pcp sas:

vpn-gw1-east#debug crypto ipsec

00:50:02: ISAKMP:(0:1:SW:1):Checking IPSec proposal 1
00:50:02: ISAKMP: transform 1, ESP_3DES
00:50:02: ISAKMP:    attributes in transform:
```

Example 9-22 *Relevant Configuration and Debug Output for IPSec SA establishment—Step 4 (Continued)*

```
00:50:02: ISAKMP:        encaps is 1 (Tunnel)
00:50:02: ISAKMP:        SA life type in seconds
00:50:02: ISAKMP:        SA life duration (VPI) of  0x0 0x20 0xC4 0x9B
00:50:02: ISAKMP:        SA life type in kilobytes
00:50:02: ISAKMP:        SA life duration (VPI) of  0x0 0x46 0x50 0x0
00:50:02: ISAKMP:        authenticator is HMAC-SHA
00:50:02: ISAKMP:(0:1:SW:1):atts are acceptable.
00:50:02: IPSEC(validate_proposal_request): proposal part #1,
  (key eng. msg.) INBOUND local= 9.1.1.35, remote= 9.1.1.154,
    local_proxy= 0.0.0.0/0.0.0.0/0/0 (type=4),
    remote_proxy= 10.254.254.201/255.255.255/0/0 (type=1),
    protocol= ESP, transform= esp-3des esp-sha-hmac  (Tunnel),
    lifedur= 0s and 0kb,
    spi= 0x0(0), conn_id= 0, keysize= 0, flags= 0x2
00:50:02: ISAKMP:(0:1:SW:1): processing NONCE payload. message ID = -1537648483
00:50:02: ISAKMP:(0:1:SW:1): processing ID payload. message ID = -1537648483
00:50:02: ISAKMP:(0:1:SW:1): processing ID payload. message ID = -1537648483
00:50:02: ISAKMP:(0:1:SW:1): asking for 1 spis from ipsec
00:50:02: ISAKMP:(0:1:SW:1): Creating IPSec SAs
00:50:02:        inbound SA from 9.1.1.154 to 9.1.1.35 (f/i)  0/ 1
        (proxy 10.254.254.201 to 0.0.0.0)
00:50:02:        has spi 0xA5C427BD and conn_id 0 and flags 2
00:50:02:        lifetime of 2147483 seconds
00:50:02:        lifetime of 4608000 kilobytes
00:50:02:        has client flags 0x0
00:50:02:        outbound SA from 9.1.1.35 to 9.1.1.154 (f/i) 0/1
        (proxy 0.0.0.0 to 10.254.254.201)
00:50:02:        has spi -800670461 and conn_id 0 and flags A
00:50:02:        lifetime of 2147483 seconds
00:50:02:        lifetime of 4608000 kilobytes
00:50:02:        has client flags 0x0
00:50:02: ISAKMP:(0:1:SW:1): sending packet to 9.1.1.154 my_port 500 peer_port 500 (R)
  QM_IDLE
00:50:02: ISAKMP:(0:1:SW:1):Node -1537648483, Input = IKE_MESG_FROM_IPSEC,
  IKE_SPI_REPLY
00:50:02: ISAKMP:(0:1:SW:1):Old State = IKE_QM_SPI_STARVE  New State = IKE_QM_R_QM2
00:50:02: IPSEC(key_engine): got a queue event with 2 kei messages
00:50:02: IPSEC(initialize_sas): ,
  (key eng. msg.) INBOUND local= 9.1.1.35, remote= 9.1.1.154,
    local_proxy= 0.0.0.0/0.0.0.0/0/0 (type=4),
    remote_proxy= 10.254.254.201/0.0.0.0/0/0 (type=1),
    protocol= ESP, transform= esp-3des esp-sha-hmac  (Tunnel),
    lifedur= 2147483s and 4608000kb,
    spi= 0xA5C427BD(2781095869), conn_id= 0, keysize= 0, flags= 0x2
00:50:02: IPSEC(initialize_sas): ,
  (key eng. msg.) OUTBOUND local= 9.1.1.35, remote= 9.1.1.154,
    local_proxy= 0.0.0.0/0.0.0.0/0/0 (type=4),
    remote_proxy= 10.254.254.201/0.0.0.0/0/0 (type=1),
    protocol= ESP, transform= esp-3des esp-sha-hmac  (Tunnel),
    lifedur= 2147483s and 4608000kb,
    spi= 0xD046BD03(3494296835), conn_id= 0, keysize= 0, flags= 0xA
```

Example 9-22 *Relevant Configuration and Debug Output for IPSec SA establishment—Step 4 (Continued)*

```
00:50:02: IPSEC(rte_mgr): VPN Route Added 10.254.254.201 255.255.255.255 via 9.1.1.154
  in vpn1
00:50:02: IPSEC(rte_mgr): VPN Peer Route Added 9.1.1.154 via 9.1.1.33 in vpn1
00:50:02: IPSEC(create_sa): sa created,
  (sa) sa_dest= 9.1.1.35, sa_proto= 50,
    sa_spi= 0xA5C427BD(2781095869),
    sa_trans= esp-3des esp-sha-hmac , sa_conn_id= 3001
00:50:02: IPSEC(create_sa): sa created,
  (sa) sa_dest= 9.1.1.154, sa_proto= 50,
    sa_spi= 0xD046BD03(3494296835),
    sa_trans= esp-3des esp-sha-hmac , sa_conn_id= 3002
```

Step 5 The packet flow sequence from this step onwards is the same as in the branch site terminating into the IPSec aggregator explained in the previous section.

If the telecommuter VPN client is using Main Mode, then one option is to use RSA-SIG with certificates. In the case of certificates, you can match fields in the certificate to bind the session to a VRF as shown in Example 9-23. The certificate map defined is 'foo'. Customer Premise Equipment (CPE) or clients that match on the OU=EAST and O=VPN1 fields in the certificate presented by them to VPN-GW1-EAST will be bound to VRF VPN1.

Example 9-23 *Use of Certificates Fields to Match and Bind to a VRF*

```
vpn-gw1-east#show running-config

version 12.3
service timestamps debug datetime
service timestamps log datetime msec
no service password-encryption
!
hostname vpn-gw1-east
aaa new-model
!
aaa authentication login vpn1 group radius
aaa authorization network vpn1 group radius
aaa accounting update periodic 5
aaa accounting network vpn start-stop group radius
aaa session-id common
ip subnet-zero
!
!
ip vrf vpn1
 rd 200:1
 route-target export 200:1
 route-target import 200:1
!
ip vrf vpn2
 rd 201:1
 route-target export 201:1
 route-target import 201:1
!
```

Example 9-23 *Use of Certificates Fields to Match and Bind to a VRF (Continued)*

```
crypto isakmp profile vpn1-ra
  vrf vpn1
  ca trustpoint vpn1
  match certificate foo
  client configuration group vpn1group
  client authentication list vpn1
  isakmp authorization list vpn1
  client configuration address respond
  accounting vpn
!
crypto ca certificate map foo

 subject-name co ou=EAST
 subject-name co o=VPN1
```

In case of remote access clients, you can also statically assign a group using the "client configuration group <groupname>" to support extended authentication [XAUTH] and Mode Configuration [MODE-CFG]. The primary use of this is in cases in which the group information used cannot be retrieved from the certificate and needs to be statically assigned to support X-AUTH.

Termination of IPSec on a Unique IP Address Per VRF

If an IPSec tunnel needs to terminate on a unique IP address per VPN on the aggregation PE router, a unique interface or sub-interface is needed in the FVRF. These can be either unique VLANs, ATM PVCs, or Frame Relay sub-interfaces on the same router. The primary motivation for a unique IP address per VPN for IPSec termination is for cases in which the IPSec spokes use Main Mode with pre-shared key authentication and are assigned IP addresses dynamically on the WAN interface. In this case, match identity based on IP address does not work; it is not known what the tunnel endpoint address will be. This is an inherent limitation of the IPSec protocol itself. To overcome the issue, a unique IP address and unique VRF is assigned per VPN customer.

Figure 9-5 illustrates this scenario and Example 9-24 shows the configuration of the aggregation PE.

Figure 9-5 *IPSec Termination on a Unique Interface per VRF*

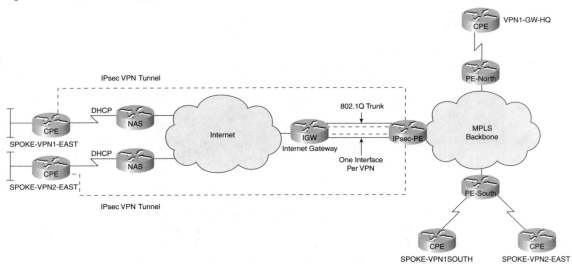

Example 9-24 *Configuration on VPN-GW1-EAST Terminating each VPN on a Unique Interface to Support Wild Card Keys*

```
vpn-gw1-east#show running-config
hostname vpn-gw1-east
!
ip vrf vpn1
 rd 200:1
 route-target export 200:1
 route-target import 200:1
!
ip vrf vpn2
 rd 201:1
 route-target export 201:1
 route-target import 201:1
!
crypto keyring vpn1 vrf vpn1
  pre-shared-key address 0.0.0.0 key vpn1aes
crypto keyring vpn2 vrf vpn2
  pre-shared-key address 0.0.0.0 key vpn2ikev2
!
crypto isakmp policy 1
 authentication pre-share
 group 2
!
crypto isakmp keepalive 10 10
!
crypto isakmp profile vpn1
vrf vpn1 description IVRF
```

Example 9-24 *Configuration on VPN-GW1-EAST Terminating each VPN on a Unique Interface to Support Wild Card Keys (Continued)*

```
keyring vpn1
match identity address 0.0.0.0 0.0.0.0 vrf vpn1
!
crypto isakmp profile vpn2
vrf vpn2 description IVRF
keyring vpn2
match identity address 0.0.0.0 0.0.0.0 vrf vpn2
!
crypto ipsec transform-set vpn1 esp-3des esp-sha-hmac
crypto ipsec transform-set vpn2 esp-3des esp-md5-hmac
!
!
interface Loopback0
 ip address 9.2.1.100 255.255.255.255
!
interface FastEthernet0/0.1
 description FVRF
 encapsulation dot1q 100
 ip vrf forwarding vpn1
 ip address 9.1.1.35 255.255.255.252
 duplex full
 random-detect
 crypto map vpn1
!
interface FastEthernet0/0.2
 description FVRF
 encapsulation dot1q 101
 ip vrf forwarding vpn1
 ip address 9.1.1.37 255.255.255.252
 duplex full
 random-detect
 crypto map vpn2
!
interface FastEthernet2/0
 ip address 100.1.1.147 255.255.255.0
 duplex full
!
interface FastEthernet4/0
 ip address 9.2.1.1 255.255.255.252
 duplex full
 tag-switching ip
!
ip route vrf vpn1 0.0.0.0 0.0.0.0 9.1.1.36
ip route vrf vpn2 0.0.0.0 0.0.0.0 9.1.1.38
!
access-list 100 permit ip 10.0.1.0 0.0.0.255 any
access-list 101 permit ip 10.0.1.0 0.0.0.255 any
```

IPSec CPE and VPN clients for customers VPN1 and VPN2 are configured with two different tunnel endpoint addresses of the gateway, which in this case are 9.1.1.35 and 9.1.1.37, respectively. It is important to note that you should have a default route per VRF and the router that front ends the PE on FastEthernet 0/0 should also be configured with 802.1q-encapsulated sub-interfaces.

Network-Based VPN Deployment Scenarios

This section looks at some common deployment scenarios for the network-based VPN solution:

- IPSec to MPLS VPN over GRE
- IPSec to Layer 2 VPN
- PE-PE encryption

IPSec to MPLS VPN over GRE

The most common application for the network-based VPN solution is to extend the MPLS VPN service provider footprint over the Internet. You learned the operation of this scenario in the previous section. You also learned from previous chapters that *dynamic routing* is desirable for site-to-site VPNs. Because an MPLS VPN provides dynamic routing capabilities, it would be very desirable to extend the dynamic routing capabilities to the extended sites over IPSec. The need for dynamic routing forces the use of IPSec over GRE. Figure 9-6 shows the topology that we use to describe this deployment model.

Figure 9-6   *IPSec to MPLS VPN over GRE*

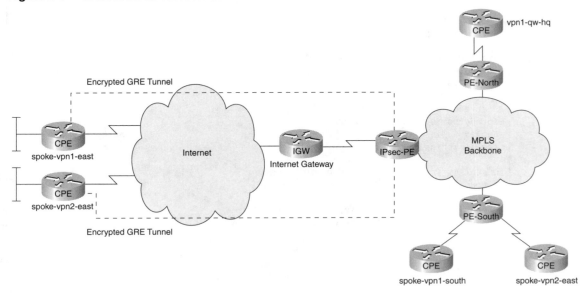

SPOKE-VPN2-EAST is the spoke that will have a GRE tunnel protected by IPSec to VPN-GW1-EAST. EIGRP is the routing protocol between the hub and spoke. At the hub that is also the MPLS VPN PE, one could redistribute the spoke routes into MP-BGP and advertise it to remote PEs.

Similarly, routes from remote PEs can be advertised to the spoke by redistributing into EIGRP from MP-BGP. Example 9-25 shows the configuration of the hub.

Example 9-25 *Configuration on VPN-GW1-EAST Terminating GRE Tunnels into a VRF*

```
vpn-gw1-east#show running-config
!
hostname vpn-gw1-east
!
!
!
ip vrf vpn1
 rd 200:1
 route-target export 200:1
 route-target import 200:1
!
ip vrf vpn2
 rd 201:1
 route-target export 201:1
 route-target import 201:1
!
ip cef
mpls label protocol ldp
tag-switching ip default-route
!
crypto keyring vpn1
  pre-shared-key address 9.1.1.146 key vpn1aes
crypto keyring vpn2
  pre-shared-key address 9.1.1.150 key vpn2ikev2
!
crypto isakmp policy 1
 authentication pre-share
 group 2
crypto isakmp keepalive 10 10
crypto isakmp profile vpn2
   keyring vpn2
   match identity address 9.1.1.150 255.255.255.255
!
!
crypto ipsec transform-set vpn1 esp-3des esp-sha-hmac
crypto ipsec transform-set vpn2 esp-3des esp-md5-hmac
 mode transport
!
crypto ipsec profile tunnel
 set transform-set vpn2
!
```

Example 9-25 *Configuration on VPN-GW1-EAST Terminating GRE Tunnels into a VRF (Continued)*

```
!
interface Tunnel0
 ip vrf forwarding vpn2
 ip address 10.2.1.1 255.255.255.0
 tunnel source 9.1.1.35
 tunnel destination 9.1.1.150
 tunnel protection ipsec profile tunnel
!
interface Loopback0
 ip address 9.2.1.100 255.255.255.255
!
interface FastEthernet0/0
 ip address 9.1.1.35 255.255.255.248
 duplex full
 crypto map vpn
!
interface FastEthernet2/0
 ip address 100.1.1.147 255.255.255.0
 duplex full
!
interface FastEthernet4/0
 ip address 9.2.1.1 255.255.255.252
 duplex full
 tag-switching ip
!
router eigrp 1
 auto-summary
 !
 address-family ipv4 vrf vpn2
 redistribute bgp 1001 metric 10000 100 255 1 1500
 network 10.2.1.0 0.0.0.255
 auto-summary
 autonomous-system 1
 exit-address-family
!
router ospf 1
 log-adjacency-changes
 redistribute static subnets
 network 9.2.1.0 0.0.0.3 area 0
 network 9.2.1.100 0.0.0.0 area 0
!
router bgp 1001
 no synchronization
 bgp log-neighbor-changes
 neighbor 153.1.1.1 remote-as 1001
 neighbor 153.1.1.1 update-source Loopback0
 no auto-summary
 !
 address-family vpnv4
 neighbor 153.1.1.1 activate
```

Example 9-25 *Configuration on VPN-GW1-EAST Terminating GRE Tunnels into a VRF (Continued)*

```
 neighbor 153.1.1.1 send-community extended
 exit-address-family
 !
 address-family ipv4 vrf vpn2
 redistribute connected
 redistribute static
 redistribute eigrp 1
 no auto-summary
 no synchronization
 exit-address-family
 !
 address-family ipv4 vrf vpn1
 redistribute connected
 redistribute static
 no auto-summary
 no synchronization
 exit-address-family
!
ip local pool vpn1pool 192.168.1.1 192.168.1.100 group vpn1group
ip classless
ip route 0.0.0.0 0.0.0.0 9.1.1.33
no ip http server
no ip http secure-server
!
end
```

The key part of the configuration is that the GRE tunnel is configured to be in a VRF. Once the IPSec packet gets decrypted, it is handed over to the GRE tunnel and, as the GRE tunnel is in a VRF, the IP packet flows are mapped into the appropriate VRF.

DMVPN and VRF

The IPSec GRE scenario can be extended to use DMVPN, an option that is explored in this section. In Chapter 7, "Auto-Configuration Architectures for Site-to-Site IPSec VPNs," you learned how Dynamic Multipoint VPN (DMVPN) drastically reduces configuration complexity at the hub for a hub-and-spoke VPN. DMVPN can be used to scale the configuration of the PE in the network-based solution. Each VPN in this solution requires a unique mGRE interface terminated in a VRF. Figure 9-7 shows this scenario and Example 9-26 represents a typical configuration on the PE.

Figure 9-7 *DMVPN Tunnel into a VRF*

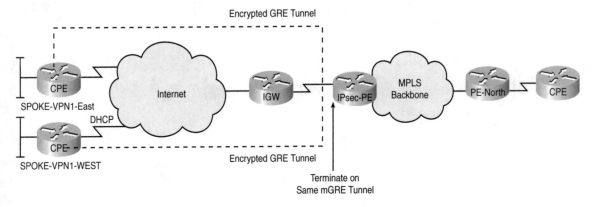

Example 9-26 *DMVPN Configuration on VPN-GW1-EAST Mapped to VRFs*

```
vpn-gw1-east#show running-config
version 12.3
service timestamps debug datetime
service timestamps log datetime msec
no service password-encryption
!
hostname vpn-gw1-east
!
ip vrf vpn1
 rd 200:1
!
ip vrf vpn2
 rd 201:1
!
ip cef
mpls label protocol ldp
tag-switching ip default-route
no ftp-server write-enable
!
crypto keyring vpn1
  pre-shared-key address 9.1.1.146 key vpn1aes
crypto keyring vpn2
  pre-shared-key address 9.1.1.150 key vpn2ikev2
!
crypto isakmp policy 1
```

Example 9-26 *DMVPN Configuration on VPN-GW1-EAST Mapped to VRFs (Continued)*

```
 authentication pre-share
 group 2
crypto isakmp keepalive 10 10
!
crypto ipsec transform-set dmvpn esp-3des esp-md5-hmac
 mode transport
!
crypto ipsec profile tunnel
 set transform-set dmvpn
!
!
interface Tunnel0
 ip vrf forwarding vpn1
 ip address 10.2.1.1 255.255.255.0
 ip mtu 1400
 ip nhrp authentication coke
 ip nhrp map multicast dynamic
 ip nhrp network-id 100
 ip nhrp holdtime 600
 no ip split-horizon eigrp 1
 tunnel source Loopback0
 tunnel key 100
 tunnel protection ipsec profile tunnel shared

 !
interface Tunnel1
 ip vrf forwarding vpn2
 ip address 10.3.1.1 255.255.255.0
 ip mtu 1430
 ip nhrp authentication vpn2
 ip nhrp map multicast multicast
 ip nhrp network-id 101
 ip nhrp holdtime 600
  no ip split-horizon eigrp 1
 ip nhrp nhs 10.1.1.1
tunnel source Loopback0
 tunnel key 101
 tunnel protection ipsec profile tunnel shared

interface Loopback0
 ip address 9.2.1.100 255.255.255.255
 !
interface FastEthernet0/0
 ip address 9.1.1.35 255.255.255.248
 duplex full
!
interface FastEthernet2/0
 ip address 100.1.1.147 255.255.255.0
 duplex full
!
interface FastEthernet4/0
```

Example 9-26 *DMVPN Configuration on VPN-GW1-EAST Mapped to VRFs (Continued)*

```
ip address 9.2.1.1 255.255.255.0
duplex full
mpls-ip
!
router eigrp 1
 auto-summary
 !
 address-family ipv4 vrf vpn2
 redistribute static
 redistribute connected
 network 10.3.1.0 0.0.0.255
 auto-summary
 autonomous-system 1
 exit-address-family
 !
 address-family ipv4 vrf vpn1
 redistribute static
 redistribute connected
 network 10.2.1.0 0.0.0.255
 auto-summary
 autonomous-system 1
 exit-address-family
 !
ip route 0.0.0.0 0.0.0.0 9.1.1.33
no ip http server
no ip http secure-server
!
```

In the configuration example shown in Example 9-26, the tunnel addresses used by the tunnels are on unique subnets for the sake of clarity. The subnets used on the mGRE tunnels for each VRF can be overlapping if so desired. One last statement with respect to the configuration is that if both tunnels are sharing the same IPSec profiles, they can be unique per tunnel if desired.

NOTE   If the spokes in the DMVPN solution are assigned IP addresses dynamically, this becomes an issue on the hub as the only possible option today is to have wild card keys for all VPNs if you want to use pre-shared Keys. A better option would be to use RSA-SIG [CERTS] authentication.

IPSec to L2 VPNs

This scenario is similar to mapping a site into an MPLS VPN over IPSec, except that in this case, the traffic after decryption at the PE is mapped into an outbound interface that is also in a VRF.

This scenario is useful for a Layer 2 provider (such as an ATM or Frame-Relay provider) to extend their footprint. The provider could terminate CPEs and remote access clients via IPSec to a PE at the edge of their cloud and map them to appropriate customer VRFs. Each of these VRFs is also mapped to the corresponding VPN customer's L2 Virtual Circuit (Ethernet VLAN, ATM, or Frame Relay VC). The IPSec packets coming in through the Internet are decrypted and mapped to the right VRF; once they are in the VRF, a route lookup is done before they are sent out through the right L2 Virtual Circuit. Figure 9-8 shows this scenario and Example 9-27 shows the configuration for this scenario.

Figure 9-8   *Mapping IPSec into L2VPN*

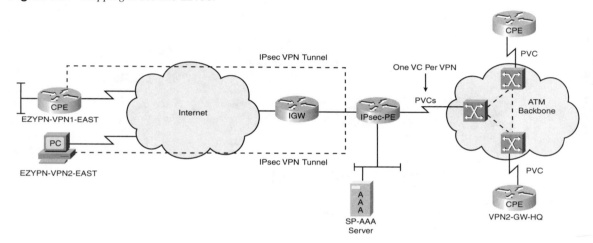

Example 9-27   *Configuration on VPN-GW1-EAST Showing Termination of an IPSec Session and Mapping Them to Routed ATM Interfaces*

```
vpn-gw1-east#show running-config
version 12.3
service timestamps debug datetime
service timestamps log datetime msec
no service password-encryption
!
hostname vpn-gw1-east
aaa new-model
!
aaa authentication login vpn group radius
aaa authorization network vpn group radius
aaa accounting update periodic 5
aaa accounting network vpn start-stop group radius
aaa session-id common
ip subnet-zero
!
!
ip vrf vpn1
 rd 200:1
!
```

Example 9-27 *Configuration on VPN-GW1-EAST Showing Termination of an IPSec Session and Mapping Them to Routed ATM Interfaces (Continued)*

```
ip vrf vpn2
 rd 201:1
!
ip cef
mpls label protocol ldp
tag-switching ip default-route
no ftp-server write-enable
!
crypto keyring vpn1
  pre-shared-key address 9.1.1.146 key vpn1aes
crypto keyring vpn2
  pre-shared-key address 9.1.1.150 key vpn2ikev2
!
crypto isakmp policy 1
 authentication pre-share
 group 2
crypto isakmp keepalive 10 10
crypto isakmp profile vpn1
    vrf vpn1
    keyring vpn1
    match identity address 9.1.1.146 255.255.255.255
crypto isakmp profile vpn1-ra
    vrf vpn1
    match identity group vpn1group
    client authentication list vpn
    isakmp authorization list vpn
    client configuration address respond
    accounting vpn
crypto isakmp profile vpn2
    vrf vpn2
    keyring vpn2
    match identity address 9.1.1.150 255.255.255.255
!
!
crypto ipsec transform-set vpn1 esp-3des esp-sha-hmac
crypto ipsec transform-set vpn2 esp-3des esp-md5-hmac
 mode transport
!

!
!
crypto dynamic-map dynamic 1
 set transform-set vpn1
 set isakmp-profile vpn1-ra
 reverse-route remote-peer 9.1.1.33
!
!
crypto map vpn 1 ipsec-isakmp
set peer 9.1.1.146
set transform-set vpn1
```

Example 9-27 *Configuration on VPN-GW1-EAST Showing Termination of an IPSec Session and Mapping Them to Routed ATM Interfaces (Continued)*

```
set isakmp-profile vpn1
reverse-route remote-peer address 9.1.1.33
match address 101
crypto map vpn 2 ipsec-isakmp
set peer 9.1.1.150
set transform-set vpn2
set isakmp-profile vpn2
reverse-route remote-peer address 9.1.1.33
match address 102

crypto map vpn 3 ipsec-isakmp dynamic dynamic
!
interface FastEthernet0/0
 ip address 9.1.1.35 255.255.255.248
 duplex full
 crypto map vpn
!
interface FastEthernet2/0
 ip address 100.1.1.147 255.255.255.0
 duplex full
!
interface ATM 4/0
 no ip address
interface ATM4/0.1
 ip address 9.2.1.1 255.255.255.252
 ip vrf forwarding vpn1
 pvc 0/101
 encapsulation aal5snap
 broadcast
interface ATM4/0.2
ip address 9.2.1.1 255.255.255.252
ip vrf forwarding vpn2
pvc 0/102
encapsulation aal5snap
broadcast
!
router eigrp 1
 auto-summary
 !
 address-family ipv4 vrf vpn2
 redistribute static
 network 9.2.1.0 0.0.0.255
 auto-summary
 autonomous-system 1
 exit-address-family
!
address-family ipv4 vrf vpn1
 redistribute static
 network 9.2.1.0 0.0.0.255
 auto-summary
```

Example 9-27 *Configuration on VPN-GW1-EAST Showing Termination of an IPSec Session and Mapping Them to Routed ATM Interfaces (Continued)*

```
autonomous-system 1
exit-address-family


ip local pool vpn1pool 192.168.1.1 192.168.1.100 group vpn1group
ip classless
ip route 0.0.0.0 0.0.0.0 9.1.1.33
no ip http server
no ip http secure-server
!
radius-server host 100.1.1.4 auth-port 1645 acct-port 1646
radius-server key cisco
radius-server vsa send accounting
!
end
```

In this example, all traffic from the remote CE is decrypted and mapped into the ATM sub-interface of the appropriate VPN.

PE-PE Encryption

One of the primary requirements for a VPN service is *security*. Traditional CE-based IPSec VPNs offer data security by encrypting data from CE-CE. For an MPLS VPN, the security comes from the separation of routing contexts (VRFs) at the PE. Of course, one could have an IPSec overlay of CEs over an MPLS VPN to provide data encryption, which means that every CE on that VPN has to build a full mesh of encrypted tunnels to every other CPE on that VPN over the provider's backbone. The overlay model defeats the scalability and any-to-any optimal routing of MPLS VPNs.

The primary driver for providers to encrypt PE-PE traffic is to extend MPLS VPN (RFC 2547bis) service across IP backbones that they have no control over (for example, the Internet). Also, this solution provides end-to-end encryption CE to PE, PE to PE, and PE to CE. Figure 9-9 shows the PE-PE encryption scenario.

One of the requirements used for PE-PE encryption is to build an MPLS-in-GRE packet between the PEs and encrypt the GRE-encapsulated packet using IPSec.

NOTE   The IETF MPLS VPN service using GRE is very well documented in the IETF draft [draft-ietf-l3vpn-gre-ip-2547-03.txt].

Figure 9-9   *PE-PE Encryption*

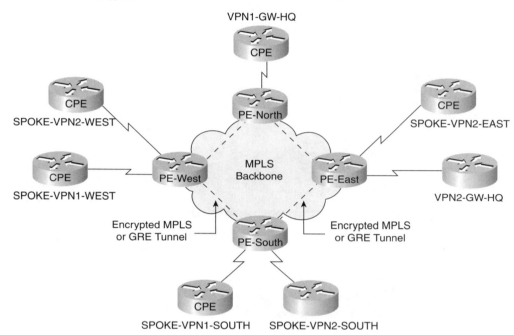

The deployment technique shown here for PE-PE encryption is to run LDP and MP-BGP over the GRE tunnel. One could also run MP-BGP outside the GRE tunnel and set the next_hop for the vpn prefixes via the GRE tunnel. Note that the use of GRE point-to-point tunnels for any-to-any PE-PE encryption requires a full mesh of GRE tunnels between the PEs. Example 9-28 shows the configuration for PE-PE encrypted GRE tunnel running MPLS VPNs.

Example 9-28   *Configuration on VPN-GW1-EAST Showing PE-PE Encryption*

```
vpn-gw1-east#show running-config

hostname vpn-gw1-east
!
ip vrf vpn1
 rd 200:1
 route-target export 200:1
 route-target import 200:1
!
ip vrf vpn2
 rd 201:1
 route-target export 201:1
 route-target import 201:1
!
mpls label protocol ldp
tag-switching tdp router-id Loopback0
```

Example 9-28 *Configuration on VPN-GW1-EAST Showing PE-PE Encryption (Continued)*

```
tag-switching ip default-route
!
crypto keyring vpn1
  pre-shared-key address 9.1.1.145 key vpn1aes
crypto keyring vpn2
  pre-shared-key address 9.1.1.149 key vpn2ikev2
!
crypto isakmp policy 1
 authentication pre-share
 group 2
!
crypto isakmp keepalive 10 10
!
crypto isakmp profile vpn1
 vrf vpn1 description IVRF
 keyring vpn1
 match identity address 9.1.1.145 255.255.255.255
 accounting vpn
!
crypto isakmp profile vpn1-ra
  vrf vpn1
  match identity group vpn1group
  client authentication list vpn
  isakmp authorization list vpn
  client configuration address respond
  accounting vpn
!
crypto isakmp profile vpn2
 vrf vpn2
 keyring vpn2
 match identity address 9.1.1.149 255.255.255.255
 accounting vpn
!
crypto ipsec transform-set vpn1 esp-3des esp-sha-hmac
crypto ipsec transform-set vpn2 esp-3des esp-md5-hmac
!
crypto dynamic-map dynamic 1
 set transform-set vpn1
 set isakmp-profile vpn1-ra
 reverse-route remote-peer 9.1.1.33
!
crypto map vpn 1 ipsec-isakmp
set peer 9.1.1.146
set transform-set vpn1
set isakmp-profile vpn1
reverse-route remote-peer address 9.1.1.33
match address 101
crypto map vpn 2 ipsec-isakmp
set peer 9.1.1.150
set transform-set vpn2
set isakmp-profile vpn2
```

Example 9-28 *Configuration on VPN-GW1-EAST Showing PE-PE Encryption (Continued)*

```
reverse-route remote-peer address 9.1.1.33
match address 102
crypto map vpn 3 ipsec-isakmp dynamic dynamic
!
interface Tunnel0
 ip address 100.1.1.1 255.255.255.252
 tunnel source 9.2.1.100
 tunnel destination 9.2.1.101
 mpls-ip
 tunnel protection ipsec profile tunnel
!
interface Loopback0
 ip address 9.2.1.100 255.255.255.255
!
interface FastEthernet0/0
 description FVRF
 ip address 9.1.1.35 255.255.255.248
 duplex full
 random-detect
 crypto map vpn
!
interface FastEthernet2/0
 ip address 100.1.1.147 255.255.255.0
 duplex full
!
interface FastEthernet4/0
 ip address 9.2.1.1 255.255.255.252
 duplex full
!
router ospf 1
 log-adjacency-changes
 network 9.2.1.0 0.0.0.3 area 0
!
router bgp 1001
 no synchronization
 bgp log-neighbor-changes
 neighbor 100.100.1.2 remote-as 1001
 neighbor 100.100.1.2 update-source tunnel0
 no auto-summary
 !
 address-family vpnv4
 neighbor 100.100.100.2 activate
 neighbor 100.100.100.2 send-community extended
 exit-address-family
 !
 address-family ipv4 vrf vpn2
 redistribute connected
 redistribute static
 no auto-summary
 no synchronization
 exit-address-family
```

Example 9-28 *Configuration on VPN-GW1-EAST Showing PE-PE Encryption (Continued)*

```
!
address-family ipv4 vrf vpn1
redistribute connected
redistribute static
no auto-summary
no synchronization
exit-address-family
!
ip route 0.0.0.0 0.0.0.0 9.1.1.33 (default route to the Internet)
ip route 153.1.1.1 255.255.255.255 Tunnel0
!
access-list 100 permit ip 10.0.1.0 0.0.0.255 any
access-list 101 permit ip 10.0.1.0 0.0.0.255 any
```

```
vpn-gw1-east#show ip route vrf vpn1

Routing Table: vpn1
Codes: C - connected, S - static, R - RIP, M - mobile, B - BGP
       D - EIGRP, EX - EIGRP external, O - OSPF, IA - OSPF inter area
       N1 - OSPF NSSA external type 1, N2 - OSPF NSSA external type 2
       E1 - OSPF external type 1, E2 - OSPF external type 2
       i - IS-IS, su - IS-IS summary, L1 - IS-IS level-1, L2 - IS-IS level-2 S- static
  route

Gateway of last resort is not set

     9.0.0.0/32 is subnetted, 1 subnets
S       9.1.1.146 [1/0] via 9.1.1.33
     10.0.0.0/24 is subnetted, 2 subnets
B       10.1.1.0 [200/0] via 100.100.100.2, 00:23:17
S       10.0.68.0 [1/0] via 9.1.1.146
```

```
vpn-gw1-east#show mpls ldp nei
    Peer LDP Ident: 153.1.1.1:0; Local LDP Ident 9.2.1.100:0
        TCP connection: 153.1.1.1.11056 - 9.2.1.100.646
        State: Oper; Msgs sent/rcvd: 785/783; Downstream
        Up time: 00:25:33
        LDP discovery sources:
          Tunnel1, Src IP addr: 100.100.100.2
        Addresses bound to peer LDP Ident:
          153.1.1.1       163.1.1.1       100.100.100.2
```

```
vpn-gw1-east#show ip bgp vpn vrf vpn1
BGP table version is 51, local router ID is 9.2.1.100
Status codes: s suppressed, d damped, h history, * valid, > best, i - internal,
              r RIB-failure, S Stale
Origin codes: i - IGP, e - EGP, ? - incomplete

   Network          Next Hop            Metric LocPrf Weight Path
Route Distinguisher: 200:1 (default for vrf vpn1)
*  9.1.1.146/32     9.1.1.33                 0          32768 ?
*> 10.0.68.0/24     9.1.1.146                0          32768 ?
```

Example 9-28 *Configuration on VPN-GW1-EAST Showing PE-PE Encryption (Continued)*

```
*>i10.1.1.0/24      100.100.100.2          0    100     0 ?
* i                 153.1.1.1              0    100     0 ?

vpn-gw1-east#show ip cef vrf vpn1
10.1.1.0/24, version 20, epoch 0
0 packets, 0 bytes
  tag information set
    local tag: VPN-route-head
    fast tag rewrite with Tu1, point2point, tags imposed: {498}
  via 100.100.100.2, 0 dependencies, recursive
    next hop 100.100.100.2, Tunnel1 via 100.100.100.0/24
    valid adjacency
    tag rewrite with Tu1, point2point, tags imposed: {498}
```

From the different outputs, you can see that the next hop for the BGP learned routes in the routing table for each of the VRFs and the LDP neighbor on VPN-GW1-EAST is learned via the tunnel. The forwarding information for the VRF VPN1 learned routes point toward the far-end PE tunnel IP address (100.100.100.2) with the appropriate VPN label (498).

The downside to PE-PE encryption is that PE-CE data is still in the clear. Of course, one could also encrypt data on the PE-CE link in addition to PE-PE encryption. But, then the PE has to do much more work. It has to decrypt data from the CE-PE and re-encrypt the data for the PE-PE.

Summary

In this chapter, you reviewed a new type of VPN service known as network-based VPNs, which allow service providers to offer value-added services. The most common application for network-based VPNs is for MPLS VPN providers to extend their footprint to sites where they have no direct connectivity to the CEs. You reviewed various connection methods with which remote sites used IPSec to reach a network-based VPN. The various connection options (that is, IPSec, EzVPN, IPSec over GRE, and DMVPN) each provide unique capabilities and constraints. Service providers may offer a combination of these IPSec access methods based on the requirements of the customer's CE site or remote access client. The customer may choose the IPSec access protocol that best meets the needs of the VPN.

The service provider's value in providing IPSec access to network-based VPNs is to assume the role of traffic management and capacity planning. The PE effectively plays the role of the enterprise "hub" VPN gateway, but does so in a distributed manner. The provider is now responsible for managing the scalability and performance of the enterprise IPSec "hub," using the same principles described in the previous chapters. The enterprise is also able to leverage the provider's investment in redundant infrastructure. Likewise, the enterprise achieves any-to-any data paths between CE sites without having to invest in expensive CE equipment capable of building a full mesh of IPSec tunnels.

The primary drawback to the network-based VPN is that customer traffic is decrypted at the PE. The network-based VPN does require more coordination between the enterprise and provider with regards to ensuring that packet QoS attributes are treated appropriately and routing updates are processed appropriately. Despite the fact that traffic segregation is retained at the PE, many customers require encryption from CE to CE. CE to CE encryption requires a per-peer relationship. Running end-to-end encryption between the CE devices through the MPLS VPN negates many of the advantages of the MPLS VPN. Most significant losses are the any-to-any data connectivity, the optimized provisioning with O(1) changes per site, and the scalable routing relationships. These are significant trade-offs that network designers must consider when building a network-based VPN. The decision to use end-to-end IPSec or CE-PE IPSec in the context of a network-based VPN will be determined by taking into account security risks and potential threats.

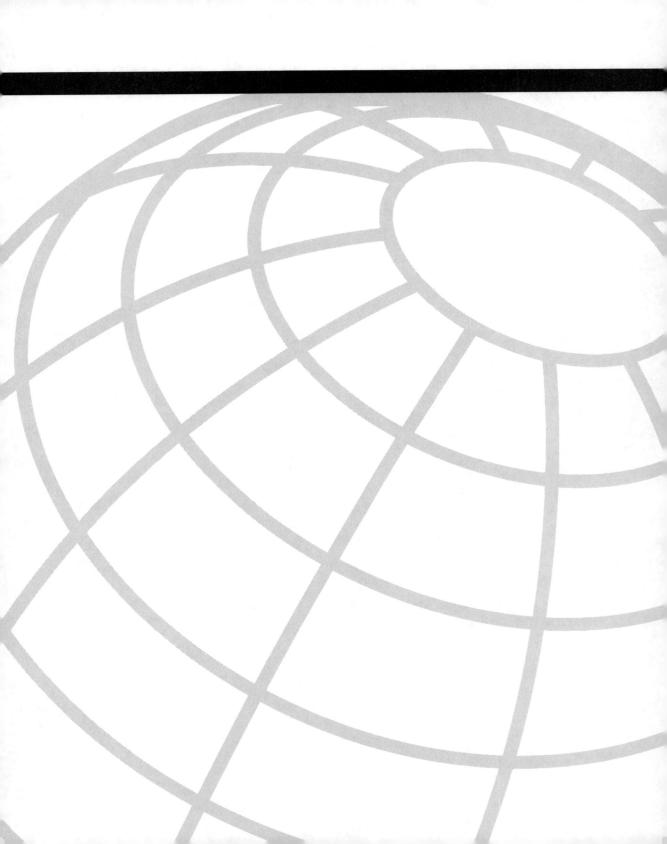

INDEX

A-B

access links
  fault tolerance, 175–176
    multiple IKE identities, 176–182
    single IKE identity with MLPPP, 188–189
    with single IKE identity, 183–187
active/standby stateful failover model, 213–214
advanced IPSec features
  DPD, 43–47
  idle timeout, 47–50
  IKE keepalives, 41–42
  IPSec pass-through, 83
  look ahead fragmentation, 69
  NAT-T, 77–82
  RRI
    and HSRP, 53–56
    configuring, 50–53
  stateful failover, 56
    configuring with SSO, 63
    configuring with SSP, 57–63
    SADB synchronization, 57
    SADB transfer, 57
Aggressive mode (IKE), 27–28
AH (Authentication Header), 19
  and NAT, 76
  transport mode, 21
anti-replay loss, mitigating in voice/data flows, 270
asymmetric cryptographic algorithms, 13–14
asymmetric routing problem, 192–194
authentication
  digital certificates, 103
    CA enrollment, 104
    revocation, 105–106

IKE, 28
  digital signature authentication, 29–30
  pre-shared key authentication, 28
MODECFG, 94–95
XAUTH, 89, 92–93
auto-configuring site-to-site IPSec VPNs
  TED, 217–221

backbone networks, fault tolerance, 174

C

CAs (certificate authorities)
  certificate revocation, 105–106
  enrollment, 104
CE configuration of network-based VPNs, 306–315
Certificate Revocation List (CRL), 105
ciphers, 12
Cisco Easy VPN. *See* EzVPN
Cisco IOS software
  enabling network-based VPNs, 296
    crypto keyrings, 297
    ISAKMP profiles, 297–299
  IPsec packet processing, 34–39
  SLB, 205
Cisco VPN 3000 clustering, peer redundancy, 210–212
classifying packets, 258
  attribute preservation of GRE tunnels, 262
  internal attribute preservation, 264
  IPSec transport mode, 260
  IPSec tunnel mode, 261
  transitive QoS applied to IPSec, 264

P

R

Q

S

V

X-Z

Cisco Press

CISCO CERTIFICATION SELF-STUDY
#1 BEST-SELLING TITLES FROM CCNA® TO CCIE®

Look for Cisco Press Certification Self-Study resources at your favorite bookseller

Learn the test topics with **Self-Study Guides**

Gain hands-on experience with **Practical Studies** books

Prepare for the exam with **Exam Certification Guides**

Practice testing skills and build confidence with **Flash Cards and Exam Practice Packs**

Visit **www.ciscopress.com/series** to learn more about the Certification Self-Study product family and associated series.

Learning is serious business.
Invest wisely.

CISCO SYSTEMS

Cisco Press

CCIE PROFESSIONAL DEVELOPMENT
RESOURCES FROM EXPERTS IN THE FIELD

CCIE Professional Development books are the **ultimate resource for advanced networking professionals**, providing practical insights for effective network design, deployment, and management. **Expert perspectives, in-depth technology discussions, and real-world implementation advice** also make these titles essential for anyone preparing for a CCIE® exam.

CCIE® Professional Development
Routing TCP/IP
Volume I

A detailed examination of interior routing protocols

ciscopress.com   Jeff Doyle, CCIE No. 1919

Look for CCIE Professional Development titles at your favorite bookseller

Cisco BGP-4 Command and Configuration Handbook
ISBN: 1-58705-017-X

Cisco LAN Switching
ISBN: 1-57870-094-9

Cisco OSPF Command and Configuration Handbook
ISBN: 1-58705-071-4

Inside Cisco IOS Software Architecture
ISBN: 1-57870-181-3

Network Security Principles and Practices
ISBN: 1-58705-025-0

Routing TCP/IP, Volume I
ISBN: 1-57870-041-8

Routing TCP/IP, Volume II
ISBN: 1-57870-089-2

Troubleshooting IP Routing Protocols
ISBN: 1-58705-019-6

Troubleshooting Remote Access Networks
ISBN: 1-58705-076-5

Visit **www.ciscopress.com/series** for details about the CCIE Professional Development series and a complete list of titles.

Learning is serious business.
Invest wisely.

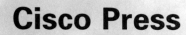

Cisco Press

Learning is serious business.
Invest wisely.

CISCO SYSTEMS

Cisco Press

NETWORKING TECHNOLOGY GUIDES
MASTER THE NETWORK

Turn to Networking Technology Guides whenever you need **in-depth knowledge of complex networking technologies**. Written by leading networking authorities, these guides offer theoretical and practical knowledge for **real-world networking applications and solutions**.

Look for Networking Technology Guides at your favorite bookseller

Cisco Access Control Security: AAA Administration Services
ISBN: 1-58705-124-9

Cisco CallManager Best Practices: A Cisco AVVID Solution
ISBN: 1-58705-139-7

Designing Network Security, Second Edition
ISBN: 1-58705-117-6

Network Security Architectures
ISBN: 1-58705-115-X

Optical Network Design and Implementation
ISBN: 1-58705-105-2

Top-Down Network Design, Second Edition
ISBN: 1-58705-152-4

Troubleshooting Virtual Private Networks
ISBN: 1-58705-104-4

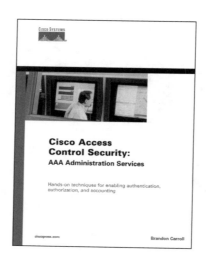

CISCO SYSTEMS

Cisco Access Control Security:
AAA Administration Services

Hands-on techniques for enabling authentication, authorization, and accounting

ciscopress.com

Brandon Carroll

Visit **www.ciscopress.com/series** for details about Networking Technology Guides and a complete list of titles.

Learning is serious business.
Invest wisely.

Learning is serious business. **Invest wisely.**

SEARCH THOUSANDS OF BOOKS FROM LEADING PUBLISHERS

Safari® Bookshelf is a searchable electronic reference library for IT professionals that features more than 2,000 titles from technical publishers, including Cisco Press.

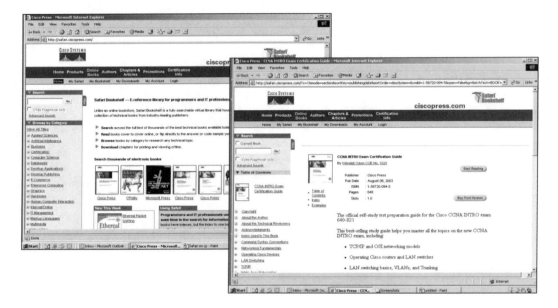

With Safari Bookshelf you can

- **Search** the full text of thousands of technical books, including more than 70 Cisco Press titles from authors such as Wendell Odom, Jeff Doyle, Bill Parkhurst, Sam Halabi, and Karl Solie.

- **Read** the books on My Bookshelf from cover to cover, or just flip to the information you need.

- **Browse** books by category to research any technical topic.

- **Download** chapters for printing and viewing offline.

With a customized library, you'll have access to your books when and where you need them—and all you need is a user name and password.

TRY SAFARI BOOKSHELF FREE FOR 14 DAYS!

You can sign up to get a 10-slot Bookshelf free for the first 14 days.
Visit **http://safari.ciscopress.com** to register.

Cisco Press

Learning is serious business.
Invest wisely.

CISCO SYSTEMS

Cisco Press

3 STEPS TO LEARNING

STEP 1

First-Step

STEP 2

Fundamentals

STEP 3

**Networking
Technology Guides**

STEP 1 **First-Step**—Benefit from easy-to-grasp explanations.
No experience required!

STEP 2 **Fundamentals**—Understand the purpose, application,
and management of technology.

STEP 3 **Networking Technology Guides**—Gain the knowledge
to master the challenge of the network.

NETWORK BUSINESS SERIES

The Network Business series helps professionals tackle the
business issues surrounding the network. Whether you are a
seasoned IT professional or a business manager with minimal
technical expertise, this series will help you understand the
business case for technologies.

Justify Your Network Investment.

Look for Cisco Press titles at your favorite bookseller today.

Visit **www.ciscopress.com/series** for details on each of these book series.

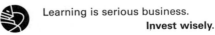

DISCUSS

NETWORKING PRODUCTS AND TECHNOLOGIES WITH CISCO EXPERTS AND NETWORKING PROFESSIONALS WORLDWIDE

VISIT NETWORKING PROFESSIONALS
A CISCO ONLINE COMMUNITY
WWW.CISCO.COM/GO/DISCUSS

CISCO SYSTEMS

THIS IS THE POWER OF THE NETWORK. now.